UNITED KINGDOM
REPUBLIC OF IRELAND
England
Wales
Irish Sea
English Channel
Isle of Man
Belfast
Dublin
Galway
Shannon
Waterford
Cork
Blackpool
Leeds
York
Liverpool
Manchester
Chester
Nottingham
Snowdon 1085 m
Birmingham
Norwich
Rugby
Cambridge
Stratford-upon-Avon
Oxford
London
Swansea
Cardiff
Bristol
Bath
Thames
Canterbury
Dover
Folkestone
Euro-tunnel
Calais
Salisbury
Southampton
Brighton
Great Torrington
Plymouth
Isle of Wight
Land's End
Scilly Islands
Channel Islands
0 50 100 miles
0 50 100 km
TM, p. 321
Folio 14

CAMDEN MARKET 3

Lehrerfassung zum Schülerband

Erarbeitet von
Ruth Barker, Michael Biermann, Otfried Börner, Simone Collenberg, Hannelore Debus, Pamela Hanus, Phil Mothershaw-Rogalla, Ingrid Preedy, Tanja Ripke, Kathleen Unterspann und Jürgen Wrobel

unter Mitwirkung der Redaktion
Dr. Anne Grimm, André Schmitt und Henriette Vahle

Herausgeber der bisherigen Reihe und Berater der Programmleitung:
Otfried Börner, StD a.D.,
Dr. phil. h.c. Christoph Edelhoff, StD a.D.,
Vorsitzender THE ENGLISH ACADEMY

Fachliche Beratung
Sigrid Boinski, Bianka Gehler, Julia Grossmann, Petra Günther, Kathrin Hough, Holger Nürnberg, Alexander Schülting und Gisela Vogt

Diesterweg

CAMDEN MARKET 3

Materialien für Schülerinnen und Schüler
- Textbook 3 (ISBN 978-3-425-**73803**-1)
- Workbook 3 mit Lernsoftware und Audio-CD (ISBN 978-3-425-**73833**-8)
- Workbook 3 mit Audio-CD (ISBN 978-3-425-**73823**-9)
- Lernsoftware 3
  - Einzelplatzlizenz (ISBN 978-3-425-**73883**-3)
  - Schullizenz (ISBN 978-3-425-**73893**-2)
- Arbeitsheft Inklusion 3 mit Audio-CD (ISBN 978-3-425-**73783**-6)
- Kit 3 (ISBN 978-3-425-**73843**-7)
- Vocab-App 3 – kostenfreier Download unter https://play.google.com/store, Stichwort: „Diesterweg"
- Zoom-App 3 – Link zum Download unter www.zoom-app.de
- Digitales Schulbuch 3 – Online-Jahres-Einzellizenz (ISBN WEB-**73797**)

Materialien für Lehrkräfte
- Workbook 3 mit Lösungen und Audio-CD (ISBN 978-3-425-**73813**-0)
- Teacher's Manual mit Lösungen 3 (ISBN 978-3-425-**73863**-5)
- Vorschläge für Lernerfolgskontrollen 3 (ISBN 978-3-425-**73913**-7)
- Audio-CD + DVD 3 für Lehrkräfte (ISBN 978-3-425-**73853**-6)
- Interaktive Whiteboard-Software 3
  - Einzelplatzlizenz (ISBN 978-3-425-**73933**-5)
  - Schullizenz (ISBN 978-3-425-**73993**-9)
- Folien 3 (ISBN 978-3-425-**73923**-6)
- Differenzierende Kopiervorlagen 3 (ISBN 978-3-425-**73873**-4)
- Differenzierende Kopiervorlagen für offenen Unterricht 3 (ISBN 978-3-425-**73953**-3)
- Digitale Lehrermaterialien 3
  - Einzellizenz auf DVD-ROM (ISBN 978-3-425-**73967**-0)
  - Einzellizenz (ISBN WEB-425-**73973**)
  - Schullizenz (ISBN WEB-425-**73979**)

Druck A[1] / Jahr 2015
Alle Drucke der Serie A sind im Unterricht parallel verwendbar.

Redaktion: Caroline Byrt, Dr. Anne Grimm, André Schmitt und Henriette Vahle
Vokabelanhang: Lea Gonsior
Herstellung: Sandra Grünberg
Layout und Satz: Visuelle Lebensfreude, Hannover
Illustrationen: Ulf Marckwort, Kassel
Umschlaggestaltung: Blum Design und Kommunikation, Hamburg
Druck: westermann druck GmbH, Braunschweig

ISBN 978-3-425-**73983**-0

CLASSROOM PHRASES

Wenn man ankommt oder geht

Good morning.	Guten Morgen.
Sorry, I'm late.	Tut mir leid, dass ich zu spät komme.
Sorry, I don't have my exercise book with me.	Tut mir leid, ich habe mein Heft nicht dabei.
Sorry, I don't have my homework with me.	Tut mir leid, ich habe meine Hausaufgaben nicht dabei.
What's for homework?	Was haben wir als Hausaufgabe auf?
See you tomorrow.	Bis morgen.

Wenn es ein Problem gibt

What's the matter with you?	Was ist mit dir los?
I'm fine./I feel sick.	Mir geht's gut./Mir ist schlecht.
I've got a headache.	Ich habe Kopfschmerzen.
Can I open the window, please?	Kann ich bitte das Fenster öffnen?
Can I go to the toilet, please?	Kann ich bitte zur Toilette gehen?

Wenn man Hilfe braucht

Can you help me, please?	Können Sie/Kannst du mir bitte helfen?
I've got a question.	Ich habe eine Frage.
I don't understand this.	Ich verstehe das hier nicht.
How can I do this exercise?	Wie mache ich diese Aufgabe?
What's … in English/German?	Was heißt … auf Englisch/Deutsch?
What does … mean?	Was bedeutet … ?
Can you write it on the board, please?	Können Sie/Kannst du das bitte an die Tafel schreiben?
Can you say it again, please?	Können Sie/Kannst du das bitte noch einmal sagen?
Sorry, I don't know.	Tut mir leid, das weiß ich nicht.
What page, please?	Auf welcher Seite bitte?

Wenn man zusammen arbeitet oder spielt

Whose turn is it?	Wer ist dran?
I (don't) like this story.	Diese Geschichte gefällt mir (nicht).
I think it's good/interesting/funny.	Ich finde … gut/interessant/komisch.
I think it's terrible/boring/sad.	Ich finde … schrecklich/langweilig/traurig.
Do you want to work with me?	Möchtest du mit mir arbeiten?

937.715 aus **Camden Market 3** (ISBN 978-3-425-73803-1)

CLASSROOM PHRASES

Wenn man mit dem Computer arbeitet

What's your email address?	Was ist deine E-Mail-Adresse?
You can click on this link.	Du kannst auf diesen Link klicken.
Can I print it out/download it?	Kann ich das ausdrucken/herunterladen?
I saved it.	Ich habe es abgespeichert.
My computer has crashed.	Mein Computer ist abgestürzt.

Was die Lehrerin oder der Lehrer sagt

Open your books at page ...	Öffnet eure Bücher auf Seite ...
Turn to page ...	Blättert zu Seite ...
Look at line ...	Seht euch Zeile ... an.
Read the text on page ...	Lies/Lest den Text auf Seite ...
Work in pairs.	Arbeitet zu zweit.
Work in groups of four/five/...	Arbeitet zu viert/fünft/...
Sit in a circle.	Bildet einen Sitzkreis.
Listen to the CD/MP3/...	Hör/Hört die CD/MP3/... an.
Write about ...	Schreibe/Schreibt über ...
Talk about ...	Sprich/Sprecht über ...
Ask questions about ...	Stelle/Stellt Fragen zu ...
Answer the question, please.	Beantworte/Beantwortet bitte die Frage.
Match the sentences.	Ordne/Ordnet die Sätze zu.
Who wants to read the text?	Wer möchte den Text vorlesen?
Write down the answers.	Schreibe/Schreibt die Antworten auf.
Act out the dialogue.	Spiel/Spielt den Dialog vor.
Change roles.	Tauscht die Rollen.
Make your own dialogue.	Entwirf/Entwerft selbst ein Gespräch.
Take a card.	Nimm/Nehmt eine Karte.
Come to the blackboard, please.	Komm/Kommt bitte zur Tafel.
Collect the exercise books, please.	Sammle/Sammelt bitte die Hefte ein.
Do this exercise at home, please.	Mach/Macht diese Aufgabe bitte zu Hause.
Please be quiet.	Sei/Seid bitte ruhig.
Please sit down.	Setz dich/Setzt euch bitte.
Please speak up.	Sprich/Sprecht bitte lauter.
You can do better.	Du kannst das besser.
Try again.	Versuch es noch einmal.
That's it.	Das ist alles.
Well done.	Gut gemacht.

937.715 aus **Camden Market 3** (ISBN 978-3-425-73803-1)

Herzlich willkommen in der Lehrerfassung zu Camden Market 3!

Worin unterscheidet sich die vorliegende Lehrerfassung vom Schülerband (ISBN 978-3-425-73803-1)?

In der Lehrerfassung sind die Seiten 3 bis 151 des Schülerbandes mit blauen Symbolen, Zusatzinformationen und z. T. Lösungen versehen, die Ihnen die Unterrichtsvorbereitung und die Arbeit im Unterricht erleichtern sollen. (Die Seiten 152 bis 284 des Schülerbandes sind unverändert übernommen.)

Vorne zwischen Impressum und Seite 3 und hinten nach Seite 284 sind zusätzliche, blau unterlegte Seiten eingefügt, so wie diese, die Sie vor sich sehen. Diese Seiten folgen einer vom Schülerband abgekoppelten Seitenzählung: LF1–64 (LF für „Lehrerfassung").
Auf den Seiten LF4–13 finden Sie mehrere Doppelseiten zur Konzeption von **Camden Market,** insbesondere zum erweiterten Differenzierungskonzept ab Band 3.
Im hinteren Teil, ab Seite LF15, finden Sie den Lösungsanhang: die Lösungen, die sich aus Platzgründen nicht auf den Schülerband-Seiten eintragen ließen.

Inhaltsverzeichnis der blau unterlegten LF-Seiten

In der Lehrerfassung verwendete Abkürzungen

- TB Textbook, d. h. der Schülerband (ISBN 978-3-425-**73803**-1)
- TM Teacher's Manual (ISBN 978-3-425-**73863**-5)
- KV Differenzierende Kopiervorlagen (ISBN 978-3-425-**73873**-4)
- IWS Interaktive Whiteboard-Software (ISBN 978-3-425-**73933**-5)
- LSW Lernsoftware (ISBN 978-3-425-**73883**-3)
- LF Lehrerfassung

Wegweiser durch die Lehrerfassung

TM: Seitenverweis auf die Unterrichtsempfehlungen im **Teacher's Manual** (ISBN 978-3-425-**73863**-5).

W plus Seitenzahl: Verweis auf die chronologischen Wortlisten hinten im TB – zur schnelleren Orientierung.

Wo immer möglich, sind die **Lösungen an Ort und Stelle** eingetragen.
Alle weiteren Lösungen finden Sie auf den blau unterlegten **Seiten LF15–64** am Ende der Lehrerfassung.
Eine entsprechende Seitenangabe – z. B. ➡ p. LF35 – hilft beim Auffinden.

Bei jeder **Parallelaufgabe** (→ LF4) im **Basis**-Teil: knappe Informationen zur Pendant-Aufgabe im **More**-Teil.

Belegstellen für ein **neues Grammatikpensum** sind beim ersten Vorkommen blau unterstrichen.

Auszeichnung von neuem Vokabular:
- ein dunkleres Blau für aktiven Wortschatz (in den Wortlisten hinten im TB fett gedruckt)
- ein helleres Blau für passiven Wortschatz.

BASIS Street festivals

W p. 219 | TM, p. 140

11 The Notting Hill Carnival

➡ p. LF35

Look at the programme. Find out:
- When is the carnival? in August: 24th–26th
- How long does the carnival last? three days
- What can you see at the carnival?

Notting Hill Carnival – Official Events

Date & Time	Event
Saturday August 24 7 pm – 11 pm	**National Steel Band Competition** The UK's top steel bands compete for the title: National Champions of Steel
Sunday August 25 9 am – 7 pm	**Children's Day Parade** Children and teenagers in colourful costumes parade through the streets of Notting Hill.
Monday August 26 10 am – 7 pm	**Main Parade** Groups and clubs in amazing costumes dance to the rhythms of mobile sound systems or steel bands.

12 At the carnival

// Geschichte inhaltlich identisch, aber sprachlich anspruchsvoller

M5 M p. 76

a) Read about the carnival. Why are the friends so excited? they are waiting to see Charlie's little sister Sharon in the Children's Day Parade

Caroline, Gillian, Charlie and Rajiv love the Notting Hill Carnival. They love watching the crowds of people who walk, dance and sing in the streets of Notting Hill. They love listening to the singers and bands. There are a lot of dancers and brightly coloured floats which pass by in the parade – and many tourists who take photos. But there are also pickpockets who try to steal wallets and watches. The police put up posters which tell everybody to be careful.

Today is the Children's Day Parade. The four friends watch it excitedly. They are waiting to see Charlie's sister, Sharon, who is in the parade this year. There is a group of children dressed up as sunshine dancers. Behind them is a children's steel band which is playing Caribbean music. Sharon and her group are close behind a music float. They have got colourful skirts and fantastic headdresses of flowers and feathers. The girls look like tropical birds of paradise. They are all dancing to the rhythm of the steel drums.

When Sharon sees Charlie, she runs over and gives him a big hug. Charlie is so proud of his little sister.

b) There are lots of different people at the carnival. Who are they? What do they do?
c) Imagine YOU could take part in a parade. How would you feel?

64 sixty-four

14 **Minimalweg und Vertiefungsmöglichkeiten**
Während im Schülerband alle Aufgaben mit weißer Ziffer gestaltet sind, markieren in der Lehrerfassung **blaue Ziffern** die Aufgaben, die Vertiefungsmöglichkeiten bieten (und ggf. ausgelassen werden können), also nicht Bestandteil des für die Progression notwendigen Minimalweges sind.

LSW: Verweis auf die **Lernsoftware** (ISBN 978-3-425-**73883**-3); die dreistellige Ziffer gibt den Code an, mit dem man zu einer bestimmten Übung der Software gelangt.

Verweise, inkl. Seitenzahl und Übungsnummer, wo sich ein Ausweichen auf das **Camden Market Arbeitsheft Inklusion** (ISBN 978-3-425-**73783**-6) anbietet, das die sechs *Themes* auf leichterem Niveau bereithält.

BASIS Robinson Crusoe

4 Oh, yeah! LSW 405 p. 56/2

a) Listen to Gillian, Charlie and Rajiv. What are they talking about?

Robinson Crusoe • a perfect island • wild animals

b) Listen again. Who wants to live on an island with …
- a high mountain? Gillian – a big waterfall? Gillian
- a beautiful lake? Charlie – a big forest? Rajiv

c) What else can you understand?

Beschriftung der Lehrwerksfiguren: als Erinnerungshilfe für L.

5 What is home?

a) Look at these English sayings. What do you think they mean? Folie 10

Home is where the heart is. My home is my castle. Home, sweet home.
There is no place like home. East, west – home is best.

Verweis auf die **Folien** (ISBN 978-3-425-**73923**-6).

b) Work with a partner and make a word web about home. KV48 ↓↑

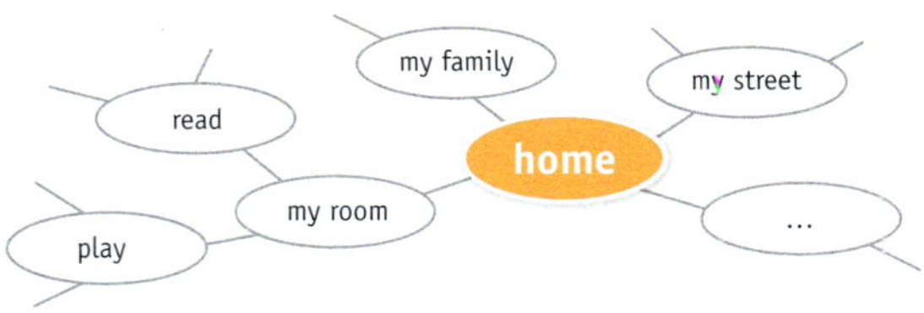

KV: Verweis auf die **Differenzierenden Kopiervorlagen** (ISBN 978-3-425-**73873**-4), mit Pfeilen, in welche Richtung jeweils differenziert wird.

c) Use the word web to talk about YOUR home. What do you like? What don't you like?

I love my room. There I can …

I like playing …

I hate/enjoy …

13 p. 191 Gerundium nach bestimmten Verben

Bei den **LiF-Verweisen in der Randspalte** ist im Gegensatz zum Schülerband nicht nur die Nummer, also z. B. „13", genannt, sondern auch **das eigentliche Pensum.**

6 Choose an activity

You can …
- imagine you are stranded on an island. One day you find an empty bottle on the beach. Write a "message in a bottle".
- write down the 20 English words you would teach Man Friday first. Why have you chosen them?
- find out more about Daniel Defoe. Make a fact file or give a short talk. IWS

Dear Finder,

Please rescue me! I am stranded. Our ship hit a rock two days after we passed Hawaii and I swam to this lonely island.
Send help soon! At night I hear strange noises. Maybe there are wild animals or cannibals on the island. …

eighty-three 83

IWS: Verweis auf die **Interaktive Whiteboard-Software** (ISBN 978-3-425-**73933**-5).

Differenzieren mit Basis und More

(am Beispiel von Seite 40 und 53)

Camden Market ermöglicht die **Differenzierung mit einem Band.** Der **Basis**-Teil deckt die Grundanforderungen ab.
Der **More**-Teil bietet Zusatzangebote für das mittlere und höhere Niveau.

BASIS Keeping fit

4 Karate with Jessica

a) **Watch the clip. What can you understand?**
b) **Watch the clip again. Then read the statements. Are they right or wrong?**
1. Jessica started karate training two years ago.
2. Jessica usually trains four times a week.
3. The training sometimes starts with a warm-up.
4. Stretching different parts of your body is important.
5. Jessica's team uses punchbags.

c) **Watch the clip a third time and check your answers.**
d) **What colour is Jessica's belt? Do you know what the colour stands for? Try to find out.**

In jedem *Theme* gibt es sog. **Parallelaufgaben:** die eine im **Basis**-Teil, das Pendant im **More**-Teil.

5 Different sports

14
p. 192

What do you think: What is important for different sports? Write five or more sentences.

Someone who	plays football/tennis/… goes swimming/cycling/… does karate/… …	must be doesn't have to be	slim • tall • fit • fast • cool • small • strong • careful • young • clever • fair • …

6 Eine orange-grüne Aufgabennummer im **Basis**-Teil zeigt an: Hierzu gibt es eine parallel einsetzbare Aufgabe im **More**-Teil. Entsprechend in der Randspalte der Verweis auf die **More**-Aufgabe.

6 A sportsperson

M3 a-c M
p. 53

a) **Who is YOUR favourite sportsperson? Make a fact file.**

Name:
Age:
Country:
Sport:
Titles:
Other information:

Diese parallel (und in den meisten Fällen auch additiv) einsetzbaren Aufgaben erleichtern die Arbeit mit **heterogenen Lerngruppen:** Während leistungsschwächere S die **Basis**-Aufgabe bearbeiten, wenden sich leistungsstärkere S der entsprechenden Aufgabe im **More**-Teil zu.
In der Phase der Ergebnissicherung ist dann ein Zusammenführen von **Basis**- und **More**-Niveau nicht nur denkbar, sondern wünschenswert.
Die Parallelaufgaben wurden genau im Hinblick darauf konzipiert.

Alle Kompetenzen werden im **Basis**-Teil integriert auf einfachem Niveau angeboten. Stärkere Lerner finden im **More**-Teil passende anspruchsvollere Materialien und Aufgaben. So tragen alle S gemeinsam zum Klassendiskurs bei.

MORE Keeping fit 2

M3 A sportsperson

a) You will read an article about Sally Brown, a sprinter from the UK. Look at her picture first. What would you like to ask her? Make notes.
b) Now read about Sally. Can you find answers to your questions in the text?

Nothing can stop Sally

Sally Brown from Belfast in Northern Ireland started running when she was 10 years old. She soon found that she was a talented sprinter. Sally was born in 1995 with problems with her left arm: It did not develop from below the elbow.

Sally has taken part in national and international competitions. In 2011 she won a bronze medal in the 200 m at the Paralympic World Championships in New Zealand. Since then her life has changed a lot. Training is much tougher and journalists want to know all about her.

The biggest event in her career has been the Paralympics in London in 2012 where she finished the 100 m final in sixth place. To prepare for this major event Sally trained six days a week. She ran three times a week and did fitness training. At the time she still went to comprehensive school.

The biggest sacrifice for her sport is her social life. She can't go out on a Saturday night because she usually trains. She also has to eat healthy food – chocolate and other sweets are not allowed.

It is hard for Sally to train and concentrate on her education at the same time. She hopes to go to university one day.

Sally's dream is to become Paralympic champion. She wants to prove that although she is disabled, she can run as well as people who aren't.

M3 Grün-orange Aufgabennummern im **More**-Teil zeigen an:
Hierzu gibt es eine parallel einsetzbare Aufgabe im **Basis**-Teil.
Entsprechend in der Randspalte der Rückverweis auf die **Basis**-Aufgabe.

c) Make a fact file about Sally.

Name:
Age:
Country:
Sport:
Titles:
Other information:

B 6a p. 40

d) Work with a partner and prepare an interview with Sally. Think of at least six questions you would like to ask her.

Where? What? Why? When? How? ... ?

One of you takes Sally's role and gives the answers. Present your interview to the class.

10R p. 189
WB M3 p. 39

Die **Parallelaufgaben** sind die direktesten, aber nicht die einzigen Querverbindungen zwischen **Basis**- und **More**-Teil.
Weitere Informationen: → LF8f.

Weiter differenzieren mit Sonne und Mond

(am Beispiel von Seite 16 und 77)

Das **Mond**-Symbol kennzeichnet besonders leichte Aufgaben im **Basis**-Teil.

Darüber hinaus bietet das Workbook **parallel einsetzbare Varianten** von TB-Aufgaben: Randspaltenverweise im TB verweisen auf parallel einsetzbare **Mond**- und **Sonnen**-Aufgaben im Workbook.

2 b) → WB 1
Die **Mond**-Variante im WB bietet vereinfachte Speisekarten. **Binnendifferenzierung:** So können leistungsstärkere Lerngruppen oder S mit dem TB arbeiten, leistungsschwächere mit dem WB. Beide Wege führen zum selben Ergebnis, sodass die **Ergebnissicherung für alle gemeinsam** im Plenum stattfinden kann.

BASIS Places to eat

1 A food and drink ABC

How to … work with others p. 176

a) Think: What food and drink words do you know? Write down your alphabet.
b) Pair: Work with a partner and complete your alphabets.

What did you write for A?
Apple. What have you got?
I've got avocado. What did you write for B?
…

A - apple, …
B - banana, …
C - cake, …
D - delicious, …
E - eat, …
F - …

c) Share: Sit together with another pair and put your food and drink words in groups (fruit, vegetables, for breakfast, …).

2 Places to eat

1 p. 7

a) What is YOUR favourite place to eat?
b) Look at the menus and the pictures of the restaurants on these two pages. Choose one restaurant you would like to go to. Make notes on what you like about it. Then talk about it in class.

I'd like to go to	Burger Queen the Windsor Castle Pizza World	because	the food is … my favourite food is … I love … I'd like to try … it's not too expensive. …

Pizza World

Pizzas	regular	large
Ciao Bambino *(tomatoes, cheese)*	£5.95	£7.75
Via Veneto *(ham, olives, garlic)*	£7.95	£10.35
Mexicana *(beans, chillies, olives, onions)*	£8.95	£11.65
Capri *(salami, mushrooms, onions)*	£9.45	£12.25
Verde (vegetarian) *(onions, broccoli, mushrooms)*	£9.45	£12.25

Fresh Salads	
Italian salad	£6.45
Tomato salad	£5.45
Chicken salad	£7.45

Drinks	
Soft drinks	£1.50
Glass of wine	£4.70
Coffee/tea	£1.45

16 sixteen

Das **Sonnen**-Symbol kennzeichnet anspruchsvolle Texte und Aufgaben im **More**-Teil. Dies ermöglicht Differenzierung bis hin zum **gymnasialen Niveau.**

Auch **More**-Aufgaben werden mit Workbook-Übungen unterstützt: Randspaltenverweise im TB verweisen auf **anspruchsvollere, parallel einsetzbare Varianten** im Workbook.

MORE Street festivals

M7 The pickpocket

a) Look at the pictures in number 15 again. How would you describe the pickpocket to the police?
- What does he look like?
- How old is he?
- What was he wearing at the parade?
- … ?

b) Work in small groups. Describe a pickpocket to your partners. They must guess which pickpocket you are talking about. Take turns.

WB M8 p. 58
wordbank People p. 159 Clothes p. 161
WB M9 p. 58

M7 b) → WB 9
Zu dieser Teilaufgabe gibt es eine anspruchsvollere, parallel einsetzbare **Sonnen**-Variante im Workbook: eine Illustration, die fünf weitere Verdächtige zeigt. Die S beschreiben die Männer und arbeiten Gemeinsamkeiten heraus. (Drei der abgebildeten Männer sind durch ein gemeinsames Merkmal, die rote Mütze, als Mitglieder einer Diebesbande o. Ä. erkennbar. Die S sollen das erkennen und begründen, wie sie zu ihrer Entscheidung gekommen sind.)

M8 What Mr Harley saw

Mr Harley saw the incident at the Notting Hill Carnival. What can he tell the police about it? Look at the pictures and the newspaper article in number 15 again. Write it down. You can start like this:
Well, this morning I went to … I was watching …
Suddenly I felt … I turned round and …

M9 Guess what it is

a) Read the definitions. Who or what is it?
1. It is a thing that people stand on in a parade.
2. It is a thing which people keep money in.
3. It is a person who visits a place on holiday.
4. It is a thing which you can make music with.
5. It is a person that tries to catch criminals.
6. It is a thing that you can wear at a carnival.
7. It is a person who steals wallets.
8. It is an animal which has colourful feathers.

b) Look at the definitions in a) again. When do you use 'who'? When do you use 'which'? When do you use 'that'? Look at LiF 14 on page 192 for help.

c) Write down definitions which have something to do with carnival, music and street festivals. Then test your partner.

It is	a thing a person	who which that	…

14 p. 192
How to … work with grammar p. 178

Aufgaben mit **Sonnen**-Symbol finden sich auf jeder **More**-Doppelseite.

Weitere Differenzierungsmöglichkeiten und parallel einsetzbare Varianten von TB- und WB-Aufgaben bieten die **Differenzierenden Kopiervorlagen** (ISBN 978-3-425-**73873**-4).
Pfeile nach oben oder unten auf den Vorlagen zeigen jeweils an, in welche Richtung differenziert wird.

Zusammenspiel von Basis und More

(am Beispiel von Seite 62 und 75)

Die **Basis**-Teile erkennen Sie an den **orangen** Elementen und dem Schriftzug BASIS, weiß auf orangem Grund, oben auf jeder Seite.

3 BASIS Things we can do

8 A musical

a) The Lambrakis want to take their children to a musical in London. It's called "The Lion King". Read the story of "The Lion King". Would you like to see the film or the musical? Say why.

King Mufasa is a powerful lion and the king of the Pridelands in Africa. He is a very good king and all the animals look up to him. Mufasa has a son, Simba. He will be the next king when his father dies. But Simba's uncle, Scar, is jealous: He wants to become the new king.

Scar tries to kill Simba but Mufasa rescues his son. Then Scar tries to kill Simba a second time: He takes him to a valley. In the valley Scar and some hyenas scare all the other animals. The animals run away in panic and trample down everything. Mufasa saves Simba again, but Mufasa dies and Scar makes Simba believe that he has killed his father. Scar tells Simba to run away.

Simba runs away and almost dies. Some other animals find him and they stay together.

Later Simba meets his friend Nala. Nala tells Simba that Scar is the king now. She asks him to come back because he is the true king. Simba returns to the Pridelands and meets his uncle Scar. Scar tells Simba that he killed Mufasa, not Simba. They fight and Scar dies. Now Simba is the lion king with his new wife, Nala.

Enge Verzahnung von **Basis** und **More** über Randspaltenverweise im **Basis**-Teil: **Grüne, mit M gekennzeichnete Randspaltenverweise** zeigen an, welche **More**-Aufgaben zu einer Aufgabe passen.
So erfahren die S hier in **Basis 8,** dass die *Lambraki family* das Musical *The Lion King* in London besuchen möchte. **M4** knüpft daran an und bietet eine Aufgabe zum Leseverstehen: Die S lesen kurze Kommentare/Kritiken zum Musical *The Lion King* in London. (Gefolgt von einer **Sonnen**-Teilaufgabe für Leistungsstärkere: *Write YOUR review of a musical, film, book or game.*)

b) Read the story again. Who is ... ?

Mufasa Simba Scar Nala

M4 p. 75 M

c) What else do you learn about the four lions?

9 A closer look

a) Look at number 8 again. Sort words from the text in a grid like this:

words I know	words I can guess	words I don't know
lion	trample down	jealous
...	...	...

How to ... work with a dictionary

b) Write down the words you don't know again.
– First sort them from A-Z.
...ich meaning fits best?
...ish word.

→ Beispiel aus Theme 2
Im **Basis**-Teil, Seite 46, erteilen die S den in einer Wartezimmer-Illustration dargestellten Patient/innen Ratschläge.
In **M6,** Seite 54, durchforsten sie den Basis-Teil nach Redemitteln zu *at the doctor's* und gestalten anschließend einen eigenen Dialog *at the doctor's*.
Zusammenführen der Niveaus: Die **More**-S spielen ihre Dialoge den **Basis**-MitS vor. Die rezeptiven Fähigkeiten sind meist besser ausgebildet als die produktiven, d. h. den Szenen *at the doctor's* folgen können auch leistungsschwächere Basis-S.

Grün ist die Farbe des **More**-Teils: **grüne** Elemente und der Schriftzug MORE, weiß auf grünem Grund, oben auf jeder Seite.
Pro *Theme* gibt es zwei **More**-Doppelseiten, passgenaue zusätzliche Aufgaben für stärkere Lerner.

→ **WB**
Selbstverständlich werden auch **More**-S mit zusätzlichen Übungen im WB gefordert.

MORE Things we can do **3**

M3 An advert

Make an advert for YOUR best idea for raising money.
Write down:
- what you are offering
- when and where
- what you will use the money for
- why people should say yes to your offer

Present your advert in class.

M4 p. 56

M4 King of the musicals?

a) **"The Lion King" is a world-famous musical. Read the reviews of the London show that people have posted on the Internet. What did they like about the show? What didn't they like?**

News (230) ▾ Favourites ▾

COMMENTS PLEASE LET US KNOW WHAT YOU THINK !

Posted by bnorth25 — October 22nd
The show was brilliant! I enjoyed every minute of it. It couldn't have been better. The only negative thing was that lots of mobile phones were ringing during the performance.

Posted by Max4u — October 23rd
This is the best show I have ever seen in my life - full of colour, surprises and the most wonderful singing and music. I can't wait to see it again!

Posted by Anonymous — October 23rd
The singing, the acting and the costumes were great. But to be honest: The tickets are far too expensive!

Posted by kiki1234 — October 27th
Very disappointed! Very bad quality of singing, background singing not loud enough, cold actors, no feeling.

Posted by Sus@n — November 1st
The costumes, make-up, acting were fantastic, the music truly magical! The whole show was amazing from beginning to end.
I would recommend it to all ages (it may be a bit scary for children under the age of 9).

b) **Read the reviews again. What do you think: How many stars ★★★★★ (1 to 5) did each person give the show?**
c) **Write YOUR review of a musical, film, book or game. Look at the reviews in a) for help.**

Einsatzmöglichkeiten des More-Teils im Unterricht
- gemeinsame Erarbeitung, sofern die Lerngruppe leistungsstark ist
- in leistungsheterogenen Klassen in Einzel- und Partnerarbeit, z. B. in Freiarbeitsphasen oder im Rahmen des Wochenplans; L sollte den S die Selbstkontrolle ihrer Ergebnisse ermöglichen, z. B. indem er/sie ihnen Lösungsblätter zur Verfügung stellt (die TB-Lösungen liegen dem **TM** gebündelt bei)
- **Pupils as tutors: More**-S sollten die Möglichkeit haben, ihren MitS, die ausschließlich den **Basis**-Teil erarbeiten, ihre Ergebnisse sowie mögliche neue Storyline-Inhalte mitzuteilen. Am Ende von arbeitsteiligen Phasen (leistungsstark vs. leistungsschwächer) sollte immer eine Zusammenführung der Niveaus stehen.

→ **Beispiel aus Theme 4**
In **Basis 13**, Seite 88, erzählt Gillian (Hörverstehen), wie es für sie war, als ihre Eltern sich scheiden ließen. In **M9**, Seite 97, trifft sich Gillian mit ihren Freunden im Café und teilt ihnen mit (Leseverstehen), dass ihr Vater seine Freundin Ronda heiraten möchte und dass Ronda schwanger ist. Gillian ist sehr unglücklich.
Zusammenführen der Niveaus: Die **More**-S informieren ihre **Basis**-MitS nach **M9**, welche „dramatische" Wendung die Storyline um Gillian genommen hat.

In jedem *Theme* gibt es darüber hinaus sog. **Parallelaufgaben:** die eine im **Basis**-Teil, das Pendant im **More**-Teil. → LF4f.

Differenzierung und individuelle Förderung
(am Beispiel von Seite 124 und 51)

Jede Lerngruppe ist heterogen und Lernen ist ein individueller Prozess. Dies muss bei der Unterrichtsgestaltung berücksichtigt werden. Individualisierung bedeutet jedoch nicht, jeder/m S ein eigenes Lernangebot zu machen. Individualisierung, individuelle Förderung und Differenzierung werden im Alltag eher durch ein **Bündel von Prinzipien** realisiert, die bei der Planung und Durchführung von Lernarrangements berücksichtigt werden.

Die **Individualisierung des Lernens durch Einzelarbeitsphasen** ist ein wesentlicher Bestandteil von **kooperativen** Lernformen.
Folgende Methoden des kooperativen Lernens sind in **Camden Market** verankert und werden auf ***How to work with others,*** Seite 176f., erklärt:
- Think – pair – share
- Buzz groups
- Milling around
- Dramatic reading
- Double circle und
- Placemat.

Think – pair – share gilt als das Grundprinzip des kooperativen Lernens.

BASIS Planning a holiday

1 Holiday

a) Listen to the song 'Summer holiday' by Cliff Richard and read or sing along.

We're all going on a summer holiday
No more working for a week or two
Fun and laughter on our summer holiday
No more worries for me or you
For a week or two
We're going where the sun shines brightly
We're going where the sea is blue
We've seen it in the movies
Now let's see if it's true

Everybody has a summer holiday
Doing things they always wanted to
So we're going on a summer holiday
To make our dreams come true
For me and you
For me and you

b) Read the song lyrics. What do people like about holidays?

2 YOUR summer holidays

Double circle: What are you going to do in the summer holidays? What would you like to do?

In the summer holidays I'm going to ... And you?

I'd like to ...

stay ... | meet ... | see ... | visit ... | go to ... | do ... | ...

3 Holidays without parents

a) Look at the picture. What can you see? What is happening?
b) Talk about the people. What do you think:
- What are the parents thinking? How do they feel?
- What are the children thinking? How do they feel?

124 one hundred and twenty-four

→ **Choose-an-activity**-Aufgaben (→ LF12), ein oder zwei pro **Basis**-Teil, sind *task*-orientierte, offene Aufgaben mit Wahlmöglichkeit, bei denen sich die S je nach Neigung, Lerntyp oder bevorzugter Sozialform/Methode für einen Arbeitsauftrag entscheiden können.

→ **Camden Market Arbeitsheft Inklusion**
(ISBN 978-3-425-**73783**-6)
Falls manche Aufgaben zu komplex für einzelne S sind, kann L auf das **Camden Market Arbeitsheft Inklusion** ausweichen. Dort gibt es die *Themes* auf leichterem Niveau. Gleiche Inhalte, aber
- reduziertes Layout,
- vereinfachte Hörtexte,
- kleinschrittigere Aufgabenführung,
- reduzierte und vereinfachte Inhalte.

Camden Market bietet zahlreiche Möglichkeiten zur **Differenzierung und Individualisierung** sowie ein umfassendes und systematisches Übungsangebot. Dabei werden gleichermaßen Angebote für leistungsstärkere S bereitgestellt, lernschwächere S gefördert sowie unterschiedliche Lernertypen einbezogen.

Practice, jeweils zwischen **Basis**- und **More**-Teil, jeweils vier Seiten: Hier werden die **sprachlichen Mittel gefestigt und schriftlich gesichert**, die im *Theme* vorrangig mündlich behandelt werden. Durch entsprechende Randverweise im **Basis**-Teil ist die Verzahnung gewährleistet. Es empfiehlt sich, die Übungen an passender Stelle **binnendifferenzierend** in den Unterricht „einzuflechten", zum Üben und als Zusatzaufgaben, wenn L Defizite feststellt (bei der Klasse oder bei einzelnen S). L weist die Übungen den S zu, die Defizite aufzuarbeiten haben. Lernschwächeren S hilft L, ein Minimum zu bewältigen, während anderen zusätzliche Aufgaben gestellt werden. Auch können die S ihren individuellen Interessen folgend an den Übungen arbeiten.

PRACTICE At the doctor's

P11 Oh, Mum!

a) **When Gillian's mum comes home from work, she has got a lot of questions. Write down what she asks Gillian.**

drink – tea? • eat – fruit? • sleep – enough? • take – medicine? • watch – TV?

b) **What do you think are Gillian's answers?**

P12 A broken leg

George has got a broken leg. Write about what he *is able to do* **and what he** *is not able to do***.**

read comics • play football • play computer games • watch films • walk to school • go swimming • ...

George is able to read comics.
He is not able to ...
He ...

P13 Can you help?

These people have got some questions but they don't speak German. Tell them what they need to know.

fifty-one 51

Auslassungspunkte ... finden sich oft in **Camden Market**. Die S, insbesondere leistungsstärkere, sollten die Punkte nicht ignorieren, sondern als Aufforderung verstehen, eine Aufgabe um eigene Ideen zu erweitern. L: *Not only does it mean you CAN add your own ideas. In fact, it means you SHOULD add ideas of your own.*

Da die **Practice**-Übungen **nicht Teil des für die Progression notwendigen Minimalweges** sind, sind die Übungsziffern in der Lehrerfassung blau eingefärbt (→ LF2).

→ **WB Test yourself** und **WB Extra practice**
Mithilfe von **Test yourself** stellen die S gezielt fest, was sie schon beherrschen und was sie noch üben müssen. Im Anschluss hält **Extra practice** Aufgaben zur Differenzierung bereit. Wer bei **Test yourself** Schwierigkeiten mit einer bestimmten Aufgabe/Fertigkeit hat, bearbeitet als Nächstes die entsprechende Aufgabe in **Extra practice.**

→ Der fakultative **Reading-is-fun**-Anhang (ab Seite 143) bietet auf die *Themes* abgestimmte authentische Lesetexte aus der Erfahrungswelt der S. Ziel u. a.: Heranführen an englischsprachige Literatur.

Schülerorientierung und Handlungsorientierung

(am Beispiel von Seite 22 und 63)

Choose an activity ist ein wiederkehrendes Aufgabenformat im **Basis**-Teil, ein oder zwei pro *Theme*. Die S wenden **Gelerntes in neuen Zusammenhängen** an und stellen ihre kommunikative Kompetenz unter Beweis. Visuelle, auditive und haptisch orientierte Lerner gleichermaßen werden angesprochen und motiviert.

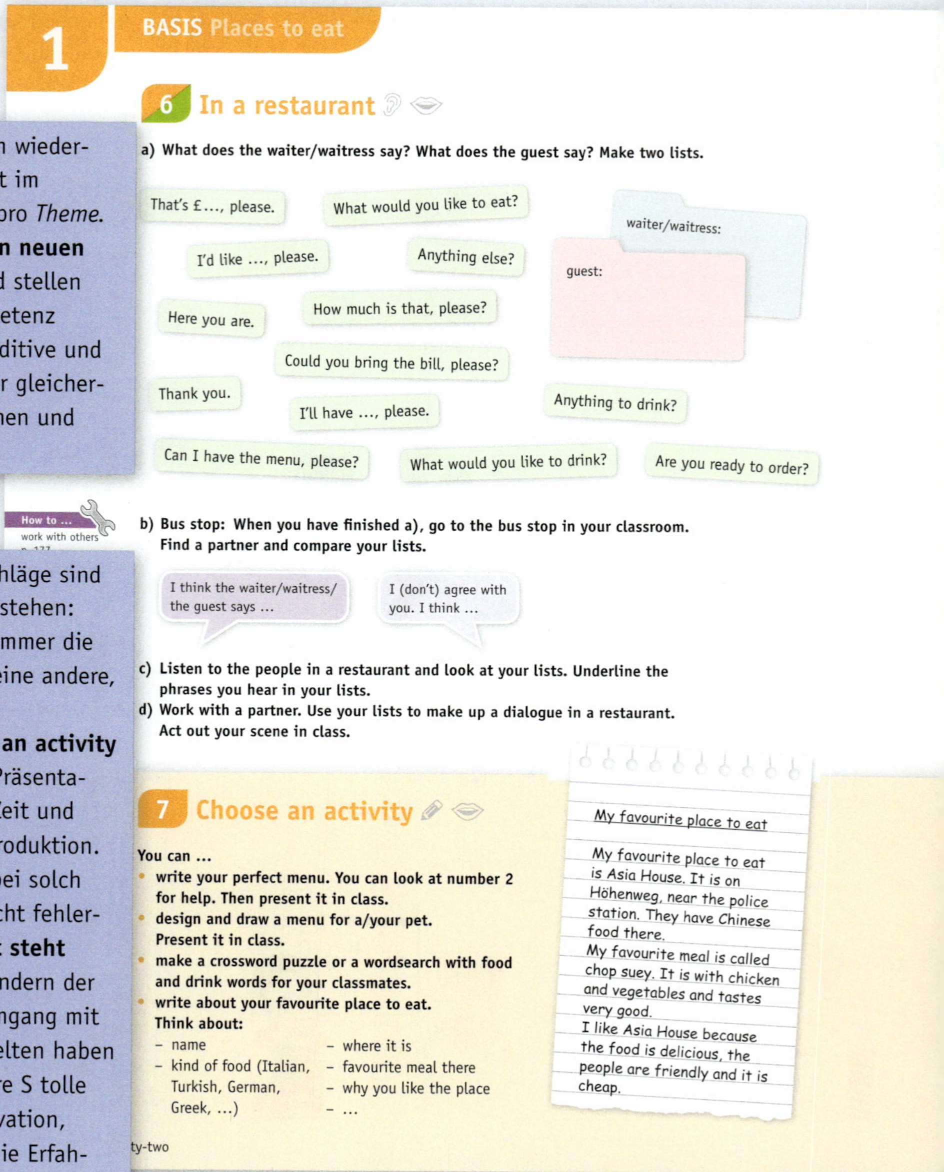

1 BASIS Places to eat

6 In a restaurant

a) What does the waiter/waitress say? What does the guest say? Make two lists.

That's £..., please. | What would you like to eat? | I'd like ..., please. | Anything else? | Here you are. | How much is that, please? | Could you bring the bill, please? | Thank you. | I'll have ..., please. | Anything to drink? | Can I have the menu, please? | What would you like to drink? | Are you ready to order?

waiter/waitress:

guest:

How to ...
work with others

b) Bus stop: When you have finished a), go to the bus stop in your classroom. Find a partner and compare your lists.

I think the waiter/waitress/ the guest says ...

I (don't) agree with you. I think ...

c) Listen to the people in a restaurant and look at your lists. Underline the phrases you hear in your lists.

d) Work with a partner. Use your lists to make up a dialogue in a restaurant. Act out your scene in class.

7 Choose an activity

You can ...

- write your perfect menu. You can look at number 2 for help. Then present it in class.
- design and draw a menu for a/your pet. Present it in class.
- make a crossword puzzle or a wordsearch with food and drink words for your classmates.
- write about your favourite place to eat. Think about:
  - name
  - kind of food (Italian, Turkish, German, Greek, ...)
  - where it is
  - favourite meal there
  - why you like the place
  - ...

My favourite place to eat

My favourite place to eat is Asia House. It is on Höhenweg, near the police station. They have Chinese food there. My favourite meal is called chop suey. It is with chicken and vegetables and tastes very good. I like Asia House because the food is delicious, the people are friendly and it is cheap.

ty-two

Choose-an-activity-Vorschläge sind immer als eben das zu verstehen: Vorschläge. Die S sollten immer die Möglichkeit haben, auch eine andere, eigene *activity* zu wählen.
Dabei gilt immer: **Choose an activity and present it,** d. h. der Präsentation gebührt ebenso viel Zeit und Aufmerksamkeit wie der Produktion. Zwar sind die Ergebnisse bei solch kreativen Aufgaben oft recht fehlerhaft, aber die **Korrektheit steht nicht im Vordergrund,** sondern der möglichst unbefangene Umgang mit der Fremdsprache. Nicht selten haben gerade leistungsschwächere S tolle Ideen und eine hohe Motivation, freie Texte zu schreiben. Die Erfahrung, den leistungsstärkeren MitS zumindest ebenbürtig zu sein, sollte L ihnen unbedingt von Zeit zu Zeit ermöglichen.

Vorsicht sollte L bei der **Fehlerkorrektur** in selbstständig erarbeiteten sprachlichen Produkten walten lassen. **Die Produkte zeigen den jetzigen Lernstand.** Bitte Fehler nicht rot im Produkt anstreichen. Der Einsatz von Klebezetteln stellt eine bewährte Alternative dar.

Camden Market wartet wiederholt (Seite 63, 69 und 131) mit einem **Projektvorschlag** auf. So werden Inhalte, Wortschatz und Strukturen eines *Theme* umgewälzt, und die S wenden ihr Wissen in einer Transferleistung, also in einem neuen Kontext, an.

BASIS Things we can do

10 A project – A magazine about YOUR area

PLAN IT

- **Work together in small groups.**
- **Make notes on what you already know about your area. Think about:**
  - what young people can do in your area/ your city/a town near you
  - where you can spend time after school
  - where you would like to take visitors
- **Collect more information:**
  - interview classmates, your family, …
  - check local newspapers
  - search the Internet
  - …

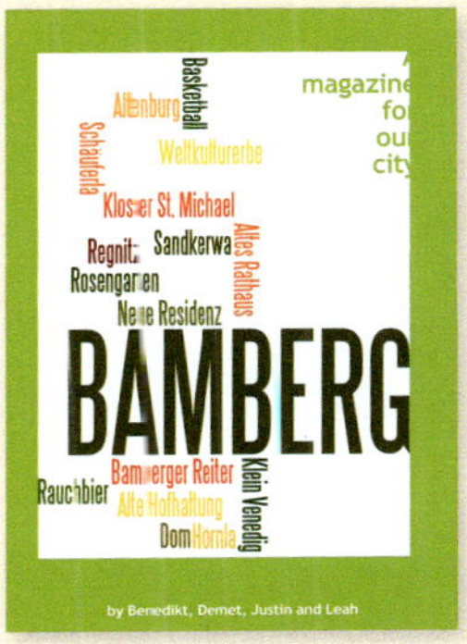

DO IT

Decide: Which member of your group is going to do what?

→ Choose an activity:

You can …

- **write down the information on different pieces of paper (also think about opening times, prices, how to get there, …).**
- **take photos or find other pictures.**
- **create a cover for your magazine.**

CHECK IT

- **Is the English OK?**
- **Do the pictures match?**
- **Is it interesting? Add details.**
- **Show it to other classmates or your teacher.**
- **Edit it. Use a dictionary.**
- **Stick the texts and pictures on the pages of your magazine. Add the cover.**

PRESENT IT

- **Present your magazines at your next Open Day at school or to exchange students.**

Die S haben bei **Projektaufgaben** viele Freiheiten:
- ob sie allein, zu zweit oder in der Gruppe arbeiten,
- welchen Aspekt des Themas sie wählen,
- wie sie ihre Ergebnisse präsentieren.

Manche S fühlen sich von diesen Freiheiten allerdings überfordert. Entsprechend sammelt L mit den S Ideen (um die Fantasie bei weniger kreativ veranlagten S in Gang zu bringen, aber auch um die Vor- und Nachteile bestimmter Vorgehensweisen zu beleuchten), bevor die S sich auf ein Thema/einen Arbeitsablauf festlegen.

Abschließend **Besprechen der Projektarbeit:** Wie seid ihr zurechtgekommen? Wie klappte die Zusammenarbeit? War die Zeit ausreichend? Was ist euch gut gelungen? Was habt ihr gelernt? Was würdet ihr beim nächsten Mal anders machen? Sollen wir so etwas wieder machen? Rückmeldung möglich als **Daumenfeedback**/Handzeichen im Plenum: *Thumbs up if you enjoyed the project./ Thumbs down if you didn't enjoy it./ And thumbs sideways if you're not sure.* (L demonstriert jeweils.)

Die S können Interviews und Ähnliches mit Smartphone oder dem **Easi-Speak-Mikrofon** (ISBN 978-3-425-**72990**-9) aufnehmen.

Mögliche Checkliste für die *magazine pages* der S:
- *Keep your work clear and tidy!*
- *Give your page some structure by making use of headings.*
- *Make use of pictures, photos and graphs.*
- *Make use of colours. But be careful: not too many different colours!*
- *If you don't use the computer: make sure people can read your handwriting.*
- *Don't put too much text on a page. Use keywords and short sentences.*
- *Remember to either sign your page or put your name somewhere so people know whose page it is.*

TM, p. 16

Mr Batson
Mr Lambraki
Mrs Lambraki
Mrs Collins
Mrs Batson
Mr Patel
Mrs Patel
Sheree Patel
Josephine Batson
George Lambraki
Rajiv Patel
Gillian Collins
Sharon Batson
Caroline Lambraki
Charlie Batson
Karla Marshall
Patch
Mrs Killmouskey

TM, p. 16 Folie 1 KV2

Who's who in CAMDEN MARKET

Gillian Collins

- 13 years old
- birthday is on 26th April
- lives with her mum, sees her dad at the weekend
- lives next door to Caroline
- has got a cat, Mrs Killmouskey
- likes animals, football and music

Charlie Batson

- 13 years old
- birthday is on 22nd June
- family came to England from Barbados
- has got a younger sister, Sharon (8), and an older sister, Josephine (19)
- has got a goldfish, Fritz
- likes football, is an Arsenal fan

Rajiv Patel

- 13 years old
- birthday is on 8th February
- grandparents came to England from India
- parents have got a small shop
- sometimes helps his parents in the shop
- has got an older sister, Sheree (16)
- likes music, plays the guitar

Caroline Lambraki

- 13 years old
- birthday is on 21st May
- moved from Manchester to Camden two years ago
- lives next door to Gillian
- father came to England from Greece
- has got a twin brother, George
- has got a rabbit, Daisy, and a dog, Patch
- likes football and music

Karla Marshall

- 14 years old
- birthday is on 10th October
- has got a younger brother, Josh (7)
- has got a rabbit, Hoppity
- is in a wheelchair
- likes sports, plays wheelchair basketball

Welcome!

Mit der *Camden Market* Rallye kannst du dein Englischbuch kennenlernen. Bei dieser Rallye geht es darum, Fragen zu den verschiedenen Teilen des Buches zu beantworten. Du musst also ein bisschen blättern, um die Antworten zu finden. Wenn du alle Fragen richtig beantwortet hast, erhältst du einen Lösungssatz, den du vorne in dein Workbook eintragen kannst. Los geht's!

Ready to start

1 Auf Seite 4 werden die Hauptfiguren von *Camden Market* vorgestellt. Welcher Junge hat zwei Schwestern?
E Rajiv — (R) Charlie

2 Wie viele Kapitel *(Themes)* gibt es?
F acht — (E) sechs

3 Jedes *Theme* hat ein Hauptthema. Blättere die Seiten 37 bis 56 durch. Worum geht es in *Theme* 2?
(A) Sport und Fitness — I Reisen

4 Jedes *Theme* hat einen blauen Extra-Teil mit Übungen. Wie heißt er?
G *Camden Chronicle* — (D) *Practice*

5 Bilder können Themen veranschaulichen. Zu welchem Thema kannst du auf den Seiten 20 und 21 Fotos sehen?
L London — (Y) Essengehen

6 Die Land & Leute-Kästen erzählen dir viel über das Leben in englischsprachigen Ländern. Worum geht es in dem Kasten auf Seite 65?
(T) eine Veranstaltung — A Geld

7 Auf den *Wordbanks*-Seiten findest du Wörter und Wendungen zu ausgewählten Themen. Auf welcher Seite befindet sich die *Wordbank* zum Thema „Menschen"?
H Seite 163 — (O) Seite 159

8 Außen an den Seiten findest du Symbole, die dir bei der Arbeit mit dem Buch helfen, wie z. B. dieses: 8 p. 187
Worum geht es hier?
D ein Projekt — (S) Grammatik

9 Finde dieses Symbol: WB 17 p. 13
Was bedeutet es?
(T) Aufgabe im Workbook — F Hausaufgabe

10 Jedes *Theme* hat eine Wortliste, in der du die Wörter findest, die ihr gerade im Unterricht besprecht. Auf welcher Seite beginnt die Wortliste für *Theme* 1?
P Seite 203 — (A) Seite 206

11 Auf den Seiten 235 bis 278 befinden sich Wörter, die nach dem Alphabet geordnet sind. Welche Wörter kannst du hier nachschlagen?
C nur englische — (R) englische und deutsche

12 Auf den *How to …*-Seiten lernst du Techniken zum Englischlernen. Sie beginnen auf Seite 166. Wie viele *How to …*-Seiten gibt es?
(T) vierzehn — H acht

Jetzt kann es losgehen! In deinem Englischbuch gibt es noch viel zu entdecken. Viel Spaß mit

CAMDEN MARKET

Die Struktur von CAMDEN MARKET

Aufbau der *Themes* 1–6

BASIS (Grundanforderungen)

- Erfüllt die **Grundanforderungen** für Klasse 7
- Umfasst zwei Themenkreise zu einem Oberthema
- Ist eng verzahnt mit dem Practice-Teil: P6 P p. 29
  und dem More-Teil: M4 M p. 33
- Besonders einfache Texte und Aufgaben sind gekennzeichnet:
- Jeder Themenkreis schließt mit einer farbig hinterlegten Zielaufgabe *(target task)*, wie z. B. Choose an activity oder Project.

PRACTICE (Übungsteil zum Trainieren und Wiederholen)

- **Übungsteil** zu beiden Themenkreisen des Basis-Teils
- Mit Übungen zu Wortschatz, Aussprache und Strukturen sowie Sprachmittlung

MORE (Differenzierung für mittleres und höheres Niveau)

- Bietet **Zusatzmaterial** zur Differenzierung für **mittleres** und **höheres Niveau**
- Ist inhaltlich mit den beiden Themenkreisen des Basis-Teils verknüpft
- Mit zusätzlichen und alternativ und/oder parallel zum Basis-Teil einsetzbaren Aufgaben
- Parallel einsetzbare Aufgaben M3 können zeitgleich zu einer Aufgabe im Basis-Teil bearbeitet werden. Im Anschluss werden die Ergebnisse von Basis- und More-Aufgabe zusammengeführt.
- Besonders anspruchsvolle Texte und Aufgaben sind gekennzeichnet:

CAMDEN CHRONICLE (Magazinseite)

- Magazinseite mit Fragen zum *Theme*, interkulturellen Hinweisen und authentischen Texten

Anhang

Reading is Fun	Optionaler Lesestoff zu den *Themes*
Wordbanks	Thematische Wortschatzsammlungen
How to …	Lern- und Arbeitstechniken
Language in Focus	Grammatikanhang zum Nachschlagen
Words W	Chronologisches Wörterverzeichnis
Dictionary D	Alphabetisches Wörterverzeichnis

Theme 1: Are you hungry?

Die Angebote in *Camden Market* sind nicht linear abzuarbeiten. Die Auswahl der Übungen und Übungsteile richtet sich nach den Schwerpunkten des schulinternen Curriculums.

R = *revision* (Wiederholung)

Theme 2: Are you fit?

Theme 3: What's on in your area?

Die Angebote in *Camden Market* sind nicht linear abzuarbeiten. Die Auswahl der Übungen und Übungsteile richtet sich nach den Schwerpunkten des schulinternen Curriculums.

R = *revision* (Wiederholung)

Theme 4: You're not alone

Seite	Themen	Kompetenzen	Target task
	BASIS		
79	**Robinson Crusoe**	Gefühle beschreiben • Sich auf Gegenstände für eine einsame Insel einigen • Sagen, was *home* für einen bedeutet Die Geschichte von Robinson Crusoe kennenlernen Einer Unterhaltung Informationen entnehmen Eine Bildergeschichte nacherzählen Einer digitalen Diashow Informationen entnehmen	**Choose an activity:** • Eine Flaschenpostnachricht schreiben • Eine Auswahl wichtiger Vokabeln treffen • Ein *fact file* über Daniel Defoe erstellen
84	**Dealing with problems**	Über Gefühle und Sorgen und mögliche Lösungen sprechen • Ratschläge geben Briefe und einen Text über persönliche Probleme lesen Eine Unterhaltung über persönliche Probleme verstehen • Einen Songtext verstehen Sein Lieblingslied beschreiben	**Choose an activity:** • Familienmitglieder vorstellen • Eine Szene zu einem Bild schreiben • Ein Lied vorstellen
	PRACTICE		
90	**Robinson Crusoe**	Aussprache • Wortschatz: Gegensatzpaare Strukturen: R: *Simple past* • R: *Word order* Sprachmittlung: Eine Flaschenpostnachricht weitergeben	
92	**Dealing with problems**	Aussprache • Wortschatz Strukturen: R: *Will-future* • *Conditional clauses, type I* Sprachmittlung: Einen Brief an eine *agony aunt* vermitteln	
	MORE		
94	**Robinson Crusoe**	Fragen an Robinson beantworten • Einen Vortrag über Robinson Crusoe halten Einem Sachtext über einen Film Informationen entnehmen Einen Tagebucheintrag auf einer einsamen Insel verfassen Einer Unterhaltung Informationen entnehmen	
96	**Dealing with problems**	Einem Dialogtext über persönliche Probleme Informationen entnehmen Einem Telefongespräch Informationen entnehmen Einen Brief an eine *agony aunt* verfassen • Einen Dialog schreiben	
98	**CAMDEN CHRONICLE**	• *Did you get it all?:* Fragen zum *Theme* • *Good to know:* interkulturelle Hinweise • authentische Texte: Witz, Gedicht	

Die Angebote in *Camden Market* sind nicht linear abzuarbeiten. Die Auswahl der Übungen und Übungsteile richtet sich nach den Schwerpunkten des schulinternen Curriculums.

R = *revision* (Wiederholung)

Theme 5: Everyday science

Optional: Bilingual module HISTORY

Theme 6: Up and away

Seite	Themen	Kompetenzen	Target task
	BASIS		
123	**Planning a holiday**	Über Urlaubspläne sprechen • Sich auf einem Bahnhof orientieren • Zugverbindungen erfragen Ein Anmeldeformular verstehen • Einer Anzeigetafel Zugverbindungen entnehmen Ein Gespräch am Fahrkartenschalter verstehen • Einer Unterhaltung über Feriencamps folgen	**Choose an activity:** • Ein Feriengedicht verfassen • Über einen Feriencampaufenthalt schreiben • Eine Szene am Bahnhofsschalter schreiben und vorspielen
128	**Go Britain**	Eine Befragung zu Freunden aus anderen Ländern durchführen • Sich über Sehenswürdigkeiten unterhalten Infotexte zu Reisezielen verstehen • Einem Dialogtext über Reisevorbereitungen folgen Einen Dialog über Ferienplanung verstehen • Britische Akzente kennenlernen **Photo Gallery:** Reiseziele in Großbritannien	**Projekt:** • Einen Landesteil Großbritanniens in einem *gallery walk* vorstellen
	PRACTICE		
134	**Planning a holiday**	Aussprache • Wortschatz: Reisen Strukturen: R: *Going to-future* • *Simple present with future meaning* Sprachmittlung: Ein Ticket am Fahrkartenautomaten kaufen	
136	**Go Britain**	Aussprache • Wortschatz: Reisen Strukturen: R: *Simple past* • R: *Word order* Sprachmittlung: Eine Werbebroschüre erklären	
	MORE		
138	**Planning a holiday**	Eine Fahrkarte am Schalter kaufen Einer Feriencamp-Website Informationen entnehmen Regeln in einem Feriencamp verstehen Über Urlaub schreiben • Feriencamp-Regeln notieren	
140	**Go Britain**	Redemittel für Urlaubssituationen sammeln Aussagen in verschiedenen Akzenten verstehen Ein Rollenspiel über eine Zimmerbuchung entwickeln • Über ein interessantes Reiseziel schreiben	
142	**CAMDEN CHRONICLE**	• *Did you get it all?:* Fragen zum *Theme* • *Good to know:* interkulturelle Hinweise • authentische Texte: E-Mail	

Die Angebote in *Camden Market* sind nicht linear abzuarbeiten. Die Auswahl der Übungen und Übungsteile richtet sich nach den Schwerpunkten des schulinternen Curriculums.

R = *revision* (Wiederholung)

ANHANG

LEGENDE

Symbole und Verweise

Übungs-/Differenzierungsangebot

P6 P p. 25	Verweis auf Übungen im Practice-Teil.
M1 M p. 32	Verweis auf Aufgaben im More-Teil.
6	Hierzu gibt es eine parallel einsetzbare Aufgabe im More-Teil.
M3 // M p. 33	Verweis auf die parallel einsetzbare Aufgabe im More-Teil.
M3	Hierzu gibt es eine parallel einsetzbare Aufgabe im Basis-Teil.
6 // B p. 22	Rückverweis auf die parallel einsetzbare Aufgabe im Basis-Teil.
xx p. xx WB	Hierzu gib es im Workbook weitere Übungen.
	Der Mond kennzeichnet im Basis-Teil besonders einfache Aufgaben.
xx p. xx WB	Von dieser Aufgabe gibt es eine einfachere, parallel einsetzbare Variante im Workbook.
	Die Sonne kennzeichnet schwierige Texte und Aufgaben im More-Teil.
xx p. xx WB	Von dieser Aufgabe gibt es eine anspruchsvollere, parallel einsetzbare Variante im Workbook.
portfolio	Das Ergebnis kann im Portfolio-Ordner abgeheftet werden.

Referenzteil

wordbank Health p. 154	In den Wordbanks befinden sich die wichtigsten Wörter zu einem Thema.
How to ... read p. 170	Die Techniken auf den How to ...-Seiten helfen beim Englischlernen.
8 p. 187	Hierzu gibt es eine Erklärung im Grammatik-Teil Language in Focus.

Medien

L xx	Dieser Text ist auf der CD für Lehrer.
L xx S xx	Dieser Text ist auf der CD für Lehrer und auf der CD für Schüler.
DVD	Das Video befindet sich auf der DVD für Lehrer.

Kompetenzbereiche

- Sprechen
- Leseverstehen
- Schreiben
- Hörverstehen
- Hörsehverstehen
- Sprachmittlung

THEME 1

TM, p. 25
KV17: Lernlandkarte

ARE YOU HUNGRY?

In diesem *Theme* ...

» unterhältst du dich über Restaurants und Essen.
» lernst du, englische Speisekarten zu lesen und zu verstehen.
» übst du, auf Englisch Essen zu bestellen.
» sprichst du über Schulessen und gesunde Ernährung.
» beschäftigst du dich mit Essgewohnheiten in anderen Ländern.

W p. 206 TM, p. 25

➡ p. LF15

1 A food and drink ABC

IWS KV3 p. 8f./1+2

How to ... work with others p. 176

a) **Think:** What food and drink words do you know? **Write down** your alphabet.
b) **Pair:** Work with a partner and **complete** your alphabets.

What did you write for A?

Apple. What have you got?

I've got avocado.
What did you write for B?

...

A - apple, ...
B - banana, ...
C - cake, ...
D - delicious, ...
E - eat, ...
F - ...

c) **Share:** Sit together with **another** pair and put your food and drink words in groups (fruit, vegetables, for breakfast, ...).

LSW 101

➡ p. LF15

2 Places to eat

LSW 102 p. 11/4

WB 1 p. 7

a) What is YOUR favourite place to eat?
b) Look at the **menus** and the pictures of the restaurants on these two **pages**. Choose one restaurant you would like to go to. **Make notes** on what you like about it. Then talk about it in class.

I'd like to go to	Burger Queen the Windsor Castle Pizza World	because	the food is ... my favourite food is ... I love ... I'd like to try ... it's not too expensive. ...

Pizza World

Pizzas	regular	large
Ciao Bambino *(tomatoes, **cheese**)*	£5.95	£7.75
Via Veneto *(**ham**, olives, garlic)*	£7.95	£10.35
Mexicana *(**beans**, chillies, olives, **onions**)*	£8.95	£11.65
Capri *(salami, **mushrooms**, onions)*	£9.45	£12.25
Verde (**vegetarian**) *(onions, broccoli, mushrooms)*	£9.45	£12.25

Fresh Salads	
Italian salad	£6.45
Tomato salad	£5.45
Chicken salad	£7.45

Drinks	
Soft drinks	£1.50
Glass of wine	£4.70
Coffee/tea	£1.45

The Windsor Castle

Starters

Soup of the day	£3.75
Tomato soup	£2.95
Garden salad *mixed green salad with tomatoes and carrots*	£3.95
Windsor Castle salad *lettuce, tomatoes, bacon and crispy chicken*	£4.95
Fresh melon salad *with cucumber, orange and mint*	£3.50
Garlic bread	£2.25

Main Courses

Chicken curry	£12.00
Roast lamb and mint sauce	£14.95
Roast beef and Yorkshire pudding	£13.45
Fish pie	£12.75
Vegetarian lasagne	£9.50

Desserts

Apple and blackberry crumble	£4.50
Chocolate and strawberry cake	£4.50
Fruit salad	£4.60
Ice cream	£4.60

Beverages

Soft drinks	£1.90
Tea, coffee or hot chocolate	£1.95

BURGER QUEEN

Queen Hamburger	£2.95
Queen Cheeseburger	£3.50
Queen Burger & Beans	£3.95
Queen Special *(Burger, Chips & Salad)*	£4.95
Queen Hot Dog	£2.95
Queen Onion Rings	£2.00
Sweet Queen Donut	£1.50
Soft drinks	£1.10

c) Work with a partner. Look at the menus. Ask and answer questions like these:

How much does the Queen Hamburger at Burger Queen cost?

It's £2.95.

How many desserts are there at the Windsor Castle?

There are …

How much is … ?

…

Mengenangaben 11R p. 190
How to … talk p. 172

d) You have got £15 and want to go to one of the restaurants. What do you want to eat and drink? Write it down and tell your partner.

P1 + F4 p. 28

W p. 206

➡ p. LF15

3 Friday evening

Folie 2 p. 10/3

L 1.1 S 1

WB 2+3 p. 8

a) What do you think: What are Mrs Collins, Gillian and Charlie talking about? Look at the title and the pictures.
b) Now listen. Were you right in a)?
c) Listen again and read along: Which restaurants are they talking about? What kind of food have these restaurants got?

Gillian: Mum, we are so hungry. What's for dinner tonight?

Mrs Collins: Well, I haven't done any shopping this week. So there isn't anything in the fridge to cook for you. But we could go out for dinner. The last time we went out was ages ago.

Gillian: Great idea. Let's go to Burger Queen. That's my favourite place! They've got some really delicious burgers on the menu – and it's not very expensive.

Mrs Collins: But the weather is so beautiful today and you can't sit outside there. It's too hot and noisy inside. And you eat too many hamburgers and chips anyway. What would you like, Charlie? Do you know any other good places to eat?

Charlie: Well, I'm not sure. We could try that new pizza place – Pizza World.

Gillian: Sorry, but I really don't want any pizza today. I'm going to have some at Dad's house tomorrow.

Mrs Collins: Oh, Gillian! OK, then why don't we go to that pub on Westbourne Street? It's called the Windsor Castle, I think. They've got great food and you can sit outside. I'm sure they'll have something you like. The salads taste really good there …

Gillian: Salad? Salad is boring!

Charlie: But you don't have to order a salad. There are other things on the menu. I've been there with my family. It's quite nice.

Mrs Collins: What do you think, Gillian? Would you like to go there? Or have you got any other ideas?

Gillian: I really fancy some Indian food tonight. Something that's hot and spicy! Can we please order some takeaway food from Bengal Tiger, Mum? We don't have to buy any drinks and we can have some ice cream for dessert. What do you think, Charlie?

Charlie: Takeaway sounds good to me. And we could watch a film afterwards.

Mrs Collins: OK then. But you two have to phone and order the takeaway. Here's the menu. Let's have a look …

d) **Now read the dialogue again. Who wants to eat what and where?**

Mrs Collins Gillian Charlie	wants to doesn't want to	eat … go to …

e) **Act out the scene in groups of three.**

P3 p. 28

M2 p. 33

\\ eigener Dialog, in dem sich die S auf ein Restaurant einigen

4 Ready to order?

Gillian is phoning the Indian restaurant. Read the questions first. Then listen to Gillian and take notes.

1. What is Gillian's phone number? 020 7709 7234
2. How does Mrs Collins like her favourite meal? hot
3. How much does the food cost? £17.40
4. How long do they have to wait for their dinner? about 40 minutes

LSW 103 p. 11/4

Bengal Tiger
115 Westbourne Grove
London W2 4UP
Phone: 020 7908 1991
Fax: 020 7908 1992

Main Dishes

Tandoori Chicken	£4.50
Lamb Tikka	£5.10
Tandoori Mixed Grill	£6.80
Chicken Madras	£4.50
Murgh Masala	£4.95
Lamb Curry	£5.50
Chicken Vindaloo	£5.50
Garlic Chicken Tikka	£5.50

Side Orders

Boiled Rice	£1.10
Bombay Potato	£2.10
Cucumber Raita	£1.90
Naan Bread	£1.50

L 1 2 S 2

WB 4 p. 8

M1 p. 32

WB 5 p. 9

5 Any ideas?

➡ p. LF16

a) **Look at these sentences from number 3. Who says them? What are they in German?**

Have you got any other ideas?

I really don't want any pizza today.

They've got some delicious burgers on the menu.

WB 6 + 7 p. 9/10

b) **Find more sentences with "some" or "any" in number 3. Write them in a grid like this:**

KV18 ↓

+	–	?
They've got some delicious burgers on the menu.	I really don't want any pizza today.	Have you got any other ideas?
…	…	…

c) **When do you use "some"? When do you use "any"? What about "something" and "anything"? Tell your classmates in German.**

Mengenangaben

How to … work with grammar p. 178

11R p. 190

P5 + P6 p. 29

Rootmaster

73
TEL: 0171-247 7122
786
Established 1992
Muhib Indian Cuisine
TANDOORI AND VEGETARIAN ALSO BALTI SPECIALIST
FULLY AIR CONDITIONED
TAKE AWAY SERVICE AVAILABLE
73 FULLY LICENSED MUHIB EST.1992

LAND & LEUTE

Essengehen in Großbritannien

Manche Leute behaupten, dass britisches Essen langweilig ist und nicht gut schmeckt. Das stimmt aber nicht, denn es gibt so viele verschiedene Restaurants in Großbritannien.

Britische Familien gehen gerne zum Essen in einen *pub*. Das Essen und die Getränke werden an der Theke bestellt und gleich bezahlt. Manche *pubs* sind nach berühmten Personen benannt *(The Queen Victoria)*, andere nach Orten *(Windsor Castle)* und wieder andere nach Tieren *(Rat and Parrot)*. Viele *pubs* haben auch lustige Namen *(The Hairy Lemon, The Dog's Breakfast)*.

Ein beliebtes britisches Gericht ist *fish and chips*. Das ist panierter und frittierter Fisch mit dicken Pommes frites, die man meist zum Mitnehmen in *fish and chip shops* kauft. Ein anderes traditionelles Gericht ist das so genannte *Sunday roast*, das es häufig sonntags mittags gibt. Dabei handelt es sich um einen Braten, z. B. *Roastbeef*, der meist mit Gemüse, Sauce und einem Gebäck namens *Yorkshire pudding* serviert wird.

Briten essen aber nicht nur traditionelle britische Gerichte; viele lieben auch indisches, chinesisches, mexikanisches oder italienisches Essen. Da in Großbritannien Menschen verschiedenster Herkunft leben, kannst du dort auch die unterschiedlichsten Gerichte probieren.

Welche Restaurants gibt es in deiner Gegend?
Welche typisch deutschen Gerichte kennst du?

Folie 3A+B IWS p. 12–13

W p. 207

➡ p. LF16

wordbank
Food and drink
p. 152

M3 // M
p. 33
// zusätzliche Redemittel für einen Restaurantdialog

6 In a restaurant

IWS   LSW 104   p. 14/6

a) What does the waiter/waitress say? What does the guest say? Make two lists.

That's £ …, please.
What would you like to eat?
I'd like …, please.
Anything else?
Here you are.
How much is that, please?
Could you bring the bill, please?
Thank you.
I'll have …, please.
Anything to drink?
Can I have the menu, please?
What would you like to drink?
Are you ready to order?

waiter/waitress:

guest:

How to …
work with others
p. 177

b) Bus stop: When you have finished a), go to the bus stop in your classroom. Find a partner and compare your lists.

I think the waiter/waitress/ the guest says …

I (don't) agree with you. I think …

L 1.3

c) Listen to the people in a restaurant and look at your lists. Underline the phrases you hear in your lists.

P2 + P7 P
p. 28/29

d) Work with a partner. Use your lists to make up a dialogue in a restaurant. Act out your scene in class.

KV13   KV19 ↓   KV20 ↑

M4 M
p. 33
8 WB
p. 10
portfolio

7 Choose an activity

You can …

- write your perfect menu. You can look at number 2 for help. Then present it in class.
- design and draw a menu for a/your pet. Present it in class.
- make a crossword puzzle or a wordsearch with food and drink words for your classmates.
- write about your favourite place to eat. Think about:
  - name
  - kind of food (Italian, Turkish, German, Greek, …)
  - where it is
  - favourite meal there
  - why you like the place
  - …

wordbank
Food and drink
p. 152

➡ p. LF17

My favourite place to eat

My favourite place to eat is Asia House. It is on Höhenweg, near the police station. They have Chinese food there.
My favourite meal is called chop suey. It is with chicken and vegetables and tastes very good.
I like Asia House because the food is delicious, the people are friendly and it is cheap.

TM, p. 48

8 Clever, isn't he?

SW 105 · KV21 · KV22 · p. 16/8 · ➡ p. LF17 · WB 9 + 10 p. 11

a) Look at the picture. What can you see? What is happening?

That isn't very healthy, is it?

What do you mean? Chips are potatoes, aren't they? And there is tomato in ketchup, isn't there? And eggs are good for you! And I'm sure there is orange juice in this lemonade. So what's wrong with you? You don't look very happy, do you?

b) Now look at the speech bubbles in a). What are they in German? Which is YOUR favourite translation for the question tags?

Question tags 12 p. 191 · P P10 p. 30

..., nicht wahr? | ..., oder? | ..., nicht? | ... ?

9 Hands up!

LSW 106 · p. 15/7 · ➡ p. LF17

a) Do a survey in class. Ask the questions and collect the number of answers (yes/no/sometimes) on the board. Hands up!

Do you ...

1. have breakfast before school?
2. eat fruit each day?
3. only drink sugary drinks?
4. bring a snack to school?
5. eat vegetables once a day?
6. buy fast food like hamburgers or chips more than once a week?
7. eat sweets every day?
8. eat crisps/peanuts/... every day?
9. ... ?

b) Report about the results of the survey.

Satzstellung 193 p. 197/198

... people in our class	always sometimes never	have breakfast before school. eat ... (each day). drink sugary drinks. ...

W p. 208

➡ p. LF17

11 p. 12 WB

10 Good for you?

p. 16/8

a) Look at these food items. What do you think is healthy? What isn't healthy? Talk to a partner.

I think … is/are healthy/unhealthy.

I (don't) agree.

smoothie | cereal | dark chocolate | sugary drinks | spinach | yoghurt

M5 p. 34 M

b) Now read what a food expert writes about the food items in a). What is new to you? What do you find surprising?

News (230) ▾ Favourites ▾

EAT BETTER FOOD!

- Start the day with a good breakfast. Some cereals with milk are healthy. But be careful: A lot of cereals have too much sugar. If you like yoghurt for breakfast, choose unsweetened yoghurt and put in small pieces of fruit or some honey.
- Eat five portions of fruit and vegetables each day. Green vegetables are very healthy, especially peas, beans, broccoli and spinach. Fruit is delicious but be careful with smoothies: Some of them contain a lot of sugar.
- Sugary drinks are bad for your health – and your teeth! Drink lots of water instead. And don't eat too many sweets. If you can't live without chocolate, it's healthier to eat dark chocolate.

➡ p. LF18

11 Lunch at school

LSW 107

12 p. 12/13 WB

a) One of Rajiv's subjects is food technology. Yesterday he had to interview his classmates about school lunches. Read Karla's statement and take notes in a grid like this:

name	likes	doesn't like
Karla	…	…
…	…	…

Karla

I eat at the school cafeteria every day. You can get fish, meat or a vegetarian dish. You can also get vegetables, for example carrots, peas and cabbage. The food is OK … My favourite school lunch is pasta. And I usually eat a dessert afterwards because I have a sweet tooth. What I absolutely hate eating at school is potatoes. They are always too soft and just taste disgusting.

L 1.4 S 3

13 p. 13 WB

b) Now listen to Jack and Shima and complete your grid.

c) Compare your notes with a partner.

d) Double circle: What do you think about the food at YOUR school? What do/don't you like? Why?

KV23 ↓

How to … work with others p. 177

12 A school lunch recipe

IWS LSW 108 p. 17/9 ➡ p. LF18

WB 14 + 15 p. 13-15

a) **Unhealthy food can make students overweight and ill. This is why school lunches should be healthy. Read this recipe for a healthy school lunch. Put the pictures in the right order.**

PASTA WITH LEEKS AND FETA CHEESE

For 4 people you need:
- 200 g tomatoes
- 1-2 green or red chillies
- 1 bunch of parsley
- 2-3 leeks
- 3 tbs olive oil
- 1 tsp paprika powder
- salt
- pepper
- 1 tbs black cumin seeds
- 300 g pasta (small macaroni)
- 200 g feta cheese

1. Wash the tomatoes and cut them into small pieces with a knife. Wash the chilli and cut it open. Take out the middle and the seeds. Then cut the chilli into small pieces. Wash and dry the parsley. Cut the leaves into very small pieces. Cut off the ends of the leeks. Wash the leeks and cut them into thin strips.
2. Mix the tomatoes, chilli and parsley with 1 tablespoon of olive oil. Add the paprika powder, salt and pepper.
3. Heat the rest of the oil in a pan. Then cook the leeks and the black cumin seeds for 5-10 minutes at a low temperature. Stir every few minutes.
4. Cook the pasta in boiling salted water until it is ready to eat. Pour the water out of the pasta.
5. Break the feta cheese into small pieces and add it to the leeks. Take the pan off the stove.
6. Mix the pasta with the tomatoes, feta cheese and leeks. Put on a plate and enjoy.

A

B

C

D

E

F

b) **Read the recipe again. Find cooking words and write them down.**

P 12 p. 31

things you use	what you do	food you need
knife	cook	pasta
…	…	…

W p. 209

➡ p. LF18

13 Very British?

LSW 109 KV24 ↓↑ p. 18/10

a) Rajiv also asked some other students from his school about their favourite food. Look at their answers. What would YOU answer Rajiv?

Katie

I like green tea and Thai food. It's spicy and good!

Taylor

My family is from Italy so my favourite food is Italian. I like all kinds of pasta and pizza.

I like nachos with cheese.

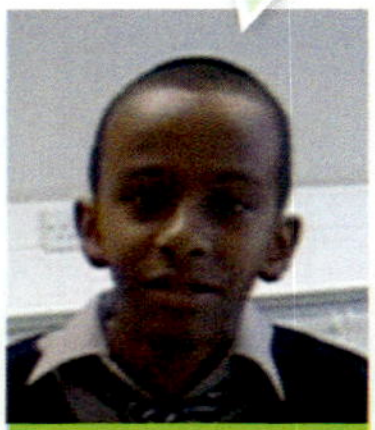
Yusuf

My favourite food is fast food – hamburgers and chips and a cola.

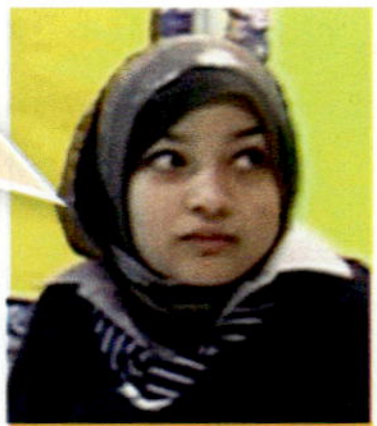
Safia

Daniel

I love curry. My friend from India makes the best curry!

…

Present perfect
9R p. 188/189
P11 P p. 31
M6 M p. 34

b) Walk around the classroom and interview your classmates.

KV25, KV26

Have you ever	eaten drunk had tried …	green tea? curry? sushi? Thai food? … ?

Yes, I have. It was …

No, I haven't but I have …

14 Eating habits around the world

LSW 110

How to … read p. 170

a) People in different countries have different ways of eating and cooking food. Match the pictures with the texts.

A-4 B-5 C-3 D-2 E-1

I think picture A goes with text …

Britain E 1

In Britain some people put the peas onto the back of a fork with a knife. They also do this to eat small pieces of meat and potatoes.

A

Iran D 2

Family meals are very important. The family usually sits on the floor around a large cloth. There are many kinds of food and they come on different plates.

Italy
C 3

Italy is famous for its many different kinds of pasta. It is not easy to eat spaghetti. You roll them around a fork. You never cut spaghetti with a knife.

D

C

India
A 4

People don't usually use knives or forks. They pick up their food with pieces of chapati (a kind of flat bread). Then they make a little ball of food with three fingers and the thumb of the right hand and eat it.

B

E

China
B 5

In China people eat food with chopsticks. You hold them between your fingers. The food is served in bowls.

b) Find a picture of a typical German meal – or a typical meal from your parents' country. What is it and how do people eat it?

➡ p. LF19

WB 16 p. 15

P P8 + P9 p. 30

M M7 p. 35

15 Choose an activity

You can ...

- **make a poster with your favourite food and label it. Show the poster to your class and say why you like the food.**
- **write a food diary for one week. What do you eat and drink for breakfast, lunch and dinner? What snacks do you have?**
- **present different food items and tell the class why they are healthy or unhealthy. You can look at number 10 for help.**
- **write a menu for your perfect school lunches for one week.**
- **write down your favourite recipe in English:**
  - What do you need?
  - How do you make it?
  - Where does it come from?

You can look at number 12 for help. p. 19/11

PERFECT SCHOOL LUNCHES

Monday:
lasagne, Italian salad, chocolate pudding

Tuesday:
pizza with ham and mushrooms, ice cream

Wednesday:
Schnitzel with chips, peas and carrots, fruit salad

Thursday:
Spaghetti Carbonara, donut

Friday:
fish fingers, potato salad, jelly

➡ p. LF19

portfolio

wordbank
Food and drink
p. 152

test yourself
p. 15/17

W p. 210 TM, p. 63

P1 Food words

➡ p. LF20

LSW 111

wordbank
Food and drink
p. 152

a) Make a list of food words that are similar to German food words. You can look at number 2 for help.

English	German
tomato	Tomate
butter	Butter
…	…

b) Compare your list with a partner.

P2 Pairs

Find the missing words and write down the pairs.

drink
salad – eat
tea – ???

waiter/waitress
school – teacher
restaurant – ???

vegetable
apple – fruit
broccoli – ???

chicken curry – main course
ice cream – ??? dessert

steak – knife and fork
soup – ??? spoon

sugar – cupboard
milk – ??? fridge

P3 Sound check

➡ p. LF20

LSW 112

L 1.5

a) Listen to the words and repeat them.
b) Make three lists. Write the words in the correct list.

fish • much • Gillian • chips • shopping • fridge • delicious • sure • Charlie • age • question • juice • chocolate • dish • German • cheeseburger • English • she • ketchup • enjoy

/ʃ/	/dʒ/	/tʃ/
fish	Gillian	much
…	…	…

P4 The menu, please

Look at the menu from the *Windsor Castle* on page 17. It has different parts:

starters • main courses • desserts • beverages

Which part of the menu is it?

– You want to eat some curry. Where is it on the menu? main courses
– You want a soup or a salad before the curry. Where are they on the menu? starters
– What is the word for things like ice cream or fruit salad? desserts
– You would like something to drink. Where can you find it on the menu? beverages

P5 A special burger

LSW 113

➡ p. LF20

11R p. 190 Mengenangaben

a) What do you like on a burger? Choose from these things (or other things you like) and write them down.

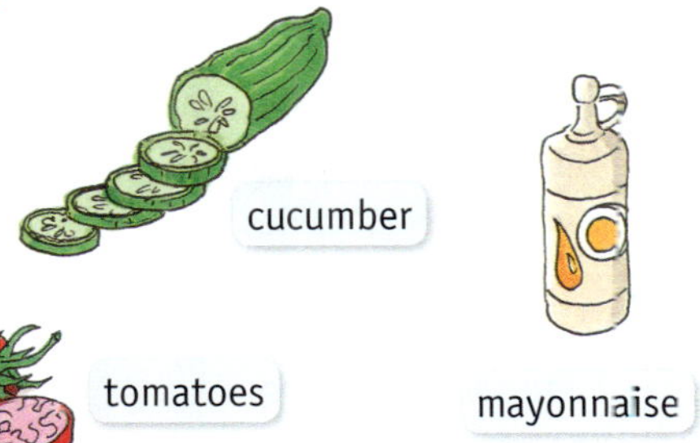

b) Tell a partner about YOUR special burger.

I like some tomatoes, some … and … on my burger. I don't like any … on it. What about your burger?

P6 So many questions

11R p. 190 Mengenangaben

a) Complete the questions with *much* or *many*.

1. How XX eggs have you eaten this week? many
2. How XX water do you drink each day? much
3. How XX meals do you have each day? many
4. Guess: How XX time do you spend eating each day? much
5. How XX money do you spend on sweets each week? much
6. What do you think: How XX students in this class can cook spaghetti? many

b) Look at the questions in a) again. Ask and answer them with a partner.

➡ p. LF21

P7 Eating out

How to … help out p. 179

You and your mother are in a restaurant in England. She doesn't speak much English. The waiter doesn't understand German. Can you help them?

1. **Kellner:** What would you like to eat?
2. **Du:** Was möchtest du … ? Was möchtest du essen?
3. **Mutter:** Ich hätte gern eine Tomatensuppe und einen großen Salat.
4. **Du:** She'd like … She'd like a tomato soup and a large salad.
5. **Kellner:** Would you like anything to drink?
6. **Du:** … ? Möchtest du etwas trinken?
7. **Mutter:** Oh ja, ein Glas Wasser und einen Kaffee, bitte.
8. **Du:** … My mum would like a glass of water and a (cup of) coffee, please.

W p. 210 TM, p. 65

➡ p. LF21

P8 Give me five!

Look at Theme 1 and find:
- 5 things you can use to eat food
- 5 kinds of vegetables
- 5 kinds of fruit
- 5 adjectives to talk about food
- 5 drinks

P9 Food poems

L 1.6

a) Listen to these two funny food poems and read along.

I eat my peas with honey.
I've done it all my life.
It makes the peas taste funny
But it keeps them on my knife.

A vegetarian called Pam
Wouldn't eat pork or ham.
Well, to tell the truth,
She had a sweet tooth
And all she would eat was jam.

b) Say the poems yourself. Then choose one of them and learn it by heart.

P10 You can do it, can't you?

LSW 114

12 p. 191 Question tags

a) Match the question tags with these sentences.
1. Charlie likes chips, XX ? doesn't he
2. Salad is healthy, XX ? isn't it
3. You know how to cook spaghetti, XX ? don't you
4. Curry can be very hot and spicy, XX ? can't it
5. didn't she Gillian ordered some takeaway food, XX ?
6. aren't there There are lots of pubs in Britain, XX ?
7. You have got a favourite meal, XX ? haven't you

L 1.7

b) Listen and check your sentences.

c) Listen again and repeat what you hear.

P11 Have you tried it?

LSW 115

p. LF21

5R+9R p. 185+188/189

5R: Simple past
9R: Present perfect

Which of these dishes have you tried? Did you like it? What else have you tried? Write about at least four dishes.

1 a baked potato

2 tomato soup

3 spaghetti

4 chicken curry

5 …

I have tried … I have had …	and I liked it. but I didn't like it.

It was/wasn't …	delicious. great. good. OK. terrible. disgusting. …

I have tried chicken curry and I liked it.
It was delicious.
…

P12 A recipe from India

LSW 116

Für dieses Rezept braucht man …

Man muss …

p. LF21

How to … help out p. 179

Look at the recipe for chicken curry. What do you need? What do you have to do? Tell a classmate in German.

Chicken Curry

You need:
300 g chicken breast
150 g yoghurt
1 tablespoon curry paste
salt, pepper
2 onions, 1 red chilli
oil

1. Cut 300 g chicken breast into pieces.
2. Mix 150 g yoghurt and 1 tablespoon curry paste.
3. Put the chicken pieces into a flat dish. Add some salt and pepper. Then cover them with the yoghurt mixture.
4. Cut two onions and one red chilli into thin slices and fry them in oil.
5. Add the chicken to the pan and cook it slowly for 40 minutes.
6. Serve with rice.

W p. 210 · TM, p. 69

➡ p. LF22

How to ... read p. 170

M1 WB p. 20

M1 Indian food in Britain

LSW 117, 118

a) Have you ever tried Indian food? What was it like?
b) Read the magazine article. What typical Indian dishes are mentioned?

chicken tikka masala

Many Indians live in Britain, so Indian food has become more and more popular there. You can find Indian takeaways or restaurants in most towns. In these restaurants you can eat all kinds of Indian meals, for example curries. The Indian curry is a meal with vegetables or meat in a special sauce. You eat it with rice.

A lot of dishes you get in Indian restaurants in Britain are a bit different from original Indian food because they are sweeter and milder. Traditionally, Indians use a lot of different spices, some of which are really hot like chillies. One very hot dish is curry vindaloo. Eating it can be a test of courage for some people.

naan

Vindaloo became very popular in Britain during the World Cup in 1998. There was even a famous football chant called "Vindaloo" because football fans ate lots of vindaloo with beer after the football matches.

daal

British people also eat many other types of Indian food, for example daal (lentil soup), naan bread (typical Indian bread) and chicken tikka masala. It is often just called CTM. There is a story that the British wanted some sauce with their chicken tikka. So the Indian cooks added masala, a sauce that has got yoghurt, coconut cream and many different spices in it. So CTM is probably the first Indian dish that started to make Indian food popular in Britain.

curry vindaloo

c) Read the article again. Find words in the article that match these expressions:

a word or phrase that people shout or sing many times • red or green hot fruits • another word for kind or sort • not hot • a restaurant selling meals that you can take home

d) Find answers to these questions. Take notes. Then tell somebody who hasn't read the article about Indian food in Britain.

1. Why can you find a lot of Indian restaurants in Britain?
2. What is Indian curry?
3. What spices are used?
4. Which curry dish is very hot?
5. What other types of Indian food do British people like?
6. What is special about CTM?

I've read an article about …
I found out that …

M2 Friday evening

LSW 119

➡ p. LF22

a) Three friends want to go out for dinner. They are trying to decide what restaurant to go to and what they can eat there. Write their dialogue.

How to ... talk p. 172

Let's go out for dinner. What do you think?

That's a great idea. Who wants to go to a Chinese restaurant?

I can't stand Chinese food. Have you got any other ideas?

...

WB M2 + M3 p. 21

KV27

b) Act out your dialogue in a group.

B 3 d + e p. 19

M3 In a restaurant

IWS KV28

➡ p. LF22

L 1.3

a) Listen to the scene in a restaurant. What kind of restaurant is it?
b) Listen again and write down the sentences with the same meaning.

Can I have the menu, please?	And please can I see the menu?
Are you ready to order?	Can I take ... ?
I'll have ..., please.	...
Anything to drink?	...
Here you are.	...
Could you bring the bill, please?	...
That's £..., please.	...

How to ... talk p. 172

c) Work with a partner. Use your lists to make a dialogue in a restaurant. Act out your scene in class.

KV13

B 6 p. 22

M4 Anything else?

➡ p. LF23

What are these people saying or thinking? Write speech and/or thought bubbles.

1

2

3

W p. 211 TM, p. 76

➡ p. LF23

wordbank
Food and drink
p. 152

M4 WB
p. 22

M5 A healthy food plate

LSW 120, 121

a) Look at the diagram. It shows what you should eat and drink every day.
Work with a partner and name the food items. How many words do you know?

b) Look at the diagram again and read the statements. Are they right or wrong?

1. You should eat more fruit than vegetables.
2. You shouldn't eat fish.
3. You should drink a lot of water.
4. Half of your food should be fruit and vegetables.

c) Use the diagram and the words from a) to put together a really healthy meal plan for one day. Then present it in class.

A healthy meal plan
- breakfast:
  banana, ...
- lunch: ...
- dinner: ...

➡ p. LF23

M6 Rajiv's curry party

LSW 122, 124

a) Look at the picture on the next page. What is everybody doing?
What has happened to Gillian?

L 1.9 S 4

b) Listen and find out: How does the curry taste in the end?

M5 WB
p. 22

Rajiv is a great cook. It's Saturday and he has invited some friends for an Indian meal: Gillian, Charlie, Caroline and Karla. They are making a curry.

Karla: Mmm. Smells good, doesn't it?
Rajiv: I always cook it like my grandmother did. When she came here from India, she brought lots of spices with her.

Charlie: I thought you could buy everything at the supermarket.
Rajiv: Well, now you can. But when she came here, people knew nothing about Indian food. Now there are lots of Indian supermarkets and I can buy everything I need.
Gillian: How many onions do you want? Ow, my eyes are watering. I can't see a thing … ouch! – Now I've cut my finger.
Caroline: Poor you! Here. Hold your finger under the tap. Then it won't hurt.
Gillian: Thanks, Caroline.
Caroline: Do you want some of this extra-hot chilli paste, Rajiv?
Rajiv: Sure. We like our curry hot, you know.
Caroline: Mmm, you have to try it. It's delicious!
Gillian: Well, it burns your mouth a bit.
Karla: Phew, it's sooo hot! I need a glass of water.
Charlie: Don't! That will make it worse. Eat some bread.
Rajiv: Looks like we put in too much chilli paste, doesn't it, Caroline?
Caroline: Why don't we … ?

c) Now read the dialogue. Take notes on: *who, where, when, what*? Then compare your notes with a partner. KV9
d) What do you think Caroline will suggest?
e) Listen and find out. What do you think about the ideas?

I (don't) think …

I (don't) agree with … because …

How to … read p. 170
WB M6 p. 23
L 1.10

M7 It's different, isn't it?

LSW 123

a) Read the statements. Do you agree with them?
1. You don't cut spaghetti with a knife.
2. The Chinese use chopsticks.
3. Chopsticks aren't very expensive.
4. You can't read a Chinese menu.
5. A chapati is a kind of flat bread.
6. Peas are the most popular vegetable in Britain.
7. Germans love sauerkraut.

b) Add the question tags to the statements. Then check with a partner.
1. You don't cut spaghetti with a knife, do you?
2. The Chinese use chopsticks, … ?
3. Chopsticks …
4. …
…

c) Work with a partner. One of you writes down a new statement on a piece of paper, the other adds the question tag. Take turns.

Question tags 12 p. 191
WB M7 p. 23
➡ p. LF24

W p. 211 TM, p. 80 IWS

CAMDEN CHRONICLE
LEARN ENGLISH THE CAMDEN WAY

DID YOU GET IT ALL? ➡ p. LF24

- Why don't Gillian, her mum and Charlie cook dinner at home?
- What is Gillian's favourite restaurant?
- What kind of restaurant is the Windsor Castle?
- What does Rajiv eat in the school cafeteria?
- Who likes to eat desserts in the school cafeteria?
- What is Shima's favourite dish at school?
- How do many British people eat their peas?
- Where do people use chopsticks for eating?

GOOD TO KNOW ...

Wenn du in Großbritannien gefragt wirst, ob du etwas *pudding* möchtest, dann ist damit nicht unbedingt die Speise gemeint, die auch auf Deutsch Pudding heißt. Auf Englisch ist *pudding* nämlich oft ein Oberbegriff für jede Art von Dessert. Doch ein *pudding* kann auch ein herzhaftes Gericht sein, z. B. ein Gebäck wie *Yorkshire pudding* oder ein Fleischgericht wie *black pudding* (Blutwurst).

A traditional British speciality:

Lemon Curd

There are only three ingredients in this British speciality: eggs, sugar and ... lemons, of course! You cook them together to make a thick yellow cream. Many people eat it on toast or scones, but it is often put in a dessert called lemon meringue pie, too. Or you can just eat it with a spoon!

A poem

A millionaire's son went on trips
In jets and luxury ships,
But all he would eat
In cold and in heat,
Were platefuls of burgers
and chips.

THEME 2 TM, p. 81 KV29: Lernlandkarte

ARE YOU FIT?

In diesem *Theme* ...

- » unterhältst du dich über Sport und Fitness.
- » liest du über ein Fußball-Freundschaftsspiel.
- » erfährst du, welche Bedeutung Wohltätigkeitsveranstaltungen in Großbritannien haben.
- » lernst du, ein Gespräch zwischen Arzt/Ärztin und Patient/in zu verstehen.
- » übst du, gesundheitliche Probleme zu beschreiben.

W p. 212 TM, p. 81

➡ p. LF25

1+2 p. 24 WB

1 Test your fitness

IWS KV13 KV30 p. 22f./1+2

a) Read this fitness test. Can you do it? Write down your guesses on a piece of paper first.
b) Now do the test with a partner. Write down your answers.

1. Jump up and down for 30 seconds. Are you out of breath?
   A No, not at all.
   B A little bit.
   C Yes, I am!

2. Can you walk backwards?
   A Yes, I can.
   B I can, but it's difficult.
   C No, I can't.

3. Run up and down 20 stairs quickly. Are you out of breath?
   A No, I'm not. That's easy.
   B Just a little.
   C Yes, I am!

4. Can you balance like this for 15 seconds?
   A Yes, I can.
   B Not quite.
   C Sorry, I can't do it.

5. Can you press your back against the wall like this for one minute?
   A Yes, of course.
   B I can, but it's not easy.
   C No, I can't. It's too hard.

You have answered mostly …

A: Very fit! Keep up the good work!
B: Not bad! But you can do better!
C: Oh dear! Time to do more sports!

Gerundium als Subjekt 13 p. 191

c) Now report to the class:

LSW 202

Jumping Walking Running Balancing Pressing	my back against the wall for one minute for 15 seconds up and down for 30 seconds up and down 20 stairs quickly backwards	was	easy. no problem. difficult. really hard. too hard. …

Jumping up and down for 30 seconds was easy.

Walking …

2 All kinds of sports

LSW 201

Work with a partner and write a list.
Find at least three sports you can do:

- alone
- with a partner
- in a team
- inside
- outside
- …

alone: swimming, …
with a partner: …
…

You can go swimming alone.

You can go/play/do …

WB 3 p. 25
wordbank Free time p. 153
➡ p. LF25

3 Favourite sports

p. 25/4

➡ p. LF25

a) Read about the sports these Haverstock students do. Take notes in a grid.

KV31

I like hockey
I really like playing hockey. It is my favourite sport because it is exciting and fast. I think that it is better than ice hockey because we don't need special equipment like helmets or special clothes. I train twice a week. I enjoy playing outside. It is nicer than being inside a sports hall.
Telisha, 15

MY FIRST MINI-TRIATHLON
Last week I had my first mini-triathlon. A triathlon has three parts: swimming, running and cycling. It's great fun because you do different kinds of sports in a short time. Cycling was a bit of a problem because my bike broke down in the middle of the race. I still did really well because I was the fastest swimmer. I can't wait until my next triathlon! Then I want to do even better! Caitlin, 11

Skateboarding
I started skateboarding five years ago. It is a great sport because you can do it whenever you want. There is a skate park near my house and I meet my friends there after school. We practise different tricks and have a lot of fun together.
Amar, 13

name	age	what sport?	why do they like it?	other information
Telisha	15	hockey	…	…
…	…			

b) Compare your notes with a partner.
c) Talk to your partner about the sports YOU do.

I play/do/go …

I like it because …

I train twice/… a week.

I started … years ago.

P P1 + P4 p. 48
M M1 + M2 p. 52
WB 4 + 5 p. 25/26

W p. 212

➡ p. LF25

DVD

WB 6 p. 27

4 Karate with Jessica

a) Watch the clip. What can you understand?
b) Watch the clip again. Then read the statements. Are they right or wrong?
   1. Jessica started karate training two years ago. wrong
   2. Jessica usually trains four times a week. ✓
   3. The training sometimes starts with a warm-up. wrong
   4. Stretching different parts of your body is important. ✓
   5. Jessica's team uses punchbags. ✓
c) Watch the clip a third time and check your answers.

WWW

d) What colour is Jessica's belt? Do you know what the colour stands for? Try to find out.

Relativsätze 14 p. 192

➡ p. LF25

5 Different sports

p. 24+26/3,5,6

What do you think: What is important for different sports?
Write five or more sentences.

Someone who	plays football/tennis/… goes swimming/cycling/… does karate/… …	must be doesn't have to be	slim • tall • fit • fast • cool • small • strong • careful • young • clever • fair • …

➡ p. LF26

M3 a-c M p. 53

// Sachtext über Sally Brown, Sportlerin aus Nordirland; die S erstellen ein *fact file*

6 A sportsperson

IWS p. 27f./7+8

a) Who is YOUR favourite sportsperson? Make a fact file.

Name:
Age:
Country:
Sport:
Titles:
Other information:

Lionel Messi, Usain Bolt, Serena Williams, Christine Theiss, Sebastian Vettel, Dirk Nowitzki

b) **Work in groups of four. Look at the different fact files. Then talk about the sportspersons.**

Folie 4 LSW 203

Comparison of adjectives 16R p. 194/195
P5 p. 49
WB 7 p. 27

I think … is the	fastest fittest … most famous most successful …	basketball player. swimmer. goalkeeper. …

I don't think so. I think … is	faster fitter … more famous more successful …	than …

Yes, I think you're right.

I don't know …/
I've never heard of …

7 Sports chants

p. 30/10

p. LF26
L 1.11
Imperativ 18R p. 197
WB 8 p. 23

a) **People use chants at sports events to cheer on a team or a special person. Listen to these chants and read along.**

Give us an *A* – *A*!
Give us an *R* – *R*!
Give us an *S* – *S*!
Give us an *E* – *E*!
Give us an *N* – *N*!
Give us an *A* – *A*!
Give us an *L* – *L*!
And what have you got?
– *ARSENAL*!!!

Dribble it
Pass it
Let's make a basket!

Don't give up, Alex,
don't give in,
Fight to the end –
we want to see you win!

b) **Do you know any other sports chants? Tell your class.**

c) **Choose one of the chants in a) and practise saying it in a group.**

P2 p. 48

W p. 213

➡ p. LF26

How to ... work with others p. 176

WB 9 p. 29

8 A friendly match

IWS LSW 204 p. 29/9

a) **Buzz groups: Look at the picture. What can you see? What do you think is happening?**

b) **Read the article from the school magazine. How did the friendly match end?** 3-3 (three all)

RED NOSES FOR CHARITY

On Sunday the Haverstock Arsenal club played a friendly match against the students of William Ellis School for Boys (WES). It was a great day and the teams raised about £250 for Red Nose Day. Fans and friends paid to watch the match and see the players wear red noses.

The match took place on the William Ellis sports fields. When it started at 2 pm, the Haverstock fans were chanting excitedly "Let's go Haverstock, let's go!" After ten minutes team captain Charlie Batson scored the first goal.

The Haverstock fans went wild. The WES crowd didn't look very happy, but five minutes later Adam Perry scored a goal for his team. At half time the score was 1-1.

The second half didn't start well for Haverstock because some of the players had trouble with their red noses – they kept falling off! Things got worse when Josh Chang from WES ran towards the goalkeeper and scored a goal. Shortly afterwards Thomas West, a player from the WES team, ran into Charlie Batson and knocked him down. The crowd cried "Foul! Foul!" but the referee didn't listen. Charlie was able to get up with the help of a WES player. That was good sportsmanship! Charlie played the rest of the match injured!

There was more bad luck for Haverstock when WES scored a third goal in the middle of the second half. But Haverstock didn't give up. There were only five minutes left, and the Haverstock crowd were cheering loudly when Nick Hull scored a second goal for Haverstock. Then in the last minute Charlie Batson ran forward quickly and scored a third goal for Haverstock! So the friendly match ended in a draw and everyone went home happy.

It was a great match and we were also glad to raise so much money for charity!

P3 + P6 P p. 48/49

c) **Read the article again and complete the sentences.**

1. Haverstock played a friendly match against ... William Ellis School for Boys (WES).
2. The players wore ... red noses.
3. At 2.10 pm Charlie ... scored the first goal.
4. Thomas West ran into Charlie and ... knocked him down.
5. But Charlie was able to ... get up with the help of a WES player.
6. In the last minute Charlie scored ... a third goal for Haverstock.

KV32

LAND & LEUTE

Red Nose Day

Oft brauchen Vereine oder Organisationen dringend Geld für einen guten Zweck: beispielsweise für Menschen, die durch Katastrophen wie Hochwasser in Not geraten sind, oder für ein Krankenhaus, das ein Spielzimmer für kranke Kinder einrichten möchte. Das nötige Geld kann auf unterschiedlichste Weise beschafft werden: Es kann z. B. ein Konzert, ein Fußballturnier, ein Flohmarkt oder ein Marathon veranstaltet werden und der Erlös geht an die Hilfsorganisation.

In Großbritannien gibt es alle zwei Jahre im März einen ganz besonderen Wohltätigkeitstag, den so genannten *Red Nose Day*. Leute spenden Geld für einen wohltätigen Zweck und tragen als Zeichen an diesem Tag eine rote Plastiknase. Im Fernsehen läuft eine spezielle Sendung, in der Spenden gesammelt werden. Viele berühmte Menschen machen dort mit. An einem *Red Nose Day* kommen so viele Millionen Pfund für Hungernde, Obdachlose oder Kranke zusammen.

Seit 2003 gibt es auch *Red Nose Day*-Veranstaltungen in Deutschland. Hast du schon davon gehört? Gibt es an deiner Schule Wohltätigkeitsveranstaltungen? Was könntest du tun, um Geld für einen wohltätigen Zweck zu sammeln?

P P7 p. 49

9 An interview

a) **Listen to Charlie and a reporter from the school magazine. What are they talking about?**

healthy food • tips on how to keep fit • Charlie's visit to the doctor

b) **Read the reporter's notes. Then listen again. What did she get wrong?**

KV33

Interview with Charlie Batson
- captain of Haverstock Arsenal club ✓
- football training 2x a week wrong
- warm-up: stretching, press-ups and running ✓
- in skateboarding club wrong
- gets enough sleep ✓
- special food wrong
- fair play very important ✓

L 1.12 S 5

➡ p. LF26

10 Choose an activity

You can ...
- **write about your favourite sport or make a collage. You can look at number 3 and P1 for help.**
- **write about your favourite sportsperson. Use your fact file from number 6 a).**
- **work in a small group and write a sports chant. You can look at number 7 for ideas. Present your chant in class.**

My favourite sportsperson is ...
He/She is ... old.
He/She comes from ...
He/She plays .../is a ...
He/She was .../has won ...
I like him/her because ...
...

➡ p. LF26
portfolio
wordbank Free time p. 153

W p. 214 TM, p. 97

11 Charlie's problem

p. 31/11+12

How to ... listen p. 169

a) Look at Charlie. What's wrong with him? Have a guess.

A His mum said he can't go to the match tomorrow if he doesn't go to the doctor first.

B He needs to go to the doctor because his knee still hurts. ✓

C He is afraid to go to the doctor.

L 1.13

b) Now listen and check. Were you right in a)?

c) Listen again. When is Charlie going to see the doctor?

at 5 o'clock this afternoon

12 At the doctor's

LSW 205, 206 p. 34/15

➡ p. LF26

L 1.14 S 6

WB 10 p. 30

WB 11 p. 30

a) Listen and read along. What are these words in English? Work with a partner and find them in the dialogues.

wehtun • geprellt • geschwollen • Verband • gebrochen • Röntgenbild • Rezept • Salbe

In the waiting room:

Charlie: Ow! This hurts. I can't move my leg at all.
Rajiv: Huh! You've only bruised your knee, that's all.
Charlie: But it hurts! And it's swollen. Look!
Rajiv: The doctor will put a bandage or something on it. I'm sure you'll be able to play football again soon.
Receptionist: Charlie Batson? Doctor Thompson will see you now.

In the surgery:

Dr Thompson: Now, what's the problem?
Charlie: I think I've broken my knee. I was playing football yesterday and I fell. Now my knee really hurts.
Dr Thompson: Let me see. Does this hurt?
Charlie: Ouch!
Dr Thompson: Ah, I see. We'll have to take an X-ray of your knee so we can see what the problem is. The X-ray room is the second door on the right. I'll be with you in a few minutes.

Later:

Dr Thompson: OK, Charlie. Your knee isn't broken, just bruised. I'll give you a prescription for some cream and put a bandage on your knee. And listen: You mustn't play football for two weeks.
Charlie: Two weeks? But we've got a match against Hendon School next Saturday ...

How to ... work with a dictionary p. 167

b) Check your words from a) in a dictionary.

c) Listen again. Then match the sentence parts.

1. Charlie thinks he has E
2. Rajiv thinks D
3. The receptionist tells Charlie B
4. Charlie's knee hurts F
5. Dr Thompson wants to A
6. She will give Charlie C

A take an X-ray.
B that the doctor is ready to see him.
C a prescription for some cream.
D that Charlie only needs a bandage.
E broken his knee.
F and it is swollen.

d) Dramatic reading: Practise reading the dialogues in groups of four. KV34
- Think about how your character feels.
- Then try to learn your role by heart.

How to ... work with others p. 176
P13 p. 51

13 After the friendly match

IWS

p. LF27
Modalverben 15F p. 192-194
P10 p. 50
M4 p. 54

Textproduktion: E-Mail Charlie an Uncle Joe, in der er von seiner Verletzung und dem Termin bei Dr Thompson erzählt

Look at the pictures. Write about what Charlie *has to* do, *mustn't* do or *can* do with his bruised knee.

Charlie mustn't play football. He ...

1. play football

2. wear a bandage

3. run during the breaks

4. watch sports on TV

5. put on cream twice a day

6. ...

W p. 215

➡ p. LF27

14 What's the problem?

Folie 5 KV35 p. 32f./13 + 14

12 + 13 WB p. 31

a) Look at the picture of the waiting room. What can you see? Talk to a partner.

wordbank Health p. 154

b) Look at the patients again. What's wrong with them?

stomach ache • a bad cold • backache • a cut foot • a sore leg • a broken arm

The old lady has stomach ache.

The man with the red scarf …

…

c) What's the reason?

has eaten too much • has been out in the rain • a dog has bitten him • has fallen off his bike • has stepped on some broken glass • has fallen off a chair

I think the old lady has eaten too much.

14 WB p. 32

P8 + P9, P11 P p. 50/51

M5 + M6 M p. 54

d) Imagine YOU are the doctor. What advice do you have for the patients?

You can/can't You should/shouldn't Don't	stay in bed. take some medicine. put on this cream. …

advice for the old lady: You … advice for … : …

LSW 207–210

15 Too bad

p. 35/16

Modalverben 15R p. 192-194

a) What are the patients not able to do?

The old lady The man with the red scarf ...	is not able to ...

go dancing

play basketball

➡ p. LF27

ride a bike

eat very much

clean the windows

go to work

b) Think about the last time YOU were ill.
What were you not able to do?

KV36 ↓↑

When I had a bad cold,
I wasn't able to ...

KV37 ↓

P P12 p. 51
M M7 p. 55
WB 15 + 15 p. 32/33

16 Choose an activity

➡ p. LF28
portfolio
wordbank Health p. 154
How to ... write p. 174

You can ...

- draw a stick man and label the body parts.
  Add words for health problems.
- record your dramatic reading from number 12 d).
- create your perfect prescription for a bad cold:
  watch films, ...
- write about the last time you were ill.
  Think about:
  - What was wrong with you?
  - What was the reason?
  - What did you have to do?
  - What were you not able to do?
  - ...

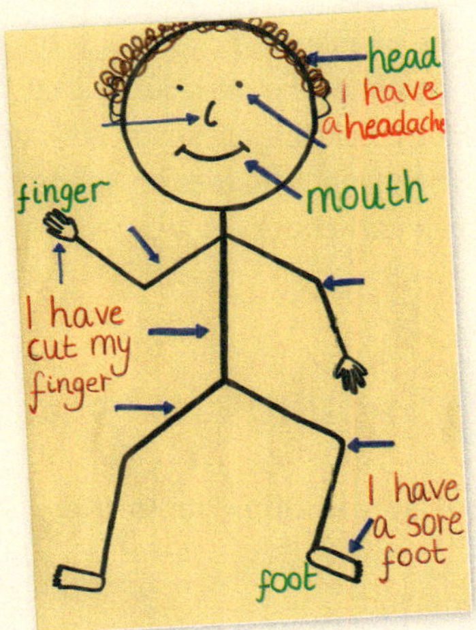

Two weeks ago I didn't feel well. I had stomach ache and couldn't go to school. I think I ate too much at my friend's birthday party.
My dad made lots of tea for me and gave me a hot-water bottle. I put it on my stomach and it really helped.
I had to stay in bed all day and wasn't able to meet my friends in the afternoon. But the next day I was fit again.

WB test yourself p. 34/35

W p. 215 TM, p. 111

P1 A sports word web

➡ p. LF28

wordbank
Free time
p. 153

How to ...
work with words
p. 166

LSW 211–213

Make a word web for your favourite sport.

P2 Sports poems

➡ p. LF28

Read the examples and write YOUR sports poem.

Anna is tall
And good at basketball

Football
Eleven players
In one team
Great fun
Football

P3 Sound check

a) Who is it?

1. The member of a football team who is in the goal is a XX. goalkeeper
2. Someone who wins a game is a XX. winner
3. The people who cheer on a team are the XX. fans
4. Someone who makes sure that the players do not break the rules is a XX. referee
5. The player who leads a sports team is a XX. captain

/ˈwɪnə/ /ˈkæptɪn/ /ˈɡəʊlˌkiːpə/ /ˌrefəˈriː/ /fænz/

L 1.15

b) Listen and check.

P4 Swimming is ...

Gerundium als Subjekt
13
p. 191

➡ p. LF28

a) What do you think about these sports? Write sentences.

Swimming Skateboarding Playing hockey Running Cycling ...	is can be isn't	fun. boring. dangerous. interesting. difficult. ...

b) Now talk to your partner.

I (don't) think swimming is ...

I think so, too.

I (don't) agree. I think ...

P5 Fit, fitter, the fittest

LSW 214

p. LF28

16R p. 194/195 Comparison of adjectives

a) Write down the adjectives and add the comparative and superlative forms.

big • happy • clean • fast • strong • small • successful • bad • exciting • good • famous

big, bigger, (the) biggest
...

b) Choose six adjectives from a) and write sports comparisons with *than* or *as ... as*.

The sports field is bigger than the swimming pool.
Running is as good as cycling.
...

P6 How do they do it?

16R + 17R p. 194-196 16R: Comparison of adjectives 17R: Adverbs of manner

a) Match the adverbs with the sentences.

hard • quickly • well • carefully • loudly

1. Fans usually cheer XX for their team. loudly
2. A goalkeeper has to move XX from side to side to guard the goal. quickly
3. The referee watches all the players XX. carefully
4. Football players have to train XX for each match. hard
5. The team captain always plays XX and is a good example to the other players. well

b) Look at these sentences and complete the rule.

It was a good start to the game. – The game started well.
The angry crowd shouted "Foul!" – The crowd shouted angrily.

Rule: Adjectives
– ... describe people, animals and things.
– ... describe actions.
Adverbs

How to ... work with grammar p. 178

P7 A special day

p. LF29

How to ... help out p. 179

Look at the article from a school magazine. What do you learn about Red Nose Day at this school? Tell a classmate in German.

A great day for charity

On Friday 15th March teachers and students in our school raised money for charity. Students could choose certain rules to break on this day only. But they had to pay £2 for each rule they wanted to break.

Many students chose to have crazy hair, wear their own clothes, eat unhealthy food during the breaks or not do their homework for the following Monday.

A huge thank you to all who helped to make this Red Nose Day a very special day and raise over £900 for charity!

W p. 215   TM, p. 113

P8 Health problems

What's wrong with the friends? Write down their health problems.

a bad cold

a headache

stomach ache

a cut finger

a sore leg

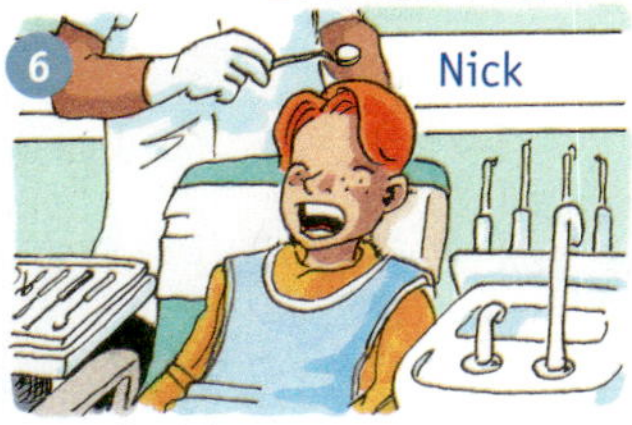

toothache

1. Gillian has got …
2. Rajiv …

…

a sore leg • a cut finger • a bad cold • stomach ache • toothache • a headache

P9 Sound check

L 1.16

a) Copy the words. Then listen: Which letters can't you hear? Underline them.

dialogue • mustn't • minute • sore • knee • medicine • bruised • wrong

b) Listen again and say the words.

P10 Rules for Gillian

LSW 215

Modalverben 15R p. 192-194

a) Gillian has got a bad cold. She has to follow her mum's rules. What are they?

can • has to • mustn't • doesn't have to

has to 1. Gillian !!! stay in bed.

doesn't have to 2. She tidy up her room.

mustn't 3. She go out.

has to 4. She !!! drink enough water and tea.

5. She !!! eat lots of fruit. has to

6. She listen to music. can

7. She kiss her mum. mustn't

8. She take out the rubbish. doesn't have to

➡ p. LF29

b) Imagine YOU are ill. What rules are there for you? Write them down.

P11 Oh, Mum!

a) When Gillian's mum comes home from work, she has got a lot of questions. Write down what she asks Gillian.

drink – tea? • eat – fruit? • sleep – enough? • take – medicine? • watch – TV?

b) What do you think are Gillian's answers?

Present perfect 9R p. 188/189
➡ p. LF29

P12 A broken leg

George has got a broken leg.
Write about what he *is able to do* and what he *is not able to do*.

read comics • play football • play computer games • watch films • walk to school • go swimming • ...

George is able to read comics.
He is not able to ...
He ...

Modalverben 15R p. 192-194
➡ p. LF29

P13 Can you help?

LSW 216

These people have got some questions but they don't speak German. Tell them what they need to know.

➡ p. LF29
How to ... help out p.179

W p. 216 TM, p. 115

➡ p. LF29

M1 The London Marathon

LSW 217, 218

a) What is a marathon? What marathons do you know or have heard of? Would you like to take part in a marathon? Talk to a partner.

b) Read this leaflet about the London Marathon. How many races are there? What are their names? What do the runners collect money for?

The London Marathon

On a Sunday in April one of the world's biggest marathons takes place on the streets of London. Each year about 30,000 runners take part in the London Marathon. The race starts at one of three starting points at Blackheath and Greenwich Park. It finishes on The Mall in front of Buckingham Palace, 26 miles or 42.195 kilometres later.

The London Marathon is not only one race. There is:

// **The Elite Race:** Women start at 9 am from the Blue Start in Blackheath. Men start at 9.30 am from the same place. The fastest men are expected to arrive at the finishing line after about 2 hours. The fastest women will probably need about 15 minutes longer than the fastest men.

// **The Mass Race:** This race starts at 9.45 am from the Red Start in Greenwich. Most runners find sponsors because they collect money for every mile they run. Then they dress up for the race. In this race fun is more important than time.

// **The Wheelchair London Marathon:** This race starts at 9.25 am from the Green Start in St John's Park. Wheelchair athletes from all over the world can take part.

// **The Mini Marathon:** This race is much shorter. It is run over the last 3 miles of the marathon. More than 2,500 children (ages 11 to 17) will run in it. It starts at 11 am.

This year the runners will collect money for these charities: The Children's Trust and the British Heart Foundation.

M1 p. 38 WB

c) Read the leaflet again. Find more details about the four races:

KV38

- Who is in the race?
- When does the race start?
- Where is the start?

Take notes. Then tell your class about the London Marathon.

KV7

➡ p. LF30

M2 Henry's big day

LSW 219

L 1.17 S 7
M2 p. 39 WB

a) Henry Edwards, 13, took part in the Mini Marathon at the London Marathon. Listen to the interview with him. Find out and take notes:

- What was Henry's result in the Mini Marathon?
- What does he think about his result?
- How did he prepare for the marathon (training, food and drink)?

b) Compare your results with a partner.

M3 A sportsperson

IWS LSW 220, 221

➡ p. LF30

a) You will read an article about Sally Brown, a sprinter from the UK. Look at her picture first. What would you like to ask her? Make notes.

b) Now read about Sally. Can you find answers to your questions in the text?

How to … talk p. 172

Nothing can stop Sally

Sally Brown from Belfast in Northern Ireland started running when she was 10 years old. She soon found that she was a talented sprinter. Sally was born in 1995 with problems with her left arm: It did not develop from below the elbow.

Sally has taken part in national and international competitions. In 2011 she won a bronze medal in the 200 m at the Paralympic World Championships in New Zealand. Since then her life has changed a lot. Training is much tougher and journalists want to know all about her.

The biggest event in her career has been the Paralympics in London in 2012 where she finished the 100 m final in sixth place. To prepare for this major event Sally trained six days a week. She ran three times a week and did fitness training. At the time she still went to comprehensive school.

The biggest sacrifice for her sport is her social life. She can't go out on a Saturday night because she usually trains. She also has to eat healthy food – chocolate and other sweets are not allowed.

It is hard for Sally to train and concentrate on her education at the same time. She hopes to go to university one day.

Sally's dream is to become Paralympic champion. She wants to prove that although she is disabled, she can run as well as people who aren't.

c) Make a fact file about Sally.

Name:
Age:
Country:
Sport:
Titles:
Other information:

B 6a p. 40

d) Work with a partner and prepare an interview with Sally. Think of at least six questions you would like to ask her.

KV13

Where? What? Why? When? How? … ?

One of you takes Sally's role and gives the answers. Present your interview to the class.

Fragen mit Fragewörtern 10R p. 139
WB M3 p. 39

W p. 217 TM, p. 120

➡ p. LF31
How to ... write a letter p. 175
15R + 20 p. 192-194 + 198
M4 WB p. 40
15R: Modalverben
20: Konjunktionen

M4 After the friendly match

LSW 222 KV39

Charlie wants to tell his uncle Joe in Birmingham about his accident in the friendly match and his visit to the doctor's. Write Charlie's email. Look at numbers 8, 12 and 13 (p. 42, p. 44-45) again. You can start like this:

To: joe.batson75@
Subject: Hi Uncle Joe!
From: c.batman@

Hi Uncle Joe,

How are you? ...
Last week the Arsenal club at my school played a friendly match against ...
The next day I went to ... because ...
Now I mustn't play football for ... and I have to wear a ... ...

Charlie

Use ...
- *time words* **(first, then, after that, ...)**,
- *linking words* **(and, because, but, ...)**,
- *modal verbs* **(have to, mustn't, ...)**,
- *adjectives* and *adverbs* to make the email interesting and to show how Charlie feels.

13 B p. 45

➡ p. LF31
How to ... talk p. 172

M5 In the surgery

IWS

a) Collect phrases that you can use when you are at the doctor's. Look at pages 44-46 and make lists for 'doctor' and 'patient'.

doctor	patient
What's the problem?	My ... hurts.
...	...

b) Work with a partner and compare your lists. Then decide what health problem you have got. Make up a dialogue at the doctor's.

KV13

➡ p. LF32
L 1.18
M5 WB p. 40

M6 Helping out at the doctor's

a) Katie, an English exchange student, is in your class. She has got a health problem. What's wrong with her? What happened? Listen to her and take notes.

b) Imagine YOU have to explain Katie's problem to a German doctor. What do you say?

M7 I won't give up!

LSW 223, 224

➡ p. LF32

WB M6 p. 41

How to … read p. 170

a) Athletes often get injured. Do you know an athlete who can't do his/her sport because of an injury? What happened to him/her?

b) Leroy Haffner from Bristol is one of the best swimmers in his local club. He takes part in national competitions. Last year he had an injury and couldn't swim. Read his blog. How did Leroy feel during that time?

News (230) Favourites

LEROY HAFFNER – SWIMMING IS MY LIFE

Tuesday — **2nd September**
Today I had to stop in the middle of training because my shoulder hurt like hell. I got out of the pool and told my coach. He said I needn't finish my training, and told me to go and see the doctor tomorrow. I don't know how I'm going to sleep tonight – swimming is my life. What if I won't be able to do it anymore?

Wednesday — **3rd September**
So this morning I went to the doctor's. The X-ray showed that no bones are broken. But the muscle is torn and it's going to take at least a month for me to recover. It means I'm not allowed to take part in the Nationals at the end of the month. I hoped I would be able to win some races there, but now all my dreams are ruined.

Wednesday — **10th September**
I've just come back from the physiotherapist. He has shown me lots of exercises, and said that I should do them all three times a day. Of course I will – I want to be back in the pool as quickly as possible! I've always been a fighter.

Saturday — **27th September**
Today we had the Nationals. I went to the competition pool to cheer on the other swimmers. My friend Michael won the 100m Butterfly: my favourite event. I tried to be happy for Michael, but I hated that he was allowed to swim and I wasn't. So frustrating!

Thursday — **2nd October**
After I was feeling down last week I spoke to my coach. He said I needn't worry, because so many athletes are able to recover from injuries and win all sorts of competitions. Just look at Usain Bolt! In 2010 he wasn't allowed to run for a month because of an injury, and two years later he was the fastest man in the world at the Olympic Games. Maybe I'll be the Usain Bolt of the water!

Tuesday — **21st October**
Wow! The physiotherapist said I'm allowed to get back in the pool this afternoon. I'm only allowed to do light training, but it's better than nothing. I can't wait to be in the water again. It's time to start swimming for success – wish me luck!

Modalverben 15R p. 192-194

c) Read the blog again. What wasn't Leroy allowed to do? What did he have to do? What was the biggest problem for him?

W p. 217 TM, p. 124 IWS

CAMDEN CHRONICLE
LEARN ENGLISH THE CAMDEN WAY

DID YOU GET IT ALL? ➡ p. LF32

» What sports do you have to do in a triathlon?
» Who scored the first goal in the friendly match between Haverstock and William Ellis School?
» What was the score at the end of the match?
» When is Red Nose Day?
» What day does Charlie go to the doctor?
» What does the doctor do to help Charlie?
» How long must Charlie wait to play football again?
» Who was bitten by a dog?

GOOD TO KNOW ...

Starke Typen kann man in Schottland bewundern. Bei den *Highland Games* messen sie ihre Kräfte in Wettkämpfen wie Baumstammwerfen *(tossing the caber)*, Tauziehen *(tug-o-war)*, Steinstoßen *(putting the stone)* und Hammerwerfen *(Scottish hammer)*. Und es gibt was auf die Ohren: Zu den Spielen gehören traditionell auch Dudelsack- und Tanzwettbewerbe.

THEME 3 TM, p. 125 KV40: Lernlandkarte

WHAT'S ON IN YOUR AREA?

In diesem *Theme* ...

- sprichst du über das Leben in der Stadt und auf dem Land.
- lernst du, Bilder genau zu beschreiben.
- erstellst du in Projektarbeit ein Veranstaltungsprogramm für deinen Wohnort.
- erfährst du etwas über den Notting Hill Carnival.
- schreibst du über ein Fest in deiner Umgebung.

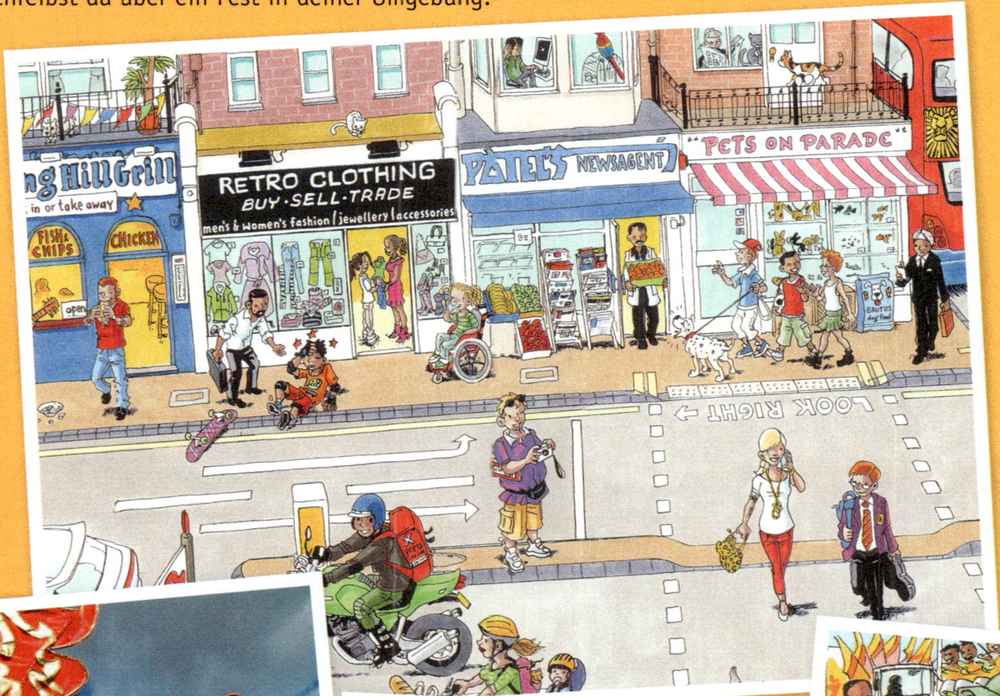

W p. 218 TM, p. 125

1 Where YOU live

➡ p. LF33
LSW 301
p. 38f./1–3
wordbank Travelling p. 156
WB 1 + 2 p. 42

a) What is there in your area?

There is/are …

youth club

shop

station

cinema

park

bus stop

…

P2 p. 70

b) Is there anything you would like to have?

2 Different places

➡ p. LF33
Folie 6
IWS
KV41
p. 38f./1+3
WB 3 p. 43
4R p. 184
How to … talk about pictures p. 173
Present progressive

a) Look at the two pictures and describe them: What can you see?

In picture A I can see …

In the middle/On the left/right there is/are …

At the top/bottom I can see …

What are the people doing?

The man and the woman on the right are sitting … The man next to them is …

LSW 302

b) Which picture do you like better? Why?

3 The city-village rap

a) Listen to the rap and read along.

L 1.19 S 8

Living in a city,
For me it is just great,
I'm always busy,
Catching the bus
To the shops or the cinema.
City life yeah –
I like living this way.

Living in a village,
For me it is just great,
Go running and climbing,
Spend time outside
Ssh! It's so quiet.
Village life yeah –
I like living this way.

Living in a city,
Or the village life,
We're all the same,
Chatting and laughing,
Having a great time
Having friends yeah –
Give me a high five!

P F1 + P3 p. 70

→ p. LF33

b) Where do YOU live? Where would you like to live? Say why.

c) Work with a partner and write your own verse about a city/a village/ where YOU live. Then present it in class.

KV13

M M1 p. 74

WB 4 p. 44

Living in …,
For me it is just/not …,
…
…
I (don't) like living this way.

a city/village/Leipzig/…

great/boring/a lot of fun/…

Children are playing • Chat with friends • Dogs are barking • Go shopping • …

W p. 218

4 A chat

LSW 303 p. 40f./4+5

5 WB p. 44

a) Gillian, Caroline and Karla are on the Internet. What is their chat about?

their plans for the weekend

Add Subject Call Video More

Coco12: Hey, I'm still doing homework. Can't wait for the weekend. Any plans yet?

KamaX: No, not really. My parents want to go to the Science Museum but I'd rather do something different.

Gi11i@n: There's a concert at the youth club on Saturday. Seeing a good band would be fun but I think it's only for people over 18.

Coco12: I think so, too. Anyway, Mum said she's got a surprise for us this weekend. Hope it's something I like and not a party with boring colleagues from work.

KamaX: Don't worry! I'm sure your mum's surprise will be a really good one.

Gi11i@n: Yeah, absolutely. I'd love to do something cool this weekend but I've already spent most of my pocket money. I've only got five pounds left.

KamaX: I think I've got something for you and me, Gill. You know my grandma, right? She lives in a village north of London. There's a car boot sale on Sunday. It's always really big and you can buy lots of things for not much money. I could ask my parents to take us there.

➡ p. LF33

P4 + P5 P p. 71

M2 + M3 M p. 74/75

How to ... work with others p. 176

b) Read the chat again. What plans and ideas do the girls have? Take notes.

c) Think – pair – share: What could you do in YOUR area without much money?

5 A car boot sale

➡ p. LF34

Folie 7 LSW 304 KV42 p. 42f./6–8

a) Look at the picture for one minute. Then close your books. Write down all the things from the picture that you can remember.

P6 P p. 71

b) Work with a partner and compare your lists. You get one point for each correct word. Who has got the most points?

6 I'll take it

LSW 305 KV43 p. 42/6, p. 44f./9 + 11

a) Listen to the three dialogues at the car boot sale. What do the customers buy?

L 1.20

How to … listen p. 169

a scarf

a pair of shoes

a book

The girl buys a book.
The man buys sunglasses.
The woman and the boy buy a scarf.

earrings

sunglasses

a vase

The girl buys …

b) Listen again. How much do the customers pay in the end? Take notes like this:

WB 6 p. 45

thing	price (£)
… book	… 2
sunglasses	12
scarf	3.50

7 Buying and selling

IWS p. 45/10 + 11

a) Read the sentences. What does the customer say? What does the seller say? Make two lists.

KV44

wordbank Shopping p. 155
→ p. LF34

Oh, that's too expensive.

It's a special offer.

What do you think about this?

Does it work?

Have you got anything cheaper?

Here's your change.

What would you like for this?

I think I'll take it.

It's £5.

OK. Let's say £4.

Have you got any … ?

How much is it?

I need something for my friend's birthday.

What size are they?

Sorry, I don't have any … but I have some …

customer:

seller:

b) Bus stop: When you have finished a), go to the bus stop in your classroom. Find a partner and compare your lists.

How to … work with others p. 177

c) Work with a partner or in a small group. Use your lists to make up a dialogue. Try to buy or sell some of these things. Act out your scene to the class.

KV13

WB 7 p. 45

KV45

old magazines • old inline skates • toy cars • a mobile phone • an old vase • …

W p. 218

➡ p. LF34

8 A musical

KV46 ↓ KV47 ↑

How to ... read p. 170

a) The Lambrakis want to take their children to a musical in London. It's called "The Lion King". Read the story of "The Lion King". Would you like to see the film or the musical? Say why.

King Mufasa is a powerful lion and the king of the Pridelands in Africa. He is a very good king and all the animals look up to him. Mufasa has a son, Simba. He will be the next king when his father dies. But Simba's uncle, Scar, is jealous: He wants to become the new king.

Scar tries to kill Simba but Mufasa rescues his son. Then Scar tries to kill Simba a second time: He takes him to a valley. In the valley Scar and some hyenas scare all the other animals. The animals run away in panic and trample down everything. Mufasa saves Simba again, but Mufasa dies and Scar makes Simba believe that he has killed his father. Scar tells Simba to run away.

Simba runs away and almost dies. Some other animals find him and they stay together.

Later Simba meets his friend Nala. Nala tells Simba that Scar is the king now. She asks him to come back because he is the true king. Simba returns to the Pridelands and meets his uncle Scar. Scar tells Simba that he killed Mufasa, not Simba. They fight and Scar dies. Now Simba is the lion king with his new wife, Nala.

8 p. 46 WB

b) Read the story again. Who is ... ?

Mufasa | Simba | Scar | Nala

M4 p. 75 M

c) What else do you learn about the four lions?

Mufasa: powerful lion, king of the Pridelands in Africa
Simba: Mufasa's son
Scar: Simba's uncle, Mufasa's brother
Nala: Simba's friend

➡ p. LF34

9 A closer look

KV47 ↑

a) Look at number 8 again. Sort words from the text in a grid like this:

words I know	words I can guess	words I don't know
lion	trample down	jealous
...	...	...

How to ... work with a dictionary p. 167

9 p. 46 WB

b) Write down the words you don't know again.
- First sort them from A-Z.
- Then look them up in a dictionary. Decide: Which meaning fits best?
- Write down the German word next to the English word.

10 A project – A magazine about YOUR area

p. 46 f./12 + 13

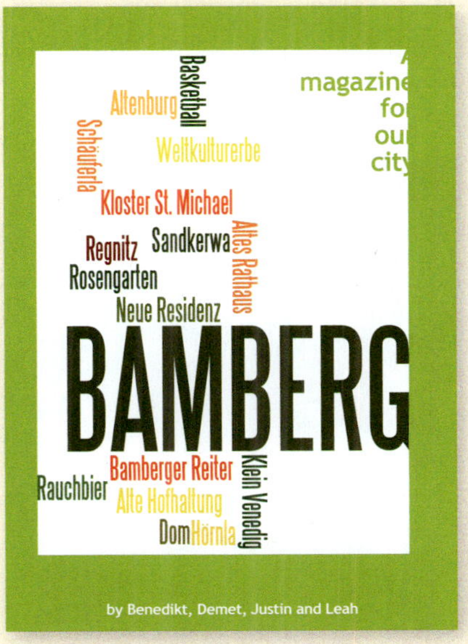

PLAN IT

- **Work together in small groups.**
- **Make notes on what you already know about your area. Think about:**
  - what young people can do in your area/ your city/a town near you
  - where you can spend time after school
  - where you would like to take visitors
- **Collect more information:**
  - interview classmates, your family, …
  - check local newspapers
  - search the Internet
  - …

DO IT

Decide: Which member of your group is going to do what?

➔ Choose an activity:

You can …

- **write down the information on different pieces of paper (also think about opening times, prices, how to get there, …).**
- **take photos or find other pictures.**
- **create a cover for your magazine.**

A great day for visitors

Part 2: afternoon & evening

2 pm: Sightseeing tour
Take your visitors on a guided tour round the historical city. Show them famous sights like the Cathedral, the Old Court, the New Residence and Rose Garden, the Old Town Hall and Little Venice.

Rose Garden

5 pm: Theatre of Shadows
Experience Bamberg's 1000-year-old history in the oldest room of the city, the small chapel near the Cathedral. (Katharinenkapelle, 15€)

8pm: Dinner at Brauhaus Schlenkerla
Choose from delicious Franconian specialities like Schäuferla or Bamberg-style sausages with sauerkraut. Adults could try the famous smokebeer.
(Dominikanerstr. 6)

Inside Brauhaus Schlenkerla

page 2

Bamberg from A to Z
~ for young people ~

Juggling
Learn how to juggle like a pro with the help of jugglers from Circus Giovanni.
Every Monday from 4 pm to 6 pm in the JuZ-Sporthalle.
(Margaretendamm 12a)

Kati learns to juggle

Jugger
"3, 2, 1 - Jugger!" Try this new team sport! It's an exciting mix between rugby and football and it's great fun.
Every Wednesday from 4 pm to 6 pm on the sports ground in Hainstraße.
There are also tournaments and championships like the "Streit um die Goldene Pompfe" on Jahnwiese in October.

Basti and Tommy playing jugger

page 5

CHECK IT

- **Is the English OK?**
- **Do the pictures match?**
- **Is it interesting? Add details.**
- **Show it to other classmates or your teacher.**
- **Edit it. Use a dictionary.**
- **Stick the texts and pictures on the pages of your magazine. Add the cover.**

PRESENT IT

- **Present your magazines at your next Open Day at school or to exchange students.**

portfolio

W p. 219 TM, p. 140

➡ p. LF35

10 + 11 WB p. 47/48

11 The Notting Hill Carnival

p. 48/14

Look at the programme. Find out:

- When is the carnival? in August: 24th-26th
- How long does the carnival last? three days
- What can you see at the carnival?

Notting Hill Carnival – Official Events

Date & Time	Event
Saturday August 24 7 pm – 11 pm	**National Steel Band Competition** The UK's top steel bands compete for the title: National Champions of Steel
Sunday August 25 9 am – 7 pm	**Children's Day Parade** Children and teenagers in colourful costumes parade through the streets of Notting Hill.
Monday August 26 10 am – 7 pm	**Main Parade** Groups and clubs in amazing costumes dance to the rhythms of mobile sound systems or steel bands.

// Geschichte inhaltlich identisch, aber sprachlich anspruchsvoller

M5 M p. 76

12 + 13 WB p. 48

How to ... read p. 170

12 At the carnival

p. 49/15

a) Read about the carnival. Why are the friends so excited? they are waiting to see Charlie's little sister Sharon in the Children's Day Parade

Caroline, Gillian, Charlie and Rajiv love the Notting Hill Carnival. They love watching the crowds of people who walk, dance and sing in the streets of Notting Hill. They love listening to the singers and bands. There are a lot of dancers and brightly coloured floats which pass by in the parade – and many tourists who take photos. But there are also pickpockets who try to steal wallets and watches. The police put up posters which tell everybody to be careful.

Today is the Children's Day Parade. The four friends watch it excitedly. They are waiting to see Charlie's sister, Sharon, who is in the parade this year. There is a group of children dressed up as sunshine dancers. Behind them is a children's steel band which is playing Caribbean music. Sharon and her group are close behind a music float. They have got colourful skirts and fantastic headdresses of flowers and feathers. The girls look like tropical birds of paradise. They are all dancing to the rhythm of the steel drums.

When Sharon sees Charlie, she runs over and gives him a big hug. Charlie is so proud of his little sister.

➡ p. LF35

b) There are lots of different people at the carnival. Who are they? What do they do?

c) Imagine YOU could take part in a parade. How would you feel?

P8 P p. 72

KV48

13 Lots to see

LSW 306

Relativsätze 14 p. 192

➡ p. LF35

a) What can you see at the carnival? Look at the pictures on pages 64-67 and read numbers 11 and 12 again for help.

There	is are	steel bands police officers a programme tourists a Children's Day Parade pickpockets …	who which	tells you what's on. you can watch on Sunday. help people. steal wallets and watches. play great music. take photos of the parade. …

b) Work with a partner and compare your sentences. Then look at them again. When do you use 'who'? When do you use 'which'?

You use 'who' for people and 'which' for things.

How to … work with grammar p. 178

M M9 p. 77

LAND & LEUTE

Notting Hill Carnival

Der Londoner Stadtteil Notting Hill ist berühmt für seinen *carnival*. Er findet jedes Jahr am letzten Wochenende im August statt.

Am Samstag geht es mit einem Wettbewerb für *steel bands* los. Die Bands spielen Musik auf *steel drums*, die aus alten Ölfässern aus Stahl hergestellt werden und das Nationalinstrument Trinidads sind.

Am Sonntag folgt dann ein Umzug, bei dem Kinder und Jugendliche in farbenprächtigen Kostümen durch die Straßen von Notting Hill ziehen.

Am Montag darauf ist in Großbritannien ein Feiertag *(bank holiday)*. Dann findet der große Umzug *(main parade)* statt. Jedes Jahr kommen bis zu 1,5 Millionen Zuschauer, um diesen großen Umzug zu sehen. Auf einer Strecke von fünf Kilometern ziehen verschiedene Gruppen und Vereine in fantastischen Kostümen durch die Straßen von Notting Hill, begleitet von Festwagen mit Musikanlagen und Bands. Dabei wird die karibische Kultur gefeiert und es herrscht ausgelassene Stimmung.

Der Notting Hill Carnival hat einen ernsten Hintergrund: 1959 wurde das Fest zum ersten Mal gefeiert, um auf rassistische Übergriffe auf Einwanderer aus der Karibik aufmerksam zu machen. Im Laufe der Zeit ist aus einer kleinen Feier ein Stadtteilfest mit einem der größten Straßenumzüge Europas geworden.

Suche im Atlas die Insel Trinidad. Dort, im karibischen Meer, findest du auch die Insel Barbados, von der Charlies Familie stammt.

IWS

Welche Straßenfeste werden in deiner Gegend gefeiert?

W p. 220

➡ p. LF35

DVD

14 Welcome to the carnival!

IWS LSW 307

p. 50f./16 + 17

a) Watch the clip. Describe what you have just seen.
b) Would YOU like to go to the Notting Hill Carnival? Say why.
c) Design YOUR costume for a carnival or party *or* design YOUR float. Describe it *or* draw and label it.

W p. 220

➡ p. LF35

15 A narrow escape

Folie 8 IWS LSW 308 p. 49/15

a) Look at the pictures. What can you see? What is happening?

b) Now read the newspaper article. Find out why the boy almost had an accident.

A pickpocket who was running away knocked the boy under a float.

Monday, 26 August

NOTTING HILL EVENING NEWS

NARROW ESCAPE

Six-year-old John Scott from Wembley had a narrow escape yesterday while he was watching the carnival parade.
A pickpocket who was running away knocked the boy under a float.

The boy's mother saw what was happening and managed to pull her son away before the front wheel of the float ran him over.
The police are now questioning a young man. Anybody with further information please phone the police: 020 8743 5520.

c) Look at the article again and find the English phrases for these German phrases.

- ist gerade noch einmal davongekommen
- stieß den Jungen unter einen Festwagen
- befragen zurzeit einen jungen Mann
- konnte ihren Sohn gerade noch wegziehen
- bevor das Vorderrad des Festwagens ihn überrollte
- wer weitere Informationen hat

P9 + P13 p. 72/73 P

M6 – M8 p. 76/77 M

14 p. 49 WB

d) Right or wrong? Correct what's wrong.

1. A boy was watching the carnival parade. ✓
2. His name is John Scott and he was there with his mother. ✓
3. A pickpocket stole a man's watch. a man's wallet
4. The pickpocket knocked the boy under a car. under a float
5. The boy's mother saw what was happening. ✓
6. She managed to pull the pickpocket away from the float. to pull her son away
7. The boy's parents are now questioning a young man. The police are questioning him.

16 A police interview

LSW 309

➡ p. LF36

L 1.21
WB 15 p. 50
Past progressive 8 p. 187
P7 + P10 – P12 p. 72/73

a) Listen to the interview. Who is the police officer talking to? a young man
b) Listen again. What is the young man's story: What was he doing yesterday afternoon? What wasn't he doing? Talk to your partner.

He	was wasn't	playing watching stealing wearing	the parade. the same jacket. TV. football. wallets.

c) What does the police officer think? What do you think: Is he right? Say why.

17 A project – YOUR festival

LSW 310

portfolio
wordbank Celebrations p. 158
How to .. write p. 174
➡ p. LF36

Write about a festival (carnival, party or street festival) that you know or have been to.

PLAN IT

- Collect words in a word web or in a list.

DO IT

- Write about the event. Give information on:
  - when it is
  - where it is
  - who is there
  - what the people do
  - why you like it
  - …

CHECK IT

- Read your text. Can you make it better? Look at these tips for help:

> ➔ Use words like *in the morning, then, after (that),* … to show when something happens.
> ➔ Use words like *and, but, because,* … to connect your ideas.
> ➔ Don't start every sentence with the same word.
> ➔ Use adjectives to make your text more interesting.
> ➔ Check your spelling. Use a dictionary for help.

- Work with a partner. Swap your texts. Tell your partner what you like about his/her text and what you would change.
- Edit it.

KV13

Our street festival

We have a fantastic street festival in summer every year. In the morning there is a children's flea market. There are a lot of bands ~~. They~~ which play music. ~~There~~ In the afternoon there are magicians and dancers. People put up lots of interesting stalls. You can buy delicious food there. We get money from the street festival. ~~The money~~ It goes to a children's home in our town. I like our street festival because I meet lots of friends there.

PRESENT IT

- Show your text to the class: Read it, record it or put it up in the classroom.

WB test yourself p. 51/52

W p. 221 TM, p. 155

➡ p. LF36

P1 City or country?

a) **Look at these words. Which ones would you sort under 'city', which ones under 'country'? Make two lists.**

farm • airport • department store • factory • park • nature • rubbish • sightseeing • fresh air • theatre • youth club • forest • chicken

b) **What other words do you know? Add them to your lists.**

P2 Sound check

a) **What are these buildings? Write them down.**

1. /tʃɜːtʃ/ church
2. /ˈeəˌpɔːt/ airport
3. /ˈsɪnəmə/ cinema
4. /skuːl/ school
5. /ˈjuːθ ˌklʌb/ youth club
6. /ˈkɑːsl/ castle
7. /laɪbrəri/ library
8. /ˈsteɪʃn/ station

L 1.22

b) **Listen and check.**

P3 A painting

How to ... talk about pictures p. 173

a) **Look at the painting and read the description. What's different? Find the six mistakes.**

This painting is called "The Sleeping Gypsy". It shows a woman who is sleeping and a tiger which is standing behind her. The sky is yellow and there aren't any clouds. The moon is on the left. The woman has long hair and she is wearing colourful trousers. She is holding a stick in her left hand. At the bottom you can see a musical instrument. Next to the musical instrument there are two vases.

➡ p. LF36

b) **Copy the description and correct the mistakes. Then compare your text with a partner.**

c) **Do you like the painting? Talk to your partner.**

I like the painting because it's nice/colourful/interesting/...

I don't like the painting. I think it's ugly/boring/...

P4 Pocket money

LSW 312

Simple present 2R p. 182/183

➡ p. LF36

a) Look at the questions and make notes.
- How often do you get pocket money?
- Do you get money for good marks at school?
- Do you get extra money?
- What jobs do you do to earn money?

b) Work with a partner. Ask and answer the questions in a).

c) What do you do with your money?

I spend my money on …

I save my money for …

downloads • make-up • tickets for … • …

P5 Last weekend

Simple past 5R p. 185

➡ p. LF37

a) What did Karla do last weekend? Write about her.

go to the youth club

read in bed

play with her rabbit

spend time with her brother

write lots of emails

watch basketball on TV

On Saturday morning Karla went to … Then she … In the afternoon … After that …

b) What did YOU do last weekend? Write about it.

P6 A poster

LSW 313

➡ p. LF37

How to … help out p. 179

Read the poster. What do you learn about the car boot sale at Haverstock School? Tell a classmate in German.

Die Haverstock Schule veranstaltet …

… findet statt am …

Es kostet …

…

Car Boot Sale

Haverstock School, Camden

Sunday, 27th May

All money goes to the Haverstock School library

STALLS	£7 prebooked £10 on the day
ENTRANCE	Adults: 20p Children: free
LOCATION	Car stalls next to Haverstock School gym
PARKING	Free parking in school car park
STALL SET-UP	From 8:00 am
SALE OPEN	From 9:00 am – 4:00 pm

For further details please contact:
Karen Dixon Tel. 60284 or Paula Knight Tel. 62058

W p. 221 TM, p. 157

P7 A word snake

LSW 311

a) **Find the carnival words in the snake. Write them down.**

band, float, parade, costume, crowd, singer, party, drum, celebration, fun, music, festival

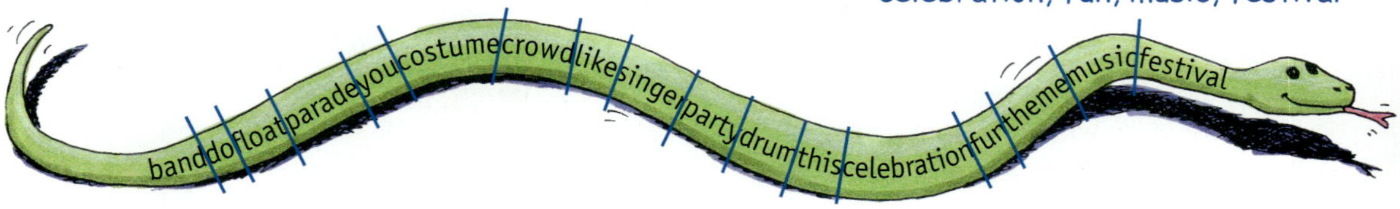

b) **The other words will make a question. Read it. And what is your answer?**

Did you like this theme? Yes, I did. I enjoyed reading about the Notting Hill Carnival. But some of the grammar was difficult!

P8 Rhyming pairs

LSW 314

a) **Find the rhyming pairs.**

crowd • sing • band •
float • steal • see •
who • bird • drum •
head • walk • dance

crowd – loud
sing – …
…

word • meal • bed •
talk • spring • hand •
chance • you • some •
loud • me • boat

L 1.23

b) **Listen and check your pairs.**

sing – spring
band – hand
float – boat

steal – meal
see – me
who – you
bird – word

drum – some
head – bed
walk – talk
dance – chance

P9 The little boy who …

LSW 315

Relativsätze 14 p. 192

Write about the parade. Match the sentence parts.

1.	John is the little boy who	who which	are playing in the parade. 5
2.	This is the float which		pulled her son away from the float. 3
3.	Mrs Scott is the woman who		almost had an accident. 1
4.	This is the phone number which		felt a hand in his pocket. 7
5.	These are the steel bands which		is talking to the police. 6
6.	Bill is the young man who		you can call to talk to the police. 4
7.	Mr Harley is the tourist who		almost ran the little boy over. 2

➡ p. LF37

P10 Check your spelling

4R p. 184 Present progressive

Copy the lists into your exercise book. Fill in the *ing*-forms of the verbs in the box.

Verdopplung des letzten Buchstabens	Wegfall des *-e*	nur *-ing* wird angehängt
run → running	have → having	watch → watching
…	…	…

run • have • happen •
watch • drive • put •
talk • take • listen •
make • write • dance •
visit • do • sit • swim

P11 What were YOU doing?

LSW 316

➡ p. LF37
8 p. 187
Past progressive

Work in small groups. Ask and answer like this:

What were you doing this morning when the teacher came in?

I was listening to music. And you?

What were you doing at six o'clock yesterday evening?

I was watching TV. And you?

Here are more ideas for questions:

… at seven o'clock this morning • … at four o'clock yesterday afternoon • … at eight o'clock last Saturday night • …

P12 What a class!

➡ p. LF38
8 p. 187
Past progressive

What were the students doing yesterday when Mr Baker came in?

When Mr Baker came in, Douglas was eating a sandwich. Aisha and Debbie were …

P13 Tips for the carnival

➡ p. LF38
How to … help out p. 179

You find these tips for the Notting Hill Carnival on the Internet. Your friend looks at them and doesn't understand everything. Tell your friend in German.

Man muss/soll …

Man darf nicht/ soll nicht …

…

Notting Hill Carnival Safety Tips

- Leave your car at home. Take the tube or bus instead.
- Wear comfortable shoes.
- Leave expensive things like jewellery or digital cameras at home.
- Don't put your wallet or mobile phone in your back pocket.
- Drink lots of water, especially if the weather is hot.
- Stay together with your friends or family all the time.

W p. 221 TM, p. 159

M1 Teenagers talking about London

LSW 317–319

L 1.24 S 9
M1 p. 55

a) A radio reporter is interviewing some teenagers about London. Listen and put the photos in the right order. B – A – C

A

B

C

➡ p. LF38

b) Listen again. Find out what the teenagers like or don't like about London. Take notes in a grid.
c) Compare your notes with a partner.

M2 Money problems

KV11, KV12 KV49
➡ p. LF38
How to ... work with others p. 177

a) Your class wants to go on a class trip but you have to raise some money to pay for it. What can you do? Work in groups of four and make a placemat.

> have a car boot sale/... • sell ... • make ... • repair ... • mow the lawn • ...

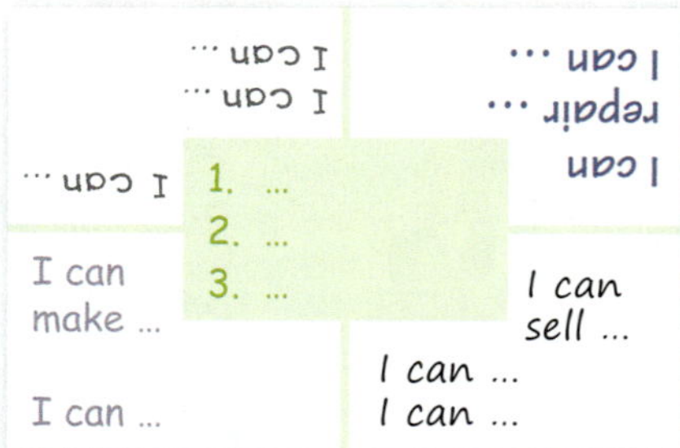

b) Talk about your ideas. Then decide on the three best ideas and write them down in the middle of the placemat.

KV50
M2 + M3 p. 55

c) Tell the class about your placemat results.

> We've talked about how to raise money for a class trip. These are our three best ideas: ...

M3 An advert

Make an advert for YOUR best idea for raising money.
Write down:
- what you are offering
- when and where
- what you will use the money for
- why people should say yes to your offer

Present your advert in class.

p. LF39
WB M4 p. 56

M4 King of the musicals?

IWS LSW 320

p. LF39
WB M5 p. 56

a) **"The Lion King" is a world-famous musical. Read the reviews of the London show that people have posted on the Internet. What did they like about the show? What didn't they like?**

News (230) ▾ Favourites ▾

COMMENTS PLEASE LET US KNOW WHAT YOU THINK !

Posted by bnorth25 — October 22nd
The show was brilliant! I enjoyed every minute of it. It couldn't have been better. The only negative thing was that lots of mobile phones were ringing during the performance.

Posted by Max4u — October 23rd
This is the best show I have ever seen in my life – full of colour, surprises and the most wonderful singing and music. I can't wait to see it again!

Posted by Anonymous — October 23rd
The singing, the acting and the costumes were great. But to be honest: The tickets are far too expensive!

Posted by kiki1234 — October 27th
Very disappointed! Very bad quality of singing, background singing not loud enough, cold actors, no feeling.

Posted by Sus@n — November 1st
The costumes, make-up, acting were fantastic, the music truly magical! The whole show was amazing from beginning to end.
I would recommend it to all ages (it may be a bit scary for children under the age of 9).

b) **Read the reviews again. What do you think: How many stars ★★★★★ (1 to 5) did each person give the show?**

c) **Write YOUR review of a musical, film, book or game. Look at the reviews in a) for help.**

W p. 222 TM, p. 167

→ p. LF39

M5 At the carnival

LSW 321, 322

12 B p. 64
M6 WB p. 57
How to … read p. 170

a) Read about the carnival. Why are the friends so excited? Find examples in the text.

It is a hot Sunday in August. Caroline, Gillian, Charlie and Rajiv are in Notting Hill for the famous carnival. The streets are packed with people who walk, dance and sing. There are many tourists who take photos of the singers, bands, dancers – and the brightly coloured floats which pass by in the parade. But there are also pickpockets who try to steal wallets, watches and mobile phones. The police put up posters which tell everybody to be careful.

Today is the Children's Day Parade. The friends are watching it excitedly. They are waiting to see Charlie's sister, Sharon, who is in the parade this year.

"Hey, guys, have you seen any pickpockets yet?" asks Rajiv and points to a police poster.

"I haven't got time to watch out for pickpockets," says Charlie. He doesn't want to miss Sharon on her big day.

There is a group of children dressed up as sunshine dancers. Their faces are painted yellow. Behind them is a children's steel band which is playing Caribbean music. The air is full of excitement.

Nick

"Guess who's in a steel band this year!" says Gillian to the others.

"Who?" asks Caroline.

"Look and see if you can find him," answers Gillian.

"Oh, wow, it's Nick. Nick's in a steel band? I didn't know he could play the steel drums," says Rajiv. They all wave at Nick and he smiles – he can't wave when he's playing!

Sharon and her group are performing close behind a music float. They are wearing colourful skirts, gold bracelets, and fantastic headdresses of flowers and feathers. The girls look like tropical birds of paradise. They are all dancing to the rhythm of the steel drums, and the crowd loves it.

"Sharon! Over here, Sharon!" shouts Charlie.

When Sharon sees Charlie, she runs over and gives him a big hug. Charlie is so proud of his little sister. She looks amazing and is really great at dancing.

b) There are lots of different people at the carnival. Who are they? What do they do?
c) Imagine YOU could take part in a parade. What would you like to do? How would you feel?

M6 Better safe than sorry

L 1.25 S 10
M7 WB p. 57
→ p. LF39

a) Listen to the interview on the radio. Find out:
- Who is Robert Taylor? police officer from Notting Hill
- When does the carnival start? next weekend
- How many important things are there to remember? six

b) Listen again. Write down the things you should or shouldn't do at the Notting Hill Carnival.

dos	don'ts
…	no high heels
…	…

M7 The pickpocket

Folie 8 LSW 323

p. LF40

WB M8 p. 58

wordbank People p. 159 Clothes p. 161

WB M9 p. 58

a) Look at the pictures in number 15 again. How would you describe the pickpocket to the police?

- What does he look like?
- What was he wearing at the parade?
- How old is he?
- ... ?

b) Work in small groups. Describe a pickpocket to your partners. They must guess which pickpocket you are talking about. Take turns.

M8 What Mr Harley saw

p. LF40

5R+8 p. 195+197 5R: Simple past 8: Past progressive

Mr Harley saw the incident at the Notting Hill Carnival. What can he tell the police about it? Look at the pictures and the newspaper article in number 15 again. Write it down. You can start like this:

Well, this morning I went to ... I was watching ...
Suddenly I felt ... I turned round and ...

M9 Guess what it is

LSW 324

p. LF40

a) Read the definitions. Who or what is it?

1. It is a thing that people stand on in a parade.
2. It is a thing which people keep money in.
3. It is a person who visits a place on holiday.
4. It is a thing which you can make music with.
5. It is a person that tries to catch criminals.
6. It is a thing that you can wear at a carnival.
7. It is a person who steals wallets.
8. It is an animal which has colourful feathers.

b) Look at the definitions in a) again. When do you use 'who'? When do you use 'which'? When do you use 'that'? Look at LiF 14 on page 192 for help.

Relativsätze 14 p. 192

How to ... work with grammar p. 178

c) Write down definitions which have something to do with carnival, music and street festivals. Then test your partner.

It is	a thing a person	who which that	...

W p. 222 TM, p. 172 IWS

CAMDEN CHRONICLE
LEARN ENGLISH THE CAMDEN WAY

DID YOU GET IT ALL? ➡ p. LF40

» How much pocket money does Gillian have left?
» Where does Karla's grandma live?
» Who becomes the new lion king?
» Who is Simba's new wife?
» When is the Children's Day Parade?
» What does Sharon wear at the Children's Day Parade?
» How old is John Scott?
» What did the pickpocket steal?

Some Notting Hill Carnival facts

- The Notting Hill Carnival is one of the largest festivals in the world.
- 20 % of visitors are tourists.
- You can see more than 15,000 costumes.
- Each costume is designed and made by hand.
- 30 million sequins, 15,000 feathers and 30 litres of body paint are used for the costumes.
- It takes one million hours to decorate all the costumes.
- Food eaten at the carnival:
  1 ton of rice and peas, 400 goats, 30,000 corn on the cob, 15,000 deep-fried bananas, 1 ton of curry chicken, 1 ton of Jamaican patties, 12,000 mangos, 16,000 coconuts, 5 million hot and cold drinks

GOOD TO KNOW ...

Für viele englische Dörfer ist „the Village Fête" die wichtigste Veranstaltung im Jahr. Dieses Dorffest findet normalerweise an einem Sommerwochenende statt. Dort werden einheimische Produkte und Lebensmittel verkauft. Dazu gibt es viel Musik, Spiele und Unterhaltung für Kinder sowie Wettbewerbe, z. B. wer die größte Sonnenblume im Garten hat oder wer die größte Zucchini angebaut hat.

TONGUE TWISTERS

Daisy Dickins dresses up and dances with Dave Donalds.

Peter Pritchett picks pockets and purses.

Sharon's sister is selling spicy samosas in the street.

THEME 4

TM, p. 173 KV51: Lernlandkarte

YOU'RE NOT ALONE

In diesem *Theme* ...

- » beschäftigst du dich mit der Geschichte von Robinson Crusoe.
- » sprichst du darüber, was *home* für dich bedeutet.
- » liest du über persönliche Probleme.
- » überlegst du, wie man mit Problemen umgehen und sie lösen kann.
- » beschreibst du dein Lieblingslied.

W p. 223 TM, p. 173

➡ p. LF41

1 p. 59 WB

1 Robinson Crusoe

Folie 9A+B IWS p. 54f./1

a) The English **writer** Daniel Defoe wrote the adventure story "Robinson Crusoe" in 1719. Have you ever heard of Robinson Crusoe? What do you know about him?

KV52

b) Read this very short **version** of the story.

York, 1st September 1651: Robinson Crusoe left his parents and **boarded a ship** to London.

London, 1st September 1659: Robinson left England on a ship to **the Caribbean**.

The ship crossed **the Atlantic Ocean**.

The Caribbean, 30th September 1659: There was a **storm** and the ship **hit** some **rocks**.

Robinson swam to an **island**.

He built a **raft** and collected a few things from the **wreck**. He **began** a new life on the island.

Robinson lived alone for many years.

One day some **cannibals** came to the island.

They had a prisoner but Robinson rescued him. He gave him the name Man Friday because he found him on a Friday.

Robinson taught Man Friday to speak English. They had a lot of adventures.

Man Friday taught Robinson how to fish.

He showed Robinson how to use plants as medicine.

19th December 1686: An English ship sailed by and rescued them.

York, 11th June 1687: Robinson arrived back in England. Home, sweet home!

c) **What do you think: How did Robinson feel in the different situations? Choose an adjective for each picture. Look up new words in the dictionary.**

LSW 401–403

In picture number 1 I think Robinson felt …

happy • excited • sad • lonely • homesick • shocked • glad • worried • proud • helpless • hungry • seasick • surprised • unhappy • …

d) **Watch the animated slide show of Robinson Crusoe's adventure. What else do you learn about Robinson?**

p. 57, 3+4

Wordbank People p. 159
P P1–P3 p. 90
M M1 p. 94
WB 2+3 p. 59
DVD

W p. 223

➡ p. LF41

4 WB
p. 60

P4 + P5 P
p. 90/91

M2 M
p. 94

// Präsentations-kompetenz: *two-minute talk* über Robinson Crusoe, unterstützt durch *wh*-Leitfragen

2 The story of Robinson

p. 56/2

a) **When Robinson Crusoe was back in York, many people asked him about his adventure. Tell his story.**
Well, I left my parents in York on
1st September 1651. I boarded a ship …
Then I left London on …

b) **Now write down his story.**

Robinson left his parents …
He … Later … Then …
After some time …
One day … …

➡ p. LF42

5 WB
p. 60

3 YOUR survival kit

IWS LSW 404

a) **Which of these things would you put in your survival kit for a lonely island?**

How to …
work with words
p. 166

b) **Think of more things you would take and write them down.**

c) **Talk about the things in groups. Agree on three things.**

KV12

I think a watch is very important. What about you?

I think you're right.

Well, I'm not sure. I think soap is more useful than a watch.

P6 P
p. 91

M3 M
p. 95

4 Oh, yeah!

LSW 405

a) Listen to Gillian, Charlie and Rajiv. What are they talking about?

Robinson Crusoe • a perfect island • wild animals

b) Listen again. Who wants to live on an island with …
- a high mountain? Gillian – a big waterfall? Gillian
- a beautiful lake? Charlie – a big forest? Rajiv

c) What else can you understand?

L 1.26

M4 p. 95

WB 6 p. 61

P7 p. 91

\\ M4: Hörtext derselbe, Auswertung anspruchsvoller: offene Fragen, *taking notes*

➡ p. LF42

WB 7 p. 61

5 What is home?

p. 58f./5+6

a) Look at these English sayings. What do you think they mean?

Home is where the heart is. My home is my castle. Home, sweet home.
There is no place like home. East, west – home is best.

b) Work with a partner and make a word web about home.

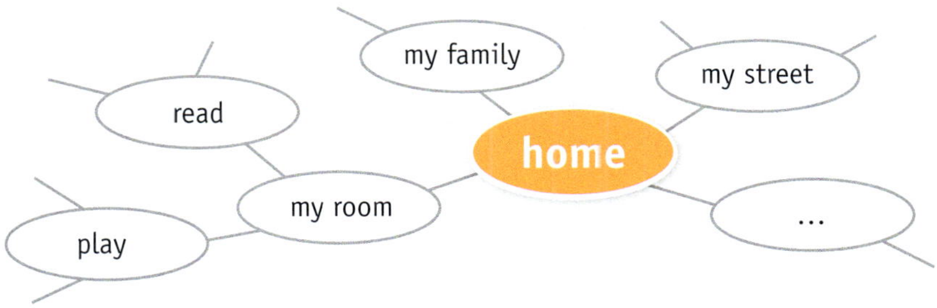

c) Use the word web to talk about YOUR home. What do you like? What don't you like?

I love my room. There I can …

I like playing …

I hate/enjoy …

13 p. 191
Gerundium nach bestimmten Verben

6 Choose an activity

You can …
- imagine you are stranded on an island. One day you find an empty bottle on the beach. Write a "message in a bottle".
- write down the 20 English words you would teach Man Friday first. Why have you chosen them?
- find out more about Daniel Defoe. Make a fact file or give a short talk.

Dear Finder,

Please rescue me! I am stranded. Our ship hit a rock two days after we passed Hawaii and I swam to this lonely island.
Send help soon! At night I hear strange noises. Maybe there are wild animals or cannibals on the island. …

➡ p. LF42

portfolio

M5 p. 95

W p. 224 TM, p. 189

7 Problem page

LSW 406 KV53 p. 60f./7+8

8+9 p. 62 WB

a) Read the letters on the next page. Find the right heading for each letter. 1-D 2-C 3-A 4-G

A Parents split up · B Problems at school · C Dad says: no dog! · D Really a best friend? · E I hate my sister · F I don't want to move · G Cyberbullying

b) Read the letters again. Who is it?

Patty *(2x)* • Jason • Tommy *(2x)* • Susan

1. XX prefers dogs. Jason
2. XX wants to live with both of his parents. Tommy
3. XX doesn't want to receive horrible messages. Susan
4. XX wants to tell her friend about her feelings. Patty
5. XX doesn't want to decide where to live. Tommy
6. XX hates sitting next to her best friend at school. Patty

8 Different people – different problems

10 p. 63 WB

a) Read Sarah's answers to the letters. Then read the following advice. Which one is correct – A, B, or C?

p. 60f./7+8

1 Try to …
- A find other friends.
- (B) talk to her to save your friendship.
- C become a basketball player, too.

2 Why don't you …
- (A) take care of a dog from a dogs' home?
- B buy a hamster and teach it to bark?
- C get a cat instead?

3 You should …
- (A) talk to your mum and dad and to others.
- B forget about your problems.
- C make a list of the things that worry you.

4 You could …
- A throw away your mobile.
- B just ignore the messages.
- (C) talk to others.

P8 + P11 p. 92 · M6 p. 96 · ➡ p. LF43

b) What do you think about Sarah's advice?

LSW 407

I think the answer to letter number	1 2 3 4	is	(very) (quite) (not very)	helpful. silly. good. …

Ask Sarah

Send all your problems to me. I can only answer some letters on this page, but I'll send an answer to everyone who writes to me.
Sarah

1

I have a big problem. I'm in love with a boy at school. He's really cute and a great basketball player. His name is Liam. I told my best friend about him and we decided she would find out if he liked me. Next thing is – he tells her she's great and now they're going out together. I can't believe she has done this to me! And we sit next to each other in school! I want to tell her how I feel, but I'll never speak to her again. I'm so disappointed – and angry. What can I do?
Patty, 14, Manchester

Dear Patty,
I know this is hard for you, but you must talk to your friend and tell her about your feelings. Of course it's not fair, but don't let a boy come between you and your best friend. Your friendship should be strong enough to get over your problems.

2

I've always wanted a dog because I love animals. My dad says no – our flat is too small. I've told him I'll feed and walk it, but he says we can't leave a dog in the flat all day. I'm sure I can find someone to look after it. My mum says I can have a cat, but I prefer dogs.
Jason, 14, Brighton

Dear Jason,
Your father is right. I'm sure you love dogs, but it isn't fair to leave them alone all day. Why don't you visit a dogs' home in your town? There you'll find lots of dogs that need a good friend. You can look after one of them and go for long walks. I know it won't be your dog, but you'll have a new friend. Perhaps when you're older your dream will come true.

3

I really need your help. My parents told my sister and me that they're going to split up! I don't know what to do. I'm so sad. Everything will change. I always thought we were a happy family and now it's all over? Do I have to decide who I want to live with? I love both my parents.
Tommy, 14, London

Dear Tommy,
It's always sad for everyone when parents split up. You're not alone. Many young people have this problem. First you – and your sister – should talk to your parents and find answers to all the questions that worry you. You have to deal with this as a family. Try to talk to others whose parents have split up. You could ask them for help, too.

4

My big problem is cyberbullying. I got a new mobile for my birthday last month. At school we shared all our numbers in my class and since then I have received some horrible messages. Someone wants to beat me up. Please help me. What can I do?
Susan, 13, York

Dear Susan,
Remember: It's not your fault. Tell your parents and your teachers. Talk about it with your friends. Maybe they have similar problems, too. Together you'll stop the bullying.

W p. 224

➡ p. LF43

9 Caroline's family

LSW 408 KV54 p. 62/9

a) Read about Caroline and her family. What are their problems?

Caroline's father, Mr Lambraki, is an engineer. Two months ago he lost his job and is now out of work. So he does the housework and the cooking. He is looking for a new job, but that is very difficult. Every morning he checks the newspaper and searches the Internet. If he doesn't find a new job soon, he will get really frustrated.

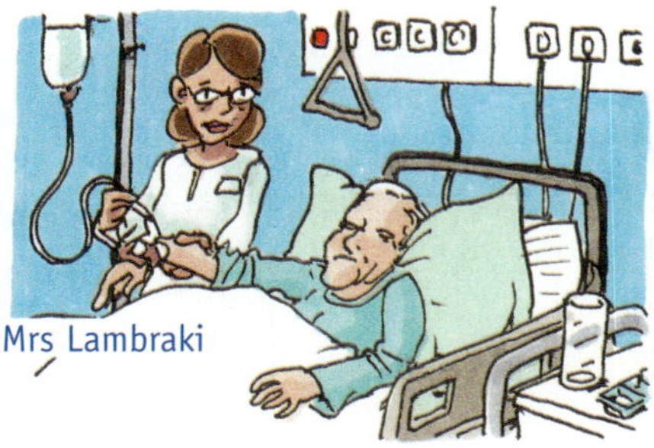

Caroline's mother, Mrs Lambraki, is a nurse at Wellington Hospital. She works very hard, but she loves her job. Looking after the patients is something she enjoys very much. She is often tired when she comes home. If her husband doesn't get a new job soon, she will have to work even more. They need the money for the family.

Caroline's twin brother, George, is 13. He never cleans his room and he doesn't like to help with the housework. Caroline often gets angry about that. After school George usually plays football or computer games. He likes football and his computer more than his homework. If he doesn't work harder for school, he won't get a good school report. But George doesn't care.

Caroline is now 13. She loves her pets and her friends. She spends a lot of time with her best friend, Gillian. They listen to music together and talk about boys. But Caroline also worries a lot: What will happen if her father doesn't find a new job soon? Will they move to a smaller house? Will her mother have to work even more? Sometimes Caroline is really worried.

11 p. 63 WB

b) Write down important facts about the family members from the text like this:

Mr Lambraki: engineer, out of work, ...
Mrs Lambraki: ...
George: ...
Caroline: ...

P10+P12+P14 P p. 92/93

How to ... give a talk p. 171

c) Now present one member of the family to the class.

10 What will happen?

IWS · LSW 409 · KV55

a) Read number 9 again. Match the sentence parts.

C 1 If Mr Lambraki doesn't find a new job soon,
E 2 If her husband doesn't get a new job soon,
A 3 If George doesn't work harder for school,
B 4 If her father doesn't find a new job soon,
D 5 If Mrs Lambraki works even more,

A he won't get a good school report.
B Caroline will worry even more.
C he will get really frustrated.
D she won't have time for her family.
E Mrs Lambraki will have to work even more.

b) Look at the sentences in a) again. What are they in German? Tell a partner.
c) What do you think: What will happen if Mr Lambraki finds a new job?

If Mr Lambraki finds a new job,	he Mrs Lambraki George Caroline	will won't	get more pocket money. be happy again. work less. have more time for her family. be worried (anymore). ...

Bedingungssätze, Typ I 23 p. 201
P13 p. 93
WB 12 + 13 p. 64
p. LF43

11 Welcome to my life

p. LF43
L 1.27
WB 14 p. 55

a) When Caroline feels unhappy, she likes listening to music.
Listen to one of her favourite songs. What can you understand?

Do you ever feel like breaking down?
Do you ever feel out of place?
Like somehow you just don't belong
And no one understands you
Do you ever want to run away?
Do you lock yourself in your room?
With the radio on, turned up so loud
That no one hears you screaming
No, you don't know what it's like
When nothing feels alright
You don't know what it's like
To be like me ...

To be hurt, to feel lost
To be left out in the dark
To be kicked when you're down
To feel like you've been pushed around
To be on the edge of breaking down
And no one's there to save you
No, you don't know what it's like
Welcome to my life
...

I think the song is about ...

I (don't) like the melody/rhythm/lyrics.

b) Listen again and read or sing along. Then talk about the song.

The music is fast/slow.

The music sounds happy/sad/angry/...

W p. 225

12 How to deal with problems

LSW 410 KV56

➡ p. LF43

How to ... work with others p. 177

a) **Placemat:** What can YOU do to deal with your problems? Work in groups of four and make a placemat.

talk to ... • listen to ... • write to ... • write ... • do ... • make ... • go ... • ...

parents • friends • teacher • music • letter • email • running • cycling • ...

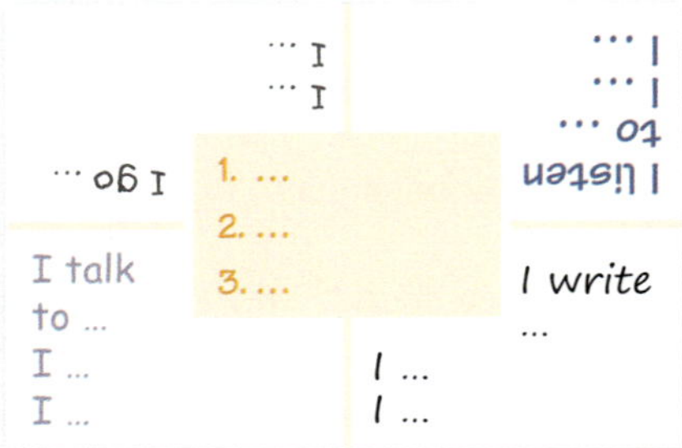

b) Talk about your ideas. Find the three most popular ideas and write them in the middle of the placemat.

15 p. 65

c) Tell the class about your placemat results.

When I have a problem, I talk to my sister.

Me too. And I write emails to my friends.

13 Girls talk

Folie 10

➡ p. LF44

a) Look at the pictures. What do you think the girls are talking about?

L 1.28

b) Now listen to Caroline and Gillian. Put the pictures in the right order. A – C – B – D

M7 - M10 M p. 96/97

c) Look at the letters on page 85 again. Which two letters are the girls talking about? letters 1 and 3

14 YOUR favourite music

IWS

➡ p. LF44

a) What is your favourite group or singer at the moment?
What is your favourite song? Talk to a partner.

I listen to … a lot.

I think … is/are cool.

My favourite … is …

I like … because …

b) **Milling around:** Tell each other about your favourite music.

c) Write about your favourite song. You can use these phrases:

How to … work with others p. 176

P9 p. 92

- My favourite song is …
- The singer is …
- The style is …
- I like the melody/rhythm/lyrics.
- I can understand some of the words: The song is about …
- …

My favourite song is "Diamonds". The singer is Rihanna. The style is electronic and pop. I like the melody and the rhythm – it is slow, but has a cool beat. I can understand some of the words: The song is about love. The girl and her boyfriend are happy together. They are like diamonds in the sky.

You can add pictures to your text.
Put it up in the classroom for everyone to read.

15 Choose an activity

p. 63/10

➡ p. LF44

portfolio

You can …

- look at this picture. What do you think is happening? Work with a partner and write some sentences for a dialogue. Then act it out in class.

KV13

- present members of your family to the class.
- bring a song with the lyrics to class. Play the song and say what it is about.

wordbank People p. 159

WB test yourself p. 66/67

W p. 225 TM, p. 203

P1 Missing letters

a) What are these words from number 1?

1. s■■p (ship)	3. i■■■■■d (island)	5. m■■■■■■e (medicine)	7. c■■■■■■■s (cannibals)
2. p■■■■■■r (prisoner)	4. s■■■m (storm)	6. r■■t (raft)	8. w■■■k (wreck)

➡ p. LF44

b) Take other words from number 1. Turn them into words with missing letters and test your partner.

➡ p. LF44

P2 Working with words

LSW 411

How to … work with a dictionary p. 167/168

a) What are the opposites of these adjectives? You can use a dictionary for help.

difficult – … · happy – … · fast – … · early – …
boring – … · unfriendly – … · expensive – … · good – …
fair – … · right – … · small – … · terrible – …

b) Use ten adjectives with nouns.
difficult tests, …

P3 Sound check

L 1.29

a) Listen to the words and repeat them.
b) Which words are spoken like *family* (Ooo)?
Which words are spoken like *computer* (oOo)?
Make two lists.

adventure • important • cannibal • September • prisoner • beautiful • excited • Robinson

Ooo	oOo
family	computer
…	…
cannibal	adventure
prisoner	important
beautiful	September
Robinson	excited

c) Listen again and check your lists.

P4 Verb search

LSW 412

Simple past 5R p. 185

➡ p. LF44

a) Look at number 1 again and find the *simple past* forms of these verbs:

swim • build • leave • collect • hit • begin • live • be • come • find • have • show • give • rescue • teach • sail

b) Check your results with a partner. Then quiz your partner. Take turns.

P5 The story in short

LSW 413

a) Write down the sentences in the correct order.

1. Robinson – on – a new life – began – an island – .
2. lived – for – He – years – many – alone – .
3. cannibals – to – island – One day – came – the – .
4. prisoner – Robinson – their – rescued – .
5. Man Friday – taught – to speak – Robinson – English – .
6. how – taught – Robinson – to fish – Man Friday – .
7. rescued – sailed by – ship – and – A – them – .

b) Listen and check your sentences.

Satzstellung 19R p. 197/198
➡ p. LF45
L 1.30

P6 A message in a bottle

You and your friend find this message in a bottle.
Your friend doesn't speak much English. Answer his/her questions.

Von wem ist die Flaschenpost?

Warum hat der Junge sie geschrieben?

Was sollen wir als Finder jetzt tun?

Wozu braucht der Junge unsere Adresse?

55 Camden High Street
London NW1 7JH

Dear Finder,

My name is Rajiv Patel and I am in year 9 at Haverstock School in London, UK.
This letter is part of our science project to study oceans and learn about people in far away countries.
Please send the date and location of the bottle with your address. I will send you my picture and tell you when and where the bottle was placed in the ocean.

Best wishes,
Rajiv Patel

➡ p. LF45
How to ... help out p. 179

P7 What did they say?

Listen to Gillian, Charlie and Rajiv again. Where do they want to go? Who do they want to take with them? Tell a partner in German.

➡ p. LF45
How to ... help out p. 179
L 1.26

W p. 226 · TM, p. 205

P8 Words, words, words

a) Look at these words. Write them with your finger on the desk or on your partner's back. Can he/she guess the words?

angry • feeling • worry • love • prefer • mobile • decide • horrible • both • message

b) Now spell the words for your partner. Can he/she write them down correctly? Use other words from this Theme, too.

➡ p. LF45

P9 Finding words

a) Look through Theme 4. Find words with these letters:

-oo-	-ea-	-ie-	-ou-
good	really	friend	your
…			

b) Compare your words with a partner. Who found more words?

P10 Sound check

L 1.31

a) Listen to the words and repeat them.
b) Make two lists. Write the words in the correct list.

look • food • good • moon • book • tooth • school • cook • room • too • soon • foot

/ʊ/	/uː/
look	food
… good	… moon
book	tooth
cook	school
foot	room
	too
	soon

P11 I guess …

Will-future 22R p. 200

➡ p. LF45

Look at the letters on page 85 again. What do you think the people will or won't do? Write it down.

I think I guess I'm sure Maybe	Patty Jason Tommy Susan	will won't	tell her parents, teachers and friends. get a cat. receive more horrible messages. speak to her friend again. talk to his parents about the things that worry him. visit a dogs' home. …

P12 The Lambrakis

LSW 414

Konjunktionen 20 p. 198

Read about the Lambrakis. Pick the right word to connect the sentence parts.

1. Mr Lambraki is at home all day because/but he is out of work. because
2. He wants to find a new job because/but that is very difficult. but
3. Mrs Lambraki is often tired and/when she comes home from the hospital. when
4. She works very hard when/but she enjoys looking after the patients. but
5. George doesn't like helping in the house but/and he never cleans his room. and
6. His school report won't be very good because/but he doesn't work hard enough. because
7. Caroline talks to Gillian a lot and/when they are in Caroline's room. when

P13 On Sunday

LSW 415

Bedingungssätze, Typ I 23 p. 201

➡ p. LF45

Look at the pictures. What will the Lambrakis do on Sunday?

1. If Mrs Lambraki doesn't have to work at the hospital, she will read a book.
2. If Mr Lambraki doesn't check the newspaper, he will …
3. If it is sunny, George …
4. If it is rainy, Caroline …
5. If no one plays with Patch, he …
6. If Caroline opens the cage, Daisy …

P14 A letter

LSW 416

➡ p. LF46

How to … help out p. 179

Your English exchange student finds this letter in a German magazine. He/She doesn't speak much German. Tell him/her what Jan's problem is.

Liebe Leah,
ich hasse meine Schwester! Sie hilft nie zu Hause mit! Ich bringe montags und dienstags den Müll raus und räume den Geschirrspüler aus. Meine Schwester ist mittwochs und donnerstags dran, aber sie tut nichts. Sie trifft sich mit ihren Freunden oder spielt die ganze Zeit mit ihrem Handy. Was soll ich nur tun?
Jan, 13

W p. 226 TM, p. 207

➡ p. LF46

M1 Interviewing Robinson Crusoe

L 1.32

a) After Robinson's adventure people had lots of questions. Listen and read along.

b) What do you think: What were Robinson's answers?

A lot of things – the houses, the people, …

With a small stick.

Well, I pointed to things and told him the word.

…

7R: Entscheidungsfragen und Kurzantworten im *simple past*
10R: Fragen mit Fragewörtern
7R + 10R p. 186+189

c) Work with a partner. What would YOU ask Robinson? Write questions. Then practise the interview with a partner. You can present it to the class.

KV13

Did you … ? • When did you … ? •
What did you … ? • How did you … ? • …

➡ p. LF46

M2 The story of Robinson

KV7

2 B p. 82

How to … give a talk p. 171

Take notes on what the story of Robinson Crusoe is about.
Use them to give a two-minute talk. These questions can help you:

- Who wrote the story?
- What kind of story is it?
- Who is in the story?
- What happens?
- How does Robinson feel in different situations?
- What can you say about the other people in the story?
- What do you like about the story?
- What don't you like?

M3 Cast Away

IWS

p. LF47
WB M1 – M3 p. 70/71

a) Read about the film "Cast Away". Would you like to watch it? Say why.

Cast Away is an American film from the year 2000.

It is the year 1995 and Chuck Noland (actor Tom Hanks) is on a business trip to Malaysia. While flying through a terrible storm, his plane crashes into the Pacific Ocean.

Chuck is able to escape the sinking plane but then loses consciousness and is washed up on a lonely island. Packages from the plane also wash up on the island. Chuck opens them and finds a volleyball, a dress, ice skates and other things he doesn't need at first. A short time later he draws a face on the volleyball, calls it Wilson and starts talking to it.

Four years later a large piece of plastic washes up on the island. Chuck builds a raft and uses the piece of plastic as a sail. With the raft he overcomes the powerful waves near the beach and reaches the ocean.

After some time on the ocean a storm nearly destroys his raft. The next day Wilson falls from the raft and is lost. Chuck loses his only friend.

A few weeks later a ship finds the half dead Chuck, rescues him and takes him home.

b) Read the text again and compare Chuck Noland's story with Robinson Crusoe's story. What is similar? What is different?

similar	different
…	…

M4 Oh, yeah!

LSW 418

p. LF47
L 1.26
B 4 p. 83

a) Listen to Gillian, Charlie and Rajiv. What are they talking about?
b) Listen again. Who wants to live where and why? Take notes.
c) Compare your notes with a partner.

M5 A diary entry

IWS

p. LF47
How to … write p. 174
WB M4 p. 71

Imagine you are stranded on an island.
Write a diary entry. Think about:

- What do/don't you like about the island?
- Where do you live?
- What do you miss?
- What do you do every day?
- How do you feel?
- …

LSW 419

You can start like this:

I don't know what day it is today. Monday or maybe Tuesday?
I'm on this strange little island and I think I'm here all alone. …

W p. 226 TM, p. 215

M6 A problem letter

LSW 420 KV57–59

➡ p. LF47
How to … write a letter p. 175
M5 WB p. 72

a) Write a letter about a problem (pocket money/a party/clothes/…).
Don't write your real name at the end.
You can use these phrases and look at page 85 for help.
Then put your letter in a box in the classroom.

Dear … | I am writing to you because … | I need your help because … | The problem is … | I have a problem with … | I (don't) want … | I am … | What can I do? | Please help me. | Yours, …

b) Take a letter out of the box and write a helpful answer to it.
c) You can read the letters and answers out loud in class.

M7 A message from Gillian

M6 WB p. 72

a) Read Gillian's message. Say the letters and numbers out loud to get their meaning.

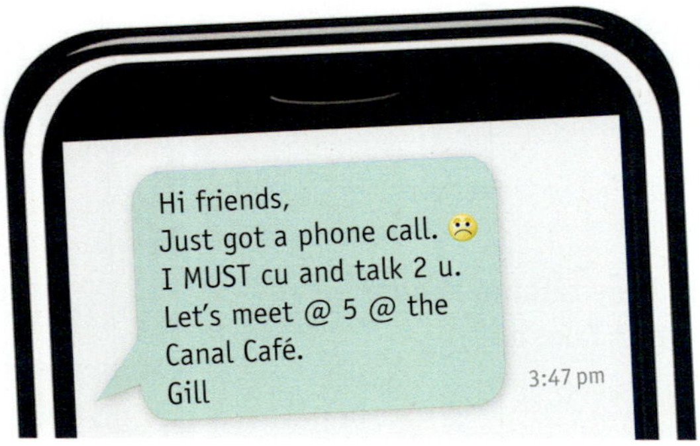

Hi friends,
Just got a phone call. (not good)
I must see you and talk to you.
Let's meet at five at the Canal Café.
Gillian

➡ p. LF48

b) Work with a partner. What do you think: What important news does Gillian want to talk about?

M8 A phone call

LSW 421, 422

➡ p. LF48
L 1.33
How to … listen p. 169

a) Listen to the phone call. Why is Rajiv calling Gillian?
b) Listen again and find out:
- What does Rajiv want to know?
- Who does Gillian want to talk about later?
- Who else is coming to the Canal Café?

Take notes.
c) Compare your notes with a partner.

M9 At the café

LSW 417, 423

➡ p. LF48
WB M7 + M8 p. 73
L 1.34

a) Read the dialogue. What is Gillian's problem?

Gillian: Thank you so much for coming.
Charlie: No problem. So, what's the matter, Gill?
Gillian: My dad phoned me this morning. He told me that he is going to marry again – his girlfriend Ronda.
Rajiv: But isn't that good news?
Gillian: No, it's not. I don't like Ronda.
Caroline: Why don't you like her?
Gillian: Well, when I visit my dad and Ronda is there, she always wants to talk to me and invite me to the cinema …
Charlie: But what's wrong about that?
Gillian: Well, I wish she would leave me alone sometimes. She tries to be nice … but she's not my mother.
Caroline: I think I know what you mean. It's hard for both of you.
Gillian: I guess you're right. But there's something else: Ronda is pregnant.
Rajiv: But isn't that great? I know you love babies, Gill.
Gillian: No, it's not great. New woman, new baby – where do I fit into that life? I always wanted to see my Dad more often and spend more time with him but it wasn't possible. And now I'm worried that Dad doesn't want to see me anymore. You're all lucky, you live with your mum and dad.
Caroline: Poor you. I feel really sorry for you.
Charlie: Cheer up, Gill. Everything is going to be OK. Why don't you talk to your dad and tell him how you feel?
Gillian: But I don't know how.
Caroline: Perhaps you could go out for dinner with him – just you and your dad.
Rajiv: That's a good idea. Then you can …

b) The next evening Gillian talks to her dad about her worries. Write their dialogue. Then present it in class.

How to … write p. 174

M10 What if … ?

LSW 424

Bedingungssätze, Typ I 23 p. 201
➡ p. LF43

Write down what will happen if …

1. Gillian – talk to her father → he – understand her better
2. Gillian – go to the wedding → Ronda and her dad – be very happy
3. Gillian – get a baby brother → she – play with him a lot
4. her dad, Ronda and the baby – go on holiday → Gillian – go with them
5. her dad and Ronda – go out in the evening → Gillian – look after the baby
6. Gillian – have a problem → her dad – listen and try to help her

1. If Gillian talks to her father, he will understand her better.
2. If …

CAMDEN CHRONICLE
LEARN ENGLISH THE CAMDEN WAY

DID YOU GET IT ALL? ➡ p. LF48

» Who wrote "Robinson Crusoe"?
» What did Man Friday teach Robinson?
» When did Robinson return to England?
» What is Patty's problem?
» What is Sarah's advice for Jason?

» Why is Mr Lambraki looking for a new job?
» Where does Mrs Lambraki work?
» How does Caroline deal with her problems?

GOOD TO KNOW ...

In Großbritannien spielt Popmusik eine große Rolle:

» Vier der sieben weltweit erfolgreichsten Musikacts aller Zeiten stammen aus Großbritannien.
» Stars wie Amy Winehouse, Adele und Leona Lewis wurden alle in Großbritannien ausgebildet.
» Selbst bei der Feier zum diamantenen Thronjubiläum der Queen traten Popstars wie Robbie Williams, Ed Sheeran und Jessie J auf.
» Die Insel bringt immer wieder neue Musikstile wie Drum and Bass, UK Garage oder Dubstep hervor.

I promise!

I didn't want to hurt you.
What I said was just not true.
I just can't stand seeing you
When you look so sad and blue.
Just, please, this once, forgive me!
I'll be better, I promise, you'll see.
From now on I will be
Almost as good a friend,
As you always are to me.

A JOKE

Two frogs sat on Robinson Crusoe's back. One said to the other: "I have to go now. But let's meet again on Friday!"

THEME 5

TM, p. 221 KV60: Lernlandkarte

EVERYDAY SCIENCE

In diesem *Theme* ...

» lernst du zu sagen, was man alles am Computer und ähnlichen Geräten machen kann.
» sprichst du darüber, wie häufig und wofür du den Computer und ähnliche Geräte benutzt.
» erfährst du, was im Londoner Science Museum zu sehen ist.
» lernst du, einen Museumsplan und eine Bastelanleitung zu verstehen.
» sprichst du über Erfindungen und Erfinder.

W p. 227 TM, p. 221

1 Computer words

LSW 501 p. 66/1

➡ p. LF49

How to … work with words p. 166

WB 1 p. 74

a) How many computer words do you know?
Write them down. You've got three minutes.

b) Now work with a partner and compare your lists.
Who has got more words?

computer words
- email
- …

2 Computers & Co.

IWS KV61 p. 66–68/2–5

wordbank Technology p. 160

a) What can you do with **electronic devices** like computers/ mobile phones/… ? chat with friends, take photos, play games, watch films

order tickets

download music

search for information

…

WB 2 p. 74

➡ p. LF49

b) What electronic devices have YOU got? What do YOU do with them?
Fill in a grid like this.

	computer	mobile phone	…
order tickets	✓	✗	…
download music	…		
…			

Fragen mit Fragewörtern 10R p. 189

c) Now work with a partner. Talk about your electronic devices.

LSW 502, 503

Have you got a computer/ mobile phone/… ?

Yes, I've got a computer/…

No, I haven't got a computer/…

How often do you use the computer/… ?

I use it very often / every day/…

I don't use it very often.

What do you use the … for?

I use it when I have to/want to …

I play …/write …/ download …/…

M1 M p. 114

3 Mobile phone fun

Do you think you spend too much time on your mobile phone? Do the test and find out.

WB 3 p. 75

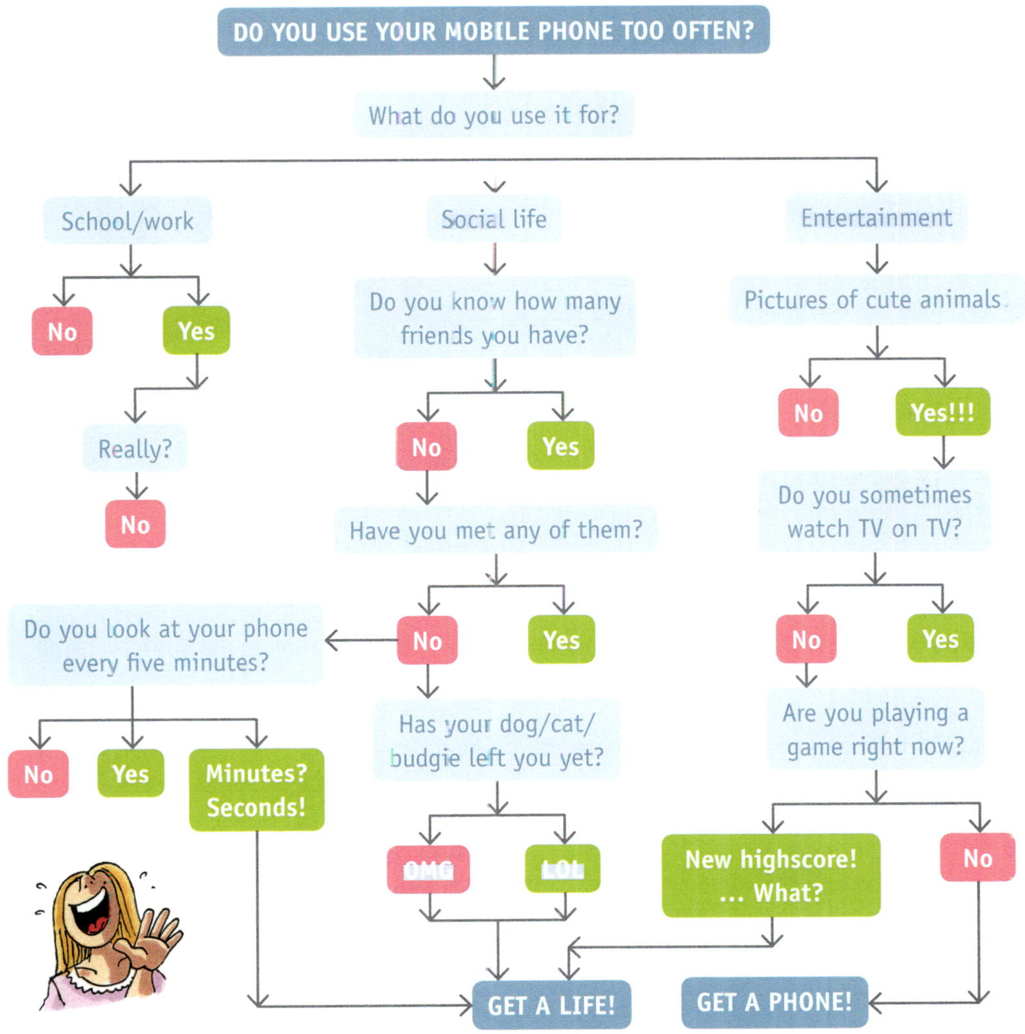

4 Text messages

a) Read the two text messages. Say the letters and the numbers out loud to get their meaning.

b) Now write a text message in English that you could send to a friend.

LSW 504 p. 69/6

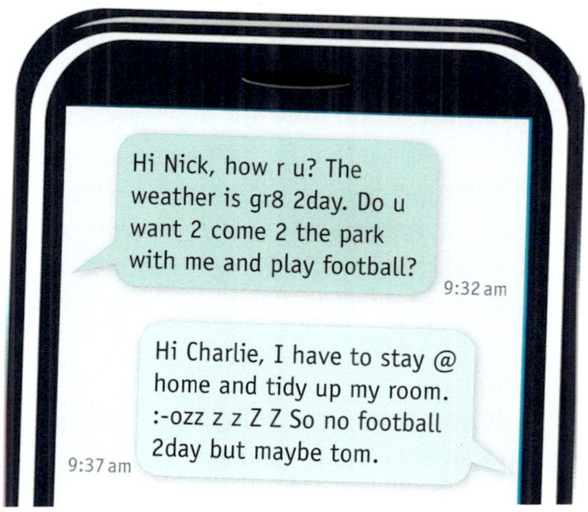

p. LF49
P1 + P3 + P6 p. 110/111
WB 4+5 p. 75/76
KV62

W p. 227

5 Home alone

LSW 505 p. 70f./7–9

How to ... work with others p. 176
L 1.35
6 p. 76

a) Buzz groups: Do you play computer or video games? What do you like about them?

b) Listen to the story and find out: Who phoned Nick? Nick's mum
Who rang the doorbell? Nick's grandmother

It was Saturday morning and Nick was alone at home. He was bored. He knew he should tidy up his room but he turned the computer on instead.

Nick started playing his favourite game, Boom Trader. In the game a girl was hiding behind a secret door. *She has to wait until the wild animals have gone*, Nick thought. *Then she'll find the key.*

Suddenly the phone rang. "Hello, Nick, it's Mum. Are you OK? Have you already had breakfast?"
"No, not yet."
"Then you haven't seen my note yet?"
"No, where is it?"
"Nick! Are you playing on the computer again?"
"Computer? What computer? I'm tidying up my room."
"Really? Well, don't forget to read my note. It's on the kitchen table. Bye."
"Bye, Mum," said Nick. He was really glad that his mother couldn't see his red face.

Nick went back to the computer. *Let me just open this door ... now where's the key? Oh no, there are some crocodiles around the next corner ... Phew! They didn't get me. Now I just have to ...*

Nick was playing really well and forgot all about his mother and the note. Then the doorbell rang. It was Nick's grandmother. She looked at him and said, "Don't tell me you've just got up."
"Well, no. I just haven't got dressed yet."
"But didn't your mum tell you?"
"Tell me what?"
"That I'm taking you out for lunch. Hurry up and get dressed. I'm already a bit hungry."

Then Nick remembered the note. He felt really bad. He got dressed quickly and then ran down the stairs. His grandmother was waiting in the hall.
"I've put all the breakfast things in the fridge – and I've turned off the computer. Are you ready to go?"

Nick couldn't believe his ears.
"You turned off the computer? You saved the game first, didn't you?"
"Saved what, dear?"

c) Now read the story. How did Nick feel ...

1. before he turned on the computer? bored
2. while he was playing the game? excited
3. when his grandmother arrived? surprised
4. when he remembered the note? bad
5. after his grandmother turned off the computer? worried

He was/felt ...

surprised · worried · excited · bored · bad

➡ p. LF49

P2 + P4 + P5 P p. 110/111
M2 M p. 115

d) What do you think: What did Nick's mother say in the note? Write it down.

6 Lunch with grandma

L 1.36 S 11

a) Listen to Nick and his grandmother. What are they talking about?

favourite free time activities • life now and then • dangers of the Internet

b) What was different when Nick's grandmother was young?

She didn't …

✓ use the Internet | have pets | ✓ go to restaurants | ✓ have a computer
get pocket money | ✓ go out in the evenings | listen to music | meet friends ✓on Sundays

p. LF50

c) What can young people do today? What things do they have?
Listen again and fill in the grid.

what they can do	things they have
go to restaurants	TV in their rooms
…	…

WB 7 p. 75/77
P7 p. 111
M3 p. 115
WB 8 p. 77

7 Choose an activity

portfolio

You can …

- look at number 5 again. What do you think Nick said to his grandmother after she turned off the computer? Work with a partner and write a short dialogue. Then act it out in class.
- ask your grandparents about life when they were young. What things did/didn't they have? What could/couldn't they do? Take notes and tell your class.
- make a crossword puzzle or a wordsearch with computer words for your classmates.
- write about your favourite computer or video game. Think about:
  - its name
  - what kind of game
  - what it is about
  - what the player can/has to do
  - why you like it
  - …
- imagine you can't use your computer, mobile phone, … for one week. What would you do instead? Make notes and tell your class.

WORDSEARCH: Computer words

D	D	L	Q	F	M	O	U	S	E
K	D	E	G	M	A	S	T	D	I
E	L	P	S	T	Q	N	M	S	N
Y	Q	S	G	K	D	A	E	D	T
B	Q	E	A	F	T	Z	A	B	E
O	X	S	M	X	U	O	I	Z	R
A	V	A	E	A	L	C	P	O	N
R	C	V	S	N	I	P	E	T	E
D	R	E	W	Q	F	L	T	E	T
Z	N	O	D	V	Z	R	R	F	F
W	D	Q	V	O	C	H	A	T	M
C	O	M	P	U	T	E	R	Z	M

wordbank Technology p. 163

W p. 227 TM, p. 235

➡ p. LF50

8 At the Science Museum

IWS p. 72/10

a) Look at the map of the Science Museum in London on the next page. Find out:

1. How many floors does the Science Museum have? seven
2. Where can you see ships? second floor
3. Where can you have something to eat? basement, ground floor, 3rd floor
4. Can a person in a wheelchair go to the museum, too? yes
5. How many toilets are there? twelve
6. Where can you buy souvenirs? museum shop on ground floor

Bedingungssätze, Typ I 23 p. 201

b) What can you do at the Science Museum?

If you	want to learn about the future, are hungry, are interested in computers, can't walk, ...	you	can should	have a meal in the café or restaurant. go to the 2nd floor. take the lift. go to the 3rd floor. ...

M4 p. 116 M

9 p. 78/79 WB

c) What do you find interesting? Where would you go first? Say why.

I'd go to the ... first because I'm interested in ...

LSW 506

➡ p. LF50

9 Around the museum

IWS p. 72/10

DVD

L 1.37

10 + 11 p. 79/80 WB

a) Watch the clip. What can you understand? Describe what you have seen.

b) Listen to the four dialogues at the Science Museum. Where are the people? Put the photos in the right order. D - B - A - C

A Agriculture: Tractor

B Exploring space: Apollo 10

C Energy: Computer terminals

D Flight: Propeller plane

c) Now look at the map on the next page. On which floor can you find the objects from b)? A → 1st floor B → ground floor C → 2nd floor D → 3rd floor

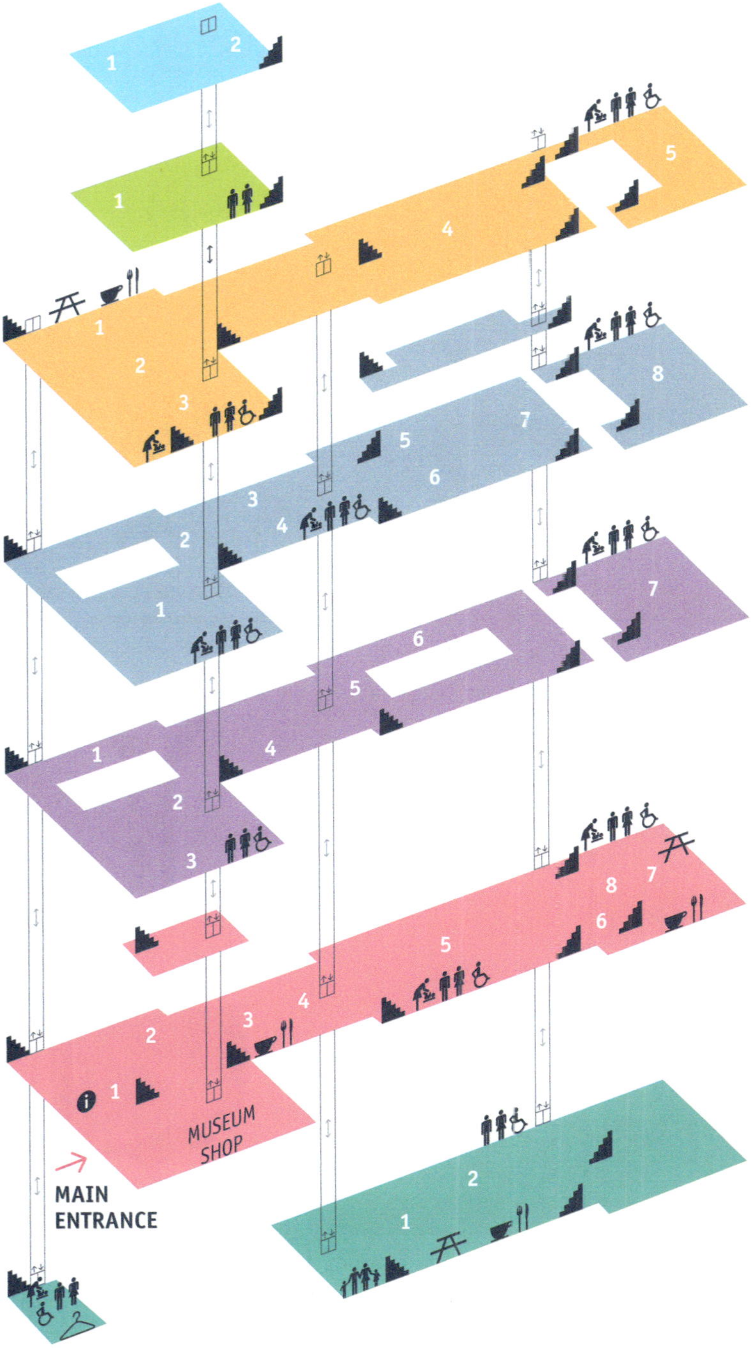

5th floor

The Science and Art of Medicine	1
Veterinary History	2

4th floor

Glimpses of Medical History	1

3rd floor

Science in the 18th Century	1
Launchpad	2
Health Matters	3
Flight	4
In Future	5

2nd floor

Public History	1
Energy	2
Computing	3
Mathematics	4
Marine Engineering	5
Ships	6
Docks and Diving	7
Atmosphere	8

1st floor

Challenge of Materials	1
Contemporary Arts	2
Telecommunications	3
Agriculture	4
Cosmos & Culture	5
Measuring Time	6
Who am I?	7

Ground floor

Energy Hall	1
James Watt and Our World	2
Foucault's Pendulum	3
Exploring Space	4
Making the Modern World	5
Pattern Pod	6
Antenna – science news	7
Cinema	8

Basement

The Garden	1
The Secret Life of the Home	2

Map Key

- Information desk
- Café/restaurant
- Picnic area
- Baby changing
- Family room
- Cloakroom
- Toilets
- Accessible toilets
- Lifts
- Stairs

W p. 228

➡ p. LF50

Satzstellung 19R p. 197/198

M5 M p. 116

// S befragen sich gegenseitig (Partnerarbeit) zu den hier abgebildeten Erfindungen.

10 Inventions

Folie 11 LSW 507 p. 73/11

a) At the Science Museum you can find out about inventions. Here are some of them. How often do YOU use these inventions?

I use the bike every day.

I never use a stamp.

My family and I sometimes use the microwave.

stamp

telephone

light bulb

chocolate chip cookies

computer

bike

matches

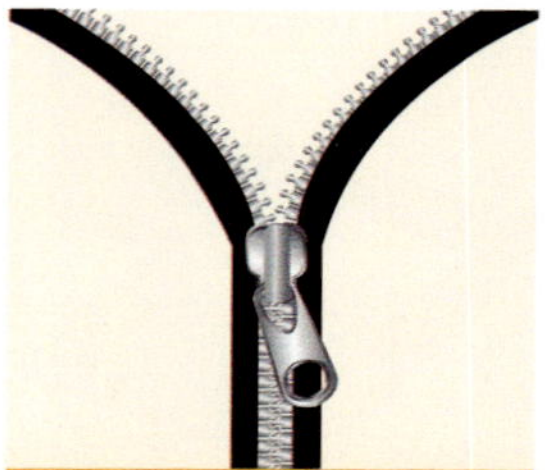
zip

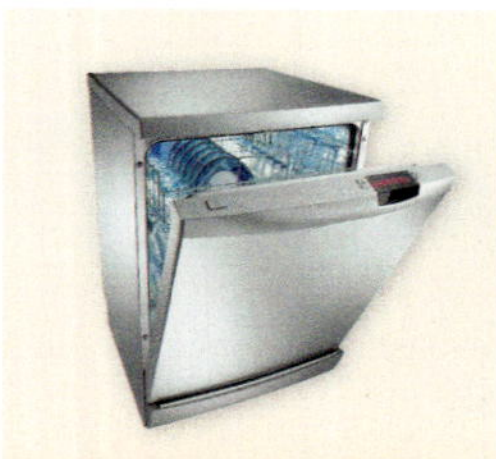
dishwasher

microwave

car

television

Comparison of adjectives 16R p. 194/195

b) What do you think about the inventions in a)?

LSW 508

The computer Matches …	is are	the most important invention for me. very important for me. more important than … good to have. not important for me.

M6 M p. 116

c) Make YOUR top five inventions list.

KV12

11 Successful inventors

IWS KV63 p. 75/13

Passiv 24 p. 202

➡ p. LF51

a) Read the information about eight of the inventions on page 106. Find out:
- Who invented what?
- When were the things invented?

The **light bulb** was invented by **Thomas Edison**. It was invented in **1879**.

Thomas Edison

USA (1879)

His invention is used to light rooms and streets. light bulb

Josephine Cochrane

USA (1885)

dishwasher

Her invention is used to wash plates, cups, glasses, …

John Walker

England (1826)

matches

His invention is used to make fire.

Karl Benz

Germany (1876)

His invention is used to travel long distances on roads. car

Ruth Wakefield

USA (1930)

Her invention is used to make your sweet tooth happy. chocolate chip cookies

Philo Farnsworth

USA (1928)

His invention is used to watch programmes. television

Alexander Graham Bell

Scotland/ USA (1876)

His invention is used to talk to people far away. telephone

John Mauchly John Eckert

USA (1945)

Their invention is used to write, search for information and play games. computer

WB 12 p. 80

Passiv 24 p. 202

b) Products are made in many different countries. Where were the things made that YOU use every day? Find out about five things or more.

My computer was made in …

My shoes were made in …

My …

LSW 509

P P8 – F13 p. 112/113

M M6 p. 116/117

W p. 228

➡ p. LF51

How to ...
work with others
p. 176

wordbank
Technology
p. 160

12 Life without electricity

LSW 510 p. 74/12

a) Think – pair – share: Which of the things in your home need electricity? Write them down in a list. Look up new words in a dictionary.

toaster

kettle

smartphone

...

b) Make a list in class and talk about it:

I need electricity for the radio.

We need electricity for cooking.

c) Why do you need electricity?

Without electricity	I we you	can't have to	watch ... listen to ... make ... eat ... cook ... ...

LAND & LEUTE

Achtung, technische Unterschiede!

Die Häuser in Großbritannien unterscheiden sich in vielerlei Hinsicht von denen in Deutschland. Hier ein paar Beispiele:

In vielen älteren Häusern öffnen die Türen nach außen. Oftmals findest du dort auch die so genannten *sash windows* – Fenster, die man nach oben schiebt, um sie zu öffnen.

In älteren Badezimmern wirst du dort vergeblich nach einem Lichtschalter suchen. Oft hängt eine Strippe von der Decke, an der man ziehen muss, damit das Licht angeht. Es kann übrigens auch vorkommen, dass du statt eines Wasserhahns am Waschbecken oder an der Badewanne jeweils zwei vorfindest. Aus dem einen fließt kaltes, aus dem anderen heißes Wasser. Man kann aber Schläuche in Form eines Y kaufen. Wenn du einen solchen Schlauch über die beiden Wasserhähne steckst, kannst du so heißes und kaltes Wasser mischen.

Für elektrische Geräte muss man einen Adapter mitnehmen. Den braucht man, weil die Steckdosen in Großbritannien ganz anders aussehen. Sie haben drei Öffnungen und heißen deshalb auch *3-pin sockets*.

Welche technischen Unterschiede fallen dir aus anderen Ländern ein?

13 Paper plane

p. 75/14

On the 3rd floor of the Science Museum you can learn a lot about all kinds of flying machines. Here is one for you to make.

1 Fold a piece of A4 paper in half.

2 Now open the paper again and fold the corners like this.

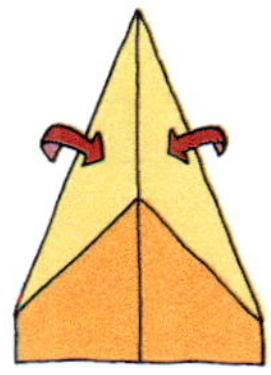

3 Fold again to the centre line.

4 Turn the plane over. Fold it along the centre line so that the sides are together.

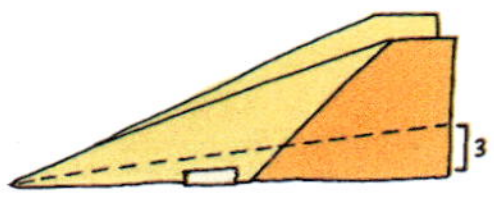

5 Make a mark 3 cm from the bottom line. Draw a line to the tip. Stick the bottom parts together.

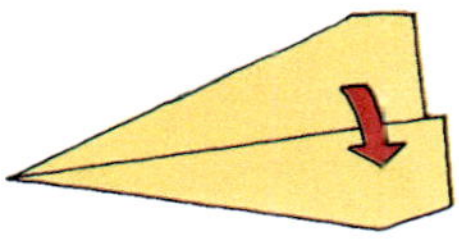

6 Fold the first wing down along the line.

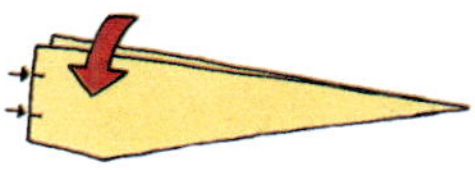

7 Do the same with the other wing. Make small cuts in both wings.

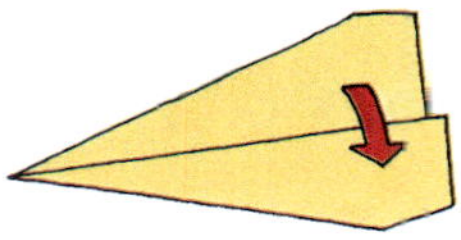

8 Open the plane. Bend the flaps up or down. Now you are ready to fly!

Work with a partner. One of you looks at the pictures and the instructions and tells the other what he/she has to do.

First you have to fold … Then you have to … Now you …

➡ p. LF51

14 Choose an activity

➡ p. LF52

portfolio

You can …

- **work with a partner or in small groups. Plan a tour through the Science Museum in London. Use the museum map and go to the museum's home page.**
  What do you want to visit? Why?
  First … Then … After that … … because …
  Present your tour to the class.
- **get a brochure from a museum in your area or find information on the Internet. What can you see and do there? Tell your class about the museum.**
- **describe some inventions and write quiz cards for your class. Look at numbers 10, 11 and P7 for help.**
- **make a list of inventions that you think no one really needs *or* that don't exist but should exist. Give reasons.**

This invention is used to close or open something, for example a jacket. What is it?

M M7 p. 117

WB test yourself p. 81/82

W p. 229 TM, p. 251

P1 Odd one out

LSW 511

a) Find the odd one out.

1. newspaper • (film) • book • magazine
2. listen to • play • download • (drink)
3. TV • (radio) • computer game • video
4. chat • (cook) • search • order
5. Internet • software • (bandage) • virus
6. (music) • email • text message • postcard

➡ p. LF52

b) Why is it the odd one out?

1. "Film" is the odd one out because you can't read it.
2. "Drink" is the odd one out because you can't do it with music.

...

c) Write a new 'odd one out' for your partner.

➡ p. LF52

P2 All kinds of words

How to ... work with words p. 166

**a) Put these words in alphabetical order.
Who can do it faster: you or your partner?**

alone • forget • save • glad • think • fridge • hungry • hide • bored • lunch • kitchen • bad • grandmother • game • remember

b) Now put the words in the correct list.

verbs	adjectives	nouns
forget	alone	fridge
hide	bad	game
remember	bored	grandmother
save	glad	kitchen
think	hungry	lunch

P3 Text messaging short forms

LSW 513

a) What do these short forms mean?

1. gr8 great
2. 2day today
3. tom tomorrow
4. np no problem
5. sry sorry
6. idk I don't know

sorry • today • no problem • great • I don't know • tomorrow

b) What other text messaging short forms do you know? Write them down. txt - text brb - be right back 4get - forget

P4 Sound check

LSW 512

L 1.38

a) Listen to these words and make lists.

websites • lunches • computers • dishes • words • games • notes • lists • fridges • jokes • emails • sentences

/s/	/z/	/ɪz/
websites	computers	lunches
notes	words	dishes
lists	games	fridges
jokes	emails	sentences

b) Listen again and say the words.

P5 How does the story go?

Konjunktionen 2C p. 198

Read number 5 again. Use *when*, *because*, *so* or *but* to connect the sentence parts.

1. Nick was bored XX he was alone at home. because
2. He knew he should tidy up his room XX he turned on the computer instead. but
3. He was playing Boom Trader XX the phone rang. when
4. He was surprised XX he saw his grandmother. when
5. His grandmother told him to hurry up XX he ran to his room to get dressed quickly. so
6. His grandmother turned off the computer XX she didn't save the game. but

P6 Texting rules

LSW 514

➡ p. LF52

How to ... help out p. 179

You find these texting rules on the Internet. Your friend looks at them and doesn't understand everything. Tell him/her the rules in German.

News (230) ▾ Favourites ▾

- Always be polite when you're texting.
- Don't send a text message when you're angry.
- If you receive horrible text messages, show them to your parents or your teachers.
- Help other kids who receive bullying text messages.
- Don't text during meals, during lessons or when you're talking to someone.
- Don't send text messages when you're riding your bike or walking down the street.
- Turn off your mobile phone at night.

Man muss/soll ...

Man darf nicht/ soll nicht ...

...

➡ p. LF52

P7 What did she say?

How to ... help out p. 179

L 1.36 S 11

Listen to Nick's grandmother again. What does she tell Nick about libraries then and now? Tell a partner in German.

W p. 229 TM, p. 253

P8 An invention quiz

LSW 515

What are the inventions?

1 stamp

It is a small piece of paper. You pay money for it. You stick it on an envelope or a postcard.

2 microwave

It looks like a box with a door. It needs electricity. You can find it in the kitchen. It cooks food very quickly.

3 match

It is a small stick. It is made of wood. It has got a head which is usually red. It is used to start a fire.

P9 Sound check

a) What can you read here? Write it down.

1. /ðə ˈsaɪəns mjuːˌziːəm‿ɪz‿ɪn ˈlʌndən/
2. /ˌðeə jə kən ˌfaɪnd‿ˈaʊt‿əˌbaʊt‿ɪnˈvenʃnz/
3. /ˌmɪstə ˈbel‿ɪnˌventɪd ðə ˈtelɪˌfəʊn/

L 1.39

b) Listen and check. 1. The Science Museum is in London.
2. There you can find out about inventions.
3. Mister Bell invented the telephone.

P10 How verbs become nouns

a) Look at these words. Half of them are verbs, the others are nouns.

invent • teach • decorate • player • celebrate • dreamer • teacher • invitation • train • reporter • worker • imagination • singer • driver • decoration • presentation • imagine • rider • present • report • invention • drive • celebration • dream • work • invite • sing • ride • trainer • play

➡ p. LF53

Make pairs and write them down like this:

verbs	nouns
invent	invention
teach	teacher
decorate	…
…	player
…	…

b) Now look at the nouns again. Which of them are things, which are people? Mark the things in red and the people in green. What do you notice?

P11 Invented by?

LSW 516

Passiv 24 p. 202

➡ p. LF53

Look at the pictures and the information. Then write about the inventions.

The … was invented by … It was invented in …

stamp

microwave

bike

zip

stamp	microwave	bike	zip
James Chalmer	Percy Spencer	Karl Drais	Whitcomb Judson
Scotland (1838)	*USA (1946)*	*Germany (1817)*	*USA (1893)*

P12 Some more facts

Passiv 24 p. 202

Complete the sentences with a word from the box.

called • spoken • written • opened • eaten • made

1. The first teddy bear was XX in 1902. made
2. The London Eye was XX to visitors in 2000. opened
3. One of the first computers was XX "Baby". cclled
4. "Harry Potter" was XX by J.K. Rowling. writ-en
5. English is XX all over the world. spoken
6. Cornflakes are usually XX with milk. eaten

P13 Josephine Cochrane

➡ p. LF53

How to … help out p. 179

Look at the information about Josephine Cochrane.
Why did she invent the dishwasher? Tell a classmate in German.

Josephine Cochrane (1839-1913) was a rich woman who often invited friends to her house for dinner. Afterwards she did not usually wash the dishes herself – she had servants to do that for her. But it always took a long time and the plates, glasses and cups sometimes broke. So she wanted a machine that could do the job faster and without breaking the dishes. She said: "If nobody else is going to invent a dishwashing machine, I'll do it myself!" And she did.

W p. 229 TM, p. 255

M1 The history of ...

LSW 517

How to ... read p. 170

a) Look at this page from a science book. What is it about?

The history of paper • The history of communication • The history of the computer

There are over 3,000 languages spoken in the world. People can use a telephone or send an email to 'talk' to other people. But how did everything start?

In the Stone Age people lived in caves in large groups. They made sounds and signs with their hands. The sounds became words. In different parts of the world people made different sounds. That is why we have different languages.

About 5,000 years ago the Egyptians invented papyrus – the first kind of paper. They also invented hieroglyphics. These were special signs used in the first letters.

There were also other ways to send messages. People used smoke signals, flags or mirrors.

The first real paper came to Europe 600 years ago. People started to write letters that riders brought to the right address – the first kind of post. It was good but not very fast. It took two weeks for a letter to get from England to Italy.

In 1876 Alexander Graham Bell invented the telephone. Now people could talk to each other – even in different countries.

In the 20th century there were thousands of inventions in the world of communication: radio, cinema, record players, televisions, ... And then the computer. The first computers were as big as a room. Now computers are everywhere: in schools, homes, hospitals, etc. We can use the Internet to get information from all over the world and send emails in seconds. What will come next?

b) Read the page and look at these keywords. Choose the right one for each of the six paragraphs.

6 computers • 2 first paper • 1 different sounds • 4 first post • 5 the telephone • 3 smoke signals

WB M1-M3 p. 85/86

➡ p. LF53

c) Look at the page again and make a timeline of dates and events. Show the timeline to your class and talk about the different events.

M2 The talking computer

LSW 518 KV9, KV10 KV64 ➡ p. LF54

How to … write p. 174

a) **Look at the pictures. What happens? Make notes on a piece of paper.**

b) **Use your notes to write the story. You can start like this:** KV65
It is Friday evening. Gina and Tim Davis are alone at home. Their parents have gone out. …

c) **Work with a partner. Swap your stories. Tell your partner what you like about his/her story and what you would change. Then edit your story and present it.** KV13

M3 Computer games: good or bad?

LSW 519, 520 KV66 ↓

L 1.40 S 12

WB M4 p. 86

a) **Some people think computer games are bad, others think they are fun. Listen to Nick and his mother. What arguments have they got for and against computer games? Take notes in a grid.**

good	bad
…	…

b) **Work with a partner. Compare your notes. Can you think of more arguments? Add them to your grids.** KV67 ↓

c) **Have a discussion in class about computer/video games. You need three groups:**
- Group one speaks for computer/video games.
- Group two speaks against computer/video games.
- Group three listens to the arguments and can take notes.

At the end of the discussion group three decides: Which group had the best arguments?

I'm for/against … because …

I (don't) agree with you.

KV12

How to … talk p. 172

➡ p. LF54

W p. 230 TM, p. 262

➡ p. LF54

How to ... help out p. 179

M5 WB p. 87

M4 Visiting the Science Museum

LSW 521

Look at the information for school visits. Your friend doesn't understand much English. Answer his/her questions.

Wie viel kostet der Eintritt?

kostenlos

Wann ist das Museum geöffnet?

täglich 10 bis 18 Uhr

Wo können wir unsere Jacken und Rucksäcke lassen?

Schließfach am Eingang

Kann man im Museum etwas zu essen kaufen?

ja: Eat Drink Shop im Keller

Können wir im Museum auch Filme ansehen?

ja: es gibt ein Kino

PLANNING A VISIT – SCIENCE MUSEUM

Opening times and admission costs
The Science Museum is open every day from 10 am to 6 pm. Entrance is free but some activities require money.

Arrive early!
If you have booked a special event or the cinema, please arrive at the museum at least 30 minutes before your scheduled time.

Eating areas
School groups can eat in the picnic area in the basement, on the benches in the museum, or in quiet areas. You can buy snacks from the Eat Drink Shop in the basement. School groups are not allowed to use the museum's cafés.

Coats and bags
At the entrance we provide lockers for coats and bags. Space is limited, so please bring as little as possible.

➡ p. LF54

10 a B p. 106

M5 Inventions

Folie 11 IWS LSW 522, 523

Look at the inventions in number 10 again. What are they good for? Ask and answer questions with a partner. Take turns.

What do you use a microwave for?

You use it to cook food very quickly.
OK, my turn. What do you need a zip for?

M6 Fantastic inventions?

IWS LSW 524

M6 WB p. 87

a) Read about some more inventions. Match them with the pictures. 1-C 2-A 3-D 4-B

1 Amphicar – the car that swims!
The "Amphicar" was designed by the German Hans Trippel in 1961. It was a boat and a car in one and could travel on land and on water. The problem was, on land it was like a fish out of water and couldn't go faster than 65 kph. It wasn't exactly a best-seller!

2 Eagle power
One of the strangest flying machines was designed in the 19th century. The idea was to use the power of eagles. They were fixed to a metal cage that carried a man. Of course, the idea didn't get off the ground!

3 Bike shower
One cyclist had a brilliant idea: His "velodouche" combined the morning shower with a bit of exercise. Pedal power was used to pump water into the shower. The more you pedalled, the more powerful the shower!

4 First parachute jump
Frenchman André Garnerin built a 7-metre wide parachute. Then he jumped from a hot-air balloon and made the first ever parachute jump. The problem was, he didn't know he needed to cut a hole in the top to let the air through. So the parachute swung so wildly that André Garnerin was very sick. But at least he landed safely!

b) Which is your favourite invention? Say why.

c) Listen to the radio report. Find out:
- What does Karen Waterman think about the Amphicar?
- What does the reporter think about it?
- What new information can you get about the Amphicar?

Take notes. Then compare them with a partner.

L 1.41

WB M7 p. 88

➡ p. LF55

M7 Are YOU a successful inventor?

Think of an invention that would make life easier or more fun. Think of a name for it and write a text that explains what your invention does. Here are some ideas:
- What is it used for?
- What special features does it have?
- When is it used?
- How often is it used?
- ...

flying bike

X-ray glasses

walk-on-walls boots

homework butler

➡ p. LF55

WB M8 p. 88

How to ... write p. 174

wordbank Technology p. 160

CAMDEN CHRONICLE
LEARN ENGLISH THE CAMDEN WAY

DID YOU GET IT ALL? ➡ p. LF55

- Who sends a text message to Nick?
- What is Nick's favourite computer game?
- Where did Nick's mother put her note?
- Where does Nick's grandmother want to take Nick?
- Can you learn about maths at the Science Museum?
- On which floor of the Science Museum can you see planes?
- What did Ruth Wakefield invent?
- Who invented the television?

GOOD TO KNOW ...

Die Briten sind Weltmeister, wenn es um Museen geht. Es gibt Museen zu fast jedem Thema: Teekannen, Rasenmäher, Spielzeug, Pferde, ... Das Besondere an den meisten Museen ist, dass man die Dinge nicht nur ansehen, sondern vieles auch anfassen und ausprobieren kann.

Can you believe it?
All the lines in this picture are straight!

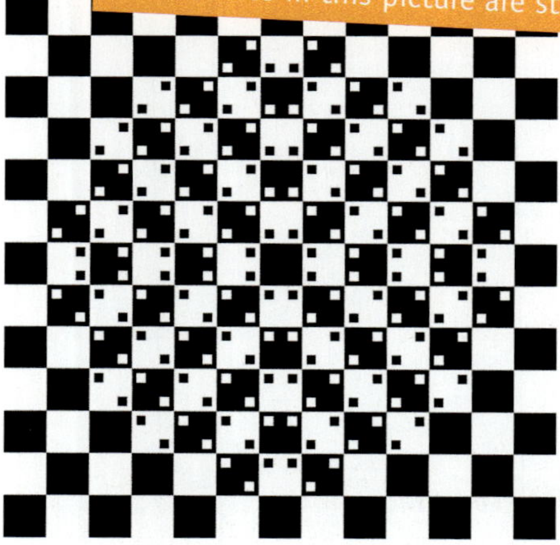

Did you know that ...

... we know more about the moon than we know about the bottom of the ocean?

... when you wear headphones for just one hour, the number of bacteria in your ear multiplies by 700?

... there is a plant that eats rats?

... rain usually falls at 11kph?

... cats can't taste sweets?

... it takes eight minutes for sunlight to travel from the sun to the earth?

... astronauts grow taller in space?

The invention of the bike

Bikes today

The bike (short for bicycle) is a fast, healthy and environmentally friendly[1] means of transport[2].
Today there are more than a billion[3] (1,000,000,000) bikes worldwide.
It was a long way to get there …

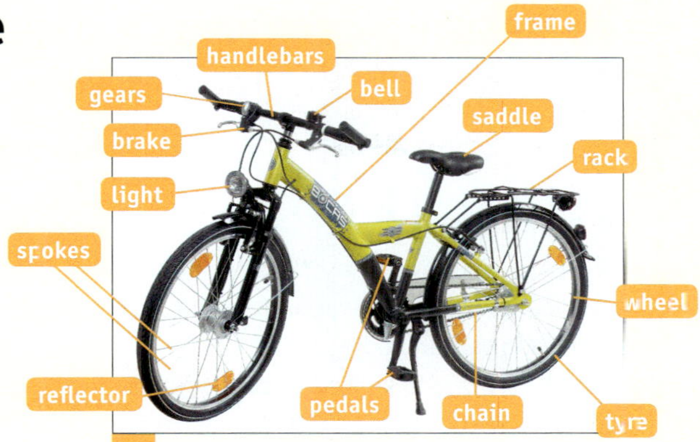

1 *A modern safe bike*

It all started with a big bang …

2 *Mount Tambora: The volcano erupted in 1815*

In 1815 the biggest volcanic eruption[4] in history happened in Indonesia. The eruption was so big that it changed the weather all over the planet: In Europe the year 1816 became known as the 'Year Without a Summer'. This meant that food did not grow well and became very expensive. In those days people used horses to get from one place to another. But after the eruption people couldn't buy food for their horses anymore. People started thinking about other quick and easy ways to travel around … and so the first kind of bike was invented!

1. Describe the developments[5] that led to the invention of the bike.

in (the year) 18… • then • after that • … years later • because of that • as a result

➡ p. LF56

Karl Drais and his Running Machine

The history of the bike begins with Baron Karl Drais from Karlsruhe in Germany. In 1817 he invented the *Laufmaschine* (Running Machine). It was the first vehicle[6] with two wheels placed in line[7]. Every part was made of wood. Riders[8] sat on a saddle and pushed themselves forward with their feet. Drais' idea was to find an alternative to the horse. The Running Machine was an international success and went by different names: *Draisine*, Velocipede, Hobby Horse or Dandy Horse.

3 *The Running Machine by Karl Drais*

2. Read about the Running Machine and look at the picture. What makes it different from the bike we know today?

[1]environmentally friendly – *umweltfreundlich*; [2]means of transport – *Verkehrsmittel*; [3]billion – *Milliarde*; [4]volcanic eruption – *Vulkanausbruch*; [5]development – *Entwicklung*; [6]vehicle – *Fahrzeug*; [7]placed in line – *hintereinander angeordnet*; [8]rider – *Fahrer/in*

The development of the bike

Two Frenchmen and their Boneshaker

The Running Machines weren't perfect. They were heavy and difficult to ride and many of them didn't have any brakes. Lots of accidents happened and in some cities Running Machines weren't allowed anymore.
So in 1818 Drais' bike began to disappear from many European roads. 50 years later, in 1867, the Frechman Pierre Lallement designed a bike with pedals on a bigger front wheel. He sold his design to a blacksmith[1] called Pierre Michaux. It was under Michaux's name that Lallement's bike was produced in factories and became famous.
The bike was made of wood and very heavy iron[2]. It took a lot of effort to turn the pedals. The British gave it the name Boneshaker because it wasn't comfortable to ride.

1 *The Boneshaker*

2 *The Penny Farthing*

James Starley and his Penny Farthing

The next step in the history of the bike was the high-wheeler. In 1869 the Frenchman Eugene Meyer built such a bike. He chose a much bigger front wheel to make the bike faster.
In 1878 the British manufacturer[3] James Starley developed the high-wheeler further. He reduced the weight[4] of the frame, used rubber[5] tyres and spokes. This bike was soon called the Ordinary or the Penny Farthing (the wheels looked like two English coins[6]: the penny and the much smaller farthing).
Penny Farthings were much faster than Boneshakers, but they needed a running start. Stopping was impossible because there were no brakes. The rider just had to jump off[7] the bike. There were many accidents with serious injuries and some people even died.

➡ p. LF56

1. Read the two texts. What problems did the inventions still have?

the problem with ...'s invention was that ... • it didn't have ... • it wasn't ... • there were no ... • you couldn't ... • it was impossible / hard / difficult to ...

[1]blacksmith – *(Huf)schmied;* [2]iron – *Eisen;* [3]manufacturer – *Hersteller, Produzent;* [4]weight – *Gewicht;* [5]rubber – *Gummi;* [6]coin – *Münze, Geldstück;* [7]jump off – *herunterspringen*

3 *Advert for John Kemp Starley's Rover*

John Kemp Starley and his Rover

In 1885 James Starley's nephew[8] John Kemp Starley presented his design: the Rover. The front wheel was smaller again and the back wheel bigger. A chain linked[9] the pedals to the back wheel. The Rover was much easier to ride than the Penny Farthing and became known as a safety bike. It was the first bike that women could ride in their dresses and skirts. Historians[10] say that the safety bike was the first modern bike.

4 *The Tricycle with three wheels is another bike that was made popular by James Starley*

2. Look at advert 3 and picture 4. What made the Rover different from the Penny Farthing?

… was / were bigger / smaller • it had / didn't have a … • it was faster / slower than …

What happened next?

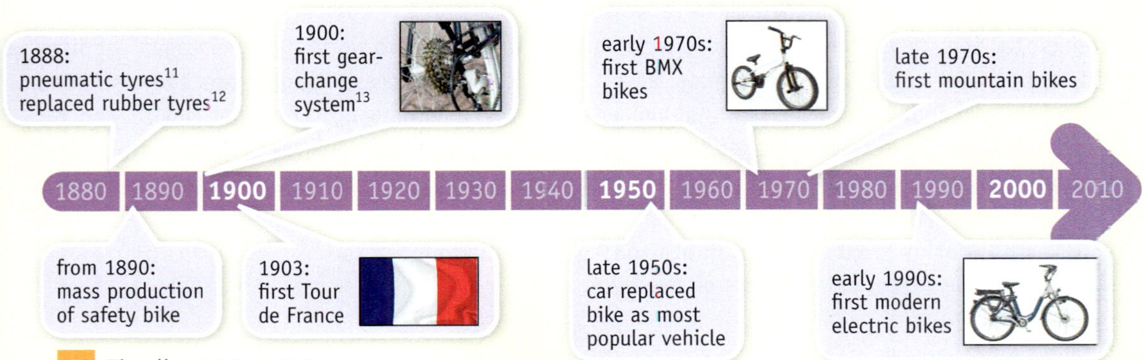

5 *Timeline 1880-2010*

3. Use timeline 5 to talk about the development of the bike from 1880 up until today.

[8]nephew – *Neffe*; [9]link – *verbinden*; [10]historian – *Historiker, Geschichtswissenschaftler*; [11]pneumatic tyre – *Luftreifen*; [12]replace – *ersetzen*; [13]gear-change system – *Gangschaltung*

How the bike changed the world

1 **"Whoever invented the bicycle deserves[1] the thanks of humanity[2]."**
Lord Charles Beresford

The first bikes were made in Europe in the 19th century. However[3], only rich people could buy them because they were so expensive. But the safety bike changed everything: It was much safer and cheaper than the older versions. From the beginning of the 20th century the bike became a popular form of transport for normal people. It helped them to travel around much more quickly.

The effect of the bike on societies[4] around the world was huge, especially for women. To be able to ride a bike, women had to change the way they dressed. Before, women had worn large dresses which weren't suitable[5] for bikes. From then on they began to wear trousers, like men. Bikes also gave women greater independence[6]. They could travel on their own more easily, and as a result women began to ask for more freedom[7] and respect.

Bikes also made a big difference to city life. By the end of the 19th century cities were badly overcrowded[8], because everyone had to live near their workplace. With a bike it became possible to live outside the city and then cycle to work. Thanks to the bike, men and women from different places could also meet more easily. So families expanded[9] because men and women could meet people who lived outside their small towns.

The technology behind the bike also helped with the invention of other, more complicated[10] machines. Henry Ford's first car and the Wright Brothers' first plane both used bicycle technology. Since the first bike these other forms of transport have become very important in society. But the bike is still the most popular form of transportation in many parts of the world. In Europe now more bikes are sold each year than cars.

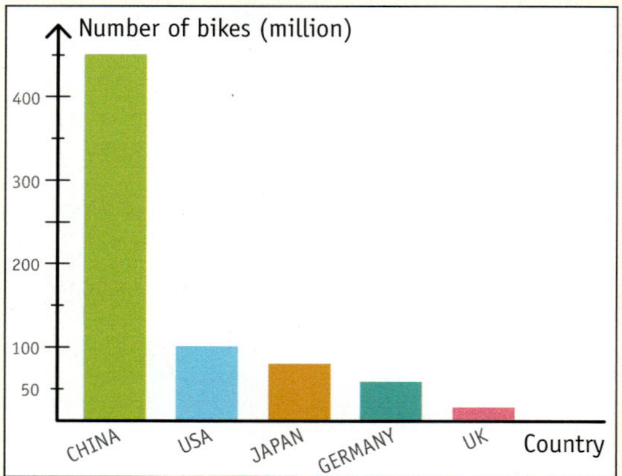

2 *Number of bikes in different countries*

In the modern world the advantages[11] of bikes are clearer than ever. Unlike cars they are good for the environment[12], for your health and for your wallet. You don't need petrol[13] to ride a bike, and it is a lot cheaper to repair them.

➡ p. LF56

1. Use information from the text, quotation[14] 1 and diagram 2 to describe the historical[15] effects of the bike.

it changed … • … made a difference … •
because of the bike … • … plays/played a big role …

2. Imagine a city where there are only bikes instead of cars or buses. Work with a partner and write a description.

KV13

[1]deserve – *verdienen;* [2]humanity – *Menschheit;* [3]however – *jedoch;* [4]society – *Gesellschaft;* [5]suitable – *geeignet;* [6]independence – *Unabhängigkeit;* [7]freedom – *Freiheit;* [8]overcrowded – *überfüllt;* [9]expand – *wachsen, sich ausbreiten;* [10]complicated – *kompliziert;* [11]advantage – *Vorteil;* [12]environment – *Umwelt;* [13]petrol – *Benzin;* [14]quotation – *Zitat;* [15]historical – *geschichtlich, historisch*

THEME 6

TM, p. 271

KV68: Lernlandkarte

UP AND AWAY

In diesem *Theme* ...

» sprichst du über Reisepläne und Ferienaktivitäten.
» lernst du, ein Anmeldeformular zu lesen und zu verstehen.
» orientierst du dich auf einem Bahnhof und erfährst, wie du Fahrkarten kaufst.
» hörst du verschiedene englische Akzente.
» arbeitest du an einem Projekt über interessante Urlaubsziele in Großbritannien.

W p. 231 TM, p. 271

1 Holiday

p. 78/1

L 1.42

WB 1 p. 89

a) Listen to the song 'Summer holiday' by Cliff Richard and read or sing along.

We're all going on a summer holiday
No more working for a week or two
Fun and laughter on our summer holiday
No more worries for me or you
For a week or two
We're going where the sun shines brightly
We're going where the sea is blue
We've seen it in the movies
Now let's see if it's true

Everybody has a summer holiday
Doing things they always wanted to
So we're going on a summer holiday
To make our dreams come true
For me and you
For me and you

➡ p. LF57

b) Read the song lyrics. What do people like about holidays?

➡ p. LF57

2 YOUR summer holidays

IWS KV69 p. 78f./1–3

How to ... work with others p. 177

P2 + P4 p. 134

wordbank Travelling p. 156

WB 2 p. 89

Double circle: What are you going to do in the summer holidays? What would you like to do?

In the summer holidays I'm going to ... And you?

I'd like to ...

stay ... | meet ... | see ... | visit ... | go to ... | do ... | ...

3 Holidays without parents

Folie 12 LSW 601

WB 3 p. 90

M1 p. 138

➡ p. LF57

a) Look at the picture. What can you see? What is happening?

b) Talk about the people. What do you think:

- What are the parents thinking? How do they feel?
- What are the children thinking? How do they feel?

4 Choosing a camp

IWS · KV70 · p. 80f./4+5

L 1.43 S 13

a) Charlie and Rajiv want to go to a summer camp. They have found some information on the Internet. Listen to them. Write down the order in which they talk about the camps.
B - D - A - C

WB 4 p. 90

water sports camp

football and rugby camp

climbing camp

musical star camp

p. LF57

b) Which camp would YOU like to go to? Why?

WB 5 p. 91
M M2 p. 138

5 Charlie's application form

LSW 602 · p. 82f./6+7 · p. LF57

a) Read the application form. Which camp did Charlie choose?

b) Read the form again and find the English words for:

Geburtsdatum • Postleitzahl • Anmeldeformular • weiblich • Einverständnis • Nachname • männlich • Unterschrift • Alter • Erziehungsberechtigte/r

c) What will happen if Charlie breaks the camp rules? will be sent home

Summer Camp Application Form

FIRST NAME: Charlie SURNAME: Batson
DATE OF BIRTH: 22nd June AGE AT CAMP: 14
SEX: MALE ☑ FEMALE ☐
ADDRESS: 4 Carol Street, London
POSTCODE: NW1 0HU TELEPHONE NUMBER: 020 [illegible]
EMAIL: c.batman@[illegible]
NAME OF SCHOOL: Haverstock School
ADDRESS: 24 Haverstock Hill, London
POSTCODE: NW3 2BQ

ACTIVITY CHOICE
CAMP: Climbing camp

AGREEMENT
I, Charlie Batson, promise to have lots of fun at the camp and follow all the rules. If I break them, a camp instructor can send me home.

SIGNATURE: Charlie Batson (Participant) A. Batson (Parent/Guardian)

M M3 p. 139

W p. 231

➡ p. LF57

6 At the station

Folie 13 IWS KV71

P1 P p. 134
How to ... talk about pictures p. 173
6 WB p. 61

a) Charlie and Rajiv are at Victoria Station. Work with a partner. Look at the picture. Ask and answer like this:

p. 84f./8+9, p. 87–89/11–13

Where is/are	the ticket counters? the platforms? the exit? the escalator? ... ?

It's They're	on the left/right. next to/behind/in front of ... opposite ... between ... and ... near ...

- coach station
- platform
- toilets
- accessible toilets
- escalator
- ticket counter
- exit
- information point
- telephone box
- cash machine

7 WB p. 91
P5 P p. 135
25 p. 202
8 WB p. 92

Simple present with future meaning

b) Look at the timetable and find out:

LSW 603

- When does the next train to Bristol/... leave?
- Which platform does the train from Plymouth/... arrive at?
- Which platform does the train to Bristol/... leave from?

It leaves at ...

It arrives at platform ...

It leaves from platform ...

DEPARTURES			ARRIVALS	
BRISTOL	CARDIFF	SWANSEA	PLYMOUTH	BRIGHTON
Time 15:47 Platform 12	Time 15:22 Platform 8	Time 13:18 Platform 6	Time 16:48 Platform 10	Time 11:33 Platform 4

7 At the ticket counter

LSW 604 KV72 p. 86/10, p. 89/14

L 1.44

a) **Charlie and Rajiv are at the ticket counter to buy their train tickets. Listen to them. How much do the tickets cost altogether?** £108

b) **Now read the dialogue. Find out:**
- What kind of ticket do the boys buy? return ticket
- Why do they have to hurry? their train leaves in five minutes

Rajiv: Two tickets to Cardiff, please.
Woman: Single or return?
Rajiv: Return, please.
Woman: OK, that's £108 pounds altogether.
Rajiv: Here you are. Oh, what platform is it, please?
Woman: Platform 8.
Rajiv: Thank you. And could you tell us when the next train leaves?
Woman: You have to hurry. It leaves in five minutes.

c) **Work with a partner and act out the dialogue.** KV13

M4: Rollenkarten für einen Dialog am Bahnhofsschalter

W3 9 + 10 p. 92/93

P3 + P6 p. 134/135

M4 p. 139

M5 p. 139

8 Choose an activity

You can …
- **write a poem about your best holiday.**
- **write about a summer camp you've been to or summer activities you've taken part in.**
  Think about:
  - what you did
  - what you liked most
  - who you went with
  - …

Best holiday

summer holiday
sleep late
meet friends
no school
that's cool!

portfolio

How to … write p. 174

wordbank Travelling p. 156

A hip hop dance workshop

Last summer my friend Lena and I took part in a hip hop dance workshop in our town.
There were twelve girls and eight boys. We met at the dance school from 10 am to 2 pm every day. Our teacher played cool music and showed us the basic moves.
At the end of the workshop we did a short performance for our parents and friends. It was great

- **work with a partner. Look at number 7 and the timetable in 6b) again. It is 1 pm. Buy or sell a ticket to Bristol, Cardiff or Swansea. Make up prices for the tickets. Present your dialogue in class.** KV13

W p. 232 TM, p. 287

Fragen mit Fragewörtern
10R
p. 189
11 WB
p. 94
How to ...
talk
p. 172
➡ p. LF58

9 Friends in foreign countries

LSW 605, 607 KV73

Are there people in your class who have friends or family in foreign countries? Interview them.

Spain • Italy • England • Turkey • Russia • France • Scotland • India • China • USA • Wales • Jamaica • Mexico • Ireland • Poland • Austria • Canada • ...

- Who is it?
- Where do they live?/ Where does he/she live?
- Have you ever visited them/him/her?
- Have they ever visited you?/ Has he/she ever visited you?
- What else do you know about them/him/her?

12 WB
p. 94
L 1.45 S 14

10 Gillian's plans for the summer

KV74

Listen to Gillian and her mother. Why is Gillian unhappy? because she has to stay at home with her mother and her mother's friends from the USA. (thinks her friends will laugh at her when she tells them about her holidays; would prefer to go to a summer camp)

➡ p. LF58
L 1.46
13 WB
p. 95

11 Friends from the USA

LSW 608 p. 90/15

a) **Listen to three dialogues. Where are the people first? And after that?**
b) **Listen to the dialogues again and read along.**

A

Mrs Collins: There they are! Hi! Welcome to London!
Mrs Hill: Gwen! I can't believe we're finally here, it's been much too long! And you must be Gillian, it's so great to meet you at last – I'm Gloria!
Gillian: Hi, nice to meet you!
Mrs Hill: And this is my husband Mark and my daughter Cheryl.
Mr Hill: Hello!
Cheryl: Hi, Gillian. Great to see you.
Gillian: How was the flight?
Cheryl: Very long, ten hours. It's hard sitting for ten hours. But there were some good movies. They also gave us some candy before the plane landed.
Gillian: Wow! Ten hours. You must be tired. But you are staying for four weeks, so you have lots of time to recover. So, let's go home.

B

Mrs Collins: So, what would you like to see first in London?
Mr Hill: Well, we'd like to see St. Paul's Cathedral. And Westminster Abbey sounds great, too.
Mrs Hill: And I really love museums. There are so many here in London.
Mrs Collins: Yes, that's right. And there are a lot of other interesting sights to see. But, Cheryl, you don't look very excited.

Cheryl: Well, you know, I thought we would do more fun things on vacation – like shopping in cool English markets or going on the London Eye. But museums and St. Paul's … Mom, Dad, do I have to go?

Gillian: And I've already been to those places.

Mrs Collins: I have an idea. Why don't you girls visit a nearby city? It'd be good for you to see something new, Gillian!

Cheryl: Awesome! What do you think, Gillian? We could go to Edinburgh. That's a big English city, right?

Gillian: Naaah, you're mixing up England and Great Britain. Edinburgh is in Scotland. And it's quite far from here.

Mrs Collins: That's true, Edinburgh is too far away. You shouldn't go there on your own. … But we could all go together.

Gillian: Then we have to go to all the museums in Edinburgh, too. No, thank you!

Mrs Collins: No no, you and Cheryl can have some time on your own – and you could climb the old volcano, "Arthur's Seat".

Gillian: Oh, that sounds amazing! Let's do it.

C

Mrs Collins: … Yes, we'd like to stay for two nights … right, from Friday to Sunday.

Receptionist: OK. Let me check … just a minute. Oh, sorry, we're booked up. But perhaps you could try our partner hotel in the south of the city? It's called 'Hotel Alexandra'.

Mrs Collins: Oh, that's too bad. But I'll try the other hotel. Thanks a lot.

Receptionist: You're welcome. Good luck and bye!

Mrs Collins: Bye.

c) Which American English words does Cheryl use for the words in the box?

WB 14 p. 95

film • sweets • holiday • mum   movie candy vacation mom

d) Put the sentences in the right order. What word do you get? PLANE

P P9 – P12 p. 136/137
M M6 + M7 p. 140

- L At home the Hills told Gillian and her mother about the places they wanted to see.
- N Gillian wasn't happy at first but then her mother had a great idea.
- P Gillian and her mother picked up the Hills at the airport.
- A Cheryl wanted to do other things: go shopping and visit the London Eye.
- E Mrs Collins phoned a hotel in Edinburgh.

W p. 232

12 Different Englishes

IWS p. 91/16

L 1.47
M8 M p. 141

// anspruchsvollere, aber ähnliche Aufgabe: sechs Varietäten des Englischen *(Ireland, England, Australian English, American English, South African English, Indian English)*

a) At the hotel in Edinburgh Gillian and Cheryl meet two girls from Scotland and Wales and two boys from England and Northern Ireland. Listen to them. Which accent can you understand best? Which one do you find the most difficult to understand?

Hi, my name's Penny. I'm from North Wales. At home I speak Welsh with my parents. But we all speak English, too.

How are you? My name's Ciaran and I'm from Belfast. I learn Irish at school but I usually speak English with my friends.

And I'm Brian. I'm from Newcastle, in the north of England. I like Edinburgh, it's a really cool city.

Hi, I'm Fiona. I come from Aberdeen. That's in the north of Scotland. How do you like Scotland?

b) What other countries do you know where people speak English?
USA, Australia, New Zealand, Canada, South Africa

13 Four places – four things to see

LSW 606

➡ p. LF58
P7 + P8 + P13 P p. 136/137
M9 M p. 141
15 + 16 WB p. 96

Read about these places. Which one do you find the most interesting? Say why.

Stonehenge
This huge monument in the south of England was built over 5,000 years ago. There's also a legend that King Arthur's father travelled to Ireland to take the huge stones to England. But the stones were too heavy. So Merlin the magician used magic to move them across the Irish Sea.

The Giant's Causeway
It is said that there was a strong Scottish giant called Benandonner who laughed at the Irish giant Finn McCool. Finn got so angry that he built a causeway across the Irish Sea.

Loch Ness
The loch (Scottish word for lake) is famous for the Loch Ness Monster. It lies in a beautiful area with forests, moors and mountains.

Mount Snowdon
Mount Snowdon is the highest mountain in Wales (1,085 m). Walk to the top and you'll have some of the best views in Britain.

14 A project – YOUR travel tips

Folie 14 | LSW 609, 610 | portfolio

p. 92/17 | WB 17 p. 97 | KV75

PLAN IT

- **Make groups for the three parts of Great Britain: England, Scotland, Wales. You can also make a group for Ireland.**
- **Make notes on what you already know about your part. Think about:**
  - what you can do there
  - what is interesting about it
- **Collect more information:**
  - interview classmates, your family, ...
  - go to the library/a travel agency
  - search the Internet
  - ...

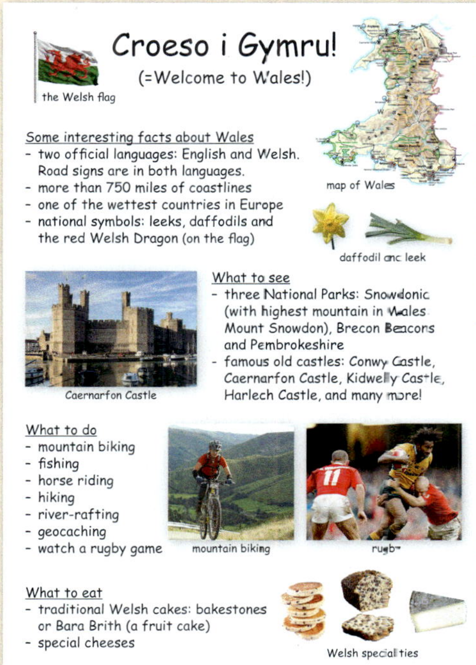

DO IT

- **Talk about the information you have found:**
  - What do you want to present?
  - How do you want to present it (poster, brochure, ...)?
- **Write down the information.**
- **Find pictures, maps, ...**
- **Prepare your presentation.**

CHECK IT

- **Is the English OK?**
- **Is it interesting? Add details.**
- **Edit it. Use a dictionary.**
- **Practise what you want to say.**

PRESENT IT

- **Put up your posters, brochures, ... in your classroom.**
- **Present them to the others in a gallery walk.**

KV8
How to ... work with others p. 176/177
WB test yourself p. 98/99

Belfast, Northern Ireland

Glencoe, Scotland

Kayaking on the River Dee, Wales

Hedge maze in Wiltshire, England

Cardiff Bay, Wales

Cornwall, England

Edinburgh Castle, Scotland

Cotswolds, England

Tower Bridge, London

The White Cliffs of Dover, England

Canterbury Cathedral, England

Brighton Pier, England

W p. 233   TM, p. 299

P1 Word groups

LSW 611

a) Find titles for these word groups.

1. swimming pool • park • cinema • market places
2. sunny • rainy • hot • nice weather
3. shorts • shirt • cap • skirt clothes
4. June • July • August • September months
5. platform • escalator • departures • ticket counter train station
6. water sports • climbing • football and rugby • musical star summer camps

clothes   train station   places   ...

➡ p. LF58

b) Now find words for these titles:

school   animals   holidays   food and drink

P2 Holiday activities

Choose the right verbs to complete these phrases.

go to • visit • have • buy • go • take • stay • write • meet

visit 1. … a castle	write 4. … postcards	visit 7. … some sights	take 10. … photos
go to 2. … a museum	go 5. … swimming	have 8. … a beach party	buy 11. … stamps
have 3. … a picnic	buy 6. … souvenirs	meet 9. … friends	stay 12. … on a campsite

P3 Sound check

LSW 614

L 1.44

Listen to the dialogue in number 7 again. Stop the recording after each sentence. Say the sentence yourself. Try to sound like Rajiv and the woman at the ticket counter.

P4 Plans

LSW 615

Going to-future
21R
p. 199

a) What are you going to do this afternoon?
What are you going to do this evening?

b) Talk to five classmates. Guess their plans and ask questions.

➡ p. LF58

This afternoon I'm going to meet a friend. Then I'm going to …
Later I'm …

This evening I'm going to …

Are you going to chat with friends?

No, I'm not.

Are you going to … ?

Yes, I am.

P5 Arrivals and departures

LSW 613

Simple present with future meaning 25 p. 202

Look at the timetable. Copy the sentences into your exercise book and complete them.

1. The next train to Canterbury leaves at … 12:36
2. The next train to Brighton leaves at … 11:40
3. The train to Eastbourne leaves from platform 6
4. The train to Canterbury leaves from … platform 8
5. The train from Dover arrives at platform … 12
6. The train from Sheffield arrives at … 12:53

DEPARTURES			ARRIVALS	
Brighton	Eastbourne	Canterbury	Dover	Sheffield
Time 11:40	Time 14:17	Time 12:36	Time 13:52	Time 12:53
Platform 10	Platform 6	Platform 8	Platform 12	Platform 5

P6 A ticket machine

➡ p. LF58

How to … help out p. 179

You are in London with your parents. They want to buy tickets for the bus at this ticket machine. Unfortunately, they don't speak much English. Answer their questions.

Was muss man denn hier zuerst machen?

Da steht *One day bus pass*. Ist der nur heute gültig?

Was ist denn ein *Single journey bus ticket*?

Gibt der Automat Wechselgeld?

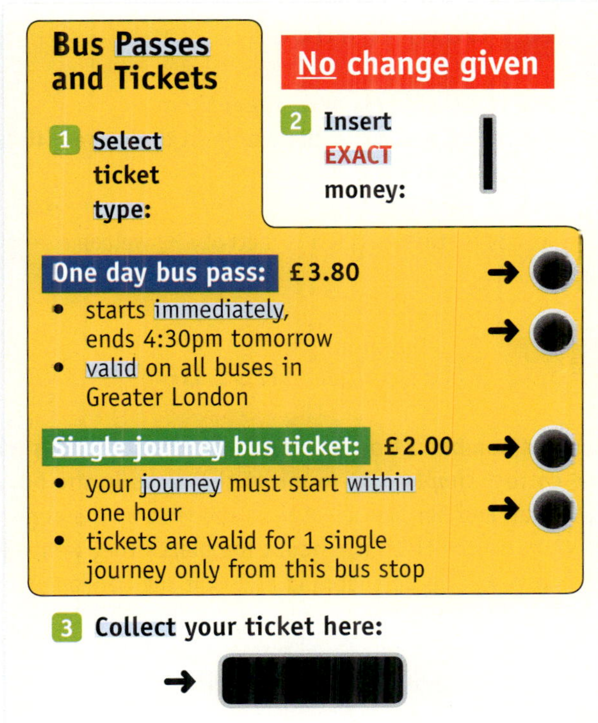

W p. 233 TM, p. 300

➡ p. LF59

P7 Give me five!

Look at Theme 6 and find:

- 5 countries in Europe
- 5 countries which are not in Europe
- 5 countries where English is spoken
- 5 things to do or see in London
- 5 cities in the UK

P8 Ten words

a) Write down ten difficult words from this Theme.
b) Spell the words for your partner. Can he/she write them down correctly?
accessible, escalator, departure, arrival, application, guardian, instructor, birth, male, female

P9 A word game

Westminster Abbey, London

a) How many English words can you make out of the letters in "Westminster Abbey"? west, best, yes, test, start, win, a, bin, … term, web, mine, wine, bat, bit, baby, wait,
b) Compare your words with a partner. Who found more words? waiter, waitress, bear, write, train, team, many

➡ p. LF59

L 1.48

P10 Sound check

a) Listen to the words and repeat them.
b) Make two lists. Write the words in the correct list.

land • ten • unhappy • spend • many • family • candy • then • plan • activity • welcome • any

/æ/	/e/
land	ten
…	…

Simple past
5R
p. 185

P11 The Hills' first day

LSW 612

Look at number 11 again. Complete the sentences with the correct *simple past* forms of the verbs in the box.

want • phone • know • pick • have • talk • be

1. Gillian and her mother XX up the Hills at the airport. picked
2. At home the Hills XX about the places they wanted to see. talked
3. Cheryl XX to go shopping and visit the London Eye. wanted
4. Gillian XX not happy because she already XX all the places. was, knew
5. But then Mrs Collins XX a great idea. had
6. She XX a hotel in Edinburgh. phoned

P12 So many questions

LSW 616

Satzstellung 19R p. 197/198

➡ p. LF59

Write down the questions in the correct order.

1. flight – was – to London – How – your – ?
2. tired – you – Are – after – flight – the – ?
3. What – see – like to – you – in London – would – ?
4. you – go – would – Where – like to – first – ?
5. want to – you – a museum – visit – Do – ?
6. don't – to Edinburgh – we – Why – go – all – ?

P13 Caves and dinosaurs

➡ p. LF59

How to ... help out p. 179

You are in Great Britain with your class and see this brochure.
Some of your classmates need help understanding it. Answer their questions.

Was gibt es dort zu sehen?

Gibt es in den Höhlen auch Dinosaurier?

Wie sind denn die Öffnungszeiten?

Was kostet der Eintritt?

Warum steht dort „sweatshirt"?

THE NATIONAL SHOWCAVES CENTRE FOR WALES

Abercrave, Swansea, UK

Explore three spectacular caves that were formed more than 315 million years ago: Dan-yr-Ogof Cave, Bone Cave and Cathedral Cave. You will leave with a better understanding of this natural wonder.

At the National Showcaves Centre for Wales we have also created one of the world's largest dinosaur parks – with over 200 life-sized dinosaur models.

Opening times: 10 am – 3 pm, open 7 days a week from March until November
Entrance fees (caves + dinosaur park): Adults £13.75 Children £8.50 (ages 3 – 16)
Clothing: Please wear a sweatshirt or a long-sleeved T-shirt and proper shoes/trainers. The temperature in the caves is a constant 12 °C. Remember you may need a raincoat for the dinosaur park.

W p. 234 TM, p. 303

➡ p. LF59

M1 Away from home

How to ... write p. 174

Have you ever been away from home without your parents?
Make notes and write about it. Here is some help:

Yes	No
Last year I went ...	I have never ...
I spent ...	My parents don't want me to go ... because ...
I had a great/wonderful/... time	I wouldn't like to ... because ...
... was most exciting.	I would like to ...
I missed/didn't miss ...	...
I (never) felt homesick/terrible/...	

M2 Summer camps

IWS LSW 617

M1 p. 102

Look at the website and answer the questions below.

News (230) Favourites

YHA Summer camps

This year there are 23 camps waiting to welcome you and give you the best week of your summer. There really is something for everyone.

Most YHA summer camps are for 10 - 16 year olds.
Remember to check the age groups for each week at the camp - just click on the activities.
Our camps are great places to make new friends, but you can also come with up to three friends.
Each camp gives you a week of action and adventure with a unique atmosphere which truly makes the summer camp experience what it is - a fantastic week shared with friends - old and new.

SUMMER ACTIVITIES

- Climbing
- Creative Writing
- Dance & Drama
- Football & Rugby

- Go Extreme
- Lights, Camera, Action!
- Mission Impossible
- Multi-activity

- Musical Star
- Robotics
- Singing
- Superweeks

1. How old do you have to be for the summer camps? between 10 and 16
2. How many camps can you choose from? 23
3. How can you find out more about the activities? click on the activities
4. How long can people stay at one of the camps? one week
5. Which activities do YOU find interesting? Say why.

➡ p. LF60

M3 Camp rules

LSW 618

➡ p. LF60
WB M2 p. 103

a) What do you think: What rules are there at the climbing camp? Make notes. Think about:
   - clothes
   - food and drink
   - rooms
   - free time
   - mobile phones
   - …

b) Then tell the class about your ideas.

Modalverben 15R p. 192-194

M4 At the ticket counter

KV13 KV76

➡ p. LF60
B 7 p. 127

You are at Victoria Station. Work with a partner and make a dialogue. Then act it out.

Partner A	Partner B
1 Sage, dass du zwei Fahrkarten nach Cardiff haben möchtest.	2 Frage A, ob es Einzelfahrkarten oder Hin- und Rückfahrkarten sein sollen.
3 Verlange Hin- und Rückfahrkarten.	4 Nenne den Gesamtpreis (£ 108).
5 Gib B das Geld. Frage, von welchem Bahnsteig der Zug abfährt.	6 Nenne den Bahnsteig (8).
7 Bedanke dich. Frage, wann der nächste Zug nach Cardiff abfährt.	8 Sage, dass der Zug in fünf Minuten abfährt und Partner A sich beeilen muss.

M5 Welcome to the camp

LSW 619

L 2.1 S 15
WB M3 p. 103

a) At the beginning of the camp, Jeff, one of the instructors, talks to everybody. Listen to Jeff. What things does he talk about?

camp activities • mobile phones • camp rules • meal times

➡ p. LF60

b) Listen again. What information is important for children who are late? Take notes. (You should find at least six things that are important.)

c) Compare your notes with a partner. Then give the information to your class.

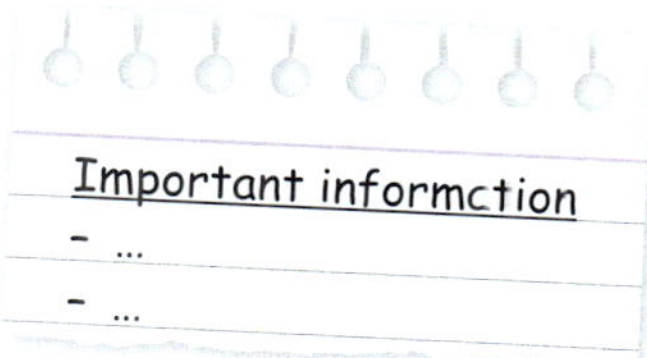

W p. 234   TM, p. 308

➡ p. LF61

M6 Making a reservation

LSW 620   KV77 ↓

M4 + M5 p. 104 WB

a) What does a customer say? What does a receptionist say? Make two lists.

OK, I've made a reservation for Friday and Saturday.

Let me check. Yes, three rooms are free.

What time is breakfast?

How much does that cost altogether?

How can I help you?

Thank you very much for your help.

Would you like to make a reservation?

Have you got three rooms for Friday and Saturday night?

No problem. Glad I could help.

Could you make a reservation for me?

receptionist:

customer:

L 2.2 S 16

b) Listen to Mrs Collins and the receptionist and look at your lists from a). Underline the phrases you hear in your lists.

c) Work with a partner. Use your lists to make up a dialogue. Act out your scene to the class. KV13

➡ p. LF61

M7 YOUR phrase book for travelling

LSW 621, 622

M6 p. 104/105 WB

a) Imagine you are going to spend your holidays in a foreign country. To prepare for the trip think about typical situations. Here are some ideas:

- going shopping
- at the station
- in a restaurant
- giving and asking for directions
- ...

b) Look through your book and your workbook. Collect words and phrases you can use in different situations.

KV6

Asking for directions:
Excuse me, can you tell me the way to the station, please?
Excuse me, how can I get to the zoo, please?
Can you show it to me on the map, please?

Giving directions:
Turn left/right at the next corner.
Walk straight on.
It's next to the cinema.
Cross the street, it's on your left/right.
Walk past the museum and then turn left/right.

M8 Different Englishes

IWS

p. LF62

L 2.3

a) Here are some travellers who were interviewed at an airport. Listen to them. What do you think: Where are they from?

Ireland • England • Australia • USA • South Africa • India

How to ... listen p. 169

Brian Fallon

Sheila Murphy

Oliver Kumalo

Sue Monkhouse

Sunit Nandi

Barbara Harmer

b) Listen to what the travellers say. Find out and take notes:
- Where are the travellers from?
- What are they going to do?
- What other information do they give?

c) Compare your results with a partner.

L 2.4

WB M7 p. 105

B 12 a p. 130

M9 More interesting places

Folie 14 LSW 623, 624

p. LF62

a) Look at number 13 again. What other places have you heard of in Great Britain? You can look at the map at the front of your book for help. Where would YOU like to go? Talk to a partner.

b) Find more information about one of these places and write a short report. Then present it in class.

How to ... write p. 174

CAMDEN CHRONICLE
LEARN ENGLISH THE CAMDEN WAY

DID YOU GET IT ALL? ➡ p. LF62

» What do Charlie and Rajiv want to do in the summer holidays?
» What is the English word for *Geburtsdatum*?
» Where do trains leave and arrive at a train station?
» Where do Charlie and Rajiv buy their train tickets?
» Who visits Gillian and her mother in the summer holidays?
» What is Mrs Collins' great idea?
» What is the American English word for "holiday"?
» Who laughed at the Irish giant Finn McCool?

To: gillian.collins@[illegible]
Subject: Thank you!
From: TheHillFamily@[illegible]

Hi everybody,
We've only been back home in the USA for three days but we're missing you already. We had such a lovely time! Gillian, would you like to come and visit us next summer? Cheryl would be so happy. We hope to hear from you soon! And thanks again.
Love,
Gloria, Mark and Cheryl

GOOD TO KNOW ...

Englisch ist die Muttersprache von ungefähr 350 Millionen Menschen in Großbritannien, Nordamerika, Australien und weiteren Ländern. Für mehr als eine Milliarde Menschen ist Englisch eine Zweitsprache, z. B. in Indien, Pakistan und Südafrika. Dort spricht man Englisch in der Schule, bei der Arbeit und in Behörden. Nur zu Hause sprechen die Leute dort ihre Muttersprache. Nahezu überall auf der Welt sprechen Menschen Englisch, wenn sie die Muttersprache des anderen nicht verstehen. Dazu gehörst auch du!

YOUR YEAR

Your year with Camden Market 3 is over. What was ...

- your favourite Theme?
- your favourite page?
- your favourite picture?
- your favourite story?

A Traditional British specialities

Read about some traditional dishes and specialities. Which of them would you like to try?

Bangers'n'Mash

This is one of the most popular meals in school cafeterias all over Britain! 'Banger' is another word for 'sausage', and 'mash' is a short form of 'mashed potatoes'[1]. So ... sausages and potatoes with a thick brown sauce called 'gravy'. You just have to try it!

Bubble and Squeak

After a big Christmas Dinner or a traditional 'Roast[2] Dinner' on Sundays, there is always lots of food left: mashed potatoes, cabbage, onions and lots more! Bubble and Squeak is a great way to use this food. You fry it together in a pan until it all sticks together. Sometimes it looks like a slice of pizza!

Welsh Rarebit

The perfect lunchtime snack, especially if you love cheese! To make Welsh Rarebit, you melt[3] cheese together with mustard[4] and beer, and then you toast it on bread. 'Rarebit' sounds a lot like 'rabbit' – and this is part of a joke. In past times[5] Welsh people didn't have the money to buy rabbit meat, so they just had cheese on toast instead.

Cock-a-Leekie

This delicious soup, made from chicken, leeks and plums[8], is a favourite of Scottish people. It is perfect in the terrible Scottish weather!

Toad-in-the-Hole

The British just love sausages – here is another speciality dish made with them! First you fry the sausages and then put them in a big pot[6] with a 'batter'[7]. A batter is a mixture of milk, flour and eggs: the same mixture that you use to make crêpes. Then you put the sausages and the batter in the oven and wait for the batter to become golden and crispy. Delicious!

➡ p. LF53

Search the Internet for more British meals. Present them in class. WWW

[1]mashed potatoes – *Kartoffelbrei*; [2]roast – *Braten*; [3]melt – *schmelzen*; [4]mustard – *Senf*; [5]in past times – *früher*; [6]pot – *Topf*; [7]batter – *Teig*; [8]plum – *Pflaume*

B The story of Christy Brown

L 2.5

Read about Christy Brown. What do you find interesting about his life? Do you know any other people with similar problems?

Christy Brown was born in Dublin, Ireland, in 1932. He had 22 brothers and sisters and they all lived in a very small house.

Christy's mother was busy all day – cooking, cleaning, washing, shopping, doing everything for her large family. Christy's father worked as a bricklayer[1] but there was never much money for the family.

When Christy was a few months old, his mother saw that he did not move like her other children. She took him to a doctor who said that he was disabled.

When Christy was older, he could not eat alone or put on his clothes. He could not walk and he could not talk. But he could move his left foot and he could hear. His mother was a very strong woman. She wanted to help Christy. But she had a very busy life because there were younger brothers and sisters. She had no machines to help her with the washing and cleaning. But she always found time to help Christy to learn the alphabet and to write with his left foot.

Christy never went to school but he was an intelligent boy. He learned to read and later he painted pictures. People bought his pictures. His brothers made a box on wheels[2] for him, so that he could sit and play in the street with them. Later they built a little house for him in the garden where he could sit, read, write and paint. When he was 18, a doctor visited him. She worked in a clinic with children and young people who were disabled like Christy. She taught him to control his body a little. His family always helped him in many ways. To thank them, he wrote a book called *My Left Foot*. He earned more money with this book than his father earned in a year as a bricklayer.

Later Christy married an English woman. He wrote more books and won many prizes[3].

Christy died in 1981. There is a film about his life called *My Left Foot*.

[1]bricklayer – *Maurer/in;* [2]wheel – *Rad;* [3]prize – *Preis, Gewinn*

C Country Mouse and City Mouse

KV9

➡ p. LF63

L 2.6

What do you think the story is about?

A country mouse invited his cousin from the city to visit him. When City Mouse sat down to dinner, he was surprised that Country Mouse only had grain[1] to eat.

"Really," he said, "you don't live well at all. You should see how I live! I've got wonderful things to eat every day. Please come and visit me in the city."

So Country Mouse went to the city with his cousin. The first place that City Mouse showed him was the kitchen cupboard of the house where he lived. There, on the lowest shelf, stood a big paper bag of sugar. City Mouse chewed a hole in the bag. The two little mice started to eat the sugar. Country Mouse thought he had never tasted anything so delicious in his life. He was just thinking how lucky City Mouse was when suddenly the kitchen door opened: The cook came in to get some flour.

"Run!" whispered City Mouse. And they ran away as fast as they could. Country Mouse was shaking[2] but City Mouse said, "That's nothing. She'll soon go away and then we can go back."

When they went back, City Mouse had something new to show: On the top shelf there were raisins[3]. This was even better than the sugar! But suddenly there was a scratching[4] at the door and a loud MIAOUW!

"What's that?" asked Country Mouse. City Mouse whispered, "Sh! Run!" and they ran as fast as they could. As soon as they were in the hole City Mouse said, "That was the cat. If she gets you, you're lost."

"This is terrible," said Country Mouse. "Let's not go back to the cupboard again."

"No," said City Mouse, "I'll take you to the cellar[5]. There's something special there."

Down in the cellar there was a big cupboard. On the shelves there were many different kinds of cheese and they all smelled so good.

Country Mouse was eating some Gouda when he saw another delicious-smelling cheese on a little piece of wood in a corner. He went over there to eat the cheese. City Mouse saw him. "Stop!" he cried. "That's a trap[6]!"

Country Mouse stopped. "What's a trap?" "That thing is a trap," said City Mouse. "As soon as you touch the cheese something comes down on your head and you'll die!"

Country Mouse looked at the trap and he looked at the cheese and he looked at City Mouse. "I think I'll go home," he said. "I'd rather have only grain and eat it in peace[7] than have sugar and raisins and cheese and be frightened all the time!"

So Country Mouse went back to his home and there he stayed for the rest of his life.

Choose an activity

- **Draw a picture for each paragraph. You can add speech bubbles, too.**
- **What does Country Mouse tell his friend when he gets home? Write a dialogue.**

[1]grain – *Korn*; [2]shake – *zittern*; [3]raisin – *Rosine*; [4]scratching – *Kratzen*; [5]cellar – *Keller*; [6]trap – *Falle*; [7]peace – *Frieden*

D About a Boy

About a Boy **is a book by British author Nick Hornby. It is a story about a boy called Marcus. Look at the pictures. What can you say about Marcus?**

KV14

"So, have you split up now?"
"Are you being funny?"
People quite often thought Marcus was being funny when he wasn't. He couldn't understand it. Asking his mum whether[1] she's split up with Roger was a perfectly sensible[2] question, he thought: They'd had a big row[3], then they'd gone off into the kitchen to talk quietly, and after a little while they'd come out looking serious, and Roger had come over to him, shaken his hand and wished him luck at his new school, and then he'd gone.
"Why would I want to be funny?"
"Well, what does it look like to you?"
"It looks to me like you've split up. But I just wanted to make sure."
"We've split up."
"So he's gone?"
"Yes, Marcus, he's gone."

He didn't think he'd ever get used to this business[4]. He had quite liked Roger, and the three of them had been out a few times; now, apparently[5], he'd never see him again. He didn't mind[6], but it was weird[7] if you thought about it. [...]

Marcus wasn't surprised that she couldn't explain what had happened. He'd heard more or less the whole argument, and he hadn't understood a word of it; there seemed to be a piece missing somewhere. When Marcus and his mum argued, you could hear the important bits: too much, too expensive, too late, too young, bad for your teeth, the other channel, homework, fruit. But when his mum and her boyfriends argued, you could listen for hours and still miss the point, the thing, the fruit and homework part of it. It was like they'd been told to argue and just came out with anything they could think of.
"Did he have another girlfriend?"
"I don't think so."
"Have you got another boyfriend?"
She laughed. "Who would that be? The guy who took the pizza orders? No, Marcus, I haven't got another boyfriend. That's not how it works. Not when you're a thirty-eight-year-old working mother. There's a time problem. Ha! There's an everything problem. Why? Does it bother[8] you?"
"I dunno[9]."
[...]
"Do you mind me having boyfriends?"
"No. Only Andrew."
"Well, yes, I know you didn't like Andrew. But generally? You don't mind the idea of it?"
"No. Course not."

[1]whether – *ob*; [2]sensible – *vernünftig*; [3]row – *Streit*; [4]business – *Angelegenheit*; [5]apparently – *offensichtlich*; [6]mind – *etw dagegen haben*; [7]weird – *seltsam*; [8]bother – *stören*; [9]dunno *(informal)* = don't know

"You've been really good about everything. Considering[10] you've had two different sorts of life."

He understood what she meant. The first sort of life had ended four years ago, when he was eight and his mum and dad had split up; that was the normal, boring kind, with school and holidays and homework and weekend visits to grandparents. The second sort was messier[11], and there were more people and places in it: his mother's boyfriends and his dad's girlfriends; flats and houses; Cambridge and London. You wouldn't believe that so much could change just because a relationship[12] ended, but he wasn't bothered. Sometimes he even thought he preferred the second sort of life to the first sort. More happened, and that had to be a good thing.

Apart from Roger, not much had happened in London yet. They'd only been here for a few weeks – they'd moved on the first day of the summer holidays – and so far it had been pretty boring. He had been to see two films with his mum, *Home Alone 2*, which wasn't as good as *Home Alone 1*, and *Honey, I Blew Up the Kids*, which wasn't as good as *Honey, I Shrunk the Kids*, and his mum had said that modern films were too commercial, and that when she was his age ... something, he couldn't remember what. And they'd been to have a look at his school, which was big and horrible, and wandered around their new neighbourhood, which was called Holloway, and had nice bits and ugly bits, and they'd had lots of talks about London, and the changes that were happening to them, and how they were all for the best,

probably[13]. But really they were sitting around waiting for their London lives to begin.

The pizzas arrived and they ate them straight out of the boxes.

"They're much better than the ones we had in Cambridge, aren't they?" Marcus said cheerfully[14]. It wasn't true: It was the same pizza company[15], but in Cambridge the pizzas hadn't had to travel so far, so they weren't quite as soggy[16]. It was just that he thought he ought[17] to say something optimistic. "Shall[18] we watch TV?"

"If you want."

He found the remote control[19] down the back of the sofa and zapped through the channels. He didn't want to watch any of the soaps, because soaps were full of trouble, and he was worried that the trouble in the soaps would remind[20] his mum of the trouble she had in her own life. So they watched a nature programme about this sort of fish thing that lived right down at the bottom of caves and couldn't see anything, a fish that nobody could see the point[21] of; he didn't think that would remind his mum of anything much.

- **Would you like to read the whole book? Why/Why not?**

➡ p. LF63

- **Describe the two lives Marcus's mum talks about. What are the differences between them?**
- **There is a film called *About a Boy*. Watch it in class. Do you like the story? Why/Why not?**

[10]considering – *wenn man bedenkt, dass*; [11]messy – *chaotisch*; [12]relationship – *Beziehung*; [13]probably – *wahrscheinlich*; [14]cheerful – *fröhlich*; [15]company – *Firma*; [16]soggy – *matschig*; [17]ought – *sollte, müsste*; [18]shall – *sollen*; [19]remote control – *Fernbedienung*; [20]remind – *erinnern*; [21]not see the point of sth – *keinen Sinn in etw sehen*

E Monstroso

KV9, KV10

Monstroso is a story about Oscar, a boy who likes computer games. One day when his parents go out, his grandfather babysits. Read and find out what happens.

Oscar didn't mind[1] too much being left alone with a normal babysitter. He could spend the whole time playing on his computer without being told to stop. But Oscar's room was used as the spare bedroom[2], so if guests came to stay, he'd be kicked out and have to sleep on a sofa in his dad's office[3] that turned into a bed. (The office didn't turn into a bed, the sofa did. It was a 'sofa bed'. Which meant that it was quite uncomfortable as a sofa and very, very uncomfortable as a bed.)

And if Grandad was in his bedroom, Oscar wouldn't be able to get at his computer. Dad kept a laptop in his study[4] but Oscar reckoned[5] it was probably[6] made in the Middle Ages[7] and was the sort of rubbish laptop that King Arthur and His Knights of the Round Table[8] would have used. It was really slow, it kept crashing, the Internet didn't work properly[9] on it and – even worse than that – Oscar wasn't allowed to install any of his games on it.

"You'll slow it down and fill the memory up," was all Dad ever said if Oscar asked him to put a decent[10] game on it. "It's not for playing with, it's for work."

What a stupid thing to say. Everyone knew that computers were for playing with; only idiots used them for work. Dad's computer was nearly as bad as the computers they had at school. There was only one game on the school computers: a really babyish fishing game that Oscar had soon realized was a trick, because it was actually[11] all about learning maths.

So not only would Oscar have to sleep in his dad's horrible office, he would also have to spend half the weekend without his computer. […]

As Oscar helped his dad open the sofa bed out on Saturday morning, Dad said what he always said when Oscar had to sleep in his office.

"You know you're not allowed to touch any of my things, don't you?"

Oscar nodded[12] and looked around the office. Why on earth[13] would he want to touch any of Dad's things? They were *Dad's things*. Dad's things weren't interesting.

But then Oscar noticed something new. There, sitting in the middle of the desk, was a brand-new laptop. […]

"You are absolutely *not* to touch that," he said. "*Absolutely not*. Do you understand?"

Oscar nodded his head dumbly[14].

"It's from my work," Dad went on. "And it's got lots of important work things on it. You are absolutely, *absolutely* not to touch it."

"I won't," said Oscar. "I promise."

Choose an activity

- **What do you think happens next? Write down your ideas.**
- **Do you have a favourite computer game? Describe it.**

[1]mind – *etw dagegen haben*; [2]spare (bed)room – *Gästezimmer*; [3]office – *Arbeitszimmer*; [4]study – *Arbeitszimmer*; [5]reckon – *glauben, vermuten*; [6]probably – *wahrscheinlich*; [7]Middle Ages – *Mittelalter*; [8]King Arthur and His Knights of the Round Table – *König Artus und seine Ritter der Tafelrunde*; [9]properly – *richtig*; [10]decent – *anständig*; [11]actually – *in Wirklichkeit*; [12]nod – *nicken*; [13]why on earth – *warum um alles in der Welt*; [14]dumb – *stumm*

F The Giant's Causeway

Read the legend of Finn McCool and the Giant's Causeway. How do you like the story?

L 2.7

Long, long ago the giant Finn McCool and his wife Oonagh lived on the north coast of Ireland. One day when Finn was on the beach, he heard someone shouting. He looked across the Irish Sea and saw another giant on the Scottish beach.

The Scottish giant shouted: "I'm Benandonner and I've heard of you! You're Finn McCool, the Irish giant. I wish I could swim because then I would come across and show you who the better giant is!"

This made Finn very angry. "If you think you're so strong, why don't you come and fight me? I'll even build you a causeway!" And with that he threw a big rock at the Scottish giant. It almost hit him but he jumped back and the rock landed on the beach. Benandonner laughed and continued[1] to shout mean things at Finn. This made Finn even more angry and he threw more rocks into the sea. But with each rock Finn became weaker[2] and weaker, and so when the causeway was finished, Finn was too tired to fight the Scottish giant.

"You're small, weak and stupid!" shouted Benandonner as he jumped onto the rock in the sea. "And soon you will die! Ha, ha, ha!" And he jumped across to the next rock.

The exhausted[3] Finn went home and told his wife that Benandonner was coming to fight him. Oonagh wasn't happy about this and she thought of a plan. She dressed Finn in clean clothes and told him to squeeze[4] into a cradle[5].

When Benandonner arrived, he saw a woman rocking[6] a baby's cradle and singing.

"Where is he?" he shouted, "where's your weak little husband, Finn McCool?"

"Ssh! Don't wake the baby or it will make my husband angry," she said.

Benandonner looked at the baby. Ugh! It was very big and very ugly!

"Excuse me," said Oonagh, "I have to feed the baby now. But you can talk to my husband. He's behind the house digging a grave[7] for a Scottish giant!"

Benandonner started to panic. Finn's baby was huge! So how big was the father? He didn't want to find out and ran back to Scotland as fast as he could. On the way back he kicked the causeway apart[8] so Finn couldn't follow him.

Today you can still see the stones in Northern Ireland.

Choose an activity

- **Which moral fits the story best? Talk to a partner.**

  Always think before you build something • A big giant isn't always the most intelligent giant • Women have always got the best ideas • …

➡ p. LF63

- **Turn the story into a play. Work in groups and act it out.**
- **Divide the text into different parts and draw pictures. Then use them to tell the story in your own words.**

[1]continue to do sth – *weiter etw tun*; [2]weak – *schwach*; [3]exhausted – *erschöpft*; [4]squeeze (into) – *sich (hinein)quetschen*; [5]cradle – *Wiege*; [6]rock (sb/sth) – *(jdn/etw) wiegen*; [7]dig a grave – *ein Grab schaufeln*; [8]apart – *auseinander*

➡ p. LF63

G The Sword in the Stone

This is one of the stories from the legend of King Arthur.
Do you know another legend? Tell it to a partner.

knight – *Ritter;* tournament – *Turnier*

sword – *Schwert*

HOW DID HE DO THAT?
BUT NO ONE CAN TAKE THE SWORD OUT OF THAT STONE!
MANY KNIGHTS HAVE TRIED!
LISTEN, GOOD KNIGHTS!
THERE IS SOMETHING I MUST TELL YOU.
FIFTEEN YEARS AGO I GAVE A BABY TO SIR ECTOR AND HIS WIFE TO LOOK AFTER, BECAUSE IT WAS IN DANGER.
THE BABY WAS OUR OLD KING UTHER'S SON. ONLY THAT SON COULD TAKE THE SWORD FROM THE STONE!
LONG LIVE KING ARTHUR!
LONG LIVE THE NEW KING!

A Food and drink

At the restaurant

choose try order have	a meal a starter the main course side orders a beverage dessert

Food can be ...

good • bad • delicious • yummy • disgusting • terrible • sweet • sugary • hot • spicy • healthy • unhealthy • fresh • old • traditional • expensive • ...

On the menu

dishes	beverages
soup • roast beef • roast lamb • pie • pork • fish and chips • pudding • lasagne • pizza • pasta • chop suey • sushi • curry • salad • burger • hot dog • nachos • ...	juice • lemonade • milk • milkshake • cola • water • coffee • tea • wine • beer • ...

Cooking your own meal

things you use	how much you use
knife • fork • pan • spoon • tablespoon • teaspoon • plate • cup • glass • stove • dish • ...	a bunch of parsley • a tablespoon of oil • a teaspoon of curry powder • a cup of flour • some pepper • ...

what you do
wash the vegetables • make a salad • cut the cucumbers • mix the tomatoes and leeks • add some pepper • heat the oil • put the sausages in the pan • stir for a few minutes • bake the pizza • use some curry powder • serve with cream •...

B Free time

Activities

meet (my) friends • listen to music • watch TV/a film • play the guitar/piano/… • play computer games/board games/chess • go to the cinema/zoo/youth club/a party/concert • dance • relax • visit a museum/castle/… • take photos • sleep over at a friend's house • phone/call a friend • chat to friends/on the Internet • read books/magazines • collect stickers/football cards/… • go shopping • be in/join a club • …

Sports

You <u>play</u> …	You <u>go</u> …	You <u>do</u> …
• table tennis	• swimming	• karate
• football	• dancing	• judo
• basketball	• cycling	• gymnastics
• volleyball	• inline skating	• kickboxing
• hockey	• riding	• …
• …	• …	

things you need (equipment)	where you do it	why you like it
ball • goal • helmet • skateboard • hockey stick • …	in a park/sports hall • at a sports centre • on a sports field • on the street • …	it is great fun/exciting/fast/… • you meet friends • you play in a team • you spend time outside • …

People in sports

sportsperson • player • dancer • runner • swimmer • athlete • team • team captain • coach • referee • goalkeeper • fan • …

Talking about sports

score a goal • catch the ball • have a (friendly) match • watch a game/match • cheer on your team • win/lose a game/match/race • practise new tricks • train once/twice/three times a week • play injured • …

C Health

Keep fit and healthy!
- Eat healthy food.
- Drink lots of water.
- Do sports.
- Get enough sleep.
- Feel good.

The body

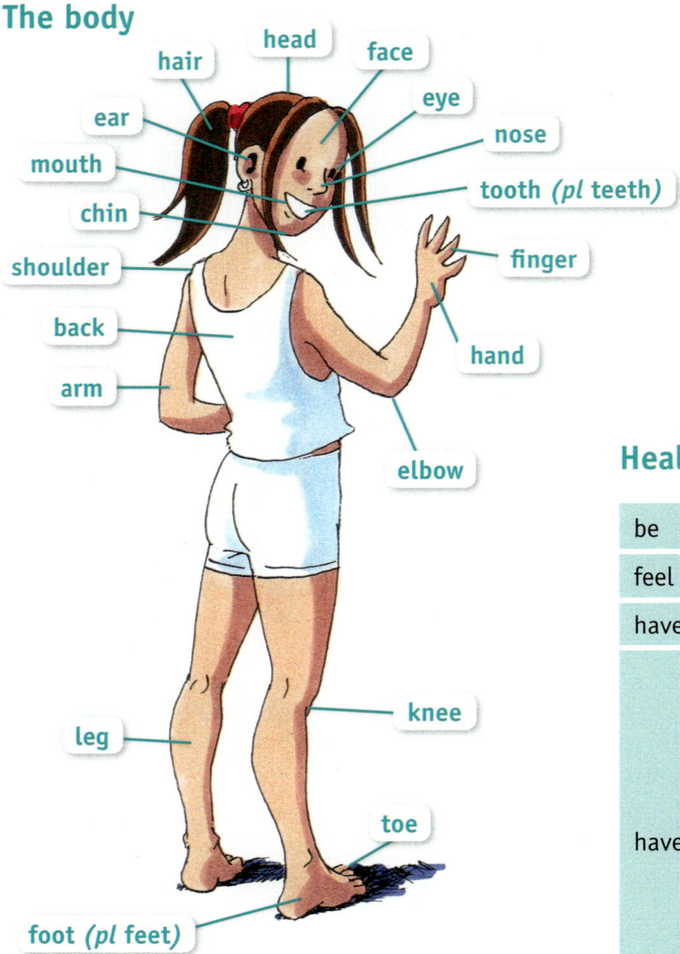

Inside the body

muscle • bone • stomach • ...

Health problems

be	ill/injured
feel	ill
have	a bike accident
have got	an injury a (bad) cold a cut foot a bruised toe a sore leg a broken arm a headache backache toothache stomach ache chickenpox

At the doctor's

What you (the patient) can say:

- My arm hurts.
- I can't move my leg.
- My hand is swollen.
- I've got stomach ache.
- I've got a headache.
- I've broken my finger.
- A dog has bitten me.
- I've fallen off my bike.
- I feel really bad.

What the doctor says:

- What's the problem?
- Where does it hurt? Let me see.
- We'll take an X-ray.
- I'll give you a prescription for some medicine.
- You need a bandage.
- You should put on this cream.
- You have to stay in bed.
- You mustn't play football for two weeks.
- Get well soon!

D Shopping

Shops

bike shop • market stall • pet shop • shopping centre • snack bar • supermarket • sweet shop • toy shop • …

supermarket

pet shop

buy a poster at a stall

go shopping at the market

look for a T-shirt/…

buy ⟷ sell

customer ⟷ seller

cheap ⟷ expensive

How much is/are … ?

Hello. I'm looking for …/ Excuse me, have you got … ?/ Can I have …, please?/ I'd like …, please.

What can I do for you?/ Can I help you?

Yes, I have./Yes, of course. Here you are.

That's too expensive for me./ I haven't got enough money.

Sorry, I don't have any … but I have some …

Have you got anything cheaper?

It's …/They are …

I think I'll take it/them.

Anything else?

No, thank you.

That's £ …

Here you are.

Thank you. Bye.

Thanks. Bye. Have a nice day.

Here's your change.

It's a special offer.

E Travelling

Places and buildings

area • city • town • village •
street • road • department store •
shop • supermarket • market •
restaurant • snack bar •
school • library • hospital •
playground • sports centre •
sports ground • skate park •
swimming pool • football stadium •
adventure centre •
cinema • theatre • museum •
church • castle • statue •
tower • bridge • zoo • park •
farm • factory • airport •
train/underground station • bus stop •
house • flat • room • hotel •
holiday apartment • campsite •
river • lake • mountain • forest •
beach • the sea • island • ...

Places can be ...

- beautiful
- famous
- quiet
- noisy
- busy
- packed with people
- interesting
- boring
- expensive
- clean
- dirty
- safe
- dangerous
- ...

Holiday activities

go sightseeing • take photos of famous sights •
visit a museum/castle/... • go to the park/beach/... •
have a picnic/barbecue • eat ice cream •
relax in the sun • enjoy the weather •
meet new people • write postcards • buy souvenirs •
go shopping/hiking/swimming/... • ...

What did you do?

I went to the zoo.

I visited a castle.

Countries

Germany • Spain •
France • Italy •
Greece • Turkey •
Russia • Poland •
Ireland • Great Britain •
the USA • Australia • ...

Getting around

by bus/train/car/bike/ motorbike/plane/underground/ boat/ship/… • on foot • take the bus/train/car/… • walk/drive/fly to … • miss the bus/train/…

How did you get to Hamburg?

I went there by train. In Hamburg I took the bus.

We went on holiday by plane. We flew to Turkey.

Giving and asking for directions

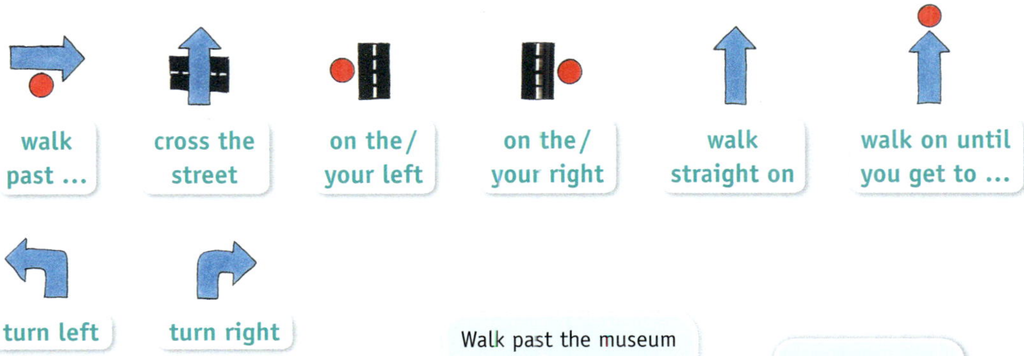

Talking about places/sights

On your left/right you can see … • In front of you there is/are … • Take a look at … • You can go inside and see … • … is the oldest/tallest/… • … is famous because … • My favourite place in town is …

F Celebrations

Happy birthday!

birthday

New Year's Eve

Happy New Year!

Merry Christmas!

Christmas

Celebrations and festivals

New Year's Eve • Halloween • Eid • Christmas • Hanukkah • Easter • wedding • Valentine's Day • birthday • carnival • Mother's Day • Diwali • St Patrick's Day • Chinese New Year • …

My favourite festival is Easter. It is in spring. We look for eggs on Easter Sunday. Afterwards we always have a big family breakfast.

Activities

go to/have a party • have a big meal • cook a special meal • make/bake a cake • go out for dinner • visit friends • celebrate with family and friends • give/get presents • write invitations • send cards • decorate the house • go to bed late • have a great time • wait for the midnight countdown • watch the fireworks • set off fireworks • make/wear a costume • dress up • wear special/traditional clothes • go to church • look for Easter eggs • sing songs • play music • dance • play games • watch a parade • …

Presents

a box of chocolates • a card • a game • flowers • a bottle of perfume • sweets • a cake with candles • a book • earrings • a scarf • a poster • …

presents

a box of chocolates

sweets

flowers

a cake with candles

cards

a book

a bottle of perfume

a scarf

Would you like to come to my party?

Sure. Thanks for the invitation.

G People

family members	other people
• mother – father (parents) • daughter – son • sister – brother • grandmother – grandfather (grandparents) • aunt – uncle • cousin – cousin • relative	• woman – man • wife – husband • girl – boy • child, teenager • friend, classmate • neighbour

Describing people

positive	neutral	negative
good-looking • beautiful • strong • pretty • brave • polite • active • honest • clever • nice • helpful • hard-working • self-confident • optimistic • charming • friendly • creative • successful • funny • ...	small • large • tall • thin • long • short • blond • dark • old • young • strict • rich • poor • careful • slow • fast • quiet • ...	angry • strange • unfriendly • ugly • terrible • mean • silly • stupid • crazy • horrible • ill • ...

Feelings

positive	negative
happy • good • great • surprised • proud • wonderful • excited • glad • fantastic • safe • ...	unhappy • bad • terrible • angry • jealous • lonely • frightened • scared • nervous • bored • sad • surprised • frustrated • shocked • embarrassed • tired • hungry • cold • worried • disappointed • horrible • homesick • ...

You can ...
- be in love with a boy/girl
- love your parents/pet/...
- laugh about a joke
- be proud of your sister/...
- be angry with your brother/...
- be nervous before a test
- be jealous of a classmate/...
- miss a friend/...
- cry because you are sad
- feel embarrassed because ...
- be scared of spiders/...
- be afraid of big dogs/...
- hate cleaning your room

(Best) friends

invite a friend • spend time together • enjoy the same things • talk about problems/... • understand a problem • ask for help • say sorry • ...

H Technology

Technology used at home

microwave • dishwasher • stove • toaster • kettle • fridge • light bulb • …

Technology used for communication

television (TV) • computer • the Internet • radio • stereo • mobile (phone) • phone • …

What we do with technology

turn on ↔ turn off

play computer games

make a presentation

chat with friends

make a phone call

use a microwave • cook a meal • heat water/food • turn on/off the lights • watch TV/a film • listen to the radio • play/download music • make a phone call • talk on the phone • take photos • make a video • work on the computer • make a presentation • search for information • surf the Internet • write/send an email • write/send a text message • order tickets • play (computer/video) games • chat with friends • …

watch TV/a film

download music

order tickets

search for information

use a dishwasher

German	English
Handy	mobile (phone)
SMS	text message
eine SMS schreiben/senden	write/send a text message

I Weather

What's the weather like?

It is ...

hot

warm

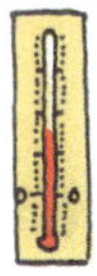

cold

J Clothes

Hurry up and get dressed!

WORDBANKS

K At school

Things in a schoolbag

In the classroom

door • window • board • bookcase • desk • chair • bin • paper • book • schoolbag • computer • map • classroom rules • poster • calendar • …

People and places at school

teacher • student • classmate • headteacher • school building • classroom • cafeteria • library • gym • sports ground • playground • …

Timetables and subjects

	lesson 1	lesson 2		lesson 3	lesson 4		
Monday	English	geography	break	PE (physical education)		lunchtime	IC
Tuesday	history	RE (religious education)		science	art		
Wednesday	ICT (information and communication technology)			maths	chemistry		En
Thursday	drama	biology		music	German		ge
Friday	science	English		maths			h

L Animals

Pets

budgie • parrot • dog • cat • mouse • goldfish • guinea pig • hamster • turtle • rabbit • …

My favourite animal is the hamster. It has got white and orange fur. I like it because it is cute and yummy.

Wild animals

lion • tiger • elephant • giraffe • hippo • kangaroo • bird • monkey • gorilla • zebra • penguin • snake • spider • otter • fish •…

Looking after a pet

feed it • talk to it • go for a walk with it • pet it • play with it • clean its cage • …

Farm animals

duck • chicken • goat • cow • pig • sheep • lamb • horse • pony • …

M Jobs

I'd like to be a firefighter! What will you be when you grow up?

jobs	what people with these jobs do
actor/actress • builder • cook • doctor • farmer • firefighter • gardener • hairdresser • (zoo) keeper • nurse • police officer • shop assistant • technician • waiter/waitress • …	act in films or plays • repair and build houses • cook meals in a restaurant • take care of ill people • work on a farm; feed farm animals • fight fires • work in a park; look after flowers, plants and trees • wash, cut and style people's hair • look after animals in a zoo • look after ill people in a hospital • catch gangsters; keep people and the streets safe • work in a shop; help customers; sell things • repair things • serve customers in a café or restaurant • …

I think I will be a nurse because I like helping people.

I'd like to be a technician. I'm good at working with my hands.

N Time

What time is it, please?

It's six forty-seven./ It's thirteen minutes to seven.

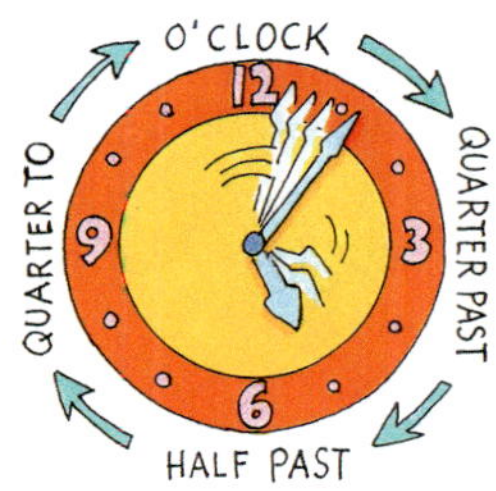

days of the week
- Monday
- Tuesday
- Wednesday
- Thursday
- Friday
- Saturday
- Sunday

months
- December, January, February – winter
- March, April, May – spring
- June, July, August – summer
- September, October, November – autumn

When?
- on Monday/ Tuesday/…
- in the morning/ afternoon/evening
- in (the year) 2014
- at the weekend
- at five o'clock
- last Monday/week/ year/…
- three days/… ago
- before
- after (that)
- afterwards
- then
- later
- finally

How often?
- always
- often
- usually
- sometimes
- never
- once/twice/three times a day/…

Wenn man ankommt oder geht

Good morning.	Guten Morgen.
Sorry, I'm late.	Tut mir leid, dass ich zu spät komme.
Sorry, I don't have my exercise book with me.	Tut mir leid, ich habe mein Heft nicht dabei.
Sorry, I don't have my homework with me.	Tut mir leid, ich habe meine Hausaufgaben nicht dabei.
What's for homework?	Was haben wir als Hausaufgabe auf?
See you tomorrow.	Bis morgen.

Wenn es ein Problem gibt

What's the matter with you?	Was ist mit dir los?
I'm fine./I feel sick.	Mir geht's gut./Mir ist schlecht.
I've got a headache.	Ich habe Kopfschmerzen.
Can I open the window, please?	Kann ich bitte das Fenster öffnen?
Can I go to the toilet, please?	Kann ich bitte zur Toilette gehen?

Wenn man Hilfe braucht

Can you help me, please?	Können Sie/Kannst du mir bitte helfen?
I've got a question.	Ich habe eine Frage.
I don't understand this.	Ich verstehe das hier nicht.
How can I do this exercise?	Wie mache ich diese Aufgabe?
What's ... in English/German?	Was heißt ... auf Englisch/Deutsch?
What does ... mean?	Was bedeutet ... ?
Can you write it on the board, please?	Können Sie/Kannst du das bitte an die Tafel schreiben?
Can you say it again, please?	Können Sie/Kannst du das bitte noch einmal sagen?
Sorry, I don't know.	Tut mir leid, das weiß ich nicht.
What page, please?	Auf welcher Seite bitte?

Wenn man zusammen arbeitet oder spielt

Whose turn is it?	Wer ist dran?
I (don't) like this story.	Diese Geschichte gefällt mir (nicht).
I think it's good/interesting/funny.	Ich finde ... gut/interessant/komisch.
I think it's terrible/boring/sad.	Ich finde ... schrecklich/langweilig/traurig.
Do you want to work with me?	Möchtest du mit mir arbeiten?

Wenn man mit dem Computer arbeitet

What's your email address?	Was ist deine E-Mail-Adresse?
You can click on this link.	Du kannst auf diesen Link klicken.
Can I print it out/download it?	Kann ich das ausdrucken/herunterladen?
I saved it.	Ich habe es abgespeichert.
My computer has crashed.	Mein Computer ist abgestürzt.

Was die Lehrerin oder der Lehrer sagt

Open your books at page ...	Öffnet eure Bücher auf Seite ...
Turn to page ...	Blättert zu Seite ...
Look at line ...	Seht euch Zeile ... an.
Read the text on page ...	Lies/Lest den Text auf Seite ...
Work in pairs.	Arbeitet zu zweit.
Work in groups of four/five/...	Arbeitet zu viert/fünft/...
Sit in a circle.	Bildet einen Sitzkreis.
Listen to the CD/MP3/...	Hör/Hört die CD/MP3/... an.
Write about ...	Schreibe/Schreibt über ...
Talk about ...	Sprich/Sprecht über ...
Ask questions about ...	Stelle/Stellt Fragen zu ...
Answer the question, please.	Beantworte/Beantwortet bitte die Frage.
Match the sentences.	Ordne/Ordnet die Sätze zu.
Who wants to read the text?	Wer möchte den Text vorlesen?
Write down the answers.	Schreibe/Schreibt die Antworten auf.
Act out the dialogue.	Spiel/Spielt den Dialog vor.
Change roles.	Tauscht die Rollen.
Make your own dialogue.	Entwirf/Entwerft selbst ein Gespräch.
Take a card.	Nimm/Nehmt eine Karte.
Come to the blackboard, please.	Komm/Kommt bitte zur Tafel.
Collect the exercise books, please.	Sammle/Sammelt bitte die Hefte ein.
Do this exercise at home, please.	Mach/Macht diese Aufgabe bitte zu Hause.
Please be quiet.	Sei/Seid bitte ruhig.
Please sit down.	Setz dich/Setzt euch bitte.
Please speak up.	Sprich/Sprecht bitte lauter.
You can do better.	Du kannst das besser.
Try again.	Versuch es noch einmal.
That's it.	Das ist alles.
Well done.	Gut gemacht.

A ... work with words

KV3–6

So kannst du Wörter notieren und besser behalten

- Sieh dir die *wordbanks* in deinem Buch an (Seite 152 bis 165). Erstelle dann zu bestimmten Themen Bildwörterbuch-Seiten für dich oder als Poster für das Klassenzimmer.

- Sammle Wörter, die zu einem Oberbegriff passen, in einer Tabelle. Du kannst auch ein Wortnetz (*word web*) zu einem Thema anlegen. Ergänze dein Wortnetz, wenn du neue Wörter zu dem Thema lernst.

nouns	verbs	adjectives
knife	cook	hot
pan	cut	delicious
...	...	...

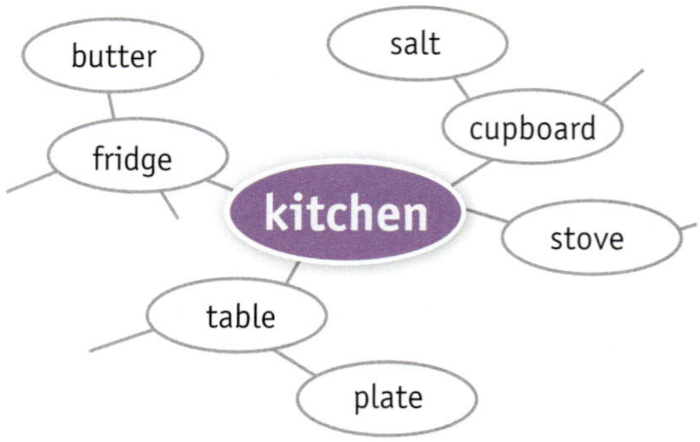

- Sammle Gegensatzpaare und schreibe sie auf.

soft ↔ *hard*　　　*delicious* ↔ *disgusting*

- Viele Wörter werden ähnlich gebildet. Notiere dir diese Wörter zusammen auf einem Zettel oder einer Karteikarte.

fair ↔ unfair
happy ↔ unhappy

rain ↔ rainy
fun ↔ funny

play ↔ player
teach ↔ teacher

- Bilde Sätze mit den Wörtern, die du dir merken willst. Sie können auch lustig sein oder sich reimen.

My mum can make a yummy cake.

- Schreibe Wörter auf Klebezettel und hänge sie zu Hause an verschiedenen Stellen auf. So hast du sie immer im Blick.

- Wenn du gerne am Computer arbeitest, dann benutze die Lernsoftware.

TIPP

- Deine Bildwörterbuch-Seiten, Tabellen, Wortnetze und vieles mehr kannst du in einem Vokabelordner abheften und dort beliebig ergänzen.
- Übe Vokabeln immer nur fünf bis zehn Minuten, aber dafür regelmäßig!
- Zu zweit macht das Vokabellernen mehr Spaß. Fragt euch gegenseitig ab. Ihr könnt auch selbst Lückentexte, Kreuzwort- oder Buchstabenrätsel für den Partner/die Partnerin erstellen.

B ... work with an English-German dictionary

Das richtige deutsche Wort finden

Wenn du ein englisches Wort nicht verstehst, kannst du ein Wörterbuch zu Hilfe nehmen.
Hier findest du ein paar Hinweise, wie das geht:

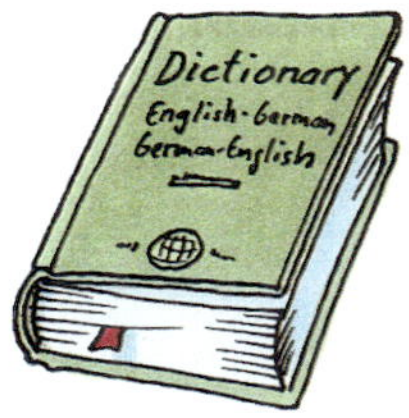

1. Wonach du suchen solltest

- Die meisten Wörter wirst du schnell finden. Manche Wörter stehen jedoch nicht so im Wörterbuch, wie man sie in englischen Texten findet. Wenn du z. B. das Wort *cheers* in dem Satz *Charlie cheers on his football team* nicht verstehst, wirst du *cheers* nicht im Wörterbuch finden. Dort steht nämlich nur die Grundform (Infinitiv) *cheer* – und danach musst du suchen.

2. Orientiere dich an den Leitwörtern

- Beim Nachschlagen im Wörterbuch kannst du dich an den Leitwörtern oben auf den Seiten orientieren. Die Leitwörter sagen dir, welche Wörter auf der jeweiligen Seite zu finden sind.

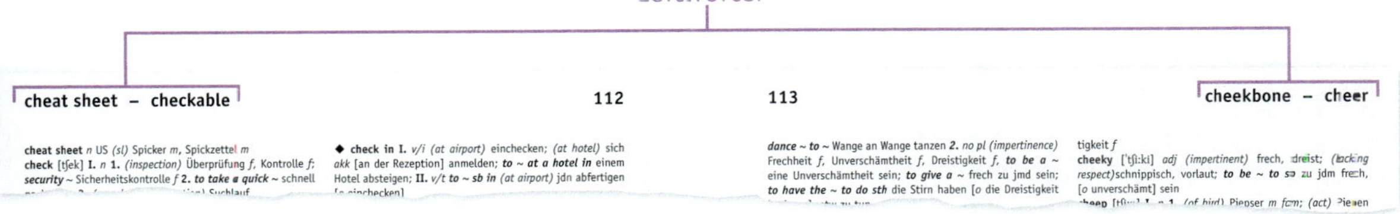

cheat sheet – checkable 112

cheat sheet *n* US *(sl)* Spicker *m*, Spickzettel *m*
check [tʃek] **I.** *n* **1.** *(inspection)* Überprüfung *f*, Kontrolle *f*; ***security*** ~ Sicherheitskontrolle *f* **2.** ***to take a quick*** ~ schnell

◆ **check in I.** *v/i (at airport)* einchecken; *(at hotel)* sich *akk* [an der Rezeption] anmelden; ***to ~ at a hotel in*** einem Hotel absteigen; **II.** *v/t* ***to ~ sb in*** *(at airport)* jdn abfertigen

113 **cheekbone – cheer**

dance ~ to ~ Wange an Wange tanzen **2.** *no pl (impertinence)* Frechheit *f*, Unverschämtheit *f*, Dreistigkeit *f*, ***to be a ~*** eine Unverschämtheit sein; ***to give a ~*** frech zu jmd sein; ***to have the ~ to do sth*** die Stirn haben [*o* die Dreistigkeit

tigkeit *f*
cheeky [ˈtʃiːki] *adj (impertinent)* frech, dreist; *(lacking respect)* schnippisch, vorlaut; ***to be ~ to sb*** zu jdm frech, [*o* unverschämt] sein

3. Finde die passende Übersetzung

- Hast du *cheer* im Wörterbuch gefunden, wirst du sehen, dass es dort mehrere Einträge gibt.
- Die Abkürzungen geben dir Auskunft über die Wortarten.

  n = *noun*
  v/i oder v/t = *verb*
  adj = *adjective*
  conj = *conjunction*

cheer [tʃɪə, US tʃɪr] **I.** *n* **1.** *(shout)* Hurraruf *m*, Beifallsruf *m*; *(cheering)* Jubel *m*; ***three ~ s for the champion!*** ein dreifaches Hoch auf den Sieger!; ***two ~s*** super! **2.** *no pl (joy)* Jubel *m*, Freude *f*
II. *v/i* ***to ~ for sb*** jdn anfeuern
◆ **cheer on** *v/t* ***to ~ sb on*** jdn anfeuern
◆ **cheer up 1.** *v/i* vergnügt[er] werden; ***~ up!*** lass denn Kopf nicht hängen!, Kopf hoch!; **2.** *v/t* ***to ~ sb up*** jdn aufheitern

Zu welcher Wortart gehört *cheers* in unserem Satz? Genau, es ist ein Verb.

- Sieh dir nun für das Verb *cheer* alle Übersetzungen an. Hier findest du auch ***cheer on*** als zusammengesetzten Ausdruck. Das Zeichen (~) ist ein Platzhalter, hier für das Verb.
- Nun kannst du den Satz *Charlie cheers on his football team* übersetzen: Charlie feuert seine Fußballmannschaft an.

C ... work with a German-English dictionary

Das richtige englische Wort finden

Auch wenn du deutsche Wörter oder Sätze ins Englische übersetzen willst, kann dir ein Wörterbuch dabei helfen.

1. Bevor du zum Wörterbuch greifst

- Überlege, ob du auch ohne Wörterbuch auskommst. Vielleicht kennst du ja ein deutsches Wort mit gleicher oder ähnlicher Bedeutung. Wenn du z. B. das englische Wort für „verlassen" nicht kennst, kannst du auch *go away* (weggehen) sagen.
- Du kannst auch versuchen, deinen deutschen Satz zu vereinfachen. Anstatt „Tom verbringt gerne Zeit im Einkaufszentrum" kannst du einfach sagen „Tom mag das Einkaufszentrum". Dafür brauchst du kein Wörterbuch.

2. Wörter nachschlagen

- Nimm nicht gleich die erste Übersetzung, wenn du Wörter im Wörterbuch nachschlägst. Für viele deutsche Wörter gibt es verschiedene Übersetzungen. Sieh dir deshalb deinen deutschen Satz genau an, bevor du wählst: „Zu Weihnachten gibt es bei uns **Plätzchen**." Hier passt die Übersetzung ***biscuit*** am besten.

f, *m* oder *nt* geben an, ob das Wort weiblich (*f*), männlich (*m*) oder sächlich (*nt*) ist.

Plätzchen *nt* **1.** *dim von* **Platz** spot, little place **2.** *(Gebäck)* biscuit *(Brit)*, cookie *(US)*

Zusätze wie *Gebäck* verraten, in welchem Zusammenhang ein Wort gebraucht wird.

US = American English
Brit = British English

- Wenn du Verben nachschlägst, solltest du immer nach der Grundform (Infinitiv) suchen. Für den Satz „Meine Tante **reist** drei Tage vor Ende des Ramadans **an**" schlägst du also „anreisen" nach.

anreisen *v/i sein* **1.** *(ein Ziel anfahren)* to travel [here/there]; ***reist du mit dem eigenen Wagen an?*** will you be travelling [*or* coming] by car? **2.** *(eintreffen)* to arrive

3. Wörter überprüfen

- Wenn du nicht sicher bist, ob das englische Wort wirklich passt, überprüfe es noch einmal. Schlage es im englisch-deutschen Teil deines Wörterbuches nach. Dort findest du oft weitere Verwendungsbeispiele und auch die Lautschrift, falls du Hilfe bei der Aussprache brauchst.

D ... listen

Ohren auf! Worum geht es überhaupt?

Du kennst ja schon einige Tricks, wie du einen Hörtext besser verstehen kannst:

1. Vor dem Hören

- Wie lautet die Überschrift des Hörtextes? Welche Hinweise gibt sie dir?
- Gibt es Bilder zum Text? Was ist zu sehen?
- Überlege: Worum könnte es wohl gehen? Was weißt du schon über das Thema? Was erwartest du?

2. Beim Hören

- Höre dir das Gespräch oder die Geschichte einmal ganz an. Du musst nicht jedes einzelne Wort verstehen. Versuche herauszufinden, worum es geht. Wer ist beteiligt? Was passiert?
  Achte auch auf die Geräusche. Sie geben dir oft Hinweise auf den Ort und das Geschehen. Wie klingen die Stimmen der Personen? Begeistert? Aufgeregt?
- Lies dir die Höraufgabe im Buch genau durch. Was sollst du herausfinden?
  Höre dir das Gespräch oder die Geschichte ein zweites Mal an. Kannst du die Höraufgabe im Buch jetzt lösen? Wenn nicht, dann höre dir den Text noch ein weiteres Mal an.
- Wenn es zu einem Hörtext keine Aufgabe gibt, können dir diese Fragen weiterhelfen:

Who? (Wer spricht? Um wen geht es?)	**Where?** (Wo findet das Gespräch/ die Geschichte statt?)	**When?** (Wann findet es/ sie statt?)	**What?** (Worüber wird gesprochen? Was passiert?)

- Mache dir Notizen zu den Fragen, auf die du eine Antwort weißt.

3. Zu guter Letzt

- Vergleiche deine Ergebnisse mit einer Partnerin oder einem Partner. Was habt ihr herausgefunden? Haben sich eure Erwartungen bestätigt?

TIPP

Nutze jede Gelegenheit, um Englisch zu hören!
- Mit der *Camden Market*-CD kannst du zu Hause dein Hörverstehen trainieren.
- Höre dir englische Musik an und achte auf den Text. Was kannst du schon verstehen?
- Sieh dir einen Film, den du schon kennst, auf Englisch an. Fast alle Filme sind mit englischem Ton (mit oder ohne Untertitel) erhältlich.

E ... read

Lesen leicht gemacht

Es gibt viele Tricks, die dir helfen, einen englischen Text leichter zu verstehen. Probiere doch einmal die folgenden Tipps beim Lesen aus:

1. Was verrät das Bild? Um was für einen Text handelt es sich? Worum könnte es in dem Text gehen?

2. Was erfährst du aus der Überschrift?

He's young, he's fast, he's great! This young man is going to make it to the top. Leroy Haffner will soon be one of Britain's best swimmers!

Leroy was born in Bristol, UK. Swimming has always been his greatest love. He started swimming at the age of four. Three years later he had already won medals for his local club. The pool became the centre of his life and he took part in one national competition after another.

Then last year Leroy had an injury and couldn't swim for nearly two months. It was the worst time of his life. But Leroy is a fighter and he didn't give up. He started swimming again – and with great success.

Next week Leroy will participate in the National Championships. His coach, Ted Henley, knows that "Leroy will do really, really well".

3. Überfliege den Text erst einmal. Versuche herauszufinden, worum es geht. Was passiert? Wer ist beteiligt? Dafür brauchst du nicht jedes Wort zu verstehen.

4. Lies den Text noch einmal gründlich. Mit den *wh*-Fragen kannst du die wichtigsten Informationen herausbekommen:
Who?
Where?
When?
What?

Mach dir Notizen!

Wenn du einen Text verstehen und eine Aufgabe dazu bearbeiten willst, können dir Notizen helfen. Dabei gibt es verschiedene Möglichkeiten:

- Lies dir die einzelnen Absätze genau durch und finde heraus, worum es in ihnen geht. Notiere dir für jeden Absatz die wichtigste Information.
- Oft ist es hilfreich, Informationen in einer Tabelle zu sammeln, z. B. positive und negative Punkte. Informationen, die voneinander abhängen, kannst du auch gut in einem Wortnetz strukturieren.

TIPP

So kannst du die Bedeutung eines Wortes ohne Wörterbuch herausfinden:

- Oft kennst du ein deutsches Wort, das ganz ähnlich aussieht, z. B. *medal* oder *centre*.
- Überlege, ob du ein englisches Wort aus der gleichen Wortfamilie, also einen „Verwandten", kennst, z. B. *fight* – *fighter*.
- Häufig kannst du die Bedeutung eines unbekannten Wortes aus dem Satzzusammenhang erschließen. Dabei helfen dir die Wörter, die vor oder nach dem unbekannten Wort stehen. Was könnten die Wörter *injury* und *participate* im Text oben bedeuten?

F ... give a talk

Wenn du etwas vor der Klasse präsentierst

1. Bevor du etwas vorträgst

- Überlege: Was ist dein Thema? Was möchtest du sagen? Wie viel Zeit hast du für deinen Vortrag?
- Sammle deine Gedanken und schreibe sie in Stichpunkten auf, z. B. in einem *word web* oder auf Karteikarten.
- Entscheide, in welcher Reihenfolge du die Dinge sagen und wie du anfangen möchtest.
- Fertige ein Poster oder eine Folie an, um deinen Vortrag anschaulich zu machen. Du kannst aber auch eine *PowerPoint*-Präsentation gestalten.
- Übe deinen Vortrag vor dem Spiegel, vor Freunden oder deiner Familie – oder nimm deinen Vortrag zur Probe auf, z. B. mit einem Handy oder einem Easi-Speak-Mikrofon.

TIPP

So sieht ein gelungenes Vortrags-Poster aus:

- ansprechende Überschrift
- interessante Informationen
- verständliche Sätze, aber: nicht zu viel Text
- große Bilder und Schrift: → Jeder im Raum muss sie sehen und lesen können.
- saubere Schrift
- Bilder mit Bildunterschriften

2. Bei deinem Vortrag

- Sprich langsam und deutlich.
- Sieh deine Zuhörer an, wenn du sprichst.
- Versuche, frei zu sprechen. Du kannst die wichtigsten Punkte von deinen Notizen, deinen Karteikarten oder deinem Poster/deiner Folie ablesen.
- Zeige deinen Zuhörern auf deinem Poster oder deiner Folie, worüber du gerade sprichst. So wird dein Vortrag für die Klasse noch interessanter.

3. Nützliche Redewendungen

Zu Beginn deines Vortrags:	*Hello, everybody. My talk is about .../I'd like to talk about ...*
	First of all, I'm going to ... Then I'll talk about ... Finally I'll ...
Im Hauptteil:	*On my poster you can see ...*
	Look at this picture. It shows ...
	Another thing I want to tell you about is ...
Wenn du mal den Faden verlierst:	*Just a moment, please./Wait a second.*
Zum Schluss:	*Thank you for listening. Have you got any questions?*

G ... talk

Du kannst reden!

Für die Partner- und Gruppenarbeit im Englischunterricht findest du hier einige nützliche Redewendungen und Tipps:

Wenn du mit jemandem zusammenarbeitest

- *Can I be Rajiv/Gillian/... ?*
- *Whose turn is it? – It's your turn.*
- *Sorry, have you finished? Can I say something now?*
- *Can you explain that, please?*
- *Can you say it again, please?*

Wenn du einen Vorschlag machen möchtest

- *Let's do it like this.*
- *You/We could write something different here.*
- *Why don't you/we change this?*

Wenn du Rückmeldung/Feedback geben möchtest

- Nenne zuerst immer die Dinge, die dir gut gefallen haben. Dann kannst du Kritik äußern und Verbesserungsvorschläge machen.

- **Zu einem Vortrag:** *Your presentation was/wasn't easy to understand. It was/wasn't really interesting. You spoke/didn't speak loudly and clearly.*
- **Zu einem Poster:** *Your poster looks/doesn't look attractive/interesting. The text is (not) too long. You could use more pictures.*
- **Zu einer Geschichte:** *I (don't) like your story because it is ... I would use more adjectives/...*
- **Zu einem Rollenspiel:** *André was/wasn't very good as Rajiv because he ...*

- Wenn dir ein Wort mal nicht einfällt, kannst du es umschreiben.
- Im Gespräch solltest du immer höflich sein. Verwende deshalb *sorry*, *please* und *thank you*.

TIPP

Sprich Englisch, sooft du kannst!
- Höre dir die *Camden Market*-CD an und lies die Texte laut mit. Versuche, die Aussprache der Sprecher nachzuahmen. Du kannst auch englische Lieder mitsingen.
- Lies einen Text aus dem Buch laut vor oder sprich Englisch und nimm dich auf. Dann kannst du dich selbst anhören und überprüfen, wie dein Englisch klingt.
- Sprich Englisch mit jemandem, der ebenfalls Englisch sprechen kann.

H ... talk about pictures

Über Bilder sprechen und sie beschreiben

Um ein Bild oder Foto zu beschreiben, gehst du am besten so vor:

1. Fange allgemein an

- Sage erst einmal, was du auf dem Bild oder Foto allgemein siehst.
  In the picture I can see a street with lots of people.

2. Wähle eine bestimmte Reihenfolge

- Sage nun, wen oder was du siehst und wo sich die Personen, Tiere und Gegenstände befinden. Dabei macht es Sinn, eine bestimmte Reihenfolge zu wählen: von links nach rechts oder von oben nach unten.
  ***In the middle**/**On the left**/**On the right** I can see ...*
  ***At the top** there is ...*
  ***At the bottom** there are ...*

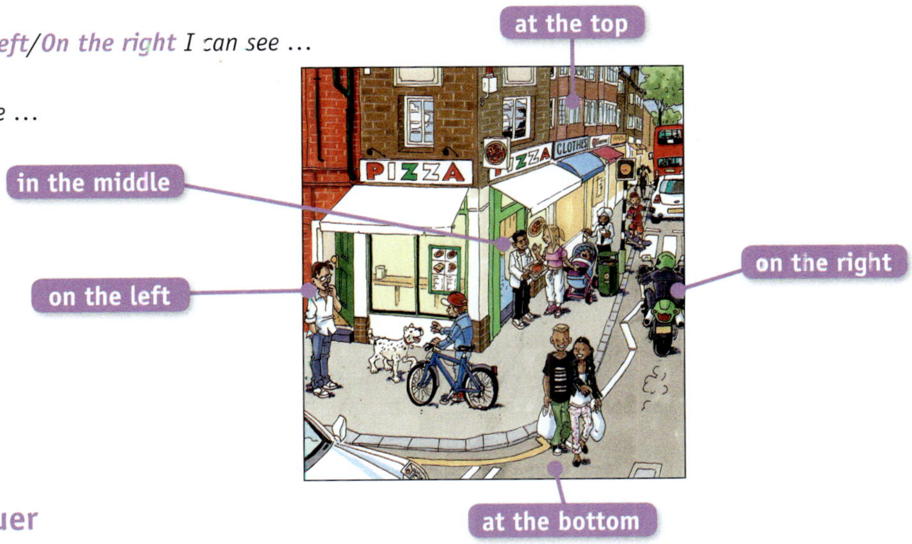

3. Werde nun genauer

- Benutze Präpositionen wie *in, on, in front of, behind, next to, between, over* oder *under*, um genauer zu beschreiben, wo sich eine Person, ein Tier oder ein Gegenstand befindet.
  *There is a dog **in front of** the pizza place.*
  *There are two cars **in** the street.*
  *The young man with the green trousers is **next to** the woman with long black hair.*

4. Beschreibe, was passiert

- Beschreibe, was die abgebildeten Personen oder Tiere tun. Benutze dazu das *present progressive*.
  *The man on the left **is watching** the boy with the red cap.*
  *The two young people at the bottom **are carrying** shopping bags.*
  *The boy with the skateboard on the right **is crossing** the street.*

I ... write

Tipps und Tricks zum Schreiben

1. Plane deinen Text

- Überlege: Was für einen Text willst du schreiben?
- Sammle Ideen und Wörter zum Thema deines Textes, z. B. in einem *word web* oder einer Liste.
- Bringe deine Ideen und Wörter in eine sinnvolle Reihenfolge.

2. Schreibe den Text

- Schreibe erst einmal kurze, einfache Sätze auf. Oder:
- Sieh dir Texte im Buch an, die sich mit dem Thema beschäftigen. Du kannst nützliche Satzanfänge und Ausdrücke übernehmen.
- Fange deine Sätze unterschiedlich an.
  Nick likes music. Nick plays the drums. ➔ *Nick likes music. He plays the drums.*
- Verbinde deine Ideen und Sätze mit *linking words* wie *and, or, but, so, because*:
  I often go to the park. I can play football there. ➔ *I often go to the park because I can play football there.*
- Benutze *time words*, um zu sagen, wann etwas geschieht, z. B. *in the morning, then, later, after (that), yesterday*:
  Karla read in bed. She played with her rabbit. ➔ *In the morning Karla read in bed. After that she played with her rabbit.*
- Adjektive und Adverbien machen deinen Text interessanter.
  Charlie ran forward and scored a goal. ➔ *Charlie ran forward quickly and scored a fantastic goal.*
- Überlege dir eine passende Überschrift.

3. Überarbeite deinen Text

- Sieh dir deinen Text noch einmal genau an. Hast du alles richtig geschrieben? Schlage schwierige Wörter im Wörterbuch nach.
- Bist du bei der Grammatik unsicher? Schau im LiF-Teil ab Seite 180 nach.
- Tauscht eure Texte untereinander aus. Sprecht darüber, was euch an dem Text gefällt, was noch ergänzt werden könnte und was verbessert werden sollte.
- Wenn du deinen Text fertig hast, schreibe ihn ins Reine.

4. Präsentiere deinen Text

- Du kannst deinen Text nun präsentieren, indem du ihn z. B. vorliest, aufnimmst, aushängst oder in einem *class book* veröffentlichst. Danach heftest du deinen Text in deiner Portfolio-Mappe ab.

J ... write a letter

So kannst du einen persönlichen Brief schreiben

Auch hier gehst du am besten Schritt für Schritt vor:

1. Deine Adresse (ohne deinen Namen) gehört in die rechte obere Ecke.

2. Das Datum folgt unter der Adresse auf der rechten Seite.

3. Beginne deinen Brief an einen Freund oder eine Freundin mit *Dear ...,* oder *Hi ...,*

4. Fange die erste Zeile mit einem Großbuchstaben an.

5. Worüber möchtest du schreiben? Vielleicht darüber, was du am Wochenende erlebt hast? Dann benutze die Vergangenheit (*simple past*): *I went, I played, ...* Denke auch an *linking words* und *time words* (siehe *How to ... write* auf Seite 174).

6. Am Ende deines Briefes kannst du deinem Freund oder deiner Freundin Fragen stellen. Du kannst ihn oder sie auch bitten, dir zurückzuschreiben.

7. So kannst du deinen Brief beenden: *Best wishes, Love, Lots of love, Yours, All the best, ...*

Waldschmidtstraße 39
60316 Frankfurt
Germany

4th April 20..

Dear Harry,

How are you?

I'm OK. Last week I had to work really hard for school: lots of homework and three tests! So I couldn't wait for the weekend.

On Saturday I went to my friend Jan's birthday party. First we played football in the park. Then we went home and made pizza. After that we watched a cool film.

On Sunday I wanted to go to the youth club but my mum was against it. I had to tidy up my room instead and help her with the cooking. It's always: "Do this, don't do that". Sometimes I really can't stand her.

What are your parents like? Do you have similar problems?

Please write back soon.

All the best,
Simon

TIPP

- Sieh dir deinen Brief noch einmal genau an. Hast du alles richtig geschrieben?
- Hast du die richtige Zeitform verwendet?
- Ist dein Ton höflich und freundlich?
- Schreibe die Adresse gut leserlich auf den Briefumschlag – und ab geht die Post!
- Übrigens: E-Mails schreibst du ganz ähnlich.

K ... work with others

Zusammen seid ihr stark!

Think – pair – share

Um Ideen zu einem Thema zu sammeln, kannst du in drei Schritten vorgehen:

1. *Think:* Sammle deine Gedanken und Ideen und mache dir Notizen.
2. *Pair:* Tausche dich mit einem Partner/einer Partnerin aus. Ergänze neue Ideen in deiner Liste.
3. *Share:* Teilt dann eure Gedanken und Ideen mit einem anderen Paar. Nun habt ihr schon Ideen und Meinungen von vier verschiedenen Leuten kennengelernt.

Buzz groups

Bei dieser Arbeitsform sprecht ihr alle mit leiser Stimme, damit sich die verschiedenen Gruppen nicht gegenseitig stören. *Buzz* heißt summen oder brummen und beschreibt den Geräuschpegel, der dabei im Raum entsteht.

1. Bildet *buzz groups* mit drei bis fünf Gruppenmitgliedern. Sprecht über das vorgegebene Thema. Ein Gruppenmitglied macht Notizen.
2. Wählt einen Sprecher/eine Sprecherin, der/die die Ergebnisse eurer *buzz group* in der Klasse vorstellt.

Milling around

Mit der Methode *milling around* (auf Deutsch: umherlaufen) kannst du dich mit deinen Klassenkameraden zu einem Thema (z. B. *favourite food*) austauschen.

1. Gehe durch die Klasse, ohne dass du dabei sprichst.
2. Wenn dein Lehrer/deine Lehrerin ein Zeichen gibt oder „Stop!“ sagt, sprich mit der Person, vor der du gerade stehst. Tauscht euch über die Aufgabe aus.
3. Notiere deine Ergebnisse und gehe weiter.

Dramatic reading

Um einen Text mit verschiedenen Rollen lebendig vorzutragen, bietet sich *dramatic reading* an:

1. Lies den Text zu deiner Rolle mit leiser Stimme mehrmals durch.
2. Schaue dir jeden Satz einzeln an und präge ihn dir ein. Sieh dann hoch und sprich den Satz nach. Schaue deine Gruppenmitglieder dabei an. Arbeite den ganzen Text auf diese Weise durch.
3. Überlege, wie sich die Person gerade fühlt, deren Rolle du liest. Ist sie verärgert, fröhlich, ... ? Versuche, die Sätze entsprechend zu lesen und zu betonen.

Double circle

Auch dies ist eine Arbeitsform, bei der du die Ideen und Gedanken von vielen verschiedenen Leuten in deiner Klasse erfährst.

1. Bildet in der Klasse zwei Kreise: einen Innenkreis und einen Außenkreis.
2. Diejenigen von euch, die sich gegenüberstehen, unterhalten sich über ein vorher bestimmtes Thema (z. B. *plans for the summer holidays*).
3. Wenn dein Lehrer/deine Lehrerin ein Zeichen gibt, dreht ihr euch in den beiden Kreisen in entgegengesetzte Richtungen weiter. Nun tauscht ihr euch mit einem neuen Partner/einer neuen Partnerin über das Thema aus.

Placemat

Auf einer *placemat* (auf Deutsch: Tischvorlage, Platzdeckchen) sammelst du mit deinen Gruppenmitgliedern zu einem Thema gleichzeitig Ideen.

1. Jede/r von euch macht auf einem Teil eines großen Bogens Papier Notizen.
2. Anschließend dreht ihr die *placemat* so lange, bis jede/r alle Beiträge gelesen hat.
3. Einigt euch dann in der Gruppe auf gemeinsame Gedanken und notiert sie in der Mitte des Blattes.
4. Schließlich stellt ein Gruppenmitglied das Ergebnis in der Klasse vor.

Bus stop

Bei dieser Arbeitsform tauscht du dich mit einem Mitschüler/einer Mitschülerin über ein Arbeitsergebnis aus.

1. Arbeite alleine an der vorgegebenen Aufgabe.
2. Gehe, wenn du fertig bist, mit deinem Arbeitsergebnis zu einem Treffpunkt im Klassenzimmer. Dieser ist als *bus stop* gekennzeichnet.
3. Warte dort auf einen Mitschüler/eine Mitschülerin, der/die ebenfalls fertig ist, und vergleicht eure Ergebnisse.

Gallery walk

Wenn verschiedene Arbeitsgruppen Produkte (z. B. Poster) erstellt haben, könnt ihr einen Rundgang in der Klasse durchführen.

1. Hängt die Poster an verschiedenen Stellen im Klassenzimmer auf.
2. Findet euch dann in neuen Gruppen zusammen, sodass in jeder Arbeitsgruppe ein Mitglied jeder Arbeitsgruppe vertreten ist.
3. Die Gruppen gehen von Poster zu Poster, und der jeweilige Experte/die jeweilige Expertin erklärt sein/ihr Poster.

L ... work with grammar

Grammatikregeln auf der Spur

Versuche, Grammatikregeln selbst aufzuspüren. Auf diese Weise kannst du sie nämlich besser behalten. Das folgende Beispiel soll dir zeigen, wie das gehen kann.

1. Sammeln

Schaue dir englische Texte an. Sammle mehrere Beispiele für eine Grammatikregel, z. B. für die Zeitform *present perfect*.

2. Sortieren

Schreibe die Beispiele untereinander. Was fällt dir (bei den Verbformen) auf? Was sieht hier ähnlich aus? Unterstreiche die Stellen.

> I have been to England.
> Nikola has never eaten sushi.
> My parents have met a famous singer.

3. Beschreiben

Sieh dir deine Beispiele gut an. Was kannst du erkennen? Welche Veränderung tritt immer wieder auf? Beschreibe und notiere dann deine Regel.

> Das present perfect wird mit have oder has + dritte Verbform gebildet.

4. Überprüfen

Schaue nun im LiF-Teil ab Seite 180 nach, ob du richtigliegst. Ändere oder ergänze deine Regel falls nötig.

TIPP

- Auf den Seiten 282 und 283 findest du die Verben, die eine unregelmäßige dritte Verbform (Partizip Perfect – *past participle*) haben. Diese Verben musst du dir gut einprägen. Aber keine Sorge: Viele Verben werden ähnlich gebildet, z. B. *bring – brought – brought, buy – bought – bought, think – thought – thought* oder *sleep – slept – slept, keep – kept – kept, leave – left – left*.
- Schreibe Grammatikregeln in deinen eigenen Worten auf und ergänze Beispiele und Merksätze. Umrande die Grammatikregeln farbig und schreibe den Grammatikbegriff (z. B. *present perfect*) auf den Blattrand. So findest du die Regeln beim Nachschlagen schnell wieder.
- Versucht, euch gegenseitig Grammatikregeln zu erklären.

M ... help out

So kannst du jemandem sprachlich aushelfen

Du kannst anderen Menschen helfen, die kaum Deutsch oder Englisch verstehen.
Hier erfährst du, wie das funktioniert:

1. Gib den Sinn wieder

Du musst nicht Wort für Wort übersetzen. Wichtiger ist es, den Sinn einer Aussage oder Information wiederzugeben. Das kannst du auch in deinen eigenen Worten machen.

2. Umschreibe Wörter

Da du in solchen Situationen oft kein Wörterbuch zur Hand hast, kannst du wichtige Wörter auch umschreiben.

3. Bilde kurze Sätze

Bilde einfache, kurze Sätze, wenn du den Sinn wiedergibst.

Lemon Curd

There are only three ingredients in this British speciality: eggs, sugar and ... lemons, of course! You cook them together to make a thick yellow cream. Many people eat it on toast or scones, but it is often put in a dessert called lemon meringue pie, too. Or you can just eat it with a spoon!

Was ist denn *Lemon Curd*?

Das ist eine Creme aus Eiern, Zucker und Zitronen.

LiF steht für *Language in Focus*. Das ist der Grammatikteil von *Camden Market*, in dem die englische Sprache genauer unter die Lupe genommen wird. Du findest in LiF die grammatischen Regeln. Wenn vorne im Buch z. B. 8 p. 187 steht, kannst du in LiF unter Nummer 8 auf Seite 187 die passenden Regeln nachschlagen.
Das „R" hinter manchen Nummern steht für *revision* (Wiederholung). So gekennzeichnete Regeln kennst du bereits aus den letzten Jahren.
Auf dieser und der nächsten Seite findest du die grammatischen Begriffe auf Englisch und Deutsch.

Grammatical terms

Englisch	LiF	Deutsch	Beispiel
adjective	16R	Adjektiv	a perfect day, a big house
adverb		Adverb	
adverb of frequency	19R	Häufigkeitsadverb	often, sometimes, never, …
adverb of manner	17R	Adverb der Art und Weise	James sings badly.
article		Artikel	
definite article		bestimmter Artikel	the
indefinite article		unbestimmter Artikel	a/an
comparison		Vergleich	
comparative	16R	Komparativ	André is taller than Anne.
		(1. Steigerungsform)	The film was more interesting than the book.
superlative	16R	Superlativ	Steven is the oldest boy.
		(2. Steigerungsform)	Sue is the most beautiful girl.
conditional clause	23	Bedingungssatz	If it rains, I will stay at home.
future		Futur (Zukunft)	
simple present with future meaning	25	einfache Gegenwart mit Zukunftsbedeutung	The train arrives at 15:22.
going to-future	21R	Futur mit *going to*	She's going to buy a book.
will-future	22R	Futur mit *will*	I'm sure he will be a pop star.
genitive		Genitiv	
genitive with of		Genitiv mit *of*	the name of the ship
s-genitive		*s*-Genitiv	Bob's dog
gerund	13	Gerundium	I like going to parties.
imperative	18R	Imperativ (Befehlsform)	Please sit down! Don't shout!
infinitive		Infinitiv (Grundform)	walk, read, go, …
linking word	20	Konjunktion	and, because, but, so, …
long form	1R	Langform	I am, he is, they are, …
modal verb	15R	Modalverb	can, must, need, should, …
noun		Nomen (Hauptwort, Substantiv)	song, ball, car, dog, …
object	19R	Objekt	We've got a car.
passive	24	Passiv	My watch was made in China.
past participle	9R	Partizip Perfekt	eaten, gone, started, …
past tense		Vergangenheit	
simple past	5R-7R	einfache Vergangenheit	They played football yesterday.
past progressive	8	Verlaufsform der Vergangenheit	Emma was reading a book.

personal pronoun		Personalpronomen	
object pronoun		Objektpronomen	me, you, him, her, it, us, them
subject pronoun		Subjektpronomen	I, you, he, she, it, we, they
plural		Plural (Mehrzahl)	
regular/irregular		regelmäßig/unregelmäßig	cars, books, .../children, men, ...
possessive determiner		Possessivbegleiter	my, your, his, her, its, our, their
preposition		Präposition	in, on, next to, behind, ...
present perfect	9R	Perfekt	David has cleaned the kitchen.
present tense		Präsens (Gegenwart)	
simple present	2R, 3R	einfache Gegenwart	I often walk to school.
present progressive	4R	Verlaufsform der Gegenwart	It's raining.
question		Frage	
question word	10R	Fragewort	who, where, what, how, ...
yes/no question	1R, 3R	Entscheidungsfrage	Are you from Germany?
question tag	12	Bestätigungsfrage	Chips are potatoes, aren't they?
relative clause	14	Relativsatz	That's the man who helped me.
short answer	1R, 3R	Kurzantwort	Yes, I am./No, I'm not.
short form	1R	Kurzform	I'm, he's, they're, ...
singular		Singular (Einzahl)	dog, friend, house, ...
statement		Aussagesatz	She's from Camden./
positive/negative		bejaht/verneint	I don't like football.
subject	19R	Subjekt	School is great./Jo and I like tea.
verb		Verb	
regular/irregular	5R, 9R	regelmäßig/unregelmäßig	look, walk, .../meet, see, ...
word order		Satzstellung	
subject – verb – object	19R	Subjekt – Verb – Objekt	Sarah likes popcorn.

1R Das Verb *be* (The verb *be*)

Die Formen des Verbs *be* gibt es als Kurzformen und als Langformen. Die Kurzformen (*short forms*) verwendet man oft beim Sprechen. Beim Schreiben verwendet man die Langformen (*long forms*).

Langform	Kurzform		
I **am**	I'**m**	I'**m** eleven.	*Ich bin ...*
you **are**	you'**re**	You'**re** my friend.	*Du bist ...*
he **is**	he'**s**	He'**s** from Manchester.	*Er ist ...*
she **is**	she'**s**	She'**s** my sister.	*Sie ist ...*
it **is**	it'**s**	It'**s** late.	*Es ist ...*
we **are**	we'**re**	We'**re** hungry.	*Wir sind ...*
you **are**	you'**re**	You'**re** nice.	*Ihr seid ...*
they **are**	they'**re**	They'**re** in the garden.	*Sie sind ...*

They ***are*** *from Manchester.*

Die Formen von *be* kannst du ganz einfach verneinen, indem du ***not*** einfügst:
He ***is*** *from Camden.* → *He* ***is not*** *from Camden./He* ***isn't*** *from Camden.*
They ***are*** *friends.* → *They* ***are not*** *friends./They* ***aren't*** *friends.*

→

Wenn du eine Entscheidungsfrage mit *be* stellen möchtest, vertauschst du einfach das **Subjekt** und die Form von ***be***:

Gillian is from Camden.
Is Gillian from Camden?

Auf Entscheidungsfragen antwortet man meist nicht mit einem ganzen Satz. Es ist aber unhöflich, nur mit „*Yes.*" oder „*No.*" zu antworten. Deshalb verwendet man häufig Kurzantworten:
Is Peter from London? – ***Yes, he is./No, he isn't.***

2R Die einfache Gegenwart (The simple present)

Das *simple present* verwendest du, ...

- um über Gewohnheiten oder regelmäßige Handlungen zu sprechen:
  They ***play*** *football every Tuesday.*
- um über aufeinander folgende Handlungen zu sprechen:
  First Caroline ***gets*** *up. Then she* ***has*** *breakfast. After that she* ***goes*** *to school.*
- um über Zustände zu sprechen, die längere Zeit andauern:
  Emma and Gillian ***live*** *in London.*

simple present: **Aussagesätze**		
I often	play	football.
You sometimes	play	tennis.
He never	plays	basketball.
She	plays	the guitar.
It always	plays	with other dogs.
We	play	basketball every Monday.
You always	play	hockey.
They	play	games at the weekend.

Bei *I, you, we* und *they* hat das *simple present* dieselbe Form wie der Infinitiv.
Bei *he, she* und *it* (in der 3. Person Singular) hängst du ein *-s* an.

! Endet das Verb mit *-ss, -sh, -ch* oder *-x*, hängst du bei *he, she, it* ein ***-es*** an:
He washes his face in the morning.
She often watches TV.

! Auch bei *do* und *go* fügst du in der 3. Person Singular ***-es*** an.
Achte auf die unterschiedliche Aussprache:
do /duː/ – she does /dʌz/,
go /gəʊ/ – she goes /gəʊz/.

! Bei Verben, die auf *-y* enden (z. B. *tidy up* und *empty*), gilt folgende Regel:
Kommt ein Konsonant vor dem *-y*, so wird das *-y* zu ***-ies***:
She often tidies up her room.
He sometimes empties the dishwasher.

→

Sätze im *simple present* kannst du mit ***don't*** verneinen. Bei *he, she, it* (also in der 3. Person Singular) verwendest du ***doesn't***. Dabei verliert das Verb das *-s* am Ende. *Don't* und *doesn't* sind die Kurzformen von *do not* und *does not*. Meistens verwendet man diese Kurzformen:

	***simple present:* Verneinung**		
Singular	I	**don't play**	football.
	You	**don't like**	tennis.
	He	**doesn't work**	in London.
	She	**doesn't live**	in Manchester.
	It	**doesn't look**	like a dog.
Plural	We	**don't walk**	to school.
	You	**don't know**	Peter's sister.
	They	**don't go**	to Manchester.

*Gillian **doesn't like** rubbish.*

! Bei der Verneinung von Sätzen mit *be, can* oder *have got* brauchst du *don't* oder *doesn't* nicht:
*He **is not** from Camden.*
*I **can't** play an instrument.*
*I **haven't got** a computer.*

3R Die einfache Gegenwart: Entscheidungsfragen und Kurzantworten
(The simple present: Yes/no questions and short answers)

Entscheidungsfragen sind Fragen, auf die man mit „Ja" oder „Nein" antworten kann.

Entscheidungsfragen und Kurzantworten mit *be, can, have got*		
Are you eleven?	**Yes, I am.**	**No, I'm not.**
Can you play an instrument?	**Yes, I can.**	**No, I can't.**
Has Emma **got** a new book?	**Yes, she has.**	**No, she hasn't.**

Wenn du Entscheidungsfragen im *simple present* mit einem anderen Verb wie *play, like* oder *know* stellen möchtest, verwendest du einfach ***do*** oder ***does*** am Satzanfang und in der Kurzantwort:

Entscheidungsfragen und Kurzantworten mit *do* + Verb		
Do you **play** volleyball?	**Yes, I do.**	**No, I don't.**
Do they **like** pizza?	**Yes, they do.**	**No, they don't.**
Does George **know** Gillian?	**Yes, he does.**	**No, he doesn't.**

! Bei *he, she, it* verwendest du in den Entscheidungsfragen *does*.
Dabei verliert das Verb das *-s*:
George knows Gillian.
***Does** George know Gillian?*

4R Die Verlaufsform der Gegenwart (The present progressive)

a) Bejahte und verneinte Aussagesätze

Das *present progressive* verwendest du, wenn du sagen möchtest, was jemand gerade tut oder was gerade passiert – also für Vorgänge, die gerade ablaufen und noch nicht abgeschlossen sind:

	***present progressive:* Aussagesätze**	
Singular	I **am watching** TV. You **are writing** an email. He **is drinking** orange juice. She **is sitting** on the sofa. Oh no, it **is raining** again!	*Ich sehe (gerade) fern.* *Du schreibst (gerade) eine E-Mail.* *Er trinkt (gerade) Orangensaft.* *Sie sitzt (gerade) auf dem Sofa.* *Oh nein, es regnet schon wieder.*
Plural	We **are eating** pizza. You **are playing** football. Listen, they **are singing** a song.	*Wir essen (gerade) Pizza.* *Ihr spielt (gerade) Fußball.* *Hör mal, sie singen (gerade) ein Lied.*

Im Deutschen gibt es keine Verlaufsform. Mit Wörtern wie *gerade, im Moment* oder *jetzt* lässt sich die Verlaufsform aber gut wiedergeben:
*Caroline **is reading** a book.* – Caroline liest **gerade** ein Buch.

So bildest du das *present progressive:*
Form von *be (am, is, are)* + **Infinitiv des Verbs** + **Endung *-ing***:
He is drinking orange juice.

*The monster **is reading** the newspaper.*

! Endet das Verb auf *-e*, dann fällt das *-e* in der Verlaufsform weg.
write ➔ *writing* — *Caroline is writing a letter.*
dance ➔ *dancing* — *Rajiv is dancing.*

! Endet das Verb auf einem kurzen betonten *Vokal* + *Konsonant*, wird der Konsonant verdoppelt.
sit ➔ *sitting* — *George is sitting in the kitchen.*
run ➔ *running* — *Charlie is running.*

Für die Verneinung fügst du einfach ein ***not*** hinter die Form von be ein:
*Caroline is **not** writing a letter.* *George is**n't** reading a book. He's watching TV.*

b) Fragen und Kurzantworten

Charlie is reading a book.
Is Charlie reading a book?

Auch in der Verlaufsform kannst du Entscheidungsfragen bilden:

Is George **helping** his mum? – **Yes, he is./No, he isn't.**
Are Caroline and George **playing** basketball? – **Yes, they are./No, they aren't.**

Bei Fragen mit Fragewort stellst du das Fragewort an den Satzanfang:

What are *you* **doing**? **Where are** *you* **going**?

5R Die einfache Vergangenheit (The simple past)

Das *simple past* verwendest du, wenn du über etwas sprechen willst, das in der Vergangenheit liegt und abgeschlossen ist – z. B. wenn du berichtest, was du erlebt hast, oder wenn du eine Geschichte erzählst.

Infinitiv + ed

watched | walked

helped | started

a) Regelmäßige Verben (Regular verbs)

Das *simple past* der regelmäßigen Verben bildest du, indem du die Endung *-ed* an den **Infinitiv** anhängst:
watch + *ed* ➔ *watched*

***simple past:* regelmäßige Formen**	
Yesterday I **watched** a film about elephants.	*Gestern habe ich einen Film über Elefanten gesehen.*
Last Monday Rajiv **helped** his parents in the shop.	*Letzten Montag hat Rajiv seinen Eltern im Laden geholfen.*

! Achte auf folgende Besonderheiten in der Schreibung:
Endet das Verb auf *-e*, dann wird nur *-d* angehängt.
like ➔ *liked*
Endet das Verb auf einem kurzen betonten *Vokal* + *Konsonant*, wird der Konsonant verdoppelt.
stop ➔ *stopped*
Endet das Verb auf *Konsonant* + *-y*, dann lautet die Endung im *simple past* *-ied*.
try ➔ *tried*

b) Unregelmäßige Verben (Irregular verbs)

Bei unregelmäßigen Verben wird das *simple past* nicht mit *-ed* gebildet. Du musst ihre Formen wie neue Vokabeln lernen. Auf den Seiten 282 und 283 findest du eine Liste der unregelmäßigen Verben.

Be hat als einziges englisches Verb zwei Formen im *simple past*, *was* und *were*:
I/he/she/it was – *you/we/they were*

Weitere unregelmäßige Verben findest du in diesen Sätzen:

Infinitiv	*simple past*	
be	was/were	I **was** very hungry after school. They **were** in London last week.
have	had	Sarah **had** a great holiday.
go	went	She **went** to Spain with her family.
find	found	She and her sister **found** many nice postcards.
do	did	They **did** lots of interesting things together.

6R Die einfache Vergangenheit: Verneinung
(The simple past: Negation)

Wenn du sagen willst, was in der Vergangenheit nicht geschehen ist, verwendest du ***not*** oder die Kurzform ***n't***, die an *was/were* angehängt wird.

simple past: **bejahter Satz**	*simple past:* **verneinter Satz**
I **was** at school on Monday.	I **wasn't** at school on Monday.
They **were** friendly at the hotel.	They **weren't** friendly at the hotel.

Wenn im Satz kein *was/were* steht, musst du ***didn't (did not)*** vor das Verb stellen.
Didn't ist die Vergangenheitsform von *don't* und *doesn't*. *Didn't* ist bei allen Personen gleich. Das Verb selbst bleibt im **Infinitiv**, weil *didn't* schon die Vergangenheit anzeigt.

simple past: **bejahter Satz**	*simple past:* **verneinter Satz**
George **talked** to Gillian yesterday.	George **didn't talk** to Gillian yesterday.
I **went** to Hamburg last year.	I **didn't go** to Hamburg last year.

7R Die einfache Vergangenheit: Entscheidungsfragen und Kurzantworten
(The simple past: Yes/no questions and short answers)

Entscheidungsfragen im *simple past* bildest du, indem du ***did*** an den Satzanfang stellst.
Du antwortest, wie bei allen Entscheidungsfragen, nicht nur mit *„Yes."* oder *„No."*, sondern fügst eine zusätzliche Bestätigung oder Ablehnung hinzu.

simple past: **Entscheidungsfragen und Kurzantworten**		
Did you **go** on holiday?	**Yes, I did.**	**No, I didn't.**
Did Claire **visit** Caroline in London?	**Yes, she did.**	**No, she didn't.**

Bei Entscheidungsfragen mit *was/were* stellst du ***was*** oder ***were*** an den Satzanfang.

simple past: **Entscheidungsfragen und Kurzantworten mit** ***was/were***		
Were you at the party yesterday?	**Yes, I was.**	**No, I wasn't.**
Was it good?	**Yes, it was.**	**No, it wasn't.**

Did *Rajiv* ***buy*** *a new football yesterday?*
– ***Yes, he did.***

8 Die Verlaufsform der Vergangenheit (The past progressive)

a) Bejahte und verneinte Aussagesätze

Das *present progressive* kennst du bereits. Du verwendest es, wenn du sagen möchtest, was jemand gerade tut oder was gerade passiert: *Emma is reading a book.*
Es gibt auch für die Vergangenheit eine *progressive form*, das *past progressive*.
Es drückt aus, ...

- was jemand gerade tat oder was gerade passierte.
- was gerade vor sich ging, als etwas anderes geschah.

So bildest du das *past progressive*:
Simple past*-Form von *be* (*was/were*)** + **Infinitiv des Verbs** + **Endung *-ing.
*Rajiv **was laughing** the whole time.*
Rajiv lachte die ganze Zeit.

*All the girls **were screaming**.*
Alle Mädchen schrien.

*Emma **was reading** a book when her father came to say good night.*

past progressive	***simple past***
The students **were running** around *Die Schüler rannten herum,*	when the teacher **came**. *als der Lehrer kam.*
While she **was taking** photos, *Während sie fotografierte,*	a man **stole** her bag. *klaute ein Mann ihre Tasche.*
⟶ **was gerade passierte:** ***past progressive***	↑ **neues Ereignis:** ***simple past***

Für die Verneinung fügst du einfach ein ***not*** hinter die Form von *be* ein:
*Sheree was **not** singing a song.*
*Rajiv was**n't** screaming with the girls.*

b) Fragen und Kurzantworten

Entscheidungsfragen im *past progressive* bildest du, indem du das Subjekt und *was/were* vertauschst:

Was Rajiv laughing? – ***Yes, he was./No, he wasn't.***
Were the reporters asking many questions? – ***Yes, they were./No, they weren't.***

Bei Fragen mit Fragewörtern stellst du das Fragewort an den Satzanfang:

What was the band doing?
Where were they sitting?

9R Das Perfekt (The present perfect)

*She **has bought** new clothes.*

a) Verwendung

Das *present perfect* verwendest du, ...

- wenn etwas irgendwann, noch nie oder noch nicht geschehen ist:
  *Holly **has** never **eaten** fish.*
  Holly hat noch nie Fisch gegessen.
- wenn ein Vorgang in der Vergangenheit noch Auswirkungen auf die Gegenwart hat:
  *David **has cleaned** the kitchen.*
  David hat die Küche geputzt (sie ist noch sauber).

b) Aussagesätze

Das *present perfect* bildest du mit ***have/has*** + **Partizip Perfekt (past participle)**.
Die Verneinung bildest du mit ***haven't/hasn't*** + **Partizip Perfekt.**

***present perfect*: Aussagesätze und Verneinung**			
I	**have**	**cleaned**	the kitchen.
He	**has**	**gone**	to London.
We	**have**	**seen**	the Queen.
She	**hasn't**	**been**	to Scotland.
They	**haven't**	**helped**	him.

*The boys **have tidied up** their room.*

Das *present perfect* kannt du mit Adverbien der unbestimmten Zeit verwenden, z. B. mit *already, just, ever, never*. Es ist in solchen Sätzen nicht wichtig, wann genau etwas geschehen ist.
Die Adverbien stehen dann direkt vor dem Partizip Perfekt:

*I have **already** done my homework.* – Ich habe meine Hausaufgaben schon gemacht.
*Angela has **just** seen the Queen.* – Angela hat eben/gerade die Queen gesehen.

! Beachte die Ausnahme: *yet* steht am Satzende.
*I haven't been to Berlin **yet**.* – Ich war noch nicht in Berlin.

c) Fragen und Kurzantworten

Entscheidungsfragen im *present perfect* bildest du, indem du das Subjekt und ***have/has*** vertauschst. Bei Fragen mit Fragewörtern steht das Fragewort am Satzanfang:

***present perfect*: Fragen und Kurzantworten**					
	Have	you	**finished**	your homework?	**Yes, I have./No, I haven't.**
	Has	Jill	**bought**	a new book?	**Yes, she has./No, she hasn't.**
What	**have**	you	**done?**		
Why	**hasn't**	she	**come?**		

→

d) Das Partizip Perfekt

Bei regelmäßigen Verben bildest du das Partizip Perfekt *(past participle)* mit dem **Infinitiv** + ***-ed***.

Infinitiv	*simple past*	*past participle*
clean	cleaned	clean**ed**
help	helped	help**ed**
play	played	play**ed**

Unregelmäßige Verben haben unregelmäßige Formen. Diese solltest du wie Vokabeln lernen.

Infinitiv	*simple past*	*past participle*
be	was/were	**been**
do	did	**done**
have	had	**had**
buy	bought	**bought**

Auf den Seiten 282 und 283 findest du eine Liste der unregelmäßigen Verben.

10R Fragen mit Fragewörtern (Questions with question words)

Who, what, when, where, why und *how* sind Fragewörter. Wenn du eine Frage mit einem Fragewort stellen möchtest, stellst du das Fragewort an den Satzanfang.

Who?	Wer?
What?	Was?
When?	Wann?
Where?	Wo?
Why?	Warum?
How?	Wie?

Fragen mit Fragewörtern mit *be, can, have got*	
Where is George?	*Wo ist George?*
What was the weather like?	*Wie war das Wetter?*
When can I call you?	*Wann kann ich dich anrufen?*
Who has got an idea?	*Wer hat eine Idee?*

! Mit *who* fragst du nach Personen, mit *where* nach Orten.
Ein Merkspruch: *Who, who, who* – **wer** bist du?
Where, where, where – **wo** kommst du her?

Auch bei Fragen mit *do* stellst du das Fragewort an den Satzanfang:

Fragen mit Fragewörtern mit *do* + Verb	
Why does Amy **like** the film?	*Warum mag Amy den Film?*
Where do you **go** on holiday?	*Wo machst du Urlaub?*
When do you **leave**?	*Wann gehst du?*
What did you **do** this summer?	*Was habt ihr diesen Sommer gemacht?*
How long did you **stay** there?	*Wie lange warst du da?*

Bei Fragen mit *who* braucht man kein *do* oder *does*, wenn *who* Subjekt ist:
***Who** lives in Camden?*

11R Mengenangaben (Quantifiers)

Mit *some* und *any* werden Mengen wie z. B. „etwas" oder „einige" bezeichnet.
Die Mengenangabe *not ... any* bedeutet „kein" oder „keine".
Some und *any* werden aber oft nicht übersetzt.

In bejahten Aussagesätzen verwendest du *some*, in verneinten Aussagesätzen und in Fragen *any*.

Bejahte Aussagesätze mit *some*	**Fragen und verneinte Aussagesätze mit *any***	
There are **some** apples in the kitchen. *In der Küche sind (ein paar) Äpfel.*	Are there **any** apples? *Gibt es Äpfel?*	We haven't got **any** apples. *Wir haben keine Äpfel.*
I need **some** milk for my cornflakes. *Ich brauche (etwas) Milch für meine Cornflakes.*	Have you got **any** milk? *Hast du (etwas) Milch?*	There isn't **any** milk. *Es gibt keine Milch.*

! Wenn du jemanden höflich um etwas bittest oder ihm etwas anbietest, benutzt du **some** auch in Fragen:
*Can I have **some** milk, please?*
*Would you like **some** tea?*

Nach denselben Regeln wie *some* und *any* benutzt du auch ihre Zusammensetzungen *something* und *(not) anything*.
*I'm sure they'll have **something** you like.* *There isn't **anything** in the fridge.*

Mit ***how much*** fragst du nach unbestimmten, nicht zählbaren Mengen (z. B. *water, milk, time, chocolate, ...*):
***How much** money have we got?*
– We've got £12.

Mit ***how many*** fragst du nach der Anzahl von Dingen:
***How many** books have you got?* – *I've got twenty books.*
***How many** eggs are there?* – *There are two eggs.*

***How much** time has she got?*
– Only a little.

12 Bestätigungsfragen (Question tags)

Wenn du erwartest, dass ein Gesprächspartner dir zustimmt, kannst du eine Bestätigungsfrage stellen. Im Englischen verwendest du dafür *question tags*. Du kannst sie mit „..., oder?", „..., nicht wahr?" oder Dialektformen wie „..., gell?", „..., ne?" usw. übersetzen.

Bejahter Aussagesatz +	question tag −	Verneinter Aussagesatz −	question tag +
The book **is** great,	**isn't it?**	The film **isn't** interesting,	**is it?**
We **have** got a lot of time,	**haven't we?**	You **haven't** got time,	**have you?**
Alex **can** come with us,	**can't he?**	He **can't** see us,	**can he?**
Gillian **likes** music,	**doesn't she?**	Mia **doesn't** like apples,	**does she?**

Das Subjekt aus dem Aussagesatz erscheint im *question tag* als Personalpronomen:
***Chips** are potatoes, aren't **they**?*

Bei Sätzen mit Hilfsverben bestehen die *question tags* aus Hilfsverb und Personalpronomen:
*We **can** stay in London, **can't we?***

Bei Sätzen ohne Hilfsverb verwendest du eine Form von *do*:
*Sarah **helped** Kim, **didn't she?***

13 Das Gerundium (The gerund)

Wird ein Verb wie ein Nomen verwendet, nennt man das Gerundium (*gerund*). Im Englischen hängst du dafür ein *-ing* an den Infinitiv des Verbs:
***Reading** can be fun.* – Lesen kann Spaß machen.

a) Das Gerundium als Subjekt

Das Gerundium kann Subjekt eines Satzes sein:
***Running** keeps you fit.* – Laufen hält dich fit.

b) Das Gerundium nach bestimmten Verben

Das Gerundium folgt oft nach bestimmten Verben wie *like, love, enjoy, hate, start* und *stop*:
*He **enjoys listening** to music.* – Er genießt es, Musik zu hören.

c) Das Gerundium nach bestimmten Ausdrücken

Du benutzt das Gerundium auch nach bestimmten Ausdrücken wie *can't stand, good at* oder *bad at*:
*I'm **good at playing** basketball.* – Ich kann gut Basketball spielen.
*She **can't stand swimming**.* – Sie kann Schwimmen nicht ausstehen.

14 Relativsätze (Relative clauses)

Mit Relativsätzen kannst du eine Person oder eine Sache genauer beschreiben. Ein Relativsatz beginnt meist mit einem Relativpronomen: ***who***, ***which*** oder ***that***.

Dabei verwendest du ***who*** für Personen und ***which*** für Dinge.

	Relativsatz		
Someone	**who** plays football	must be fit.	*Jemand, der Fußball spielt, muss fit sein.*
There are many tourists	**who** take photos.		*Es gibt viele Touristen, die Fotos machen.*
They listen to a band	**which** is playing great music.		*Sie hören einer Band zu, die tolle Musik spielt.*
I've got a computer game	**which** is really good.		*Ich habe ein Computerspiel, das richtig gut ist.*

Das Relativpronomen ***that*** kannst du sowohl für Dinge als auch für Personen benutzen.
Ice hockey is a sport ***that*** *can be dangerous.* – Eishockey ist ein Sport, der gefährlich sein kann.
There are lots of people ***that*** *dance to the music.* – Es gibt viele Leute, die zu der Musik tanzen.

15R Modalverben (Modal verbs)

Du kennst bereits einige Modalverben wie *can*, *must*, oder *need*.
Die meisten Modalverben haben nur Formen für das *simple present*.
Im *simple past* und im *will-future* verwendest du deshalb die Ersatzformen.

a) Fähigkeit: *can/can't – be able to/not be able to* + –

Mit ***can*** kannst du sagen, ...
- was jemand tun kann
- was jemand tun darf

He **can** swim.	*Er kann schwimmen.*
You **can** watch TV.	*Du darfst fernsehen.*

Can steht mit dem Infinitiv und bleibt in allen Personen gleich.

! Die Ersatzform von *can* ist ***be able to***. Im *simple past* kannst du aber auch ***could*** benutzen.

Emma and Charlie **were able to** help Mr Miller.	*Emma und Charlie konnten Herrn Miller helfen.*
Rajiv **couldn't** do his maths homework because it was too difficult.	*Rajiv konnte seine Mathehausaufgaben nicht machen, weil sie zu schwierig waren.*

→

Could benutzt du auch für höfliche Bitten und Aufforderungen.

Could I take your pencil, please?	*Könnte ich bitte deinen Bleistift nehmen?*

b) Erlaubnis: *can/can't – be allowed to/not be allowed to – must not*

Can/can't, ***be allowed to*** und ***must not*** benutzt du, wenn du ...

- um etwas bittest
- um Erlaubnis fragst oder jemandem etwas erlaubst
- etwas verbietest.

You **can** swim in the swimming pool but you **are not allowed to** swim in the lake.	*Du kannst im Pool schwimmen, aber du darfst nicht im See schwimmen.*
Kenny Hoover **is allowed to** sleep in David's bedroom.	*Kenny Hoover darf in Davids Schlafzimmer schlafen.*
In Germany cars **mustn't** drive on the left.	In Deutschland dürfen Autos nicht links fahren.

! ***Must not*** oder die Kurzform ***mustn't*** klingt wie im Deutschen „muss nicht", heißt aber „etwas nicht dürfen".

You **mustn't** talk now.

Ihr dürft jetzt nicht mehr sprechen.

c) Notwendigkeit: *must/have to – needn't/don't have to*

Must klingt wie das deutsche Wort „muss" und heißt auch *müssen*.
In der Regel kannst du ***must*** auch durch ***have to/has to*** ersetzen.

I **have to** wear a school uniform.

Claire **must** tidy up her room. *oder* Claire **has to** tidy up her room.	*Claire muss ihr Zimmer aufräumen.*

Must hat keine eigene Vergangenheitsform. Daher wird die *simple past*-Form von ***have to*** benutzt.

Before there were lights, people **had to** use candles.	*Bevor es Lampen gab, mussten die Menschen Kerzen benutzen.*

→

Wenn du sagen willst, was jemand *nicht* tun muss, benutzt du ***don't/doesn't have to***.

I **have to** take out the rubbish but I **don't have to** clean the kitchen.

Auch mit ***need not*** oder ***needn't*** kannst du ausdrücken, dass etwas nicht notwendig ist.

You **needn't** do your homework now. You can do it later.	*Du brauchst deine Hausaufgaben nicht jetzt zu machen. Du kannst sie später machen.*

16R Steigerung und Vergleich von Adjektiven (Comparison of adjectives)

Mit Adjektiven lassen sich Personen oder Sachen näher beschreiben.
Wenn du Personen oder Sachen miteinander vergleichen möchtest, kannst du ein Adjektiv steigern.
Die Steigerungsformen heißen ***comparative*** (Komparativ) und ***superlative*** (Superlativ).

a) Steigerung von Adjektiven mit *-er* und *-est*

Einsilbige Adjektive (z. B. *cheap, old, young)* werden durch das Anhängen von *-er* und *-est* gesteigert.

Adjektiv	Komparativ	Superlativ
cheap	cheap**er**	(the) cheap**est**
old	old**er**	(the) old**est**
young	young**er**	(the) young**est**

Bei zweisilbigen Adjektiven, die auf *-y* enden, wird aus dem *-y* ein *-i*.

Adjektiv	Komparativ	Superlativ
pretty	pretti**er**	(the) pretti**est**
easy	easi**er**	(the) easi**est**
friendly	friendli**er**	(the) friendli**est**

→

! Bei manchen Adjektiven ändert sich die Schreibweise.

Adjektiv	Komparativ	Superlativ
nice	nicer	(the) nicest
hot	hotter	(the) hottest
big	bigger	(the) biggest

Einige Adjektive haben unregelmäßige Steigerungsformen.
Diese Formen musst du wie Vokabeln lernen.

Adjektiv	Komparativ	Superlativ
good	better	(the) best
bad	worse	(the) worst
much/many	more	(the) most

b) Steigerung von Adjektiven mit *more* und *most*

Mehrsilbige Adjektive werden mit *more* und *most* gesteigert.
Du stellst dabei *more* oder *most* vor das Adjektiv. Das Adjektiv bleibt unverändert.

Adjektiv	Komparativ	Superlativ
interesting	more interesting	(the) most interesting
beautiful	more beautiful	(the) most beautiful

c) Vergleichssätze

Willst du ungleiche Dinge miteinander vergleichen, benutzt du den Komparativ mit *than*.

Vergleichssätze	
The blue cap is **cheaper than** the green cap.	*Die blaue Kappe ist billiger als die grüne.*
The jacket is **more expensive than** the white T-shirt.	*Die Jacke ist teurer als das weiße T-Shirt.*

Rabbits are smaller than cats.

Sind die Eigenschaften von zwei Dingen oder Personen gleich, benutzt du *as ... as*.

Vergleichssätze	
Mike's brother is **as old as** Finn's brother.	*Mikes Bruder ist genauso alt wie Finns Bruder.*
Sarah is **as tall as** Anne.	*Sarah ist so groß wie Anne.*

17R Adverbien der Art und Weise (Adverbs of manner)

Wenn du eine Person, ein Tier oder eine Sache beschreibst, benutzt du ein Adjektiv.

The boys are **loud**. The garden is **big**. The sky is **blue**.

Wenn du beschreiben möchtest, wie jemand etwas tut oder wie etwas geschieht, benutzt du ein Adverb der Art und Weise. Adverbien der Art und Weise bildest du, indem du an das Adjektiv die Endung ***-ly*** anhängst:

Adjektiv	Adverb	
loud	loud**ly**	The boys speak very **loudly**.
bad	bad**ly**	Susan sings **badly**.
slow	slow**ly**	Tom walks **slowly**.

*He sings **badly**.*

Bei manchen Adverbien ändert sich die Schreibweise, wenn ***-ly*** angehängt wird. *-y* wird zu ***-ily***; *-le* wird zu ***-ly***; *-l* wird zu ***-lly***.

Adjektiv	Adverb	
happy	happ**ily**	Caroline laughed **happily**.
angry	angr**ily**	He called the police **angrily**.
terrible	terrib**ly**	Simon dances **terribly**.
beautiful	beautiful**ly**	Mona sings **beautifully**.

! Einige Adverbien haben Sonderformen, die du wie Vokabeln lernen musst.
Manche Adjektive und Adverbien sind gleich:

Adjektiv	Adverb	
good	**well**	Rajiv is a good guitar player. He plays the guitar **well**.
fast	**fast**	Jack is a fast runner. He runs **fast**.
hard	**hard**	Gillian is a hard worker. She works **hard**.

Adverbien der Art und Weise stehen nach dem Verb.
In Sätzen mit Objekt stehen sie nach dem Objekt.

Subjekt	Verb	Objekt	Adverb.
Gillian	works		**hard**.
Rajiv	plays	the guitar	**well**.

*Rajiv dances very **well**.*

18R Imperativ (The imperative)

Mit dem Imperativ (der Befehlsform) kannst du Bitten, Befehle oder Anweisungen ausdrücken:
*Please **open** the window, Lisa.*

Im Englischen hat der Imperativ dieselbe Form wie der Infinitiv und bleibt im Singular und Plural gleich.
***Help** me, please.* – Bitte **hilf** mir./Bitte **helft** mir.

Wenn jemand etwas nicht tun soll, stellst du einfach *do not* oder *don't* vor das Verb.
***Don't forget** your keys.*

! Wenn du nur den Imperativ verwendest, kann das im Englischen sehr unhöflich klingen. Höflicher ist es, wenn du ***please*** hinzufügst.

19R Die Satzstellung (Word order)

a) Satzstellung Subjekt – Verb – Objekt (S – V – O)

Die Satzstellung ist so etwas wie der „Bauplan" eines Satzes. Im englischen Aussagesatz ist die Satzstellung meist:
Subjekt – Verb – Objekt (S – V – O):

Subjekt *(subject)* S	Verb *(verb)* V	Objekt *(object)* O
I	like	ice cream.
Charlie and his friends	play	football.

b) Aussagesätze mit Häufigkeitsadverbien

Im Englischen stehen Häufigkeitsadverbien *(adverbs of frequency)* meist zwischen Subjekt und Verb:

Subjekt	Häufigkeitsadverb	Verb		
I	sometimes	help	at home.	*Ich helfe manchmal zu Hause.*
Leon	never	walks	to school.	*Leon läuft nie zur Schule.*

! Häufigkeitsadverbien stehen hinter den Formen von *be*:
*She's **always** late.*

! Häufigkeitsadverbien stehen hinter *can*:
*We can **sometimes** get up late on Saturdays.*

→

c) Ortsangaben und Zeitangaben

Orts- und Zeitangaben stehen in der Regel am Ende eines Satzes. Wenn sie zusammen in einem Satz vorkommen, steht immer „Ort" vor „Zeit".

	Ortsangabe	Zeitangabe
Robinson Crusoe lived	on the island	for many years.
He and Man Friday arrived	in York	on 11th June 1687.

Um eine Zeitangabe stärker zu betonen, kannst du sie auch an den Satzanfang stellen.

Zeitangabe		Ortsangabe
One day	some cannibals came	to the island.

20 Konjunktionen (Linking words)

Linking words sind Wörter, mit denen du Sätze verbinden kannst. Mit ihnen kannst du einen Text gut strukturieren.
Du kennst bereits eine Reihe von Konjunktionen, mit denen du zwei Hauptsätze oder einen Hauptsatz und einen Nebensatz verbinden kannst, z. B. *and*, *but*, *because*.

Konjunktionen	
Mr Brown is our German teacher **and** Mrs Thompson is our English teacher.	*... und ...*
Carol likes ice cream **but** she doesn't like chocolate.	*... aber ...*
Charlie is happy **because** he can play football.	*... weil ...*
Ben went into the house **when** it started to rain.	*... als ...*
We have enough food **so** we don't need to go shopping.	*... also ...*

21R Die Zukunft mit *going to* (The *going to*-future)

Die Zukunft mit *going to* verwendest du, wenn du sagen willst, was jemand für die Zukunft plant oder vorhat. Im Deutschen gibt es keine Zeitform, die dem *going to* entspricht.
Du hast aber verschiedene Möglichkeiten, es wiederzugeben:

We**'re going to** fly to London tomorrow.	*Wir werden morgen nach London fliegen.* *Wir möchten/wollen morgen nach London fliegen.* *Wir planen/haben vor, morgen nach London zu fliegen.*

Du bildest die Zukunft mit *going to* mit einer **Form von *be*** + ***going to*** + **Infinitiv des Verbs**.

*He **is going to buy** an ice cream.*

Zukunft mit *going to*: Aussagesätze			
I**'m**	**going to**	**fly**	to Spain next week.
Rajiv **is**	**going to**	**help**	his parents in their shop.

Für die Verneinung von *going to* verwendest du die verneinte Form von *be*. Hier steht *not* immer hinter *am, is* oder *are*.

Zukunft mit *going to*: Verneinung			
I**'m not**	**going to**	**call**	her tomorrow.
She **isn't**	**going to**	**go**	to the party.
They **aren't**	**going to**	**visit**	Emma's aunt.

Bei Entscheidungsfragen rückt auch beim *going to-future* die Form von *be (am, is, are)* an den Satzanfang.

Zukunft mit *going to*: Fragen und Antworten	
Are you **going to watch** the film tonight?	Yes, **I am.**/No, **I'm not.**
What **are** you **going to do**?	I'm going to read a book.

22R Die Zukunft mit *will* (The will-future)

Wenn du über die Zukunft sprechen willst, benutzt du das *will-future*. Mit dem *will-future* kannst du Vermutungen aussprechen und Vorhersagen oder Versprechen äußern.

Das *will-future* bildest du mit ***will*** und dem **Infinitiv des Verbs**.
Auch ***will*** hat eine Kurzform. Sie lautet ***'ll***. *Will* ist in allen Personen gleich.

Zukunft mit *will*: Aussagesätze	
I **will help** you.	*Ich werde dir helfen.*
You**'ll find** new friends.	*Du wirst neue Freunde finden.*
The weather **will be** great tomorrow.	*Das Wetter wird morgen großartig sein.*

! *Will* sieht aus wie das deutsche Wort „will". Aber es bedeutet „werden", nicht „wollen". Im Deutschen kannst du es oft weglassen, aber niemals im Englischen:

Next time I'll catch you. – Das nächste Mal krieg' ich dich!
Das nächste Mal werde ich dich kriegen!

Die Verneinung bildest du mit ***will not*** oder der Kurzform ***won't***.

Zukunft mit *will*: Verneinung	
I **won't win** the match.	*Ich werde das Spiel nicht gewinnen.*
He **won't get** a dog.	*Er wird keinen Hund bekommen.*
It **won't be** cold on Wednesday.	*Am Mittwoch wird es nicht kalt sein.*

Entscheidungsfragen mit *will* bildest du, indem du *will* an den Satzanfang stellst. Du verwendest *will* auch in der Kurzantwort.
Bei Fragen mit Fragewörtern stellst du das Fragewort an den Satzanfang.

Zukunft mit *will*: Fragen und Antworten	
Will Tom **get** a good job?	Yes, he **will**. / No, he **won't**.
Where **will** you **live** in ten years?	I think I will live in Berlin.

23 Bedingungssätze, Typ I (Conditional clauses, type I)

Ein Bedingungssatz besteht aus einem *if*-Satz *(if-clause)* und einem Hauptsatz *(main clause)*:

- Der *if*-Satz nennt eine Bedingung. Der Hauptsatz drückt aus, was passiert, wenn die Bedingung erfüllt ist.
- Im *if*-Satz steht das *simple present*, im Hauptsatz das *will-future*.

***if*-Satz** (Bedingung: *Wenn ...*)	**Hauptsatz** (Folge: *dann ...*)	
If you **miss** the bus,	you **will be** late.	*Wenn du den Bus verpasst, kommst du zu spät.*
If it **rains**,	they **won't go** outside.	*Wenn es regnet, werden sie nicht rausgehen.*

Bedingungssätze können entweder mit dem *if*-Satz oder mit dem Hauptsatz beginnen. Wenn sie mit dem *if*-Satz beginnen, werden sie mit einem Komma getrennt. Wenn sie mit dem Hauptsatz beginnen, verwendest du kein Komma:

If you go to the cinema, I'll come with you.
I'll come with you if you go to the cinema.

They won't go to the beach if it rains.

Im Hauptsatz kannst du auch Modalverben (z. B. *can, must*) oder den Imperativ verwenden:

If it snows, we can go inside. – Wenn es schneit, können wir reingehen.
If you like her, you must call her. – Wenn du sie magst, musst du sie anrufen.
If you need help, ask Lisa. – Wenn du Hilfe brauchst, frag Lisa.

! *If* und *when* kannst du beide mit „wenn" übersetzen.
Sie werden aber unterschiedlich verwendet:

- ***If*** *I see Ben on Monday, I'll give him the book.*
  Der Sprecher verwendet *if*, weil er nicht sicher ist, ob er Ben am Montag sieht.
  Du kannst *if* hier mit „wenn" oder „falls" übersetzen.

- ***When*** *I see Ben on Monday, I'll give him the book.*
  Der Sprecher hat fest vor, Ben am Montag zu sehen.
  Du kannst *when* hier mit „wenn" übersetzen, aber nicht mit „falls".

24 Das Passiv (The passive)

Bis jetzt hast du Aktivsätze gebildet. Diese Sätze sagen uns, wer oder was handelt. Wenn es aber nicht wichtig oder klar ist, wer etwas tut oder getan hat, kannst du das Passiv verwenden.

Das Passiv bildest du so: Form von *be* + **Partizip Perfekt (past participle)**

English **is spoken** all over the world.	*Englisch wird überall auf der Welt gesprochen.*
Matches **are used** to make fire.	*Streichhölzer werden zum Feuer machen benutzt.*
My computer **was made** in China.	*Mein Computer wurde in China hergestellt.*
These books **were written** in Germany.	*Diese Bücher wurden in Deutschland geschrieben.*

Wenn du in einem Passivsatz doch einmal die handelnde Person oder die Ursache für etwas nennen willst, hängst du sie mit ***by*** („von", „durch") an den Satz an:

The first car was invented ***by*** *Karl Benz.* – Das erste Auto wurde von Karl Benz erfunden.

The house was destroyed ***by*** *fire.* – Das Haus wurde durch Feuer zerstört.

25 Die einfache Gegenwart mit Zukunftsbedeutung (The simple present with future meaning)

Wenn du über einen festgelegten Zeitplan (zum Beispiel Flugpläne und Fahrpläne von Zügen oder Bussen) oder einen Programmablauf sprichst, benutzt du das *simple present*.

The train from Dover ***arrives*** *at 15:45.* – Der Zug aus Dover kommt um 15:45 an.
On Friday classes ***finish*** *at 1 pm.* – Am Freitag endet der Unterricht um 13 Uhr.
The camp ***starts*** *next Sunday.* – Das Ferienlager beginnt nächsten Sonntag.

So funktionieren die Wortlisten

Es gibt alphabetische Wortlisten *(Dictionaries)* und Wortlisten nach *Themes*.

Alphabetische Wortlisten *(Dictionaries)*

Camden Market hat zwei *Dictionaries:* Im *English-German dictionary* ab Seite 235 kannst du nachschlagen, wenn du die Bedeutung von einem englischen Wort aus dem Buch wissen möchtest. Im *German-English dictionary* ab Seite 264 kannst du nachschlagen, wenn dir mal ein englisches Wort nicht einfällt.

Wortlisten nach *Themes*

In den Wortlisten nach *Themes* ab Seite 206 findest du alle neuen Wörter in der Reihenfolge, in der sie in den *Themes* vorkommen. Hier siehst du, wie du die Wortlisten benutzen kannst:

Fett gedruckte Wörter solltest du dir merken.

(irr) bedeutet: Dieses Verb ist unregelmäßig.

(informal) bedeutet: Dieses Wort ist umgangssprachlich.

(pl halves) bedeutet: Dieses Wort hat einen unregelmäßigen Plural *(halves)*.

	/ ˌpiː em, ˌpəʊst mə rɪdiəm /	(nur hinter Uhrzeit zwischen 12 Uhr mittags und Mitternacht)	
8	chant / tʃɑːnt /	singen; einen Sprechgesang anstimmen	
	captain / ˈkæptɪn /	Kapitän/in	Charlie is the captain of his football team.
	score a goal / skɔːr‿ə ˈɡəʊl /	ein Tor schießen	Rajiv scored a goal.
	goal / ɡəʊl /	Tor	goal
	go wild *(irr)* *(informal)* / ɡəʊ ˈwaɪld /	außer sich geraten, aus dem Häuschen geraten	
	crowd / kraʊd /	(Menschen)menge, Zuschauermenge	
	half time / ˌhɑːf ˈtaɪm /	Halbzeit	
	score / skɔː /	Punktestand; *hier:* Spielstand	
	half *(pl **halves**)* / hɑːf, hɑːvz /	Hälfte	Nick scored a goal for Haverstock in the second half of the match.

(AE) bedeutet: *American English*
(BE) bedeutet: *British English*

Kleine Bilder und Beispielsätze helfen dir dabei, dir Wörter besser einzuprägen.

(no pl) bedeutet: Dieses Wort hat keinen Plural (Mehrzahl).

Die Lautschrift zeigt dir, wie man ein Wort ausspricht.

Wenn du den *More*-Teil bearbeitest, solltest du dir die **grün** gedruckten Wörter merken.

(only pl) bedeutet: Dieses Wort wird nur oder gewöhnlich im Plural benutzt.

	clothing *(no pl)* / ˈkləʊðɪŋ /	Kleidung	
	long-sleeved / ˈlɒŋˌsliːvd /	langärm(e)lig	
	proper / ˈprɒpə /	richtig	
	trainer *(BE)* / ˈtreɪnə /	Turnschuh	trainers
	constant / ˈkɒnstənt /	dauernd; *hier:* beständig, gleich bleibend	
	raincoat / ˈreɪnˌkəʊt /	Regenmantel	
M2	below / bɪˈləʊ /	unten	
	welcome / ˈwelkəm /	willkommen heißen, begrüßen	
	click / klɪk /	(an)klicken, drücken	
	up to / ˈʌp tuː /	bis (zu)	
	unique / juːˈniːk /	einzigartig	
	atmosphere / ˈætməsˌfɪə /	Atmosphäre, Stimmung	
	experience / ɪkˈspɪəriəns /	Erfahrung, Erlebnis	
	drama / ˈdrɑːmə /	Schauspielerei; *hier:* Theater	drama
	mission / ˈmɪʃn /	Auftrag, Mission	
	impossible / ɪmˈpɒsəbl /	unmöglich	
	robotics *(only pl)* / rəʊˈbɒtɪks /	Robotik, Robotertechnik	
M6	**reservation** / ˌrezəˈveɪʃn /	Reservierung	
	altogether / ˌɔːltəˈɡeðə /	völlig, ganz; *hier:* insgesamt	
M7	phrase book / ˈfreɪz bʊk /	Sprachführer	
	give directions / ˌɡɪv dɪˈrekʃnz /	den Weg beschreiben	The tourist is asking the man for directions. The man is giving him directions.
	ask for directions / ˌɑːsk fə dɪˈrekʃnz /	nach dem Weg fragen	

Folgende Abkürzungen werden noch verwendet: *sb* = *somebody*, *sth* = *something*, etw = etwas, jdm/jdn = jemandem/jemanden, jmd = jemand

English sounds

Im Englischen spricht man Wörter oft anders aus, als man sie schreibt.
Deshalb ist die Lautschrift sehr nützlich: Sie gibt an, wie ein Wort ausgesprochen wird.
Hier ist eine Liste mit Lautschriftzeichen zusammen mit Beispielwörtern, in denen der entsprechende Laut vorkommt.

Vokale

/ɑː/	**ar**m
/ʌ/	b**u**t
/e/	d**e**sk
/ə/	**a**, **a**n
/ɜː/	g**ir**l, b**ir**d
/æ/	**a**pple
/ɪ/	**i**n, **i**t
/i/	ever**y**
/iː/	**ea**sy, **ea**t
/ɒ/	**o**range
/ɔː/	**a**ll, st**or**y
/ʊ/	l**oo**k
/u/	Febr**u**ary
/uː/	f**oo**d

Doppellaute

/aɪ/	**eye**, b**uy**
/aʊ/	**our**
/eə/	th**ere**
/eɪ/	t**a**ke, th**ey**
/ɪə/	h**ere**
/ɔɪ/	b**oy**
/əʊ/	g**o**, **o**ld
/ʊə/	**you're**

Konsonanten

/b/	**b**ag, clu**b**
/d/	**d**uck, car**d**
/f/	**f**ish, lau**gh**
/g/	**g**et, do**g**
/h/	**h**ot
/j/	**y**ou
/k/	**c**an, du**ck**
/l/	**l**ot, sma**ll**
/m/	**m**ore, **m**u**m**
/n/	**n**ow, su**n**
/ŋ/	so**ng**, lo**ng**
/p/	**p**resent, to**p**
/r/	**r**ed, **r**ight
/s/	**s**i**s**ter, cla**ss** (scharfes **s**)
/t/	**t**ime, ca**t**
/z/	no**s**e, dog**s** (weiches **s**)
/ʒ/	televi**s**ion
/dʒ/	oran**ge**
/ʃ/	**s**ure, Engli**sh**
/tʃ/	**ch**ild, **ch**eese
/ð/	**th**ese, mo**th**er (weicher Laut)
/θ/	mou**th**, **th**ink (harter Laut)
/v/	**v**ery, ha**v**e
/w/	**wh**at, **w**ord

Betonungszeichen für die folgende Silbe

/ˈ/	Hauptbetonung
/ˌ/	Nebenbetonung

The English alphabet

a	/eɪ/	**h**	/eɪtʃ/	**o**	/əʊ/	**v**	/viː/
b	/biː/	**i**	/aɪ/	**p**	/piː/	**w**	/ˈdʌbljuː/
c	/siː/	**j**	/dʒeɪ/	**q**	/kjuː/	**x**	/eks/
d	/diː/	**k**	/keɪ/	**r**	/ɑː/	**y**	/waɪ/
e	/iː/	**l**	/el/	**s**	/es/	**z**	/zed/
f	/ef/	**m**	/em/	**t**	/tiː/		
g	/dʒiː/	**n**	/en/	**u**	/juː/		

Ähnliche Wörter im Deutschen und Englischen

Es gibt viele Wörter, die im Englischen und im Deutschen gleich sind. Sie unterscheiden sich oft nur dadurch, dass die meisten von ihnen im Deutschen groß geschrieben werden. Viele dieser Wörter sprechen wir gleich aus.
Diese Wörter stehen nicht in den Wortlisten, weil sie dir ja nicht neu sind. Bei denen, die ein bisschen anders ausgesprochen werden als im Deutschen, ist die Lautschrift farbig hervorgehoben.

action /ˈækʃn/
adjective /ˈædʒɪktɪv/
adverb /ˈædvɜːb/
avocado /ˌævəˈkɑːdəʊ/
baby /ˈbeɪbi/
ball /bɔːl/
band /bænd/
baseball /ˈbeɪsˌbɔːl/
basketball /ˈbɑːskɪtˌbɔːl/
beat /biːt/
blog /blɒg/
box /bɒks/
burger /ˈbɜːgə/
butler /ˈbʌtlə/
café /ˈkæfeɪ/
cafeteria /ˌkæfəˈtɪəriə/
camp /kæmp/
champion /ˈtʃæmpiən/
chapati /tʃəˈpɑːti/
chat /tʃæt/
cheeseburger /ˈtʃiːzˌbɜːgə/
clip /klɪp/
cola /ˈkəʊlə/
collage /ˈkɒlɑːʒ/
comic /ˈkɒmɪk/
computer /kəmˈpjuːtə/
cool /kuːl/
cornflakes /ˈkɔːnˌfleɪks/
cricket /ˈkrɪkɪt/
donut /ˈdəʊˌnʌt/
download /ˌdaʊnˈləʊd/
email /ˈiːmeɪl/
event /ɪˈvent/
fair /feə/
feta (cheese) /ˈfetə/
film /fɪlm/
foul /faʊl/
gold /gəʊld/
hamburger /ˈhæmˌbɜːgə/
hey /heɪ/
highscore /ˈhaɪskɔː/
hip hop /ˈhɪp hɒp/
hockey /ˈhɒki/
home page /ˈhəʊm ˌpeɪdʒ/
hot dog /ˌhɒt ˈdɒg/
hotel /həʊˈtel/
inline skate /ˈɪnlaɪn ˌskeɪt/
international /ˌɪntəˈnæʃnəl/
Internet /ˈɪntənet/
interview /ˈɪntəˌvjuː/
jet /dʒet/
journalist /ˈdʒɜːnəlɪst/
karate /kəˈrɑːti/
ketchup /ˈketʃəp/
kid /kɪd/
lasagne /ləˈzænjə/
location /ləʊˈkeɪʃn/
make-up /ˈmeɪkˌʌp/
mango /ˈmæŋgəʊ/
marathon /ˈmærəθn/
material /məˈtɪəriəl/
mayonnaise /ˌmeɪəˈneɪz/
million /ˈmɪljən/
mini /mɪni/
modern /ˈmɒdən/
monster /ˈmɒnstə/
multi /mʌlti/
museum /mjuːˈziːəm/
musical /ˈmjuːzɪkl/
nachos /ˈnɑːtʃəʊz/
national /ˈnæʃnəl/
partner /ˈpɑːtnə/
party /ˈpɑːti/
paste /peɪst/
pizza /ˈpiːtsə/
pool /puːl/
pop (music) /(ˈ)pɒp (ˌmjuːzɪk)/
portion /ˈpɔːʃn/
post /pəʊst/
poster /ˈpəʊstə/
propeller /prəˈpelə/
quiz /kwɪz/
rap /ræp/
reporter /rɪˈpɔːtə/
rest /rest/
roast beef /ˌrəʊst ˈbiːf/
rugby /ˈrʌgbi/
salami /səˈlɑːmi/
sandwich /ˈsænwɪdʒ/
sauerkraut /ˈsaʊəˌkraʊt/
scone /skɒn/
shopping /ˈʃɒpɪŋ/
shorts /ʃɔːts/
show /ʃəʊ/
sightseeing /ˈsaɪtˌsiːɪŋ/
smoothie /ˈsmuːði/
snack /snæk/
sound check /ˈsaʊnd tʃek/
souvenir /ˌsuːvəˈnɪə/
spaghetti /spəˈgeti/
sponsor /ˈspɒnsə/
sprinter /ˈsprɪntə/
star /stɑː/
steak /steɪk/
steel band /ˈstiːl bænd/
super /ˈsuːpə/
sweatshirt /ˈswetˌʃɜːt/
team /tiːm/
teenager /ˈtiːnˌeɪdʒə/
tennis /ˈtenɪs/
text /tekst/
ticket /ˈtɪkɪt/
toast /təʊst/
toaster /ˈtəʊstə/
tour /tʊə/
tourist /ˈtʊərɪst/
trainer /ˈtreɪnə/
training /ˈtreɪnɪŋ/
trick /trɪk/
T-shirt /ˈtiːʃɜːt/
vase /vɑːz/
verb /vɜːb/
video /ˈvɪdiəʊ/
virus /ˈvaɪrəs/
volleyball /ˈvɒliˌbɔːl/
website /ˈwebˌsaɪt/
wild /waɪld/
workshop /ˈwɜːkˌʃɒp/
wow /waʊ/

Theme 1 – Are you hungry?

I	theme /θiːm/	Thema; Lektion, Kapitel	
1	write down /raɪt ˈdaʊn/	aufschreiben	
	pair /peə/	Paar	
	complete /kəmˈpliːt/	vervollständigen	
	share /ʃeə/	teilen	
	another /əˈnʌðə/	ein anderer/anderes, eine andere	
2	**menu** /ˈmenjuː/	Speisekarte	The zebra likes what's on the menu.
	page /peɪdʒ/	Seite	
	make notes /meɪk ˈnəʊts/	(sich) Notizen machen	
	regular /ˈregjʊlə/	regelmäßig; *hier:* normal	
	cheese *(no pl)* /tʃiːz/	Käse	cheese
	ham *(no pl)* /hæm/	Schinken	ham
	garlic *(no pl)* /ˈgɑːlɪk/	Knoblauch	
	bean /biːn/	Bohne	
	chilli *(pl* chillies*)* /ˈtʃɪli/	Peperoni	
	onion /ˈʌnjən/	Zwiebel	I don't like the smell of onions.
	mushroom /ˈmʌʃruːm/	Pilz	
	vegetarian /ˌvedʒəˈteəriən/	Vegetarier/in; vegetarisch	Vegetarians don't eat meat.
	broccoli *(no pl)* /ˈbrɒkəli/	Brokkoli	
	wine /waɪn/	Wein	
	coffee /ˈkɒfi/	Kaffee	
	starter /ˈstɑːtə/	Vorspeise	
	soup /suːp/	Suppe	I'll have the mushroom soup, please.
	mixed /mɪkst/	gemischt	
	lettuce /ˈletɪs/	Blattsalat; Kopfsalat	
	bacon /ˈbeɪkən/	(Schinken)speck	
	crispy /ˈkrɪspi/	knusprig	
	melon /ˈmelən/	Melone	
	cucumber /ˈkjuːˌkʌmbə/	(Salat)gurke	cucumber
	mint *(no pl)* /mɪnt/	Minze	
	bread *(no pl)* /bred/	Brot	bread
	main course /ˌmeɪn ˈkɔːs/	Hauptgericht, Hauptgang	
	curry /ˈkʌri/	Curry(gericht)	Curry is a popular Indian dish.
	roast lamb /ˌrəʊst ˈlæm/	Lammbraten	
	Yorkshire pudding /ˌjɔːkʃə ˈpʊdɪŋ/	*eine Art Gebäck als Beilage zu Fleischgerichten*	
	pie /paɪ/	Pastete	
	dessert /dɪˈzɜːt/	Nachtisch, Dessert	My favourite dessert is ice cream.
	blackberry /ˈblækbəri/	Brombeere	
	crumble /ˈkrʌmbl/	*Fruchtauflauf*	I love chocolate, vanilla
	strawberry /ˈstrɔːbri/	Erdbeere	and strawberry ice cream.
	beverage /ˈbevrɪdʒ/	Getränk	
	onion rings /ˈʌnjən ˌrɪŋz/	Zwiebelringe	
	answer /ˈɑːnsə/	(be)antworten	
	cost *(irr)* /kɒst/	kosten	cost – cost – cost
3	title /ˈtaɪtl/	Titel	
	read along /ˌriːd‿əˈlɒŋ/	mitlesen	
	which /wɪtʃ/	welche(r, s)	
	tonight /təˈnaɪt/	heute Abend	What's for dinner tonight?
	well /wel/	nun (ja), tja	

	go out /gəʊ‿ˈaʊt/	(hinaus)gehen; *hier:* ausgehen	
	ages ago *(informal)* /ˈeɪdʒɪz‿əˌgəʊ/	vor einer Ewigkeit, vor langer Zeit	
	noisy /ˈnɔɪzi/	laut	noisy ↔ quiet
	inside /ɪnˈsaɪd/	drinnen; innen	inside ↔ outside
	anyway /ˈeniˌweɪ/	sowieso	
	pub /pʌb/	Kneipe, Gaststätte	
	taste /teɪst/	schmecken	Chocolate tastes sweet.
	order /ˈɔːdə/	bestellen	Are you ready to order? – Yes, I'd like the chicken curry, please.
	quite /kwaɪt/	ziemlich	
	fancy sth *(informal)* /ˈfænsi ˌsʌmθɪŋ/	auf etw Lust haben	
	hot /hɒt/	heiß; *hier:* scharf	Indian food can be very hot.
	spicy /ˈspaɪsi/	würzig; scharf	
	takeaway (food) /ˈteɪkəˌweɪ/	Essen zum Mitnehmen	
	OK then *(informal)* /ˌəʊˈkeɪ ðen/	na gut, also gut	
	have a look (at sth) /hæv‿ə ˈlʊk/	(sich) (etw) (an)schauen	
	dialogue /ˈdaɪəlɒg/	Gespräch, Dialog	
	act out /ækt‿ˈaʊt/	nachspielen	
	scene /siːn/	Szene	
	group of three /gruːp‿əv ˈθriː/	Dreiergruppe	
4	take notes /teɪk ˈnəʊts/	(sich) Notizen machen	
	main dish /meɪn ˈdɪʃ/	Hauptgericht	
	mixed grill /mɪkst ˈgrɪl/	Grillteller, Grillplatte	
	side order /ˈsaɪd‿ˌɔːdə/	Beilage	
	boiled /bɔɪld/	gekocht	
	rice *(no pl)* /raɪs/	Reis	
	raita /ˈraɪtə/	*Joghurt mit Gurke und Minze*	
5	grid /grɪd/	Gitter; *hier:* Tabelle	
	like this /laɪk ˈðɪs/	so	
6	**guest** /gest/	Gast	The waiter serves the guest some soup.
	bill /bɪl/	Rechnung	Waiter, I'd like to pay, please. – Sure. Here's your bill.
	compare /kəmˈpeə/	vergleichen	
	underline /ˌʌndəˈlaɪn/	unterstreichen	
	phrase /freɪz/	Satz; Ausdruck, (Rede)wendung	
	make up sth /ˌmeɪk‿ˈʌp ˌsʌmθɪŋ/	(sich) etw ausdenken, etw erfinden	
7	present /prɪˈzent/	präsentieren	
	design /dɪˈzaɪn/	entwerfen	
	crossword puzzle /ˈkrɒswɜːd ˌpʌzl/	Kreuzworträtsel	
	wordsearch /ˈwɜːdsɜːtʃ/	Wortsuchrätsel	
	Greek /griːk/	griechisch	
8	**mean** *(irr)* /miːn/	bedeuten; meinen	mean – meant – meant
	What's wrong? /wɒts ˈrɒŋ/	Was ist los?	
	speech bubble /ˈspiːtʃ ˌbʌbl/	Sprechblase	
	translation /trænsˈleɪʃn/	Übersetzung	
	question tag /ˈkwestʃn ˌtæg/	Bestätigungsfrage	
9	Hands up! /ˌhændz‿ˈʌp/	Hände hoch!; *hier:* Meldet euch!	
	survey /ˈsɜːveɪ/	Untersuchung, Umfrage	

TIPP

Teamwork
Zu zweit macht das Vokabellernen mehr Spaß. Fragt euch gegenseitig ab. Tauscht euch auch darüber aus, wie ihr am besten Wörter lernt. Wenn ihr Lust habt, könnt ihr selbst Lückentexte, Kreuzwort- oder Buchstabenrätsel für den Partner/die Partnerin erstellen.

	each /iːtʃ/	jede(r, s)	
	sugary /ˈʃʊgəri/	zuckerhaltig	
	a day /ə ˈdeɪ/	pro/am Tag	You should drink 5 glasses of water a day.
	a week /ə ˈwiːk/	pro/in der Woche	
	peanut /ˈpiːnʌt/	Erdnuss	
	report /rɪˈpɔːt/	berichten	
	result /rɪˈzʌlt/	Ergebnis; Folge	
10	item /ˈaɪtəm/	Artikel, Ding	
	unhealthy /ʌnˈhelθi/	ungesund	Many people love unhealthy food.
	cereal /ˈsɪəriəl/	Getreide(sorte); Frühstückszerealien, -flocken	
	spinach *(no pl)* /ˈspɪnɪdʒ/	Spinat	
	yoghurt *(no pl)* /ˈjɒgət/	Joghurt	strawberry yoghurt 
	expert /ˈekspɜːt/	Experte/Expertin	
	surprising /səˈpraɪzɪŋ/	überraschend	
	if /ɪf/	wenn, falls	
	unsweetened /ˌʌnˈswiːtənd/	ungesüßt	
	piece /piːs/	Stück	a piece of strawberry cake 
	especially /ɪˈspeʃli/	besonders	
	pea /piː/	Erbse	 peas
	contain /kənˈteɪn/	enthalten	
	health *(no pl)* /helθ/	Gesundheit	Vegetables are good for your health.
	instead (of) /ɪnˈsted (‿əv)/	stattdessen; (an)statt	
	without /wɪðˈaʊt/	ohne	without ↔ with
11	food technology /ˈfuːd tekˌnɒlədʒi/	Ernährung *(Schulfach)*	
	interview /ˈɪntəˌvjuː/	befragen; *hier:* interviewen	
	statement /ˈsteɪtmənt/	Aussage; Äußerung	
	cabbage /ˈkæbɪdʒ/	Kohl, Kraut	
	pasta *(no pl)* /ˈpæstə/	Nudeln	Spaghetti is a kind of pasta.
	have a sweet tooth /hæv‿ə swiːt ˈtuːθ/	gerne Süßigkeiten essen, eine Naschkatze sein	
	absolutely /ˈæbsəluːtli/	absolut, völlig	
	soft /sɒft/	weich	
	disgusting /dɪsˈgʌstɪŋ/	widerlich	
	note /nəʊt/	Notiz	
	double circle /ˌdʌbl ˈsɜːkl/	Doppelkreis	
12	**recipe** /ˈresəpi/	Rezept	I have a great recipe for muffins.
	overweight /ˌəʊvəˈweɪt/	übergewichtig	
	order /ˈɔːdə/	Ordnung, Reihenfolge	
	leek /liːk/	Lauch	
	bunch /bʌntʃ/	Büschel, Bund	tbs = tablespoon *(Esslöffel)*
	parsley *(no pl)* /ˈpɑːsli/	Petersilie	tsp = teaspoon *(Teelöffel)*
	oil /ɔɪl/	Öl	
	powder *(no pl)* /ˈpaʊdə/	Pulver	
	salt *(no pl)* /sɔːlt/	Salz	Most dishes taste boring
	pepper *(no pl)* /ˈpepə/	Pfeffer	without salt and pepper.
	cumin *(no pl)* /ˈkʌmɪn/	Kreuzkümmel	
	seed /siːd/	Same(n), Korn	
	macaroni *(no pl)* /ˌmækəˈrəʊni/	Makkaroni	

into /ˈɪntʊ/	in	
cut sth open /kʌt ˌsʌmθɪŋ‿ˈəʊpən/	etw aufschneiden	
middle /ˈmɪdl/	Mitte	
dry /draɪ/	trocknen	
leaf *(pl* leaves*)* /liːf, liːvz/	Blatt	
cut off /kʌt‿ˈɒf/	abschneiden	
thin /θɪn/	dünn	
strip /strɪp/	Streifen	
mix /mɪks/	(ver)mischen, anrühren	To bake a cake you need to mix eggs, flour, sugar and butter.
tablespoon /ˈteɪblˌspuːn/	Esslöffel	
add /æd/	hinzufügen	
heat /hiːt/	erhitzen	To cook pasta you have to heat water.
pan /pæn/	Pfanne	
low /ləʊ/	niedrig	
temperature /ˈtemprɪtʃə/	Temperatur	
stir /stɜː/	rühren	
few /fjuː/	paar	
boiling /ˈbɔɪlɪŋ/	kochend	
salted /ˈsɔːltɪd/	gesalzen	
pour /pɔː/	gießen, schütten	
break *(irr)* /breɪk/	(zer)brechen	break – broke – broken
off /ɒf/	weg von	
stove /stəʊv/	Herd	
cooking *(no pl)* /ˈkʊkɪŋ/	Kochen	
13 **British** /ˈbrɪtɪʃ/	britische(r, s)	
Thai /taɪ/	thailändisch	
around /əˈraʊnd/	herum, umher	
14 eating habits *(only pl)* /ˌiːtɪŋ ˈhæbɪts/	Essgewohnheiten	
around the world /əˌraʊnd ðə ˈwɜːld/	weltweit, auf der ganzen Welt	
country /ˈkʌntri/	Land	
way /weɪ/	Weg; *hier:* Art, Weise	
match (with) /mætʃ/	zuordnen	
go with /ˈgəʊ wɪð/	gehören zu, passen zu	
onto /ˈɒntə/	auf	
back /bæk/	Rücken; Rückseite	
around /əˈraʊnd/	um	They are sitting around a table.
cloth *(no pl)* /klɒθ/	Tuch, Stoff	
roll /rəʊl/	rollen	You roll spaghetti around a fork to eat them.
pick up /ˌpɪk‿ˈʌp/	aufheben; *hier:* aufnehmen	
flat /flæt/	flach	
thumb /θʌm/	Daumen	
chopstick /ˈtʃɒpˌstɪk/	(Ess)stäbchen	
hold *(irr)* /həʊld/	halten	hold – held – held
serve /sɜːv/	servieren	
bowl /bəʊl/	Schüssel	
typical /ˈtɪpɪkl/	typisch	

15	label /ˈleɪbl/	beschriften	
P1	similar /ˈsɪmɪlə/	ähnlich	
P2	missing /ˈmɪsɪŋ/	fehlend	
P3	repeat /rɪˈpiːt/	wiederholen	
P4	part /pɑːt/	Teil	
P7	eat out /iːt‿ˈaʊt/	essen gehen, auswärts essen	
P9	poem /ˈpəʊɪm/	Gedicht	
	pork *(no pl)* /pɔːk/	Schweinefleisch	
	truth /truːθ/	Wahrheit	
	yourself *(pl* yourselves*)* /jəˈself, jəˈselvz/	dich, dir; selbst/ihr, euch; selbst	
	by heart /baɪ ˈhɑːt/	auswendig	
P11	what else /wɒt‿ˈels/	was noch, was sonst	
	at least /ət ˈliːst/	mindestens, wenigstens	
	baked potato /beɪkt pəˈteɪtəʊ/	Ofenkartoffel	
P12	breast /brest/	Brust	
	dish *(pl -es)* /dɪʃ/	Gericht; *hier:* Schale	
	cover /ˈkʌvə/	bedecken	
	mixture /ˈmɪkstʃə/	Mischung	
	slice /slaɪs/	Scheibe	
	fry /fraɪ/	frittieren, braten	
M1	article /ˈɑːtɪkl/	Artikel	
	mention /ˈmenʃn/	erwähnen	
	popular /ˈpɒpjʊlə/	beliebt	Football is very popular in Germany.
	takeaway /ˈteɪkəˌweɪ/	Essen zum Mitnehmen; *hier:* Imbiss	
	original /əˈrɪdʒnəl/	ursprünglich	
	mild /maɪld/	sanft; *hier:* mild	
	traditionally /trəˈdɪʃnəli/	traditionell; üblicherweise, normalerweise	
	spice /spaɪs/	Gewürz	Rajiv puts a lot of spices in his curry.
	some of which /ˈsʌm‿əv wɪtʃ/	von denen einige	
	vindaloo /ˌvɪndəˈluː/	*sehr scharfes indisches Gericht*	
	test of courage /test‿əv ˈkʌrɪdʒ/	Mutprobe	
	World Cup /ˌwɜːld ˈkʌp/	Weltmeisterschaft	
	chant /tʃɑːnt/	Sprechgesang, Sprechchor	
	beer *(no pl)* /bɪə/	Bier	
	type /taɪp/	Art; Typ, Sorte	Spaghetti is a type of pasta.
	lentil /ˈlentɪl/	Linse	
	tikka /ˈtiːkə/	*indisches Gericht*	
	masala /məˈsɑːlə/	*würzige indische Soße*	
	just /dʒʌst/	gleich; *hier:* nur	
	that /ðæt/	dass	Charlie thinks that pizza is delicious.
	the British *(only pl)* /ðə ˈbrɪtɪʃ/	die Briten	
	add /æd/	hinzufügen	Add some more spices to the curry. Then it'll taste better.
	coconut /ˈkəʊkəˌnʌt/	Kokosnuss	
	cream *(no pl)* /kriːm/	Sahne; *hier:* Creme	
	match /mætʃ/	passen zu	

TIPP

Probier's mal mit Gemütlichkeit
Nicht nur für das Vokabellernen gilt: Du solltest dich an dem Ort, an dem du arbeitest, wohlfühlen und durch nichts abgelenkt sein! Eine gewisse Ordnung erleichtert das Arbeiten. Mache regelmäßig Pausen, in denen du z. B. das Fenster öffnest, etwas trinkst und dich bewegst. So kannst du dich besser konzentrieren.

	expression /ɪkˈspreʃn/	Ausdruck	
	who /huː/	wer; *hier:* der/die/das	
	find out /faɪnd‿ˈaʊt/	herausfinden	
M2	**go out** /ɡəʊ‿ˈaʊt/	(hinaus)gehen; *hier:* ausgehen	I like to go out in the evening.
M3	meaning /ˈmiːnɪŋ/	Bedeutung	
M4	thought bubble /ˈθɔːt ˌbʌbl/	Denkblase, Gedankenblase	
M5	diagram /ˈdaɪəɡræm/	Diagramm, Schaubild	
	name /neɪm/	(be)nennen	
	half *(pl* **halves***)* /hɑːf, hɑːvz/	Hälfte	cut an apple in half
	put together /pʊt təˈɡeðə/	zusammensetzen, zusammenstellen	
M6	in the end /ˌɪn ði‿ˈend/	letzten Endes; schließlich	
	well /wel/	nun (ja), tja	
	ow /aʊ/	au	
	water /ˈwɔːtə/	gießen; *hier:* tränen	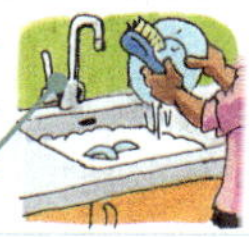
	ouch /aʊtʃ/	aua, autsch	
	poor you /pɔː ˈjuː/	du Arme(r)	
	tap /tæp/	Wasserhahn	tap
	hurt *(irr)* /hɜːt/	wehtun, schmerzen	hurt – hurt – hurt
	phew /fjuː/	puh	
	put in /pʊt‿ˈɪn/	hineinsetzen/-legen/-stellen; *hier:* hineintun	
M7	piece of paper /ˌpiːs‿əv ˈpeɪpə/	Blatt Papier, Zettel	
	take turns /ˌteɪk ˈtɜːnz/	sich abwechseln	
CC	chronicle /ˈkrɒnɪkl/	Anzeiger	
	the … way /ðə ˈweɪ/	auf die … Art	
	get *(irr)* /ɡet/	erhalten, bekommen; *hier:* verstehen	
	traditional /trəˈdɪʃnəl/	traditionell	
	speciality /ˌspeʃiˈæləti/	Spezialität	
	lemon curd *(no pl)* /ˌlemən ˈkɜːd/	*Creme aus Eiern, Zucker und Zitronensaft*	
	ingredient /ɪnˈɡriːdiənt/	Zutat	
	lemon /ˈlemən/	Zitrone	
	thick /θɪk/	dick	
	cream *(no pl)* /kriːm/	Sahne; *hier:* Creme	
	lemon meringue pie /ˌlemən məˌræŋ ˈpaɪ/	*Zitronen-Baiser-Torte*	
	millionaire /ˌmɪljəˈneə/	Millionär/in	
	luxury /ˈlʌkʃəri/	Luxus	
	cold /kəʊld/	Kälte	
	heat *(no pl)* /hiːt/	Wärme; Hitze	
	a plateful of /ə ˈpleɪtfʊl‿əv/	ein Teller (voll)	
	save /seɪv/	retten; *hier:* aufheben	
	cookie /ˈkʊki/	Keks, Plätzchen	

TIPP

Mache sie zu deinen Wörtern!
Am besten kannst du dir Wörter merken, die du selbst verwendet hast. Darum: Bilde Sätze mit den Wörtern, die du dir merken willst. Sie können auch lustig sein oder sich reimen:
My mum can make a yummy cake.

Theme 2 – Are you fit?

1	**test** /test/	prüfen, testen	
	guess /ges/	Vermutung	
	piece of paper /ˌpiːs‿əv ˈpeɪpə/	Blatt Papier, Zettel	
	up and down /ˌʌp‿ən ˈdaʊn/	auf und ab	He is jumping up and down angrily.
	second /ˈsekənd/	Sekunde	60 seconds = one minute
	out of breath /aʊt‿əv ˈbreθ/	außer Atem, atemlos	
	not at all /nɒt‿ət‿ˈɔːl/	überhaupt nicht	
	backwards /ˈbækwədz/	rückwärts	
	stair /steə/	(Treppen)stufe	
	just /dʒʌst/	gleich; *hier:* nur	Are you hungry? – Yes, but just a little.
	balance /ˈbæləns/	das Gleichgewicht halten	
	not quite /nɒt ˈkwaɪt/	nicht ganz	
	press /pres/	drücken, pressen	
	answer /ˈɑːnsə/	(be)antworten	Please answer my question.
	mostly /ˈməʊstli/	größtenteils; hauptsächlich; meistens	
	keep up sth /ˌkiːp‿ˈʌp ˌsʌmθɪŋ/	etw fortführen, etw weiterhin tun	
	work /wɜːk/	Arbeit	
	Oh dear! /əʊ ˈdɪə/	Du meine Güte!	
3	ice hockey /ˈaɪs ˌhɒki/	Eishockey	
	equipment *(no pl)* /ɪˈkwɪpmənt/	Ausrüstung, Ausstattung	
	helmet /ˈhelmɪt/	Helm	different helmets 
	train /treɪn/	trainieren	
	twice /twaɪs/	zweimal	once, twice, three times, ...
	sports hall /ˈspɔːts hɔːl/	Sporthalle	
	skateboarding /ˈskeɪtˌbɔːdɪŋ/	Skateboardfahren	
	whenever /wenˈevə/	immer wenn, wann (auch) immer	
	skate park /ˈskeɪt pɑːk/	Skatepark	
	practise /ˈpræktɪs/	üben	
	running /ˈrʌnɪŋ/	Laufen, Rennen	Cycling is the second part of a triathlon, running is the last.
	cycling /ˈsaɪklɪŋ/	Radfahren, Radeln	
	short /ʃɔːt/	kurz	short ↔ long
	break down /ˌbreɪk ˈdaʊn/	kaputtgehen	
	race /reɪs/	Rennen	He won the race. 
	still /stɪl/	(immer) noch, noch immer; *hier:* trotzdem, dennoch	
	do well /duː ˈwel/	gut abschneiden	
	swimmer /ˈswɪmə/	Schwimmer/in	He is a good swimmer. 
	sb cannot wait (to do sth) /ˌsʌmbədi ˌkænɒt ˈweɪt/	jmd kann es kaum erwarten (, etw zu tun)	
	even /ˈiːvn/	sogar; *hier:* noch	
4	warm-up /ˈwɔːmˌʌp/	Warm-up, Aufwärmen	
	stretch /stretʃ/	(sich) dehnen	
	punchbag /ˈpʌntʃˌbæg/	Sandsack, Boxsack	
	colour /ˈkʌlə/	Farbe	
	belt /belt/	Gürtel	
	stand for sth /ˈstænd fə ˌsʌmθɪŋ/	für etw stehen, etw bedeuten	
	find out /faɪnd‿ˈaʊt/	herausfinden	

5 **who** /huː/	wer; *hier:* der/die/das	Someone who does a lot of sport is often slim and fit. This gorilla isn't. 
slim /slɪm/	schlank, schmal, dünn	
5 **sportsperson** /ˈspɔːtsˌpɜːsn/	Sportler/in	A swimmer is a sportsperson.
fact file /ˈfækt ˌfaɪl/	Steckbrief	
country /ˈkʌntri/	Land	China is a very big country.
successful /səkˈsesfl/	erfolgreich	
goalkeeper /ˈɡəʊlˌkiːpə/	Tormann/Torfrau	This goalkeeper was not very successful. 
7 chant /tʃɑːnt/	Sprechgesang, Sprechchor	
cheer on /tʃɪər‿ˈɒn/	anfeuern	
dribble /ˈdrɪbl/	dribbeln	
pass /pɑːs/	vorbeikommen; *hier:* abgeben, abspielen	
give up /ˌɡɪv‿ˈʌp/	aufgeben	The football team didn't play well. But the players didn't give up and they were successful in the end.
give in /ˌɡɪv‿ˈɪn/	nachgeben	
8 friendly match /ˈfrendli mætʃ/	Freundschaftsspiel	
buzz group /ˈbʌz ɡruːp/	*Form der Gruppenarbeit*	
article /ˈɑːtɪkl/	Artikel	
end /end/	enden	
charity /ˈtʃærəti/	Wohltätigkeitsorganisation; *hier:* wohltätige Zwecke	
raise money /reɪz ˈmʌni/	Geld aufbringen/auftreiben	
take place /teɪk ˈpleɪs/	stattfinden	
sports field /ˈspɔːts fiːld/	Sportplatz, Spielfeld	Our school has a great new sports field.
pm (= post meridiem) /ˌpiːˈem, ˌpəʊst məˈrɪdiəm/	nachmittags, abends *(nur hinter Uhrzeit zwischen 12 Uhr mittags und Mitternacht)*	pm = 12:00 to 24:00
chant /tʃɑːnt/	singen; einen Sprechgesang anstimmen	
captain /ˈkæptɪn/	Kapitän/in	Charlie is the captain of his football team. 
score a goal /skɔːr‿ə ˈɡəʊl/	ein Tor schießen	Rajiv scored a goal.
goal /ɡəʊl/	Tor	goal 
go wild *(informal)* /ɡəʊ ˈwaɪld/	außer sich geraten, aus dem Häuschen geraten	
crowd /kraʊd/	(Menschen)menge, Zuschauermenge	
half time /ˌhɑːf ˈtaɪm/	Halbzeit	
score /skɔː/	Punktestand; *hier:* Spielstand	
half *(pl* **halves***)* /hɑːf, hɑːvz/	Hälfte	Nick scored a goal for Haverstock in the second half of the match.
trouble *(no pl)* /ˈtrʌbl/	Schwierigkeiten	This surfer is in great trouble. 
keep doing sth /kiːp ˈduːɪŋ sʌmθɪŋ/	etw weiter tun	
fall off /fɔːl‿ˈɒf/	herunterfallen, abfallen	
toward(s) /təˈwɔːd(z)/	in Richtung	

	run into sb/sth /rʌn‿ˈɪntʊ ˌsʌmbədi/ˌsʌmθɪŋ/	in jdn/etw hineinrennen	
	knock down sb/sth /nɒk ˈdaʊn ˌsʌmbədi/ˌsʌmθɪŋ/	jdn/etw umstoßen	
	referee /ˌrefəˈriː/	Schiedsrichter/in	Many football fans don't like referees.
	sportsmanship *(no pl)* /ˈspɔːtsmənʃɪp/	Fairness	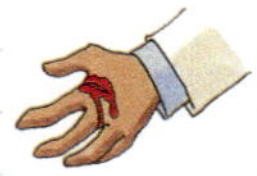
	injured /ˈɪndʒəd/	verletzt	He cut his hand. Now he is injured.
	bad luck *(no pl)* /ˌbæd ˈlʌk/	Pech	
	left /left/	(nach) links; *hier:* übrig	There are no chocolate muffins left because André ate them all.
	cheer /tʃɪə/	jubeln	They cheered when their team won the match. 
	forward /ˈfɔːwəd/	nach vorn(e)	
	end in a draw /ˌend‿ɪn‿ə ˈdrɔː/	unentschieden ausgehen	
9	how to /haʊ tə/	wie man	
	keep fit /ˌkiːp ˈfɪt/	sich fit halten	
	visit /ˈvɪzɪt/	Besuch	
	press-up /ˈpres ʌp/	Liegestütz	
	sleep *(no pl)* /sliːp/	Schlaf	
11	have a guess /ˌhəv‿ə ˈges/	raten, schätzen; *hier:* vermuten	
	need to /ˈniːd tə/	müssen	
	still /stɪl/	(immer) noch, noch immer	I'm not angry with you anymore. Don't worry, I'm still your friend.
	hurt *(irr)* /hɜːt/	wehtun, schmerzen	hurt – hurt – hurt
12	waiting room /ˈweɪtɪŋ ˌruːm/	Wartezimmer	
	ow /aʊ/	au	
	huh /hʌ/	häh?	
	bruise /bruːz/	sich prellen/stoßen	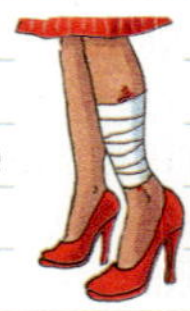
	swollen /ˈswəʊlən/	geschwollen	
	bandage /ˈbændɪdʒ/	Verband	She has to wear a bandage around her leg.
	receptionist /rɪˈsepʃnɪst/	Sprechstundenhilfe	
	surgery /ˈsɜːdʒəri/	(Arzt)praxis	
	fall *(irr)* /fɔːl/	fallen	fall – fell – fallen 
	ouch /aʊtʃ/	aua, autsch	
	I see. /aɪ siː/	Aha!, Ich verstehe.	
	X-ray /ˈeksˌreɪ/	Röntgenstrahl(en); *hier:* Röntgenbild	
	so /səʊ/	deshalb; also; hier: damit, sodass	
	a few /ə ˈfjuː/	einige	a few ⟷ many
	bruised /bruːzd/	geprellt	
	prescription /prɪˈskrɪpʃən/	Rezept, Verschreibung	
	cream /kriːm/	Creme, Salbe	cream 
	dictionary /ˈdɪkʃənri/	Wörterbuch	
	character /ˈkærɪktə/	Charakter; Figur	
	role /rəʊl/	Rolle	
13	during /ˈdjʊərɪŋ/	während	
	put on /pʊt‿ˈɒn/	anziehen; *hier:* auftragen	She is putting cream on her leg.

14	**patient** /ˈpeɪʃnt/	Patient/in	When you are at the doctor's because you are ill, you are his/her patient.
	stomach ache /ˈstʌmək ‿ˌeɪk/	Magenschmerzen, Bauchschmerzen	 The dog has got stomach ache.
	bad /bæd/	schlecht; *hier:* schlimm, stark	The old lady has got a bad cold. 
	cold /kəʊld/	Kälte; *hier:* Erkältung, Schnupfen	
	backache /ˈbækeɪk/	Rückenschmerzen	The girl has got backache. 
	cut foot /ˌkʌt ˈfʊt/	Schnittwunde am Fuß	
	sore /sɔː/	wund, entzündet	She has got a sore leg.
	broken /ˈbrəʊkən/	zerbrochen, kaputt; *hier:* gebrochen	His arm is broken. 
	reason /ˈriːzn/	Grund	
	out /aʊt/	draußen	
	rain /reɪn/	Regen	They played football in the rain.
	step on sth /ˈstep‿ɒn ˌsʌmθɪŋ/	auf etw treten	
	imagine /ɪˈmædʒɪn/	sich vorstellen	
	advice *(no pl)* /ədˈvaɪs/	Rat	
	medicine *(no pl)* /ˈmedsn/	Medizin, Medikament(e)	
15	too bad /ˌtuː ˈbæd/	wirklich schade; *hier:* so ein Pech	
	think about (sb/sth) /ˈθɪŋk‿əˌbaʊt/	an (jdn/etw) denken; über (jdn/etw) nachdenken	
16	stick man /ˈstɪk ˌmæn/	Strichmännchen	
	record /rɪˈkɔːd/	aufnehmen, aufzeichnen	
	dramatic /drəˈmætɪk/	dramatisch	
	reading /ˈriːdɪŋ/	Lesen; Lesung	
	create /kriˈeɪt/	erschaffen; gestalten	
P1	word web /ˈwɜːd web/	Wortnetz	
P2	example /ɪɡˈzɑːmpl/	Beispiel	
P3	make sure /ˌmeɪk ˈʃɔː/	sich versichern, darauf achten	
	that /ðæt/	dass	
	lead *(irr)* /liːd/	(an)führen, leiten	
P5	comparative (form) /kəmˈpærətɪv/	Komparativ	
	superlative (form) /sʊˈpɜːlətɪv/	Superlativ	
	comparison /kəmˈpærɪsn/	Vergleich	
P6	guard /ɡɑːd/	bewachen	
	start /stɑːt/	Anfang, Beginn	
	describe /dɪˈskraɪb/	beschreiben	
	action /ˈækʃn/	Handlung; Aktion	
P7	certain /ˈsɜːtn/	gewisse(r, s), bestimmte(r, s)	
	crazy /ˈkreɪzi/	verrückt	
	following /ˈfɒləʊɪŋ/	folgende(r, s)	
	huge /hjuːdʒ/	riesig, riesengroß	
	thank you /ˈθæŋk juː/	Dankeschön, Danke	
P8	toothache /ˈtuːθeɪk/	Zahnschmerzen	
	headache /ˈhedeɪk/	Kopfschmerzen, Kopfweh	
P9	copy /ˈkɒpi/	abschreiben	
	letter /ˈletə/	Brief; Buchstabe	

TIPP

Unregelmäßige Verben
(irregular verbs)
erkennst du im Wörterverzeichnis an der Kennzeichnung *(irr)*. Sie haben unregelmäßige Formen für die Vergangenheit, die du dir gut einprägen musst. Eine Liste der unregelmäßigen Verben findest du auf den Seiten 283 und 284.

M1	leaflet /ˈliːflət/	Prospekt, Broschüre	
	take place /teɪk ˈpleɪs/	stattfinden	The New York City Marathon takes place on the first Sunday in November.
	starting point /ˈstɑːtɪŋ ˌpɔɪnt/	Start, Startpunkt	
	point /pɔɪnt/	Punkt	1 mile ≈ 1.609 kilometres 1 kilometre ≈ 0.6214 miles
	mile /maɪl/	Meile	
	kilometre /ˈkɪləˌmiːtə/	Kilometer	
	elite /ɪˈliːt/	Elite; *hier:* Wettkampf-	
	am (= ante meridiem) /ˌeɪˈem, ˌænti məˈrɪdiəm/	morgens, vormittags *(nur hinter Uhrzeit zwischen Mitternacht und 12 Uhr mittags)*	am = 24:00 to 12:00
	expect /ɪkˈspekt/	erwarten	
	finishing line /ˈfɪnɪʃɪŋ ˌlaɪn/	Ziellinie	
	mass /mæs/	Masse	
	dress up (as) /dres‿ˈʌp/	sich verkleiden (als)	Gillian likes to dress up as a vampire for Halloween.
	athlete /ˈæθliːt/	Athlet/in	athlete = sportsperson
	from all over the world /frəm‿ɔːl‿ˌəʊvə ðə ˈwɜːld/	aus der ganzen Welt	
	charity /ˈtʃærəti/	Wohltätigkeitsorganisation	Charities often collect money to help people who need help.
	detail /ˈdiːteɪl/	Detail, Einzelheit	
M2	**result** /rɪˈzʌlt/	Ergebnis; Folge	Caroline is preparing for a test. She'll get good marks as a result.
	prepare /prɪˈpeə/	(sich) vorbereiten	
M3	**stop** /stɒp/	aufhören; beenden; *hier:* aufhalten	
	Northern Ireland /ˌnɔːðn‿ˈaɪələnd/	Nordirland	Northern Ireland is a part of the UK.
	talented /ˈtæləntɪd/	talentiert, begabt	She is a talented singer. 
	develop /dɪˈveləp/	(sich) entwickeln	
	below /bɪˈləʊ/	unter(halb)	
	The Paralympic World Championships /ðə ˌpærəˌlɪmpɪk ˌwɜːld ˈtʃæmpiənʃɪps/	*Leichtathletik-Weltmeisterschaften der Behinderten*	
	New Zealand /nju ˈziːlənd/	Neuseeland	
	since then /ˌsɪns ˈðen/	seitdem, seither	
	tough /tʌf/	robust, zäh, tough; *hier:* hart	
	career /kəˈrɪə/	Beruf; Karriere	Muhammad Ali had a great career as a boxer. He was very successful.
	major /ˈmeɪdʒə/	bedeutend, wichtig	
	sacrifice /ˈsækrɪfaɪs/	Opfer	
	social /ˈsəʊʃl/	sozial	
	night /naɪt/	Nacht; *hier:* Abend	
	allowed /əˈlaʊd/	erlaubt	You are not allowed to play football here.
	education *(no pl)* /ˌedjʊˈkeɪʃn/	(Aus)bildung	
	at the same time /æt ðə seɪm ˈtaɪm/	gleichzeitig	
	university /ˌjuːnɪˈvɜːsəti/	Universität	

	Paralympic /ˌpærəˈlɪmpɪk/	paralympisch	
	prove /pruːv/	beweisen	I can prove that I did a bungee jump. Just look at this photo of me.
	although /ɔːlˈðəʊ/	obwohl, obgleich	
	disabled /dɪsˈeɪbld/	behindert	 Karla is in a wheelchair. She is disabled.
	title /ˈtaɪtl/	Titel	
14	accident /ˈæksɪdnt/	Unfall	
	the next day /ðə ˌnekst ˈdeɪ/	am nächsten Tag	
	linking word /ˈlɪŋkɪŋ wɜːd/	Bindewort	
16	help out /ˌhelp‿ˈaʊt/	(aus)helfen, unterstützen	
	exchange /ɪksˈtʃeɪndʒ/	(Aus)tausch-	
17	**injury** /ˈɪndʒəri/	Verletzung	Charlie wasn't allowed to play football because of his injury.
	local /ˈləʊkl/	örtlich	
	shoulder /ˈʃəʊldə/	Schulter	shoulder 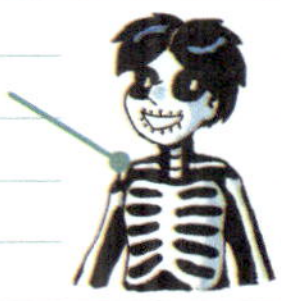
	like hell /laɪk ˈhel/	wie verrückt, höllisch	
	coach /kəʊtʃ/	Trainer(in)	
	tonight /təˈnaɪt/	heute Abend; *hier:* heute Nacht	
	bone /bəʊn/	Knochen	Rajiv is wearing a costume with just bones and no muscles on it.
	muscle /ˈmʌsl/	Muskel	
	tear *(irr)* /teə/	(zer)reißen	
	at least /ət ˈliːst/	mindestens, wenigstens	You should do sports at least twice a week. It's fun and keeps you fit.
	recover /rɪˈkʌvə/	sich erholen	
	the Nationals /ðə ˈnæʃnəlz/	*nationaler Wettkampf*	
	ruined /ˈruːɪnd/	zerstört, ruiniert	
	just /dʒʌst/	gleich; *hier:* gerade	
	physiotherapist /ˌfɪziəʊˈθerəpɪst/	Physiotherapeut/in, Krankengymnast/in	
	exercise /ˈeksəsaɪz/	Übung	Press-ups and crunches are exercises.
	possible /ˈpɒsəbəl/	möglich	
	fighter /ˈfaɪtə/	Kämpfer(in)	This boxer is a fighter. 
	butterfly /ˈbʌtəˌflaɪ/	Schmetterling	
	frustrating /ˈfrʌˌstreɪtɪŋ/	frustrierend	
	down *(informal)* /daʊn/	niedergeschlagen, down	
	light /laɪt/	leicht	
	success *(no pl)* /səkˈses/	Erfolg	Muhammad Ali had a lot of success in his career as a boxer.
	luck *(no pl)* /lʌk/	Glück	I have an English test tomorrow. – Good luck!
C	popular /ˈpɒpjʊlə/	beliebt	
	Gaelic /ˈɡeɪlɪk/	Gälisch; gälisch	
	table tennis /ˈteɪbl ˌtenɪs/	Tischtennis	
	kickboxing /ˈkɪkˌbɒksɪŋ/	Kickboxen	
	wrestling /ˈreslɪŋ/	Ringen, Ringkampf	
	skiing /ˈskiːɪŋ/	Skifahren, Skilaufen	
	archery /ˈɑːtʃəri/	Bogenschießen	

TIPP

Nur 10 Minuten!
Übe Vokabeln immer nur ca. 10 Minuten, aber dafür regelmäßig! Das bringt mehr als mal eine ganze Stunde oder nur zweimal im Monat.

Theme 3 – What's on in your area?

I	What's on? /wɒts‿ˈɒn/	Was ist los?	
	area /ˈeəriə/	Gebiet, Region; *hier:* Viertel, Gegend	
2	**at the top (of)** /æt ðə ˈtɒp/	oben, am oberen Ende (von), an der Spitze (von)	He is at the top of the mountain.
	at the bottom (of) /æt ðə ˈbɒtəm/	unten, am unteren Ende (von)	There is a number at the bottom of this page.
3	catch *(irr)* /kætʃ/	fangen; *hier:* erwischen, kriegen	
	yeah *(informal)* /jeə/	ja	
	this way /ˈðɪs weɪ/	so, auf diese Art und Weise	
	the same /ðə ˈseɪm/	der-/die-/dasselbe; *hier:* gleich	
	give sb a high five /gɪv ˌsʌmbədi ə ˌhaɪ ˈfaɪv/	jdn abklatschen	
	verse /vɜːs/	Strophe	
4	be about /bi‿əˈbaʊt/	handeln von	
	yet /jet/	schon; bis jetzt	
	rather /ˈrɑːðə/	ziemlich; *hier:* lieber	
	be (great) fun /biː (ˌgreɪt) ˈfʌn/	(viel) Spaß machen	 Dancing is great fun.
	anyway /ˈeniˌweɪ/	jedenfalls	
	colleague /ˈkɒliːg/	Kollege/Kollegin; Mitarbeiter/in	You see your colleagues at work every day.
	work /wɜːk/	Arbeit	
	sb would love (to) /ˌsʌmbədi wʊd ˈlʌv/	jmd möchte sehr gern	Charlie would love some ice cream. 
	most (of) /məʊst/	das meiste (von), ein Großteil	Jake slept during most of the lesson.
	pocket /ˈpɒkɪt/	Tasche	Dad carries his keys in his pocket.
	pocket money *(no pl)* /ˈpɒkɪt ˌmʌni/	Taschengeld	
	right /raɪt/	richtig; *hier:* oder	
	north /nɔːθ/	nördlich, Nord-	Hamburg is north of Hanover.
	car boot sale /ˌkɑː ˈbuːt ˌseɪl/	*Verkauf persönlicher Gegenstände aus dem Kofferraum auf einem Parkplatz*	
5	point /pɔɪnt/	Punkt	
6	**pair** /peə/	Paar	I really need a new pair of jeans.
	in the end /ˌɪn ði‿ˈend/	letzten Endes; schließlich	
7	**special offer** /ˌspeʃl‿ˈɒfə/	Sonderangebot	
	work /wɜːk/	arbeiten; *hier:* funktionieren	
	change /tʃeɪndʒ/	(Ver)änderung; *hier:* Wechselgeld	
	size /saɪz/	Größe	
	toy /tɔɪ/	Spielzeug	
8	**powerful** /ˈpaʊəfl/	mächtig	
	Africa /ˈæfrɪkə/	Afrika	
	look up to /lʊk‿ˈʌp tə/	aufblicken zu	
	jealous /ˈdʒeləs/	eifersüchtig	Dan is jealous of me.
	kill /kɪl/	töten	
	rescue /ˈreskjuː/	retten	
	valley /ˈvæli/	Tal	mountain ↔ valley
	hyena /haɪˈiːnə/	Hyäne	
	scare /skeə/	Angst machen, erschrecken	Zombies scare him. 

panic /ˈpænɪk/	Panik	Caroline felt panic. 
trample down /ˌtræmpl ˈdaʊn/	niedertrampeln, zertrampeln	
save /seɪv/	retten	
make sb believe sth /meɪk ˌsʌmbədi bɪˈliːv ˌsʌmθɪŋ/	jdn etw glauben machen, jdm etw weismachen	
almost /ˈɔːlməʊst/	fast, beinahe	Patch ate almost all the sausages.
return /rɪˈtɜːn/	zurückkehren	When will you return from the trip?
close /kləʊs/	nah(e); *hier:* genau	
sort /sɔːt/	sortieren	
look up /lʊk‿ˈʌp/	nachschlagen	
meaning /ˈmiːnɪŋ/	Bedeutung	
fit *(irr)* /fɪt/	passen (zu)	
best /best/	am meisten/liebsten/besten	
10 project /ˈprɒdʒekt/	Projekt	
plan /plæn/	planen	
think about (sb/sth) /ˈθɪŋk‿əˌbaʊt/	an (jdn/etw) denken; sich (etw) überlegen	
town /taʊn/	Stadt	
visitor /ˈvɪzɪtə/	Besucher/in	
interview /ˈɪntəˌvjuː/	befragen	
local /ˈləʊkl/	örtlich	
newspaper /ˈnjuːzˌpeɪpə/	Zeitung	
search /sɜːtʃ/	(durch)suchen	
opening times *(only pl)* /ˈəʊpnɪŋ ˌtaɪmz/	Öffnungszeiten	
get *(irr)* /get/	erhalten, bekommen; *hier:* (an)kommen	
cover /ˈkʌvə/	Titelseite, Cover	
match /mætʃ/	passen (zu)	
detail /ˈdiːteɪl/	Detail, Einzelheit	
edit /ˈedɪt/	bearbeiten, redigieren	
stick *(irr)* /stɪk/	kleben	
Open Day /ˈəʊpən ˌdeɪ/	Tag der offenen Tür	
exchange /ɪksˈtʃeɪndʒ/	(Aus)tausch-	
1 **carnival** /ˈkɑːnɪvl/	Karneval	
last /lɑːst/	(an)dauern	
official /əˈfɪʃl/	offiziell	
top /tɒp/	oberes Ende; *hier:* Top-, Spitzen-	
compete (for) /kəmˈpiːt/	wetteifern (um), kämpfen (um)	
title /ˈtaɪtl/	Titel	
steel *(no pl)* /stiːl/	Stahl	
am (= ante meridiem) /ˌeɪˈem, ˌænti məˈrɪdiəm/	morgens, vormittags *(nur hinter Uhrzeit zwischen Mitternacht und 12 Uhr mittags)*	
parade /pəˈreɪd/	Parade, Umzug	The people in the parade are wearing costumes.
parade /pəˈreɪd/	einen Umzug machen, durch die Straßen ziehen	
main /meɪn/	Haupt-	
rhythm /ˈrɪðəm/	Rhythmus, Takt	
mobile /ˈməʊbaɪl/	mobil	

TIPP

Schwierige Wörter
Wenn du merkst, dass du bei der Schreibweise einiger englischer Wörter Schwierigkeiten hast, kannst du Folgendes tun: Schreibe das Wort auf ein großes Blatt und markiere die Stelle, die dir Probleme macht. Hänge das Blatt in deinem Zimmer auf. Du wirst merken, dass du das Wort bald richtig schreiben kannst.

	sound system /ˈsaʊnd ˌsɪstəm/	Stereoanlage, Hi-Fi-Anlage	
12	**dancer** /ˈdɑːnsə/	Tänzer/in	Gillian is a good dancer.
	brightly /ˈbraɪtli/	hell, leuchtend	
	coloured /ˈkʌləd/	bunt, farbig	
	float /fləʊt/	Festwagen	
	which /wɪtʃ/	welche(r, s); *hier:* der/die/das	
	pass by /pɑːs baɪ/	vorbeifahren, vorbeigehen	
	pickpocket /ˈpɪkˌpɒkɪt/	Taschendieb/in	A pickpocket stole her bag.
	wallet /ˈwɒlɪt/	Portemonnaie, Brieftasche	
	watch /wɒtʃ/	(Armband)uhr	a watch
	put up /pʊt‿ˈʌp/	aufhängen	
	everybody /ˈevriˌbɒdi/	jede(r); alle	
	dress up (as) /dres‿ˈʌp/	sich verkleiden (als)	Mr Smith dressed up as Batman.
	sunshine *(no pl)* /ˈsʌnˌʃaɪn/	Sonnenschein	
	Caribbean /ˌkærɪˈbiːən/	karibisch	
	close /kləʊs/	nah(e)	
	headdress /ˈhedˌdres/	Kopfschmuck	
	feather /ˈfeðə/	Feder	
	tropical /ˈtrɒpɪkl/	tropisch, Tropen-	
	bird of paradise /bɜːd‿əv ˈpærədaɪs/	Paradiesvogel	
	over /ˈəʊvə/	hinüber, herüber	
	drum /drʌm/	Trommel	a drum
	hug /hʌg/	Umarmung	
13	lots (= a lot) *(informal)* /lɒts/	viel, jede Menge	
14	just /dʒʌst/	gleich; *hier:* gerade	
15	narrow /ˈnærəʊ/	eng, schmal; *hier:* knapp	
	escape /ɪˈskeɪp/	Flucht; *hier:* Entkommen	
	accident /ˈæksɪdnt/	Unfall	
	while /waɪl/	während	
	knock sb /ˈnɒk ˌsʌmbədi/	jdn stoßen	
	manage /ˈmænɪdʒ/	es schaffen	
	pull /pʊl/	ziehen	You have to pull the door to open it.
	front wheel /frʌnt ˈwiːl/	Vorderreifen, Vorderrad	
	run over sb /rʌn‿ˈəʊvə ˌsʌmbədi/	jdn überfahren	
	question sb /ˈkwestʃn ˌsʌmbədi/	jdn befragen	The police questioned everyone.
	anybody /ˈeniˌbɒdi/	(irgend)jemand	
	further /ˈfɜːðə/	zusätzlich, noch mehr, weiter	
	correct /kəˈrekt/	korrigieren	
16	interview /ˈɪntəˌvjuː/	Interview; *hier:* Befragung	
	who /huː/	wer; *hier:* wen, wem	
17	tip /tɪp/	Tipp	
	connect /kəˈnekt/	verbinden	
	spelling /ˈspelɪŋ/	Rechtschreibung	
	swap /swɒp/	tauschen	
	change /tʃeɪndʒ/	(sich) (ver)ändern	
	flea market /ˈfliː ˌmɑːkɪt/	Flohmarkt, Trödelmarkt	
	magician /məˈdʒɪʃn/	Zauberer/Zauberin	
	put up /pʊt‿ˈʌp/	aufhängen; *hier:* aufstellen	
	children's home /ˈtʃɪldrənz ˌhəʊm/	Kinderheim	

TIPP

Kim's game
Schreibe zehn Wörter auf ein Blatt Papier. Nimm dir drei Minuten Zeit, um sie dir einzuprägen.
Dann drehe das Blatt um. Versuche nun, alle Wörter auswendig auf die Rückseite zu schreiben.
Wie viele hast du dir gemerkt?

P1	air *(no pl)* /eə/	Luft	
	theatre /ˈθɪətə/	Theater	
P3	painting /ˈpeɪntɪŋ/	Bild, Gemälde	
	description /dɪˈskrɪpʃn/	Beschreibung	
	mistake /mɪˈsteɪk/	Fehler, Irrtum	
	gypsy /ˈdʒɪpsi/	Zigeuner/in	
	sky /skaɪ/	Himmel	
	cloud /klaʊd/	Wolke	
	stick /stɪk/	Stock	
	musical instrument /ˌmjuːzɪkl‿ˈɪnstrʊmənt/	Musikinstrument	
P4	mark /mɑːk/	(Schul)note	
	earn /ɜːn/	verdienen	
	save /seɪv/	retten; *hier:* sparen	
P6	prebooked /ˌpriːˈbʊkt/	im Voraus gebucht	
	entrance /ˈentrəns/	Eingang; *hier:* Eintritt(sgebühr)	
	adult /ˈædʌlt/	Erwachsene/r	
	parking /ˈpɑːkɪŋ/	Parken; Parkmöglichkeit, Parkplatz	
	car park /ˈkɑː ˌpɑːk/	Parkplatz	
	set-up /ˈsetʌp/	Aufbau	
	sale /seɪl/	(Aus)verkauf	
	contact sb /ˈkɒntækt ˌsʌmbədi/	jdn kontaktieren, sich mit jdm in Verbindung setzen	
P8	rhyming pair /ˈraɪmɪŋ peə/	Reimpaar	
P10	fill in /fɪl‿ˈɪn/	ausfüllen; *hier:* einsetzen	
P11	this morning /ðɪs ˈmɔːnɪŋ/	heute Morgen	
P13	safety *(no pl)* /ˈseɪftɪ/	Sicherheit	
	leave *(irr)* /liːv/	verlassen; *hier:* lassen	
	jewellery *(no pl)* /ˈdʒuːəlri/	Schmuck	
	digital /ˈdɪdʒɪtl/	digital, Digital-	
	camera /ˈkæmrə/	Kamera, Fotoapparat	
	back pocket /bæk ˈpɒkɪt/	Hintertasche, Gesäßtasche	
M2	placemat /ˈpleɪsˌmæt/	Set, Platzdeckchen	
	mow *(irr)* /məʊ/	mähen	
	lawn /lɔːn/	Rasen	
M3	**advert (= advertisement)** /ˈædvɜːt, ədˈvɜːtɪsmənt/	Anzeige, Inserat	
	offer /ˈɒfə/	Angebot	a special offer
M4	world-famous /ˈwɜːldˌfeɪməs/	weltberühmt, weltbekannt	
	review /rɪˈvjuː/	Kritik, Rezension	
	post sth /ˈpəʊst ˌsʌmθɪŋ/	etw schicken; *hier:* etw ins Internet stellen	
	comment /ˈkɒment/	Kommentar, Bemerkung	Send us your comments online.
	brilliant *(informal)* /ˈbrɪljənt/	toll, hervorragend	The Ramones are a brilliant band.
	only /ˈəʊnli/	einzige(r, s)	
	negative /ˈnegətɪv/	negativ	
	ring *(irr)* /rɪŋ/	klingeln, läuten	
	performance /pəˈfɔːməns/	Vorführung, Darbietung	

TIPP

Für gute Zuhörer
Du kannst dir Vokabeln auch merken, indem du sie dir immer wieder anhörst. Das funktioniert super! Nimm das englische Wort auf, das du lernen willst – aber vergiss die deutsche Übersetzung nicht! Höre dir die Wörter regelmäßig an, und du wirst bald feststellen, dass du sie gelernt hast.

	sb cannot wait (to do sth) /ˌsʌmbədi ˌkænɒt ˈweɪt (‿tə duː ˌsʌmθɪŋ)/	jmd kann es kaum erwarten (, etw zu tun)	
	anonymous /əˈnɒnɪməs/	anonym	
	acting /ˈæktɪŋ/	Schauspielerei	
	far /fɑː/	weit; *hier:* viel	
	quality /ˈkwɒləti/	Qualität	
	background /ˈbækˌgraʊnd/	Hintergrund	
	truly /ˈtruːli/	wirklich	
	magical /ˈmædʒɪkl/	magisch	
	beginning /bɪˈgɪnɪŋ/	Anfang	beginning ↔ end
	recommend /ˌrekəˈmend/	empfehlen	
M5	**packed** /pækt/	voll	The stadium was packed.
	pass by /pɑːs baɪ/	vorbeifahren, vorbeigehen	
	guys *(only pl) (informal)* /gaɪz/	Leute	
	point (to) /pɔɪnt/	deuten/zeigen (auf)	
	watch out (for) /wɒtʃ‿ˈaʊt/	aufpassen (auf), sich in Acht nehmen (vor)	Watch out for cars when you cross the road.
	sunshine *(no pl)* /ˈsʌnˌʃaɪn/	Sonnenschein	Let's enjoy the sunshine in the park.
	excitement /ɪkˈsaɪtmənt/	Aufregung, Spannung	
	if /ɪf/	wenn, falls; *hier:* ob	
	wave /weɪv/	winken	
	perform /pəˈfɔːm/	vorführen; aufführen	
	bracelet /ˈbreɪslət/	Armband, Armreif	
	feather /ˈfeðə/	Feder	
	rhythm /ˈrɪðəm/	Rhythmus, Takt	This song has a slow rhythm.
	over here /ˌəʊvə ˈhɪə/	hier drüben	
M6	Better safe than sorry. /ˌbetə ˌseɪf ðæn ˈsɒri/	Vorsicht ist besser als Nachsicht.	
	high heels *(only pl)* /haɪ ˈhiːlz/	hochhackige Schuhe, High Heels	
M8	incident /ˈɪnsɪdnt/	Vorfall	
	this morning /ðɪs ˈmɔːnɪŋ/	heute Morgen	This morning I drank a cup of coffee.
	turn round /tɜːn ˈraʊnd/	(sich) umdrehen	He turns round to wave at her.
M9	definition /ˌdefəˈnɪʃn/	Definition, Erklärung	
CC	fête /feɪt/	Fest	
	fact /fækt/	Fakt	
	sequin /ˈsiːkwɪn/	Paillette	
	litre /ˈliːtə/	Liter	
	paint /peɪnt/	Farbe	
	take *(irr)* /teɪk/	(mit)nehmen; *hier:* brauchen	
	ton *(pl - or -s)* /tʌn, tʌnz/	Tonne	
	corn on the cob /ˌkɔːn‿ɒn ðə ˈkɒb/	Maiskolben	
	deep-fried /ˌdiːpˈfraɪd/	frittiert	
	Jamaican /dʒəˈmeɪkən/	jamaikanisch	
	patty /ˈpæti/	Pastetchen	
	coconut /ˈkəʊkəˌnʌt/	Kokosnuss	
	tongue twister /ˈtʌŋ ˌtwɪstə/	Zungenbrecher	
	pick pockets /pɪk ˈpɒkɪts/	Taschendiebstahl begehen	
	purse /pɜːs/	Portemonnaie	
	samosa /səˈməʊsə/	*gefüllte Teigtasche*	

TIPP

Gegensätze
Neue Vokabeln musst du nicht immer in Listen schreiben. Du kannst sie auch anders sortieren, zum Beispiel indem du Gegensätze zusammenstellst. Wie viele Wörter kennst du schon, die sich so zusammenstellen lassen?
girl ↔ boy
black ↔ white

Theme 4 – You're not alone

home /həʊm/	Zuhause, Heim	My home is my castle. 
writer /ˈraɪtə/	Schriftsteller/in, Autor/in	
version /ˈvɜːʃn/	Version, Fassung	
board (a ship) /bɔːd/	(ein Schiff) besteigen	
the Caribbean /ðə ˌkærɪˈbiːən/	die Karibik; die Karibischen Inseln	
the Atlantic (Ocean) /ði‿ətˌlæntɪk(‿ˈəʊʃn)/	der Atlantische Ozean	
storm /stɔːm/	Sturm	
hit *(irr)* /hɪt/	schlagen; treffen; stoßen (gegen)	hit – hit – hit
rock /rɒk/	Stein, Fels(en)	
island /ˈaɪlənd/	Insel	an island 
raft /rɑːft/	Floß	
wreck /rek/	Wrack	
begin *(irr)* /bɪˈgɪn/	anfangen, beginnen	begin – began – begun
cannibal /ˈkænɪbl/	Kannibale/Kannibalin, Menschenfresser/in	
prisoner /ˈprɪznə/	Gefangene/r	
rescue /ˈreskjuː/	retten	Help! Please rescue me!
teach *(irr)* /tiːtʃ/	unterrichten; *hier:* beibringen	teach – taught – taught
fish /fɪʃ/	fischen, angeln	Can you teach me how to fish? 
sail /seɪl/	segeln	
by /baɪ/	bei, in der Nähe; *hier:* vorbei	
Home, sweet home! /həʊm swiːt ˈhəʊm/	Trautes Heim, Glück allein!	
situation /ˌsɪtʃuˈeɪʃn/	Situation, Lage	
feel homesick /fiːl ˈhəʊmsɪk/	Heimweh haben	
shocked /ʃɒkt/	schockiert, entsetzt	I am shocked to hear it!
worried /ˈwʌrid/	beunruhigt, besorgt	Mum is worried about you.
helpless /ˈhelpləs/	hilflos	
seasick /ˈsiːˌsɪk/	seekrank	
unhappy /ʌnˈhæpi/	unglücklich	unhappy 
animated /ˈænɪˌmeɪtɪd/	animiert	
slide show /ˈslaɪd ʃəʊ/	Diashow	
survival kit /səˈvaɪvl kɪt/	Überlebensausrüstung	
rope /rəʊp/	Seil	
axe /æks/	Axt, Beil	
soap *(no pl)* /səʊp/	Seife	 soap
plastic /ˈplæstɪk/	Plastik, Kunststoff	
bag /bæg/	Tasche; *hier:* Tüte, Beutel	
trumpet /ˈtrʌmpɪt/	Trompete	
packet /ˈpækɪt/	Packung, Schachtel	
spade /speɪd/	Spaten, Schaufel	
match /mætʃ/	Streichholz, Zündholz	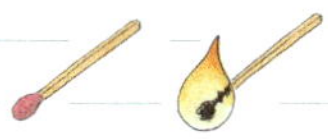 matches
first aid kit /fɜːst‿ˈeɪd kɪt/	Erste-Hilfe-Ausrüstung, Verbandskasten	
toothbrush /ˈtuːθˌbrʌʃ/	Zahnbürste	a toothbrush 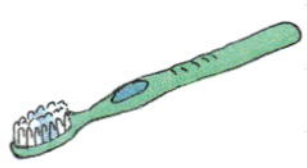
think of /ˈθɪŋk‿əv/	denken an; sich ausdenken	
agree on /əˈgriː‿ɒn/	einer Meinung sein über; *hier:* sich einigen auf	
useful /ˈjuːsfl/	nützlich, hilfreich	

4	lake /leɪk/	See	
	waterfall /ˈwɔːtəˌfɔːl/	Wasserfall	
5	saying /ˈseɪɪŋ/	Sprichwort	
	heart /hɑːt/	Herz	a heart 
	east /iːst/	Osten	
	west /west/	Westen	
6	stranded /ˈstrændɪd/	gestrandet	
	empty /ˈempti/	leer	
	message in a bottle /ˌmesɪdʒ‿ɪn‿ə ˈbɒtl/	Flaschenpost	
	give a talk /ˌgɪv‿ə ˈtɔːk/	einen Vortrag halten	
7	**letter** /ˈletə/	Brief; Buchstabe	a letter
	page /peɪdʒ/	Seite	
	heading /ˈhedɪŋ/	Überschrift, Titel	
	be in love (with) /bi ɪn lʌv/	verliebt sein (in)	
	if /ɪf/	wenn, falls; *hier:* ob	
	each other /ˌiːtʃ‿ˈʌðə/	einander	
	disappointed /ˌdɪsəˈpɔɪntɪd/	enttäuscht	
	feeling /ˈfiːlɪŋ/	Gefühl	different feelings
	friendship /ˈfrendʃɪp/	Freundschaft	
	get over sth/sb /get‿ˈəʊvə ˌsʌmθɪŋ/ˌsʌmbədi/	hinwegkommen über etw/jdn	
	flat /flæt/	Wohnung	We live in a small flat.
	walk the dog /ˌwɔːk ðə ˈdɒg/	den Hund ausführen	
	leave *(irr)* /liːv/	verlassen; *hier:* lassen	leave – left – left
	prefer /prɪˈfɜː/	vorziehen, bevorzugen, lieber mögen	He doesn't like cats, he prefers dogs.
	come true /ˌkʌm ˈtruː/	wahr werden	
	split up /splɪt‿ˈʌp/	sich teilen; *hier:* sich trennen	
	over /ˈəʊvə/	hinüber; *hier:* vorbei	The concert is already over.
	both /bəʊθ/	beide(s)	We're both 13 years old.
	worry sb /ˈwʌri ˌsʌmbədi/	jdn beunruhigen, jdm Sorgen bereiten	
	deal with /ˈdiːl wɪð/	sich befassen mit; *hier:* umgehen mit	
	whose /huːz/	wessen; *hier:* dessen	
	cyberbullying /ˈsaɪbəˌbʊliɪŋ/	Internetmobbing	
	since /sɪns/	seit	
	receive /rɪˈsiːv/	empfangen, erhalten	
	horrible /ˈhɒrəbl/	schrecklich	a horrible monster
	beat up /ˌbiːt‿ˈʌp/	verprügeln; *hier:* fertigmachen	
8	which one /ˈwɪtʃ wʌn/	welche(r, s)	
	throw *(irr)* /θrəʊ/	werfen	throw – threw – thrown
	ignore /ɪgˈnɔː/	ignorieren	
	helpful /ˈhelpfl/	hilfsbereit; hilfreich, nützlich	
	silly /ˈsɪli/	dumm; albern	
9	engineer /ˌendʒɪˈnɪə/	Ingenieur/in	
	out of work /aʊt‿əv ˈwɜːk/	arbeitslos	
	housework *(no pl)* /ˈhaʊsˌwɜːk/	Hausarbeit	
	check /tʃek/	überprüfen, kontrollieren; *hier:* nachsehen (in)	

	newspaper /ˈnjuːzˌpeɪpə/	Zeitung
	if /ɪf/	wenn, falls
	frustrated /frʌˈstreɪtɪd/	frustriert; enttäuscht
	hospital /ˈhɒspɪtl/	Krankenhaus
	even /ˈiːvn/	selbst, sogar; *hier:* noch
	report /rɪˈpɔːt/	Bericht; *hier:* Zeugnis
	sb does not care /ˌsʌmbədi dəz nɒt ˈkeə/	jdm ist es egal
10	less /les/	weniger
11	break down /ˌbreɪk ˈdaʊn/	kaputtgehen; *hier:* zusammenbrechen
	out of place /aʊt‿əv ˈpleɪs/	fehl am Platz(e)
	somehow /ˈsʌmhaʊ/	irgendwie
	belong /bɪˈlɒŋ/	dazugehören, hinpassen
	lock /lɒk/	(ein)schließen
	turn up /ˌtɜːn‿ˈʌp/	aufdrehen, lauter stellen
	scream /skriːm/	schreien; kreischen
	alright /ɔːlˈraɪt/	in Ordnung
	hurt /hɜːt/	verletzt, verwundet
	lost /lɒst/	verloren
	leave sb out /ˌliːv ˌsʌmbədi‿ˈaʊt/	jdn ausschließen
	dark *(no pl)* /dɑːk/	Dunkelheit
	kick /kɪk/	treten, schießen, kicken
	down *(informal)* /daʊn/	niedergeschlagen, down
	push /pʊʃ/	drücken; *hier:* schubsen, stoßen
	edge /edʒ/	Rand
	sing along /ˌsɪŋ‿əˈlɒŋ/	mitsingen
	melody /ˈmelədi/	Melodie
	lyrics *(only pl)* /ˈlɪrɪks/	(Lied)text
12	placemat /ˈpleɪsˌmæt/	Set, Platzdeckchen
	Me too. /mi ˈtuː/	Ich auch.
14	at the moment /æt ðə ˈməʊmənt/	im Moment
	mill around /mɪl‿əˈraʊnd/	umherlaufen
	style /staɪl/	Stil
	diamond /ˈdaɪəmənd/	Diamant
	electronic /ˌelekˈtrɒnɪk/	Elektro(musik)
	boyfriend /ˈbɔɪˌfrend/	(fester) Freund
P1	turn into /ˌtɜːn‿ˈɪntʊ/	umwandeln in, verändern in
P2	opposite /ˈɒpəzɪt/	Gegenteil
	noun /naʊn/	Substantiv
P4	search /sɜːtʃ/	Suche
	simple past /ˌsɪmpl ˈpɑːst/	einfache Vergangenheit
	quiz sb /ˈkwɪz‿ˌsʌmbədi/	jdn befragen/prüfen
	take turns /ˌteɪk ˈtɜːnz/	sich abwechseln
P5	in short /ɪn ˈʃɔːt/	in Kürze, kurz gefasst
P6	finder /ˈfaɪndə/	Finder/in
	study /ˈstʌdi/	studieren; *hier:* erforschen
	ocean /ˈəʊʃn/	Meer; Ozean
	location /ləʊˈkeɪʃn/	Lage; (Stand)ort
	address /əˈdres/	Adresse

a newspaper

TIPP

Falsche Freunde
Im Englischen gibt es viele Wörter, die deutschen Wörtern zwar sehr ähnlich sehen, aber eine ganz andere Bedeutung haben. Man nennt sie deshalb *false friends* (falsche Freunde). Für diese Wörter kannst du dir ein Merkblatt „Vorsicht Falle" anlegen.

also = auch (NICHT: also)
map = Karte (NICHT: Mappe)
become = werden (NICHT: bekommen)
kind = Art, Sorte (NICHT: Kind)
stall = (Verkaufs)stand (NICHT: Stall)
brave = mutig (NICHT: brav)

	place /pleɪs/	stellen, legen	
P12	pick /pɪk/	aussuchen, auswählen	
M1	**most** /məʊst/	am meisten	
	most of all /ˌməʊst‿əv‿ˈɔːl/	am (aller)meisten	
M2	talk /tɔːk/	Gespräch; Unterhaltung; *hier:* Vortrag	
M3	cast away /kɑːst‿əˈweɪ/	gestrandet	
	business trip /ˈbɪznəs trɪp/	Dienstreise, Geschäftsreise	
	crash /kræʃ/	stürzen	The plane crashed into the sea.
	the Pacific (Ocean) /ðə pəˌsɪfɪk(‿ˈəʊʃn)/	der Pazifische Ozean	
	sinking /ˈsɪŋkɪŋ/	sinkend	
	lose consciousness /luːz ˈkɒnʃəsnəs/	bewusstlos werden, das Bewusstsein verlieren	
	wash up /wɒʃ‿ˈʌp/	anspülen, anschwemmen	
	package /ˈpækɪdʒ/	Paket	
	ice skate /ˈaɪsskeɪt/	Schlittschuh	
	call /kɔːl/	anrufen; *hier:* nennen	I call my hamster "Fluffy".
	sail /seɪl/	Segel	
	overcome *(irr)* /ˌəʊvəˈkʌm/	überwinden, bewältigen	
	powerful /ˈpaʊəfl/	mächtig; *hier:* stark, heftig	
	wave /weɪv/	Welle	
	reach /riːtʃ/	erreichen	Robinson reaches the beach.
	ocean /ˈəʊʃn/	Meer; Ozean	
	destroy /dɪˈstrɔɪ/	zerstören	The waves destroyed the ship.
	half /hɑːf/	halb	
M5	entry /ˈentri/	Eintrag	
	all alone /ɔːl‿əˈləʊn/	ganz allein, mutterseelenallein	
M6	**yours** /jɔːz/	deine(r, s); eure(r, s); Ihre(r, s)	
	read out loud /ˌriːd‿ˌaʊt ˈlaʊd/	laut vorlesen	
M7	say out loud /ˌseɪ‿ˌaʊt ˈlaʊd/	laut sagen	
M8	who else /hu‿ˈels/	wer noch, wer sonst	
M9	**girlfriend** /ˈɡɜːlˌfrend/	(feste) Freundin	
	leave sb alone /ˌliːv ˌsʌmbədi‿əˈləʊn/	jdn in Ruhe lassen	
	something else /ˌsʌmθɪŋ‿ˈels/	(noch) etwas anderes	
	pregnant /ˈpreɡnənt/	schwanger	
	feel sorry for sb /ˌfiːl ˈsɒri fə sʌmbədi/	Mitleid mit jdm haben	
	Cheer up! /tʃɪər‿ˈʌp/	Lass (doch) den Kopf nicht hängen!, Kopf hoch!	Cheer up, you two! It's just a story.
	worry /ˈwʌri/	Sorge	
M10	what if /wɒt‿ɪf/	was ist/wäre, wenn	
	baby /ˈbeɪbi/	klein	
CC	blue /bluː/	blau; *hier:* traurig	
	forgive *(irr)* /fəˈɡɪv/	vergeben, verzeihen	
	joke /dʒəʊk/	Witz	
	frog /frɒɡ/	Frosch	

TIPP

Hosentaschenzettel
Schreibe dir kleine Zettel für unterwegs mit den schwierigsten oder wichtigsten Vokabeln. So hast du sie immer bei dir.

Theme 5 – Everyday science

I	everyday /ˈevrideɪ/	alltäglich, Alltags-	
2	electronic /ˌelekˈtrɒnɪk/	elektronisch	
	device /dɪˈvaɪs/	Gerät, Apparat	
	download /ˌdaʊnˈləʊd/	herunterladen, downloaden	
	search /sɜːtʃ/	(durch)suchen	
	fill in /fɪl‿ˈɪn/	ausfüllen	
3	social /ˈsəʊʃl/	sozial, gesellschaftlich	
	OMG (= Oh my god) /ˌəʊ‿em ˈdʒiː/	*Abkürzung für:* Oh mein Gott!	
	LOL (= Laugh(ing) out loud) /ˌel‿əʊ‿ˈel/	*Abkürzung für:* laut lachen(d)	
	entertainment /ˌentəˈteɪnmənt/	Unterhaltung	
4	**text message** /ˈtekst ˌmesɪdʒ/	SMS, Kurznachricht	
	say out loud /ˌseɪ‿ˌaʊt ˈlaʊd/	laut sagen	
5	**ring** *(irr)* /rɪŋ/	klingeln, läuten	ring – rang – rung
	doorbell /ˈdɔːˌbel/	Türklingel	Somebody rang the doorbell.
	turn on /ˌtɜːn‿ˈɒn/	einschalten	George turns on the computer.
	secret /ˈsiːkrət/	geheim	There are ghosts in our secret room.
	crocodile /ˈkrɒkədaɪl/	Krokodil	
	phew /fjuː/	puh	
	get dressed /get‿ˈdrest/	sich anziehen	
	take sb out /teɪk ˈsʌmbədi‿aʊt/	jdn (zum Essen) einladen	
	down /daʊn/	(nach) unten; hinunter, hinab	
	stairs *(only pl)* /steəz/	Treppe	
	hall /hɔːl/	Halle; Saal; *hier:* Flur	
	turn off /ˌtɜːn‿ˈɒf/	ausmachen, ausschalten	
	sb could not believe his/her ears /ˌsʌmbədi kʊd nɒt bɪˌliːv hɪz/hər‿ˈɪəz/	jmd traute seinen/ihren Ohren nicht	
	save /seɪv/	retten; *hier:* speichern, sichern	Don't forget to save the document.
6	then /ðen/	dann; *hier:* damals	
	danger /ˈdeɪndʒə/	Gefahr	Help! Our lives are in danger!
	go out /gəʊ‿ˈaʊt/	(hinaus)gehen; *hier:* ausgehen	
8	**floor** /flɔː/	Boden; *hier:* Stockwerk	
	toilet /ˈtɔɪlət/	Toilette, Klo	
	lift /lɪft/	Aufzug, Lift	
	key /kiː/	Schlüssel; *hier:* Legende	
	information desk /ˌɪnfəˈmeɪʃn desk/	Information(sstelle)	
	picnic /ˈpɪknɪk/	Picknick	
	area /ˈeəriə/	Gebiet, Region; *hier:* Bereich	
	baby changing /ˈbeɪbi ˌtʃeɪndʒɪŋ/	Wickelraum	
	cloakroom /ˈkləʊkˌruːm/	Garderobe	
	accessible /əkˈsesəbl/	(leicht) erreichbar; *hier:* behindertengerecht	
	basement /ˈbeɪsmənt/	Keller, Untergeschoss	
	antenna (*pl* antennae) /ænˈtenə, ænˈteniː/	Antenne; Fühler	
	pattern pod /ˈpætən pɒd/	*Erfahrungsraum zum Begreifen von Formen und Mustern*	
	explore /ɪkˈsplɔː/	erforschen, untersuchen	

	space /speɪs/	Platz, Raum; *hier*: Weltraum
	pendulum /ˈpendjʊləm/	Pendel
	hall /hɔːl/	Halle; Saal
	ground floor /ˌgraʊnd ˈflɔː/	Erdgeschoss, Parterre
	measure /ˈmeʒə/	messen
	cosmos /ˈkɒzmɒs/	Kosmos, Weltall
	culture /ˈkʌltʃə/	Kultur
	agriculture *(no pl)* /ˈægrɪˌkʌltʃə/	Landwirtschaft, Ackerbau
	telecommunications *(only pl)* /ˌtelikəˌmjuːnɪˈkeɪʃnz/	Telekommunikation
	contemporary /kənˈtempri/	zeitgenössisch; modern
	challenge /ˈtʃælɪndʒ/	Herausforderung
	atmosphere /ˈætməsˌfɪə/	Atmosphäre, Stimmung; *hier*: Erdatmosphäre
	dock /dɒk/	Dock, Kai
	diving /ˈdaɪvɪŋ/	Tauchen
	marine engineering *(no pl)* /məˌriːn‿ˌendʒɪˈnɪərɪŋ/	Schiffsmaschinenbau
	mathematics *(only pl)* /ˌmæθəˈmætɪks/	Mathematik
	computing /kəmˈpjuːtɪŋ/	Berechnen, Kalkulieren; EDV
	public /ˈpʌblɪk/	öffentlich
	flight /flaɪt/	Flug
	matter /ˈmætə/	Angelegenheit, Sache
	launchpad /ˈlɔːntʃpæd/	Startrampe, Abschussrampe
	century /ˈsentʃəri/	Jahrhundert
	glimpse /glɪmps/	(kurzer) (Ein)blick
	medical /ˈmedɪkl/	medizinisch, ärztlich
	veterinary /ˈvetnri/	tierärztlich
9	around /əˈraʊnd/	um; *hier*: in, durch
	object /ˈɒbdʒekt/	Objekt, Gegenstand, Sache
10	**invention** /ɪnˈvenʃn/	Erfindung
	find out about /faɪnd‿ˈaʊt‿əˌbaʊt/	sich informieren über
	microwave /ˈmaɪkrəˌweɪv/	Mikrowelle(nherd)
	light bulb /ˈlaɪt ˌbʌlb/	Glühbirne
	chocolate chip cookie /ˌtʃɒklət ˌtʃɪp ˈkʊki/	*Keks mit Schokoladenstückchen*
	zip /zɪp/	Reißverschluss
11	inventor /ɪnˈventə/	Erfinder/in
	invent /ɪnˈvent/	erfinden
	light /laɪt/	erhellen, erleuchten
	distance /ˈdɪstəns/	Entfernung; Strecke
	road /rəʊd/	Straße
	product /ˈprɒdʌkt/	Produkt, Erzeugnis
12	**electricity** *(no pl)* /ɪˌlekˈtrɪsəti/	Elektrizität, Strom
	kettle /ketl/	Wasserkocher
13	fold /fəʊld/	(zusammen)falten
	centre line /ˌsentə ˈlaɪn/	Mittellinie
	turn over /tɜːn‿ˈəʊvə/	(sich) umdrehen
	along /əˈlɒŋ/	entlang

TIPP

Wortbilder
Vielleicht kannst du dir Vokabeln besser merken, wenn du daraus Wortbilder machst.
Wenn du nicht gerne selbst zeichnest, kannst du auch Bilder aus Zeitschriften und Katalogen ausschneiden und auf ein Blatt Papier kleben. Schreibe die dazugehörigen Vokabeln direkt zum Bild. So kannst du englische Begriffe richtig „sehen."

The microwave is a useful invention.

Be careful when you cross the road!

	mark /mɑːk/	(Schul)note; *hier:* Markierung
	bottom /ˈbɒtəm/	untere(r, s)
	line /laɪn/	Linie
	tip/tɪp/	Tipp; *hier:* Spitze
	fold down /fəʊld ˈdaʊn/	herunterklappen
	wing /wɪŋ/	Flügel
	cut /kʌt/	Schnitt
	bend *(irr)* /bend/	biegen
	flap /flæp/	Klappe
	up /ʌp/	(nach) oben; hinauf
	instruction /ɪnˈstrʌkʃn/	Anweisung, Anleitung
14	brochure /ˈbrəʊʃə/	Broschüre
	exist /ɪgˈzɪst/	existieren, vorkommen
	give reasons /gɪv ˈriːznz/	begründen, Gründe angeben
P1	be the odd one out	aus der Reihe fallen,
	/biː ði‿ˌɒd wʌn‿ˈaʊt/	nicht dazugehören
P2	alphabetical /ˌælfəˈbetɪkl/	alphabetisch
P6	text /tekst/	SMS schicken
	at night /æt ˈnaɪt/	nachts
P8	wood /wʊd/	Holz
P10	dreamer /ˈdriːmə/	Träumer/in
	worker /ˈwɜːkə/	Arbeiter/in
	imagination /ɪˌmædʒɪˈneɪʃn/	Fantasie, Vorstellungskraft;
		Einbildung
	decoration /ˌdekəˈreɪʃn/	Dekoration, Schmuck
	presentation /ˌpreznˈteɪʃn/	Präsentation
	rider /ˈraɪdə/	Reiter/in
	mark /mɑːk/	markieren, kennzeichnen
P12	teddy bear /ˈtedi ˌbeə/	Teddybär
	the London Eye /ðə ˌlʌndən‿ˈaɪ/	*Riesenrad in London*
	all over the world	auf der ganzen Welt
	/ˌɔːl‿ˌəʊvə ðə ˈwɜːld/	
P13	herself /həˈself/	sich (selbst); selbst
	servant /ˈsɜːvnt/	Bedienstete/r
	nobody else /ˌnəʊˌbɒdi‿ˈels/	niemand anders
	myself /maɪˈself/	mich, mir; selbst
M1	communication *(no pl)*	Kommunikation
	/kəˌmjuːnɪˈkeɪʃn/	
	the Stone Age /ðə ˈstəʊn eɪdʒ/	die Steinzeit
	cave /keɪv/	Höhle
	Egyptian /iˈdʒɪpʃn/	Ägypter/in; ägyptisch
	hieroglyphics *(only pl)*	Hieroglyphen
	/ˌhaɪərəˈglɪfɪks/	
	smoke signal /ˈsməʊk ˌsɪgnl/	Rauchzeichen
	mirror /ˈmɪrə/	Spiegel
	address /əˈdres/	Adresse
	record player /ˈrekɔːd ˌpleɪə/	(Schall)plattenspieler
	everywhere /ˈevriweə/	überall
	keyword /ˈkiːˌwɜːd/	Schlüsselwort

TIPP

Verknüpfungen herstellen
Bei Wörtern, die überhaupt nicht in deinen Kopf wollen, kannst du:
- dir das Wort bildlich vorstellen,
- ein kleines Bild dazu zeichnen,
- an ein Ereignis denken, das du selbst erlebt hast,
- einen Satz auswendig lernen, in dem das Wort vorkommt,
- dir eine Eselsbrücke (z. B. einen Reim) ausdenken.

The wombat leaves its cave.

a mirror

There were snakes everywhere. It was really scary.

TIPP

Reimwörter
Damit du dir besser merken kannst, wie bestimmte Wörter ausgesprochen werden, suche Reimwörter für sie. Dir wird auffallen, dass die Reimwörter nicht immer dieselbe Schreibweise haben.
sn<u>ow</u> – g<u>o</u>
s<u>oap</u> – h<u>ope</u>

	paragraph /ˈpærəˌgrɑːf/	Absatz, Abschnitt	
	timeline /ˈtaɪmˌlaɪn/	Zeitstrahl	
M3	argument /ˈɑːgjʊmənt/	Auseinandersetzung, Streit; *hier*: Argument	
	discussion /dɪˈskʌʃn/	Diskussion	
M4	admission *(no pl)* /ədˈmɪʃn/	Eintritt, Einlass	
	cost /kɒst/	Kosten, Preis	
	require /rɪˈkwaɪə/	brauchen; erfordern	
	book /bʊk/	buchen	
	scheduled /ˈʃedjuːld/	geplant, planmäßig	
	bench /bentʃ/	Bank	
	coat /kəʊt/	Mantel, Jacke	
	provide /prəˈvaɪd/	zur Verfügung stellen, sorgen für	
	locker /ˈlɒkə/	Schließfach, Spind	
	space /speɪs/	Platz, Raum	
	limited /ˈlɪmɪtɪd/	begrenzt, eingeschränkt	
	little /ˈlɪtl/	wenig	
M6	**land** /lænd/	(Fest)land	
	kph /ˌkeɪ pi‿ˈeɪtʃ/	km/h	
	not exactly /nɒt‿ɪgˈzæktli/	nicht gerade	
	best-seller /ˌbestˈselə/	Bestseller *(Artikel mit großem Verkaufserfolg)*	
	fix /fɪks/	festmachen, befestigen	
	metal /ˈmetl/	Metall	
	carry /ˈkæri/	tragen	She carried a lot of bags.
	get off the ground /ˌget‿ˌɒf ðə ˈgraʊnd/	abheben; *hier*: verwirklicht werden	
	shower /ˈʃaʊə/	Dusche	I like to sing in the shower.
	cyclist /ˈsaɪklɪst/	Radfahrer/in	
	combine /kəmˈbaɪn/	verbinden, kombinieren	
	exercise /ˈeksəˌsaɪz/	Übung; *hier:* Bewegung	
	pedal power /ˈpedl ˌpaʊə/	Pedalkraft	
	pump /pʌmp/	pumpen	
	pedal /ˈpedl/	in die Pedale treten, strampeln	
	parachute jump /ˈpærəˌʃuːt dʒʌmp/	Fallschirmsprung	
	Frenchman/Frenchwoman /ˈfrentʃmən,ˈfrentʃˌwʊmən/	Franzose/Französin	
	wide /waɪd/	breit	The river is very wide. I'm not sure we can cross it.
	hot-air balloon /ˌhɒt ˈeə bəˌluːn/	Heißluftballon	
	swing *(irr)* /swɪŋ/	schwingen, schaukeln	
	sb is sick /ˌsʌmbədi ɪz‿ˈsɪk/	jdm ist schlecht/übel	
	land /lænd/	landen	The plane landed at JFK Airport.
M7	special feature /ˌspeʃl ˈfiːtʃə/	Besonderheit	
	boot /buːt/	Stiefel	
	X-ray /ˈeksˌreɪ/	Röntgenstrahl(en); *hier:* Röntgen-	
CC	kph /ˌkeɪ pi‿ˈeɪtʃ/	km/h	kph = kilometres per hour
	headphones *(only pl)* /ˈhedˌfəʊnz/	Kopfhörer	
	bacterium *(pl* bacteria*)* /bækˈtɪəriəm, bækˈtɪəriə/	Bakterie	

multiply by / 'mʌltɪplaɪ baɪ /	multiplizieren mit;	
	hier: sich vermehren/	
	vervielfachen um	
grow *(irr)* / grəʊ /	wachsen; *hier*: werden	
bottom of the ocean	Meeresgrund	
/ ˌbɒtəm‿əv ði‿'əʊʃn /		
sunlight / 'sʌnˌlaɪt /	Sonnenlicht	
the earth / ði‿'ɜːθ /	die Erde	

Theme 6 – Up and away

up and away / ˌʌp‿ən‿ə'weɪ /	auf und davon	
laughter *(no pl)* / 'lɑːftə /	Lachen, Gelächter	
worry / 'wʌri /	Sorge	
shine *(irr)* / ʃaɪn /	scheinen *(Sonne)*	
movie *(AE)* = film *(BE)* / 'muːvi /	(Kino-, Spiel)film	
summer camp / 'sʌmə ˌkæmp /	Ferienlager	
climbing / 'klaɪmɪŋ /	Klettern, Bergsteigen; Kletter-	Climbing is a fascinating sport.
application form / ˌæplɪ'keɪʃn ˌfɔːm /	Bewerbungsformular	
form / fɔːm /	Formular	
first name / 'fɜːst ˌneɪm /	Vorname	first name
surname / 'sɜːˌneɪm /	Familienname, Nachname	surname
date of birth / 'deɪt‿əv ˌbɜːθ /	Geburtsdatum	date of birth
sex / seks /	Geschlecht	
male / meɪl /	männlich	
female / 'fiːmeɪl /	weiblich	
address / ə'dres /	Adresse	
postcode / 'pəʊstˌkəʊd /	Postleitzahl	
choice / tʃɔɪs /	Wahl	
agreement / ə'griːmənt /	Vereinbarung, Vertrag	
instructor / ɪn'strʌktə /	Betreuer/in	
signature / 'sɪgnətʃə /	Unterschrift	
participant / pɑː'tɪsɪpənt /	Teilnehmer/in	
parent / 'peərənt /	Elternteil, Erziehungs-	
	berechtigte/r	
guardian / 'gɑːdiən /	Erziehungsberechtigte/r	
ticket counter / 'tɪkɪt ˌkaʊntə /	Fahrkartenschalter	at the ticket counter
platform / 'plætˌfɔːm /	Plattform; *hier:* Bahnsteig, Gleis	Your train leaves from platform 8.
exit / 'eksɪt /	Ausgang	
escalator / 'eskəˌleɪtə /	Rolltreppe	Use the escalator to get down.
opposite / 'ɒpəzɪt /	gegenüber(liegend)	The shop is opposite the counter.
coach station / 'kəʊtʃ ˌsteɪʃn /	Busbahnhof	
information point	Informationsstelle	
/ ˌɪnfə'meɪʃn pɔɪnt /		
telephone box / 'telɪfəʊn bɒks /	Telefonzelle	

	cash machine /ˈkæʃ məˌʃiːn/	Geldautomat	I need some money. Where's the nearest cash machine?
	timetable /ˈtaɪmteɪbl/	Stundenplan; *hier:* Fahrplan	
	leave *(irr)* /liːv/	verlassen; *hier:* abfahren	leave – left – left
	departure /dɪˈpɑːtʃə/	Abreise; Abflug; Abfahrt	
	arrival /əˈraɪvl/	Ankunft	
7	altogether /ˌɔːltəˈgeðə/	völlig, ganz; *hier:* insgesamt	
	hurry /ˈhʌri/	sich beeilen	
	single (ticket) /ˈsɪŋgl/	Einzelfahrkarte	
	return (ticket) /rɪˈtɜːn/	Hin- und Rückfahrkarte	
8	take part (in) /ˌteɪk ˈpɑːt/	teilnehmen (an)	
	sleep late /ˌsliːp ˈleɪt/	ausschlafen, lange schlafen	
	basic /ˈbeɪsɪk/	grundlegend, wesentlich; Grund-	
	move /muːv/	Bewegung; Schritt	
	performance /pəˈfɔːməns/	Vorführung, Aufführung	
9	foreign /ˈfɒrɪn/	ausländisch, fremd	
	Austria /ˈɒstriə/	Österreich	
11	it's been much too long /ɪts biːn ˌmʌtʃ tuː ˈlɒŋ/	es ist viel zu lange her	
	at last /ət ˈlɑːst/	endlich, schließlich	
	candy *(AE)* = sweets *(BE)* /ˈkændi/	Süßigkeiten	
	land /lænd/	landen	
	recover /rɪˈkʌvə/	sich erholen	
	excited /ɪkˈsaɪtɪd/	aufgeregt; *hier:* begeistert	The mice are really excited.
	vacation *(AE)* = holiday *(BE)* /vəˈkeɪʃn/	Ferien, Urlaub	
	mom *(AE)* = mum *(BE)* *(informal)* /mɒm/	Mama	
	nearby /ˌnɪəˈbaɪ/	nahe/in der Nähe gelegen, benachbart	
	awesome *(informal)* /ˈɔːsm/	super, spitze	
	naaah *(informal)* /nɑː/	ne(e)	
	mix up /mɪks‿ˈʌp/	verwechseln	
	on one's own /ɒn wʌnz‿ˈəʊn/	allein(e)	Dracula is often on his own.
	volcano *(pl* **-oes** *or* **-os***)* /vɒlˈkeɪnəʊ, vɒlˈkeɪnəʊz/	Vulkan	
	receptionist /rɪˈsepʃnɪst/	Empfangschef/in	
	just a minute /ˌdʒʌst‿ə ˈmɪnɪt/	einen Moment/Augenblick bitte	
	booked up /bʊkt‿ˈʌp/	ausgebucht	
	south /saʊθ/	Süden	
	too bad /ˌtuː ˈbæd/	wirklich schade	
	You're welcome. /ˌjɔː ˈwelkəm/	Gern geschehen., Bitte.	
	Good luck! /gʊd ˈlʌk/	Viel Glück!	
	American /əˈmerɪkən/	amerikanisch	
	pick up /ˌpɪk‿ˈʌp/	aufheben; *hier:* abholen	
12	**Northern Ireland** /ˌnɔːðn‿ˈaɪələnd/	Nordirland	
	accent /ˈæksnt/	Akzent	
	Welsh /welʃ/	Walisisch; walisisch	
	north /nɔːθ/	Norden	
13	monument /ˈmɒnjʊmənt/	Denkmal, Monument	

magic

	legend /ˈledʒ(ə)nd/	Sage, Legende	
	stone /stəʊn/	Stein	
	heavy /ˈhevi/	schwer	
	magician /məˈdʒɪʃn/	Zauberer/Zauberin	
	magic *(no pl)* /ˈmædʒɪk/	Magie, Zauber	
	move /muːv/	sich bewegen; *hier:* bewegen, verschieben	
	across /əˈkrɒs/	über	Tower Bridge is a bridge across the River Thames.
	The Irish Sea /ðiˌaɪrɪʃ ˈsiː/	die Irische See	
	Scottish /ˈskɒtɪʃ/	schottisch	
	giant /ˈdʒaɪənt/	Riese	
	laugh at sb /ˈlɑːf‿ət ˌsʌmbədi/	jdn auslachen	
	causeway /ˈkɔːzˌweɪ/	Damm	
	loch /lɒk/	See	
	lie *(irr)* /laɪ/	liegen	
	area /ˈeəriə/	Gebiet, Region	
	moor /mʊə/	Heideland, (Hoch)moor	
	view /vjuː/	Sicht; (Aus)blick, Aussicht	
14	travel /ˈtrævl/	Reise-	
	travel agency /ˈtrævl‿ˌeɪdʒnsi/	Reisebüro	
	prepare /prɪˈpeə/	(sich) vorbereiten	
	gallery walk /ˈgæləri wɔːk/	Galerierundgang	
	kayaking /ˈkaɪækɪŋ/	Kajakfahren, Kajaken	
	hedge /hedʒ/	Hecke	
	maze /meɪz/	Labyrinth, Irrgarten	
	bay /beɪ/	Bucht	
	cliff /klɪf/	Klippe, Kliff	
	cathedral /kəˈθiːdrəl/	Kathedrale, Dom	
	pier /pɪə/	Pier; Landungsbrücke	
P3	recording /rɪˈkɔːdɪŋ/	Aufnahme	
P4	this afternoon /ðɪs‿ˌɑːftəˈnuːn/	heute Nachmittag	
	this evening /ðɪs‿ˈiːvnɪŋ/	heute Abend	
P6	ticket machine /ˈtɪkɪt məˈʃiːn/	Fahrkartenautomat	
	pass /pɑːs/	Pass; *hier:* Karte	
	single journey /ˌsɪŋgl ˈdʒɜːni/	Einzelfahrt	
	select /sɪˈlekt/	(aus)wählen, aussuchen	
	type /taɪp/	Art; Typ, Sorte	
	insert /ɪnˈsɜːt/	einwerfen, (hinein)stecken	
	exact /ɪgˈzækt/	genau (abgezählt)	
	immediately /ɪˈmiːdiətli/	sofort	
	valid /ˈvælɪd/	gültig	
	journey /ˈdʒɜːni/	Reise; *hier:* Fahrt	
	within /wɪðˈɪn/	innerhalb	
	collect /kəˈlekt/	sammeln; *hier:* entnehmen	
P7	Europe /ˈjʊərəp/	Europa	
P13	cave /keɪv/	Höhle	
	dinosaur /ˈdaɪnəˌsɔː/	Dinosaurier	
	showcave /ˈʃəʊkeɪv/	Schauhöhle	
	spectacular /spekˈtækjʊlə/	atemberaubend, spektakulär	

TIPP

Vergiss es einfach!
Hast du Probleme, dir bestimmte Wörter zu merken? Sind es immer dieselben Vokabeln, die dir nicht einfallen? Dann probiere es doch mal mit Vergessen! Das geht so: Suche fünf oder sechs schwierige Wörter aus, die du unbedingt vergessen willst. Schreibe sie auf Zettel und hänge sie neben dein Bett, über deinen Schreibtisch oder an den Badezimmerspiegel. Lies sie dir bei jeder Gelegenheit durch, damit du dich daran erinnerst, welche Wörter du unbedingt vergessen willst.

	form /fɔːm/	bilden, formen
	understanding *(no pl)* /ˌʌndəˈstændɪŋ/	Verständnis
	natural /ˈnætʃrəl/	natürlich
	wonder /ˈwʌndə/	Wunder
	life-sized /ˈlaɪfsaɪzd/	in Lebensgröße, lebensgroß
	model /ˈmɒdl/	Modell
	entrance fee /ˈentrəns ˌfiː/	Eintritt(sgeld)
	clothing *(no pl)* /ˈkləʊðɪŋ/	Kleidung
	long-sleeved /ˈlɒŋˌsliːvd/	langärm(e)lig
	proper /ˈprɒpə/	richtig
	trainer *(BE)* /ˈtreɪnə/	Turnschuh
	constant /ˈkɒnstənt/	dauernd; *hier:* beständig, gleich bleibend
	raincoat /ˈreɪnˌkəʊt/	Regenmantel
M2	below /bɪˈləʊ/	unten
	welcome /ˈwelkəm/	willkommen heißen, begrüßen
	click /klɪk/	(an)klicken, drücken
	up to /ˈʌp tuː/	bis (zu)
	unique /juːˈniːk/	einzigartig
	atmosphere /ˈætməsˌfɪə/	Atmosphäre, Stimmung
	experience /ɪkˈspɪəriəns/	Erfahrung, Erlebnis
	drama /ˈdrɑːmə/	Schauspielerei; *hier:* Theater
	mission /ˈmɪʃn/	Auftrag, Mission
	impossible /ɪmˈpɒsəbl/	unmöglich
	robotics *(only pl)* /rəʊˈbɒtɪks/	Robotik, Robotertechnik
M6	**reservation** /ˌrezəˈveɪʃn/	Reservierung
	altogether /ˌɔːltəˈgeðə/	völlig, ganz; *hier:* insgesamt
M7	phrase book /ˈfreɪz bʊk/	Sprachführer
	give directions /ˌgɪv dɪˈrekʃnz/	den Weg beschreiben
	ask for directions /ˌɑːsk fə dɪˈrekʃnz/	nach dem Weg fragen
	workbook /ˈwɜːkˌbʊk/	Arbeitsbuch
M8	**traveller** /ˈtrævlə/	Reisende/r
M9	at the front /æt ðə ˈfrʌnt/	vorn(e)
CC	only /ˈəʊnli/	nur; *hier:* erst
	such /sʌtʃ/	solche(r,s)
	love /lʌv/	Liebe; *hier:* herzliche Grüße, alles Liebe

TIPP

Spell check
Buchstabiere ein Wort für eine/n Partner/in. Wechselt euch ab und kontrolliert anschließend gegenseitig, ob alles richtig geschrieben ist. Für jedes richtige Wort gibt es einen Punkt. Wer ist der *spelling king* oder die *spelling queen*?

drama

The tourist is asking for directions.

a traveller

TIPP

Unregelmäßige Verben
(irregular verbs) haben eine unregelmäßige Form für das *simple past* und auch für das Partizip Perfekt *(past participle)*. Die Formen solltest du wie Vokabeln lernen. Du findest die Formen in der Liste der unregelmäßigen Verben auf den Seiten 283 und 284. Hier sind einige Beispiele:

Infinitiv	*simple past*	*past participle*
be *(irr)*	was/were	been
take *(irr)*	took	taken
go *(irr)*	went	gone
send *(irr)*	sent	sent
do *(irr)*	did	done

Hier findest du die Wörter, die in deinem Buch vorkommen.

- Die **fett gedruckten** Wörter solltest du dir merken.
- Wenn du den *More*-Teil bearbeitest, solltest du dir auch die **grün gedruckten** Wörter merken.
- 1/1 bedeutet: Dieses Wort kommt in *Theme* 1, Aufgabe 1 vor.
- I bedeutet: Dieses Wort kommt in Band I (5. Klasse) vor. Entsprechend steht II für Band 2 (6. Klasse).
- Folgende Abkürzungen werden noch verwendet:
  P = *Practice* M = *More* CC = *Camden Chronicle*

A

a/an /ə, ən/ ein(e) I

a bit /ə ˈbɪt/ ein bisschen II

a box of chocolates /ə bɒks‿əv ˈtʃɒkləts/ eine Schachtel Pralinen II

a day /ə ˈdeɪ/ pro/am Tag 1/9

a few /ə ˈfjuː/ einige 2/12

a little /ə ˈlɪtl/ ein bisschen II

a lot (of) /ə ˈlɒt/ sehr; viel(e) I

a week /ə ˈwiːk/ pro/in der Woche 1/9

a year /ə ˈjɪə/ pro/im Jahr II

be able to do sth /bi‿ˌeɪbl tə ˈduː ˌsʌmθɪŋ/ etw tun können II

about /əˈbaʊt/ über I

about /əˈbaʊt/ ungefähr II

be about /bi‿əˈbaʊt/ handeln von 3/4

absolutely /ˈæbsəluːtli/ absolut, völlig 1/11

accent /ˈæksnt/ Akzent 6/12

accessible /əkˈsesəbl/ (leicht) erreichbar; behindertengerecht 5/8

accident /ˈæksɪdnt/ Unfall 3/15

across /əˈkrɒs/ über 6/13

act out /ækt‿ˈaʊt/ nachspielen 1/3

acting /ˈæktɪŋ/ Schauspielerei 3/M4

action /ˈækʃn/ Handlung; Aktion 2/P6

active /ˈæktɪv/ aktiv II

activity /ækˈtɪvəti/ Aktivität I

actor/actress /ˈæktə, ˈæktrəs/ Schauspieler/in I

add /æd/ hinzufügen 1/M1

address /əˈdres/ Adresse 6/5

admission *(no pl)* /ədˈmɪʃn/ Eintritt, Einlass 5/M4

adult /ˈædʌlt/ Erwachsene/r 3/P6

adventure /ədˈventʃə/ Abenteuer, Erlebnis II

advert (= advertisement) /ˈædvɜːt, ədˈvɜː tɪsmənt/ Anzeige, Inserat 3/M3

advice *(no pl)* /ədˈvaɪs/ Rat 2/14

be afraid (of sth/sb) /ˌbi‿əˈfreɪd/ (vor etw/jdm) Angst haben II

Africa /ˈæfrɪkə/ Afrika 3/8

after /ˈɑːftə/ nach I

after /ˈɑːftə/ nachdem II

after that /ˌɑːftə ˈðæt/ anschließend, danach I

afternoon /ˌɑːftəˈnuːn/ Nachmittag I

in the afternoon /ˌɪn ði‿ˈɑːftənuːn/ am Nachmittag, nachmittags I

this afternoon /ðɪs‿ˌɑːftəˈnuːn/ heute Nachmittag II

afterwards /ˈɑːftəwədz/ danach, anschließend; später II

again /əˈgen/ wieder, noch (ein)mal I

against /əˈgenst/ gegen II

age /eɪdʒ/ Alter II

(three days) ago /əˈgəʊ/ vor (drei Tagen) II

ages ago *(informal)* /ˈeɪdʒɪz‿əˌgəʊ/ vor einer Ewigkeit, vor langer Zeit 1/3

agree (with sb) /əˈgriː/ (jdm) zustimmen II

agree on /əˈgriː‿ɒn/ einer Meinung sein über; sich einigen auf 4/3

agreement /əˈgriːmənt/ Vereinbarung, Vertrag 6/5

agriculture *(no pl)* /ˈægrɪˌkʌltʃə/ Landwirtschaft, Ackerbau 5/8

air *(no pl)* /eə/ Luft I

airport /ˈeəˌpɔːt/ Flughafen II

alarm clock /əˈlɑːm ˌklɒk/ Wecker II

alien /ˈeɪliən/ Außerirdische(r), Alien II

all /ɔːl/ alle(s) I

all alone /ɔːl‿əˈləʊn/ ganz allein, mutterseelenallein 4/M5

all over the world /ˌɔːl‿ˌəʊvə ðə ˈwɜːld/ auf der ganzen Welt 5/P12

allowed /əˈlaʊd/ erlaubt 2/M3

be allowed to do sth /bi‿əˌlaʊd tə ˈduː ˌsʌmθɪŋ/ etw tun dürfen II

almost /ˈɔːlməʊst/ fast, beinahe 3/8

alone /əˈləʊn/ allein II

leave sb alone /ˌliːv ˌsʌmbədi‿əˈləʊn/ jdn in Ruhe lassen 4/M9

along /əˈlɒŋ/ entlang 5/13

alphabetical /ˌælfəˈbetɪkl/ alphabetisch 5/P2

already /ɔːlˈredi/ schon II

alright /ɔːlˈraɪt/ in Ordnung 4/11

also /ˈɔːlsəʊ/ auch I

although /ɔːlˈðəʊ/ obwohl, obgleich 2/M3

altogether /ˌɔːltəˈgeðə/ völlig, ganz; insgesamt 6/M6

always /ˈɔːlweɪz/ immer I

am (= ante meridiem) /ˌeɪˈem, ˌænti məˈrɪdiəm/ morgens, vormittags *(nur hinter Uhrzeit zwischen Mitternacht und 12 Uhr mittags)* 3/11

amazing *(informal)* /əˈmeɪzɪŋ/ toll, unglaublich II

American /əˈmerɪkən/ amerikanisch II

and /ænd/ und I

angry /ˈæŋgri/ verärgert; zornig; wütend II

animal /ˈænɪml/ Tier I

animated /ˈænɪˌmeɪtɪd/ animiert 4/1

anonymous /əˈnɒnɪməs/ anonym 3/M4

another /əˈnʌðə/ noch ein(e, r, s); ein anderer/anderes, eine andere II

another /əˈnʌðə/ ein anderer/anderes, eine andere 1/1

answer /ˈɑːnsə/ Antwort I

answer /ˈɑːnsə/ (be)antworten 2/1

antenna *(pl* antennae*)* /ænˈtenə, ænˈteniː/ Antenne; Fühler 5/8

any /ˈeni/ irgendwelche, irgendein(e); etwas II

not any /nɒt‿ˈeni/ kein(e) II

anybody /ˈeniˌbɒdi/ (irgend)jemand 3/15

not anymore /ˌnɒt eniˈmɔː/ nicht mehr II

anything /ˈeniˌθɪŋ/ (irgend)(et)was II

not anything /nɒt‿ˈeniˌθɪŋ/ nichts II

Anything else? /ˌeniθɪŋ‿ˈels/ Darf es noch etwas sein? I

anyway /ˈeniˌweɪ/ sowieso 1/3; jedenfalls 3/4

apartment /əˈpɑːtmənt/ Wohnung II

apple /ˈæpl/ Apfel II

application form /ˌæplɪˈkeɪʃn ˌfɔːm/ Bewerbungsformular 6/5

April /ˈeɪprəl/ April I

archery /ˈɑːtʃəri/ Bogenschießen 2/CC

area /ˈeəriə/ Gebiet, Region 6/13; Viertel, Gegend 3/I

area /ˈeəriə/ Bereich 5/8

argument /ˈɑːgjʊmənt/ Auseinandersetzung, Streit; Argument 5/M3

armchair /ˈɑːmˌtʃeə/ Sessel, Lehnstuhl I

around /əˈraʊnd/ um 1/14

around /əˈraʊnd/ herum, umher II

around /əˈraʊnd/ in, durch 5/9

around the world /əˌraʊnd ðə ˈwɜːld/ weltweit, auf der ganzen Welt 1/14

arrival /əˈraɪvl/ Ankunft 6/6

arrive /əˈraɪv/ ankommen I

art /ɑːt/ Kunst I

article /ˈɑːtɪkl/ Artikel 1/M1

as /əz/ als II

as ... as /əz əz/ (genau)so ... wie ... II

ask /ɑːsk/ fragen; bitten I

ask for directions /ˌɑːsk fə dɪˈrekʃnz/ nach dem Weg fragen 6/M7

astronaut /ˈæstrəˌnɔːt/ Astronaut/in II

at /æt/ auf, an, in, bei; um I

at first /ət ˈfɜːst/ anfangs, zuerst II

at last /ət ˈlɑːst/ endlich, schließlich 6/11

at least /ət ˈliːst/ mindestens, wenigstens 2/M7

ate /eɪt/ *Vergangenheitsform von „eat"*

athlete /ˈæθliːt/ Athlet/in 2/M1

the Atlantic (Ocean) /ðiˌətˌlæntɪk(‿ˈəʊʃn)/ der Atlantische Ozean 4/1

atmosphere /ˈætməsˌfɪə/ Atmosphäre, Stimmung 6/M2; Erdatmosphäre 5/8

attack /əˈtæk/ angreifen I

August /ˈɔːgəst/ August I

aunt /ɑːnt/ Tante I

Australia /ɒˈstreɪliə/ Australien II

Austria /ˈɒstriə/ Österreich 6/9

author /ˈɔːθə/ Schriftsteller/in, Autor/in II

autograph /ˈɔːtəˌgrɑːf/ Autogramm II

autumn /ˈɔːtəm/ Herbst I

away /əˈweɪ/ weg II

up and away /ˌʌp‿ən‿əˈweɪ/ auf und davon 6/I

awesome *(informal)* /ˈɔːsm/ super, spitze 6/11

axe /æks/ Axt, Beil 4/3

B

baby /ˈbeɪbi/ klein 4/M10

baby changing /ˈbeɪbi ˌtʃeɪndʒɪŋ/ Wickelraum 5/8

back /bæk/ Rücken; Rückseite I

back /bæk/ zurück II

back pocket /bæk ˈpɒkɪt/ Hintertasche, Gesäßtasche 3/P13

backache /ˈbækeɪk/ Rückenschmerzen 2/14

background /ˈbækˌgraʊnd/ Hintergrund 3/M4

backwards /ˈbækwədz/ rückwärts 2/1

bacon /ˈbeɪkən/ (Schinken)speck 1/2

bacterium *(pl* bacteria*)* /bækˈtɪəriəm, bækˈtɪəriə/ Bakterie 5/CC

bad /bæd/ schlecht I; schlimm, stark 2/14

too bad /ˌtuː ˈbæd/ wirklich schade 6/11

too bad /ˌtuː ˈbæd/ so ein Pech 2/15
bad luck *(no pl)* /ˌbæd ˈlʌk/ Pech 2/8
bag /bæg/ Tasche I
bag /bæg/ Tüte, Beutel 4/3
bake /beɪk/ backen II
baked potato /beɪkt pəˈteɪtəʊ/ Ofenkartoffel 1/P11
balance /ˈbæləns/ das Gleichgewicht halten 2/1
balloon /bəˈluːn/ Ballon I
banana /bəˈnɑːnə/ Banane I
bandage /ˈbændɪdʒ/ Verband 2/12
have a barbecue /ˌhæv‿ə ˈbɑːbɪˌkjuː/ grillen, eine Grill-party feiern II
bark /bɑːk/ bellen II
barn /bɑːn/ Scheune, (Vieh)stall I
basement /ˈbeɪsmənt/ Keller, Untergeschoss 5/8
basic /ˈbeɪsɪk/ grundlegend, wesentlich; Grund- 6/8
basket /ˈbɑːskɪt/ Korb I
bathroom /ˈbɑːθˌruːm/ Bad(ezimmer) I
bay /beɪ/ Bucht 6/14
be *(irr)* /biː/ sein I
beach /biːtʃ/ Strand II
bean /biːn/ Bohne 1/2
beard /bɪəd/ Bart II
beat up /ˌbiːt‿ˈʌp/ verprügeln; fertigmachen 4/7
beautiful /ˈbjuːtəfl/ schön I
became /bɪˈkeɪm/ *Vergangenheitsform von „become"*
because /bɪˈkɒz/ weil I
become *(irr)* /bɪˈkʌm/ werden I
bed /bed/ Bett I
bedroom /ˈbedruːm/ Schlafzimmer I
been /biːn/ *siehe „be"*
beer *(no pl)* /bɪə/ Bier 1/M1
before /bɪˈfɔː/ vor I; bevor II
began /bɪˈgæn/ *Vergangenheitsform von „begin"*

begin *(irr)* /bɪˈgɪn/ anfangen, beginnen 4/1
beginning /bɪˈgɪnɪŋ/ Anfang 3/M4
in the beginning /ɪn ðə bɪˈgɪnɪŋ/ am Anfang, zu Beginn II
behind /bɪˈhaɪnd/ hinter I
believe (in) /bɪˈliːv/ glauben (an) II
make sb believe sth /meɪk ˌsʌmbədi bɪˈliːv ˌsʌmθɪŋ/ jdn etw glauben machen, jdm etw weismachen 3/8
sb could not believe his/her ears /ˌsʌmbədi kʊd nɒt bɪˌliːv hɪz/hər‿ˈɪəz/ jmd traute seinen/ihren Ohren nicht 5/5
belong /bɪˈlɒŋ/ dazugehören, hinpassen 4/11
belong to sb/sth /bɪˈlɒŋ tə ˌsʌmbədi/ˌsʌmθɪŋ/ jdm/zu etw gehören II
below /bɪˈləʊ/ unter(halb) 2/M3; unten 6/M2
belt /belt/ Gürtel 2/4
bench /bentʃ/ Bank 5/M4
bend *(irr)* /bend/ biegen 5/13
best /best/ beste(r, s) I
best /best/ am meisten/ liebsten/besten I
best wishes /ˌbest ˈwɪʃɪz/ viele Grüße II
best-seller /ˌbestˈselə/ Bestseller *(Artikel mit großem Verkaufserfolg)* 5/M6
better /ˈbetə/ besser; lieber, mehr I
better safe than sorry /ˌbetə ˌseɪf ðæn ˈsɒri/ Vorsicht ist besser als Nachsicht 3/M6
between /bɪˈtwiːn/ zwischen I
beverage /ˈbevrɪdʒ/ Getränk 1/2
big /bɪg/ groß I
bike /baɪk/ (Fahr)rad I
ride a bike /raɪd‿ə ˈbaɪk/ (Fahr)rad fahren I
bill /bɪl/ Rechnung 1/6

bin /bɪn/ Mülleimer, Mülltonne I
biology *(no pl)* /baɪˈɒlədʒi/ Biologie I
bird /bɜːd/ Vogel II
bird of paradise /bɜːd‿əv ˈpærədaɪs/ Paradiesvogel 3/12
date of birth /ˈdeɪt‿əv ˌbɜːθ/ Geburtsdatum 6/5
birthday /ˈbɜːθdeɪ/ Geburtstag I
Happy birthday! /ˌhæpi ˈbɜːθdeɪ/ Alles Gute zum Geburtstag! I
a bit /ə ˈbɪt/ ein bisschen II
bite *(irr)* /baɪt/ beißen I
bitten /ˈbɪtn/ *siehe „bite"*
black /blæk/ schwarz I
blackberry /ˈblækbəri/ Brombeere 1/2
blue /bluː/ blau I
blue /bluː/ traurig 4/cc
board /bɔːd/ Brett; Tafel II
board (a ship) /bɔːd/ (ein Schiff) besteigen 4/1
board game /ˈbɔːd geɪm/ Brettspiel I
boat /bəʊt/ Boot; Schiff II
body /ˈbɒdi/ Körper I
boiled /bɔɪld/ gekocht 1/4
boiling /ˈbɔɪlɪŋ/ kochend 1/12
bone /bəʊn/ Knochen 2/M7
book /bʊk/ Buch I
book /bʊk/ buchen 5/M4
bookcase /ˈbʊkˌkeɪs/ Bücherregal, Bücherschrank I
booked up /bʊkt‿ˈʌp/ ausgebucht 6/11
boot /buːt/ Stiefel 5/M7
bored /bɔːd/ gelangweilt II
boring /ˈbɔːrɪŋ/ langweilig I
born /bɔːn/ geboren II
boss /bɒs/ Chef/in II
both /bəʊθ/ beide(s) 4/7
bottle /ˈbɒtl/ Flasche II
bottom /ˈbɒtəm/ untere(r, s) 5/13
at the bottom (of) /æt ðə ˈbɒtəm/ unten, am unteren Ende (von) 3/2

bottom of the ocean /ˌbɒtəm‿əv ðiˈəʊʃn/ Meeresgrund 5/CC
bowl /bəʊl/ Schüssel 1/14
boy /bɔɪ/ Junge I
boyfriend /ˈbɔɪˌfrend/ (fester) Freund I
bracelet /ˈbreɪslət/ Armband, Armreif 3/M5
brave /breɪv/ mutig, unerschrocken II
bread *(no pl)* /bred/ Brot 1/2
bread roll /ˈbred rəʊl/ Brötchen I
break /breɪk/ Pause I
break *(irr)* /breɪk/ (zer)brechen 1/12
break down /ˌbreɪk ˈdaʊn/ kaputtgehen 2/3; zusammenbrechen 4/11
breakfast /ˈbrekfəst/ Frühstück I
breast /brest/ Brust 1/P12
out of breath /aʊt‿əv ˈbreθ/ außer Atem, atemlos 2/1
bridge /brɪdʒ/ Brücke II
brightly /ˈbraɪtli/ hell, leuchtend 3/12
brilliant *(informal)* /ˈbrɪljənt/ toll, hervorragend 3/M4
bring *(irr)* /brɪŋ/ (mit)bringen I
Britain /ˈbrɪtn/ Großbritannien II
British /ˈbrɪtɪʃ/ britische(r, s) 1/13
the British *(only pl)* /ðə ˈbrɪtɪʃ/ die Briten 1/M1
broccoli *(no pl)* /ˈbrɒkəli/ Brokkoli 1/2
brochure /ˈbrəʊʃə/ Broschüre 5/14
broken /ˈbrəʊkən/ zerbrochen, kaputt; gebrochen 2/14
broken /ˈbrəʊkən/ *siehe „break"*
bronze /brɒnz/ Bronze, Bronze- II
brother /ˈbrʌðə/ Bruder I
brothers and sisters /ˌbrʌðəz‿ænd ˈsɪstəz/ Geschwister II
brought /brɔːt/ *Vergangenheitsform von „bring"*
brown /braʊn/ braun I
bruise /bruːz/ sich prellen/stoßen 2/12
bruised /bruːzd/ geprellt 2/12
brush /brʌʃ/ bürsten; putzen I
budgie (= budgerigar) /ˈbʌdʒi, ˈbʌdʒəriˌɡɑː/ Wellensittich I
build *(irr)* /bɪld/ bauen II
builder /ˈbɪldə/ Bauarbeiter/in II
building /ˈbɪldɪŋ/ Gebäude II
built /bɪlt/ *Vergangenheitsform von „build"*
bully /ˈbʊli/ Rüpel, Rabauke; jemand, der andere drangsaliert
bully /ˈbʊli/ tyrannisieren, drangsalieren, mobben II
bullying *(no pl)* /ˈbʊliɪŋ/ Mobbing II
bunch /bʌntʃ/ Büschel, Bund 1/12
burn *(irr)* /bɜːn/ (ver)brennen II
bus stop /ˈbʌs ˌstɒp/ Bushaltestelle II
business trip /ˈbɪznəs trɪp/ Dienstreise, Geschäftsreise 4/M3
busy /ˈbɪzi/ beschäftigt II
busy /ˈbɪzi/ arbeitsreich II
but /bʌt/ aber I
butterfly /ˈbʌtəˌflaɪ/ Schmetterling 2/M7
buy *(irr)* /baɪ/ kaufen I
buzz group /ˈbʌz ɡruːp/ *Form der Gruppenarbeit* 2/8
by /baɪ/ bei, in der Nähe; mit, durch; von II
by /baɪ/ vorbei 4/1
by (eight o'clock) /baɪ/ (spätestens) bis (acht Uhr) II
bye *(informal)* /baɪ/ tschüss I
bye for now /ˈbaɪ fə naʊ/ bis bald II

C

cabbage /ˈkæbɪdʒ/ Kohl, Kraut 1/11
cage /keɪdʒ/ Käfig I
cake /keɪk/ Kuchen I
calculator /ˈkælkjʊˌleɪtə/ (Taschen)rechner I
calendar /ˈkælɪndə/ Kalender I
(phone) call /(ˈfəʊn) kɔːl/ (Telefon)anruf II
call /kɔːl/ anrufen II
call /kɔːl/ nennen 4/M3
be called /biː ˈkɔːld/ heißen I
came /keɪm/ *Vergangenheitsform von „come"*
camera /ˈkæmrə/ Kamera, Fotoapparat 3/P13
campsite /ˈkæmpˌsaɪt/ Campingplatz, Zeltplatz II
can *(irr)* /kæn/ können I
candle /ˈkændl/ Kerze II
candy *(AE)* = sweets *(BE)* /ˈkændi/ Süßigkeiten 6/11
cannibal /ˈkænɪbl/ Kannibale/Kannibalin, Menschenfresser/in 4/1
cap /kæp/ Kappe I
captain /ˈkæptɪn/ Kapitän/in 2/8
car /kɑː/ Auto I
car boot sale /ˌkɑː ˈbuːt ˌseɪl/ *Verkauf persönlicher Gegenstände aus dem Kofferraum auf einem Parkplatz* 3/4
car park /ˈkɑː ˌpɑːk/ Parkplatz 3/P6
caravan /ˈkærəvæn/ Wohnwagen II
card /kɑːd/ Pappe, Karton; Karte I
get well card /get ˈwel kɑːd/ Genesungskarte II
sb does not care /ˌsʌmbədi dəz nɒt ˈkeə/ jdm ist es egal 4/9
take care of /teɪk ˈkeər‿əv/ sich kümmern um, versorgen II
career /kəˈrɪə/ Beruf; Karriere 2/M3
careful /ˈkeəfl/ vorsichtig; sorgfältig II

the Caribbean /ðə ˌkærɪˈbiːən/ die Karibik; die Karibischen Inseln 4/1
Caribbean /ˌkærɪˈbiːən/ karibisch 3/12
carnival /ˈkɑːnɪvl/ Karneval 3/11
carpet /ˈkɑːpɪt/ Teppich I
carrot /ˈkærət/ Möhre, Karotte, Mohrrübe II
carry /ˈkæri/ tragen 5/M6
cartoon /kɑːˈtuːn/ Cartoon, Karikatur; Zeichentrickfilm II
cash machine /ˈkæʃ məˌʃiːn/ Geldautomat 6/6
cast away /kɑːst‿əˈweɪ/ gestrandet 4/M3
castle /ˈkɑːsl/ Burg; Schloss II
cat /kæt/ Katze I
catch *(irr)* /kætʃ/ fangen I; festnehmen II
catch *(irr)* /kætʃ/ erwischen, kriegen 3/3
cathedral /kəˈθiːdrəl/ Kathedrale, Dom 6/14
causeway /ˈkɔːzˌweɪ/ Damm 6/13
cave /keɪv/ Höhle 5/M1
ceiling /ˈsiːlɪŋ/ (Zimmer)decke I
celebrate /ˈseləˌbreɪt/ feiern II
celebration /ˌseləˈbreɪʃn/ Feier, Fest II
centre /ˈsentə/ Zentrum, Center I
centre line /ˌsentə ˈlaɪn/ Mittellinie 5/13
century /ˈsentʃəri/ Jahrhundert II
cereal /ˈsɪəriəl/ Getreide(sorte); Frühstückszerealien, -flocken 1/10
certain /ˈsɜːtn/ gewisse(r, s), bestimmte(r, s) 2/P7
chair /tʃeə/ Stuhl I
challenge /ˈtʃælɪndʒ/ Herausforderung 5/8
chance /tʃɑːns/ Chance; Möglichkeit II
change /tʃeɪndʒ/ (Ver)änderung; Wechselgeld 3/7
change /tʃeɪndʒ/ wechseln II
change /tʃeɪndʒ/ (sich) (ver)ändern 3/17
chant /tʃɑːnt/ Sprechgesang, Sprechchor 1/M1
chant /tʃɑːnt/ singen; einen Sprechgesang anstimmen 2/8
character /ˈkærɪktə/ Charakter; Figur 2/12
charity /ˈtʃærət/ Wohltätigkeitsorganisation 2/M1; wohltätige Zwecke 2/8
charming /ˈtʃɑːmɪŋ/ bezaubernd, charmant II
chat /tʃæt/ chatten, sich unterhalten II
cheap /tʃiːp/ billig, preiswert II
check /tʃek/ überprüfen, kontrollieren I
check /tʃek/ nachsehen (in) 4/9
cheer /tʃɪə/ jubeln 2/8
cheer on /tʃɪər‿ˈɒn/ anfeuern 2/7
Cheer up! /tʃɪər‿ˈʌp/ Lass (doch) den Kopf nicht hängen!, Kopf hoch! 4/M9
cheese *(no pl)* /tʃiːz/ Käse 1/2
chemistry /ˈkemɪstri/ Chemie I
chess *(no pl)* /tʃes/ Schach(spiel) II
chew /tʃuː/ kauen II
(chewing) gum *(no pl)* /(ˈtʃuːɪŋ) gʌm/ Kaugummi II
chicken /ˈtʃɪkɪn/ Huhn; Hähnchen I
chickenpox *(no pl)* /ˈtʃɪkɪnˌpɒks/ Windpocken II
child *(pl* **children***)* /tʃaɪld, ˈtʃɪldrən/ Kind I
children's home /ˈtʃɪldrənz ˌhəʊm/ Kinderheim 3/17
chilli *(pl chillies)* /ˈtʃɪli/ Peperoni 1/2
chimney /ˈtʃɪmni/ Kamin; Schornstein I
chin /tʃɪn/ Kinn II
Chinese /ˌtʃaɪˈniːz/ Chinesisch II
Chinese /ˌtʃaɪˈniːz/ chinesisch II
chips *(only pl) (BE)* /tʃɪps/ Pommes frites II
chocolate *(no pl)* /ˈtʃɒklət/ Schokolade I
chocolate chip cookie /ˌtʃɒklət ˌtʃɪp ˈkʊki/ *Keks mit Schokoladenstückchen* 5/10
a box of chocolates /ə bɒks‿əv ˈtʃɒkləts/ eine Schachtel Pralinen II
choice /tʃɔɪs/ Wahl 6/5
choose *(irr)* /tʃuːz/ auswählen I
chopstick /ˈtʃɒpˌstɪk/ (Ess)stäbchen 1/14
chose /ʃəʊz/ *Vergangenheitsform von „choose"*
chosen /ˈtʃəʊzn/ *siehe „choose"*
Christmas /ˈkrɪsməs/ Weihnachten II
Christmas Day /ˌkrɪsməs ˈdeɪ/ erster Weihnachtsfeiertag II
Christmas Eve /ˌkrɪsməs‿ˈiːv/ Heiligabend II
chronicle /ˈkrɒnɪkl/ Anzeiger 1/CC
church /tʃɜːtʃ/ Kirche II
cinema /ˈsɪnəmə/ Kino I
circle /ˈsɜːkl/ Kreis II
city /ˈsɪti/ (Groß)stadt I
class /klɑːs/ (Schul)klasse I
classmate /ˈklɑːsˌmeɪt/ Klassenkamerad/in, Mitschüler/in I
classroom /ˈklɑːsˌruːm/ Klassenzimmer I
clean /kliːn/ sauber machen, reinigen, putzen I
clean /kliːn/ sauber I
clever /ˈklevə/ klug, gescheit, schlau II
click /klɪk/ (an)klicken, drücken 6/M2
cliff /klɪf/ Klippe, Kliff 6/14
climb /klaɪm/ (hinauf) klettern; (hinauf)steigen II
climbing /ˈklaɪmɪŋ/ Klettern, Bergsteigen; Kletter- 6/4

cloakroom /ˈkləʊkˌruːm/ Garderobe 5/8
clock /klɒk/ Uhr I
close /kləʊz/ schließen, zumachen I
close /kləʊs/ nah(e) 3/12; genau 3/9
cloth *(no pl)* /klɒθ/ Tuch, Stoff 1/14
clothes *(only pl)* /kləʊðz/ Kleider, Kleidung I
clothing *(no pl)* /ˈkləʊðɪŋ/ Kleidung 6/P13
cloud /klaʊd/ Wolke 3/P3
cloudy /ˈklaʊdi/ bewölkt, bedeckt I
club /klʌb/ Klub, Verein I
coach /kəʊtʃ/ Trainer(in) 2/M7
coach station /ˈkəʊtʃ ˌsteɪʃn/ Busbahnhof 6/6
coast /kəʊst/ Küste I
coat /kəʊt/ Mantel, Jacke 5/M4
coconut /ˈkəʊkəˌnʌt/ Kokosnuss 1/M1
coffee /ˈkɒfi/ Kaffee 1/2
coffin /ˈkɒfɪn/ Sarg II
cold /kəʊld/ Erkältung, Schnupfen 2/14
cold /kəʊld/ Kälte 1/CC
cold /kəʊld/ kalt I
colleague /ˈkɒliːg/ Kollege/ Kollegin; Mitarbeiter/in 3/4
collect /kəˈlekt/ sammeln I
collect /kəˈlekt/ entnehmen 6/P6
colour /ˈkʌlə/ Farbe I
coloured /ˈkʌləd/ bunt, farbig 3/12
colourful /ˈkʌləfl/ farbenfroh, farbenprächtig II
combine /kəmˈbaɪn/ verbinden, kombinieren 5/M6
come *(irr)* /kʌm/ kommen I
come in /kʌm‿ˈɪn/ hereinkommen I
come true /ˌkʌm ˈtruː/ wahr werden 4/7
comedy /ˈkɒmədi/ Komödie I
comfortable /ˈkʌmftəbl/ bequem I
comment /ˈkɒment/ Kommentar, Bemerkung 3/M4
communication *(no pl)* /kəˌmjuːnɪˈkeɪʃn/ Kommunikation 5/M1
comparative (form) /kəmˈpærətɪv/ Komparativ 2/P5
compare /kəmˈpeə/ vergleichen 1/6
comparison /kəmˈpærɪsn/ Vergleich 2/P5
compete (for) /kəmˈpiːt/ wetteifern (um), kämpfen (um) 3/11
competition /ˌkɒmpəˈtɪʃn/ Wettbewerb II
complete /kəmˈpliːt/ vervollständigen 1/1
completely /kəmˈpliːtli/ völlig, ganz I
comprehensive school /ˌkɒmprɪˈhensɪv ˌskuːl/ Gesamtschule II
computing /kəmˈpjuːtɪŋ/ Berechnen, Kalkulieren; EDV 5/8
concentrate /ˈkɒnsnˌtreɪt/ sich konzentrieren II
concert /ˈkɒnsət/ Konzert II
connect /kəˈnekt/ verbinden 3/17
lose consciousness /luːz ˈkɒnʃəsnəs/ bewusstlos werden, das Bewusstsein verlieren 4/M3
constant /ˈkɒnstənt/ dauernd; beständig, gleich bleibend 6/P13
contact sb /ˈkɒntækt ˌsʌmbədi/ jdn kontaktieren, sich mit jdm in Verbindung setzen 3/P6
contain /kənˈteɪn/ enthalten 1/10
contemporary /kənˈtempri/ zeitgenössisch; modern 5/8
cook /kʊk/ Koch/Köchin II
cook /kʊk/ kochen II
cookie /ˈkʊki/ Keks, Plätzchen 1/CC
cooking *(no pl)* /ˈkʊkɪŋ/ Kochen 1/12
do the cooking /ˌduː ðə ˈkʊkɪŋ/ kochen I
cool down /kuːl ˈdaʊn/ sich beruhigen II
copy /ˈkɒpi/ abschreiben 2/P9
corn on the cob /ˌkɔːn‿ɒn ðə ˈkɒb/ Maiskolben 3/CC
corner /ˈkɔːnə/ Ecke II
correct /kəˈrekt/ korrigieren 3/15
correct /kəˈrekt/ richtig, korrekt II
cosmos /ˈkɒzmɒs/ Kosmos, Weltall 5/8
cost /kɒst/ Kosten, Preis 5/M4
cost *(irr)* /kɒst/ kosten 1/2
costume /ˈkɒstjuːm/ Tracht, Kostüm II
couch /kaʊtʃ/ Couch, Sofa II
could /kʊd/ könnte(st, n, t) I
country /ˈkʌntri/ Land 2/6
test of courage /test‿əv ˈkʌrɪdʒ/ Mutprobe 1/M1
course /kɔːs/ Kurs I
cousin /ˈkʌzn/ Cousin/e I
cover /ˈkʌvə/ Titelseite, Cover 3/10
cover /ˈkʌvə/ bedecken 1/P12
cow /kaʊ/ Kuh I
crash /kræʃ/ stürzen 4/M3
crazy /ˈkreɪzi/ verrückt I
go crazy *(informal)* /gəʊ ˈkreɪzi/ durchdrehen, ausflippen I
cream /kriːm/ Sahne II; Creme, Salbe 2/12
create /kriˈeɪt/ erschaffen; gestalten II
creative /kriˈeɪtɪv/ kreativ II
criminal /ˈkrɪmɪnl/ Verbrecher/in, Kriminelle/r II
crisps *(only pl)* *(BE)* /krɪsps/ Chips I
crispy /ˈkrɪspi/ knusprig 1/2
crocodile /ˈkrɒkədaɪl/ Krokodil 5/5

cross /krɒs/ durchqueren; überqueren II
crossword puzzle /ˈkrɒswɜːd ˌpʌzl/ Kreuzworträtsel 1/7
crowd /kraʊd/ (Menschen) menge, Zuschauermenge II
crown /kraʊn/ Krone II
crumble /ˈkrʌmbl/ *Fruchtauflauf* 1/2
cry /kraɪ/ weinen; schreien II
cucumber /ˈkjuːˌkʌmbə/ (Salat)gurke 1/2
culture /ˈkʌltʃə/ Kultur 5/8
cumin *(no pl)* /ˈkʌmɪn/ Kreuzkümmel 1/12
cup /kʌp/ Tasse I
cupboard /ˈkʌbəd/ Schrank II
curry /ˈkʌri/ Curry(gericht) 1/2
curtain /ˈkɜːtn/ Vorhang II
cushion /ˈkʊʃn/ Kissen I
customer /ˈkʌstəmə/ Kunde/ Kundin II
cut /kʌt/ Schnitt 5/13
cut *(irr)* /kʌt/ schneiden II
cut foot /ˌkʌt ˈfʊt/ Schnittwunde am Fuß 2/14
cut off /kʌt‿ˈɒf/ abschneiden 1/12
cut sth open /kʌt ˌsʌmθɪŋ‿ˈəʊpən/ etw aufschneiden 1/12
cute /kjuːt/ süß, niedlich I
cyberbullying /ˈsaɪbəˌbʊliɪŋ/ Internetmobbing 4/7
cycle /ˈsaɪkl/ Rad fahren II
cycling /ˈsaɪklɪŋ/ Radfahren, Radeln 2/3
cyclist /ˈsaɪklɪst/ Radfahrer/in 5/M6

D

dad *(informal)* /dæd/ Papa, Vati I
dance /dɑːns/ Tanz II
dance /dɑːns/ tanzen I
dancer /ˈdɑːnsə/ Tänzer/in 3/12
dancing *(no pl)* /ˈdɑːnsɪŋ/ Tanzen I
danger /ˈdeɪndʒə/ Gefahr 5/6
dangerous /ˈdeɪndʒərəs/ gefährlich I
dark *(no pl)* /dɑːk/ Dunkelheit 4/11
dark /dɑːk/ dunkel I
darkness /ˈdɑːknəs/ Dunkelheit, Finsternis II
date /deɪt/ Datum I
date of birth /ˈdeɪt‿əv ˌbɜːθ/ Geburtsdatum 6/5
daughter /ˈdɔːtə/ Tochter I
day /deɪ/ Tag I
a day /ə ˈdeɪ/ pro/am Tag 1/9
one day /ˈwʌn deɪ/ eines Tages II
the next day /ðə ˌnekst ˈdeɪ/ am nächsten Tag 2/M4
dead /ded/ tot II
deal with /ˈdiːl wɪð/ sich befassen mit; umgehen mit 4/7
dear /dɪə/ liebe(r) *(Anrede)* I
Oh dear! /əʊ ˈdɪə/ Du meine Güte 2/1
December /dɪˈsembə/ Dezember I
decide /dɪˈsaɪd/ (sich) entscheiden; beschließen II
decorate /ˈdekəˌreɪt/ schmücken, dekorieren II
decoration /ˌdekəˈreɪʃn/ Dekoration, Schmuck 5/P10
deep-fried /ˌdiːpˈfraɪd/ frittiert 3/CC
definition /ˌdefəˈnɪʃn/ Definition, Erklärung 3/M9
delicious /dɪˈlɪʃəs/ köstlich, lecker II
department store /dɪˈpɑːtmənt ˌstɔː/ Kaufhaus II
departure /dɪˈpɑːtʃə/ Abreise; Abflug; Abfahrt 6/6
depressed /dɪˈprest/ deprimiert I
describe /dɪˈskraɪb/ beschreiben 2/P6
description /dɪˈskrɪpʃn/ Beschreibung 3/P3
design /dɪˈzaɪn/ entwerfen 1/7
desk /desk/ Schreibtisch I
dessert /dɪˈzɜːt/ Nachtisch, Dessert 1/2
destroy /dɪˈstrɔɪ/ zerstören 4/M3
detail /ˈdiːteɪl/ Detail, Einzelheit 2/M1
detective /dɪˈtektɪv/ (Privat)detektiv/in II
develop /dɪˈveləp/ (sich) entwickeln 2/M3
device /dɪˈvaɪs/ Gerät, Apparat 5/2
devil /ˈdevl/ Teufel II
diagram /ˈdaɪəgræm/ Diagramm, Schaubild 1/M5
dialogue /ˈdaɪəlɒg/ Gespräch, Dialog 1/3
diamond /ˈdaɪəmənd/ Diamant 4/14
diary /ˈdaɪəri/ Tagebuch II
dictionary /ˈdɪkʃənri/ Wörterbuch I
did /dɪd/ *Vergangenheitsform von „do"*
die /daɪ/ sterben II
difference /ˈdɪfrəns/ Unterschied II
different /ˈdɪfrənt/ anders, andere(r, s); verschieden, unterschiedlich II
difficult /ˈdɪfɪklt/ schwierig, schwer I
digital /ˈdɪdʒɪtl/ digital, Digital- 3/P13
dinner /ˈdɪnə/ Abendessen; Mittagessen II
dinosaur /ˈdaɪnəˌsɔː/ Dinosaurier 6/P13
direction /dɪˈrekʃn/ Richtung II
ask for directions /ˌɑːsk fə dɪˈrekʃnz/ nach dem Weg fragen 6/M7
give directions /ˌgɪv dɪˈrekʃnz/ den Weg beschreiben 6/M7
director /dəˈrektə/ Direktor/in, Leiter/in II
dirty /ˈdɜːti/ dreckig, schmutzig I

disabled /dɪs'eɪbld/ behindert 2/M3
disappointed /ˌdɪsə'pɔɪntɪd/ enttäuscht 4/7
discover /dɪ'skʌvə/ entdecken II
discussion /dɪ'skʌʃn/ Diskussion 5/M3
disgusting /dɪs'gʌstɪŋ/ widerlich 1/11
dish *(pl* **-es***)* /dɪʃ/ Gericht II
dish *(pl -es)* /dɪʃ/ Schale 1/P12
dishwasher /'dɪʃˌwɒʃə/ Geschirrspülmaschine I
distance /'dɪstəns/ Entfernung; Strecke 5/11
diving /'daɪvɪŋ/ Tauchen 5/8
do *(irr)* /du:/ machen, tun I
do well /du: 'wel/ gut abschneiden 2/3
dock /dɒk/ Dock, Kai 5/8
doctor /'dɒktə/ Arzt/Ärztin II
dog /dɒg/ Hund I
done /dʌn/ *siehe „do"*
door /dɔ:/ Tür I
doorbell /'dɔ:ˌbel/ Türklingel 5/5
double circle /ˌdʌbl 's3:kl/ Doppelkreis 1/11
down /daʊn/ (nach) unten; hinunter, hinab 5/5
down *(informal)* /daʊn/ niedergeschlagen, down 2/M7
download /ˌdaʊn'ləʊd/ herunterladen, downloaden 5/2
dragon /'drægən/ Drache I
drama /'drɑ:mə/ Schauspielerei; Theater 6/M2
dramatic /drə'mætɪk/ dramatisch 2/16
draw *(irr)* /drɔ:/ zeichnen I
end in a draw /ˌend‿ɪn‿ə 'drɔ:/ unentschieden ausgehen 2/8
dream /dri:m/ Traum I
dreamer /'dri:mə/ Träumer/in 5/P10
dress /dres/ Kleid I
dress up (as) /dres‿'ʌp/ sich verkleiden (als) 3/12
get dressed /get‿'drest/ sich anziehen 5/5
dribble /'drɪbl/ dribbeln 2/7
drink /drɪŋk/ Getränk I
drink *(irr)* /drɪŋk/ trinken I
drive *(irr)* /draɪv/ fahren II
driver /'draɪvə/ Fahrer/in II
drop /drɒp/ fallen lassen II
drum /drʌm/ Trommel 3/12
drunk /drʌŋk/ *siehe „drink"*
dry /draɪ/ trocknen 1/12
duck /dʌk/ Ente I
during /'djʊərɪŋ/ während I

E

each /i:tʃ/ jede(r, s) 1/9
each other /ˌi:tʃ‿'ʌðə/ einander 4/7
eagle /'i:gl/ Adler II
ear /ɪə/ Ohr I
sb could not believe his/her ears /ˌsʌmbədi kʊd nɒt bɪˌli:v hɪz/hər‿'ɪəz/ jmd traute seinen/ihren Ohren nicht 5/5
early /'3:li/ früh, zeitig II
earn /3:n/ verdienen II
earring /'ɪərɪŋ/ Ohrring II
the earth /ði‿'3:θ/ die Erde 5/CC
east /i:st/ Osten 4/5
Easter /'i:stə/ Ostern, Osterfest II
easy /'i:zi/ einfach; leicht I
eat *(irr)* /i:t/ essen I
eat out /i:t‿'aʊt/ essen gehen, auswärts essen 1/P7
eaten /'i:tn/ *siehe „eat"*
eating habits *(only pl)* /ˌi:tɪŋ 'hæbɪts/ Essgewohnheiten 1/14
edge /edʒ/ Rand 4/11
edit /'edɪt/ bearbeiten, redigieren 3/10
education *(no pl)* /ˌedjʊ'keɪʃn/ (Aus)bildung 2/M3
egg /eg/ Ei I
Egyptian /i'dʒɪpʃn/ Ägypter/in 5/M1
Egyptian /i'dʒɪpʃn/ ägyptisch 5/M1
elbow /'elbəʊ/ Ellbogen II
electricity *(no pl)* /ɪˌlek'trɪsəti/ Elektrizität, Strom 5/12
electronic /ˌelek'trɒnɪk/ Elektro(musik) 4/14
electronic /ˌelek'trɒnɪk/ elektronisch 5/2
elephant /'elɪfənt/ Elefant I
elite /ɪ'li:t/ Elite; Wettkampf- 2/M1
nobody else /ˌnəʊˌbɒdi‿'els/ niemand anders 5/P13
something else /ˌsʌmθɪŋ‿'els/ (noch) etwas anderes 4/M9
what else /wɒt‿'els/ was noch, was sonst 1/P11
who else /hu‿'els/ wer noch, wer sonst 4/M8
embarrassed /ɪm'bærəst/ verlegen, peinlich berührt II
empty /'empti/ ausräumen, (ent)leeren I
empty /'empti/ leer 4/6
end /end/ Ende II
end /end/ enden II
in the end /ˌɪn ði‿'end/ letzten Endes; schließlich 3/6
end in a draw /ˌend‿ɪn‿ə 'drɔ:/ unentschieden ausgehen 2/8
energy /'enədʒi/ Energie, Kraft II
engineer /ˌendʒɪ'nɪə/ Ingenieur/in 4/9
English /'ɪŋglɪʃ/ Englisch I
English /'ɪŋglɪʃ/ englisch I
in English /ˌɪn‿'ɪŋglɪʃ/ auf Englisch I
enjoy /ɪn'dʒɔɪ/ mögen; genießen I
enough /ɪ'nʌf/ genügend, ausreichend, genug II
entertainment /ˌentə'teɪnmənt/ Unterhaltung 5/3
entrance /'entrəns/ Eingang; Eintritt(sgebühr) 3/P6
entrance fee /'entrəns ˌfi:/ Eintritt(sgeld) 6/P13
entry /'entri/ Eintrag 4/M5
envelope /'envələʊp/ Briefumschlag, Kuvert II

equipment *(no pl)* /ɪ'kwɪpmənt/ Ausrüstung, Ausstattung 2/3
escalator /'eskəˌleɪtə/ Rolltreppe 6/6
escape /ɪ'skeɪp/ Flucht II
escape /ɪ'skeɪp/ Entkommen 3/15
escape /ɪ'skeɪp/ (ent)fliehen, ausbrechen; entkommen II
especially /ɪ'speʃli/ besonders 1/10
Europe /'jʊərəp/ Europa II
even /'i:vn/ selbst; sogar I
even /'i:vn/ noch 2/3
evening /'i:vnɪŋ/ Abend II
in the evening /ˌɪn ði‿'i:vnɪŋ/ am Abend, abends I
this evening /ðɪs‿'i:vnɪŋ/ heute Abend 6/P4
ever /'evə/ jemals II
every /'evri/ jede(r, s) I
everybody /'evriˌbɒdi/ jede(r); alle 3/12
everyday /'evrideɪ/ alltäglich, Alltags- 5/I
everyone /'evriwʌn/ jede(r); alle I
everything /'evriθɪŋ/ alles II
everywhere /'evriweə/ überall 5/M1
exact /ɪg'zækt/ genau (abgezählt) 6/P6
not exactly /nɒt‿ɪg'zæktli/ nicht gerade 5/M6
example /ɪg'zɑ:mpl/ Beispiel I
for example /fər‿ɪg'zɑ:mpl/ zum Beispiel I
exchange /ɪks'tʃeɪndʒ/ (Aus)tausch- 2/M6
excited /ɪk'saɪtɪd/ aufgeregt II; begeistert 6/11
excitement /ɪk'saɪtmənt/ Aufregung, Spannung 3/M5
exciting /ɪk'saɪtɪŋ/ aufregend; spannend I
excuse /ɪk'skju:s/ Entschuldigung; Ausrede I
Excuse me! /ɪk skju:z ˌmi/ Entschuldigen Sie bitte!, Entschuldigung! I
exercise /'eksəsaɪz/ Übung 2/M7; Bewegung 5/M6
exercise book /'eksəsaɪz ˌbʊk/ Heft I
exist /ɪg'zɪst/ existieren, vorkommen 5/14
exit /'eksɪt/ Ausgang 6/6
expect /ɪk'spekt/ erwarten 2/M1
expensive /ɪk'spensɪv/ teuer II
experience /ɪk'spɪəriəns/ Erfahrung, Erlebnis 6/M2
expert /'ekspɜ:t/ Experte/ Expertin 1/10
explain /ɪk'spleɪn/ erklären II
explore /ɪk'splɔ:/ erforschen, untersuchen II
expression /ɪk'spreʃn/ Ausdruck 1/M1
extreme /ɪk'stri:m/ extrem I
eye /aɪ/ Auge I

F

face /feɪs/ Gesicht I
fact /fækt/ Fakt 3/CC
fact file /'fækt ˌfaɪl/ Steckbrief 2/6
factory /'fæktri/ Fabrik; Werk II
fall *(irr)* /fɔ:l/ fallen 2/12
fall down /fɔ:l 'daʊn/ hinfallen I
fall off /fɔ:l‿'ɒf/ herunterfallen, abfallen 2/8
fallen /'fɔ:lən/ *siehe „fall"*
family /'fæmli/ Familie I
famous /'feɪməs/ berühmt I
fancy sth *(informal)* /'fænsi ˌsʌmθɪŋ/ auf etw Lust haben 1/3
fantastic *(informal)* /fæn'tæstɪk/ fantastisch, wunderbar I
far /fɑ:/ weit II
far /fɑ:/ viel 3/M4
farm /fɑ:m/ Bauernhof I
farmer /'fɑ:mə/ Bauer/ Bäuerin I
fast /fɑ:st/ schnell I
father /'fɑ:ðə/ Vater I
Father Christmas /ˌfɑ:ðə 'krɪsməs/ Weihnachtsmann II
fault /fɔ:lt/ Schuld; Fehler II
favourite /'feɪvrət/ Lieblings- I
feather /'feðə/ Feder 3/M5
February /'februəri/ Februar I
feed *(irr)* /fi:d/ füttern, zu Essen geben I
feel *(irr)* /fi:l/ (sich) fühlen I
feel sorry for sb /ˌfi:l 'sɒri fə sʌmbədi/ Mitleid mit jdm haben 4/M9
feeling /'fi:lɪŋ/ Gefühl 4/7
fell /fel/ *Vergangenheitsform von „fall"*
felt /felt/ *Vergangenheitsform von „feel"*
felt tip /'felt‿tɪp/ Filzstift I
female /'fi:meɪl/ weiblich 6/5
ferry /'feri/ Fähre II
festival /'festɪvl/ Fest; Festival II
fête /feɪt/ Fest 3/CC
few /fju:/ wenige II
few /fju:/ paar 1/12
a few /ə 'fju:/ einige 2/12
fight *(irr)* /faɪt/ kämpfen II
fighter /'faɪtə/ Kämpfer(in) 2/M7
fill in /fɪl‿'ɪn/ ausfüllen 5/2; einsetzen 3/P10
finally /'faɪnli/ schließlich, endlich; zum Schluss II
find *(irr)* /faɪnd/ finden I
find out /faɪnd‿'aʊt/ herausfinden 1/M1
find out about /faɪnd‿'aʊt‿əˌbaʊt/ sich informieren über 5/10
finder /'faɪndə/ Finder/in 4/P8
fine /faɪn/ in Ordnung, gut II
I'm fine. /aɪm 'faɪn/ Es geht mir gut. I
finish /'fɪnɪʃ/ beenden, aufhören I
finishing line /'fɪnɪʃɪŋ ˌlaɪn/ Ziellinie 2/M1
fire /faɪə/ Feuer I

firefighter /ˈfaɪəˌfaɪtə/ Feuerwehrmann/-frau II
first /fɜːst/ erste(r, s) I
first /fɜːst/ zuerst, als Erstes II
at first /ət ˈfɜːst/ anfangs, zuerst II
first aid kit /fɜːst‿ˈeɪd kɪt/ Erste-Hilfe-Ausrüstung, Verbandskasten 4/3
first name /ˈfɜːst ˌneɪm/ Vorname 6/5
first of all /ˌfɜːst‿əv‿ˈɔːl/ erstens, als erstes II
fish *(pl - or* **-es***)* /fɪʃ, fɪʃ, fɪʃɪz/ Fisch I
fish /fɪʃ/ fischen, angeln 4/1
fish tank /ˈfɪʃ tæŋk/ Aquarium I
fit *(irr)* /fɪt/ passen (zu) 3/9
keep fit /ˌkiːp ˈfɪt/ sich fit halten 2/9
fix /fɪks/ festmachen, befestigen 5/M6
flag /flæg/ Fahne; Flagge II
flap /flæp/ Klappe 5/13
flat /flæt/ Wohnung 4/7
flat /flæt/ platt II
flat /flæt/ flach 1/14
flea market /ˈfliː ˌmɑːkɪt/ Flohmarkt, Trödelmarkt 3/17
flight /flaɪt/ Flug 5/8
float /fləʊt/ Festwagen 3/12
floor /flɔː/ Boden I; Stockwerk 5/8
flour *(no pl)* /ˈflaʊə/ Mehl II
flower /ˈflaʊə/ Blume II
fly *(irr)* /flaɪ/ fliegen I
fog /fɒg/ Nebel II
foggy /ˈfɒgi/ neblig II
fold /fəʊld/ (zusammen) falten 5/13
fold down /fəʊld ˈdaʊn/ herunterklappen 5/13
folder /ˈfəʊldə/ Mappe, Schnellhefter I
follow /ˈfɒləʊ/ folgen II
following /ˈfɒləʊɪŋ/ folgende(r, s) 2/P7
food *(no pl)* /fuːd/ Essen I
food technology /ˈfuːd tekˌnɒlədʒi/ Ernährung *(Schulfach)* 1/11
foot *(pl* **feet***)* /fʊt, fiːt/ Fuß I
on foot /ɒn ˈfʊt/ zu Fuß II
football /ˈfʊtbɔːl/ Fußball I
for /fɔː/ für I
for example /fər‿ɪgˈzɑːmpl/ zum Beispiel I
for free /fɔː ˈfriː/ gratis, umsonst I
foreign /ˈfɒrɪn/ ausländisch, fremd 6/9
forest /ˈfɒrɪst/ Wald II
forget *(irr)* /fəˈget/ vergessen I
forgive *(irr)* /fəˈgɪv/ vergeben, verzeihen 4/CC
fork /fɔːk/ Gabel I
form /fɔːm/ Formular 6/5
form /fɔːm/ bilden, formen 6/P13
application form /ˌæplɪˈkeɪʃn ˌfɔːm/ Bewerbungsformular 6/5
forward /ˈfɔːwəd/ nach vorn(e) 2/8
look forward to sth /ˌlʊk ˈfɔːwəd‿tə ˌsʌmθɪŋ/ sich auf etw freuen I
found /faʊnd/ *Vergangenheitsform von „find"*
France /frɑːnts/ Frankreich I
free /friː/ frei I
for free /fɔː ˈfriː/ gratis, umsonst I
free time /ˈfriː taɪm/ Freizeit 6/2
freedom *(no pl)* /ˈfriːdəm/ Freiheit II
French /frentʃ/ Französisch II
French /frentʃ/ französisch II
Frenchman/Frenchwoman ˈfrentʃmən,ˈfrentʃˌwʊmən/ Franzose/Französin 5/M6
fresh /freʃ/ frisch II
Friday /ˈfraɪdeɪ/ Freitag I
fridge *(informal)* /frɪdʒ/ Kühlschrank II
friend /frend/ Freund/in I
friendly /ˈfrendli/ freundlich I
friendly match /ˈfrendli mætʃ/ Freundschaftsspiel 2/8
friendship /ˈfrendʃɪp/ Freundschaft 4/7
be frightened (of) /biː ˈfraɪtnd/ Angst haben, sich fürchten (vor) II
frog /frɒg/ Frosch 4/CC
from /frəm/ von, aus I
from all over the world /frəm‿ɔːl‿ˌəʊvə ðə ˈwɜːld/ aus der ganzen Welt 2/M1
at the front /æt ðə ˈfrʌnt/ vorn(e) 6/M9
in front of /ɪn ˈfrʌnt‿əv/ vor I
front wheel /frʌnt ˈwiːl/ Vorderreifen, Vorderrad 3/15
fruit /fruːt/ Frucht; Obst I
frustrated /frʌˈstreɪtɪd/ frustriert; enttäuscht 4/9
frustrating /ˈfrʌˌstreɪtɪŋ/ frustrierend 2/M7
fry /fraɪ/ frittieren, braten 1/P12
full /fʊl/ voll II
fun *(no pl)* /fʌn/ Spaß I
fun /fʌn/ lustig, witzig, spaßig I
be (great) fun /biː (ˌgreɪt) ˈfʌn/ (viel) Spaß machen 3/4
make fun of sb /meɪk ˈfʌn‿əv ˌsʌmbədi/ sich über jdn lustig machen I
funny /ˈfʌni/ lustig, witzig, komisch I
fur /fɜː/ Fell; Pelz II
further /ˈfɜːðə/ zusätzlich, noch mehr, weiter 3/15
future /ˈfjuːtʃə/ Zukunft II

G

Gaelic /ˈgeɪlɪk/ Gälisch 2/CC
Gaelic /ˈgeɪlɪk/ gälisch 2/CC
gallery walk /ˈgæləri wɔːk/ Galerierundgang 6/14
game /geɪm/ Spiel I
garden /ˈgɑːdn/ Garten I
gardener /ˈgɑːdnə/ Gärtner/in II

garlic *(no pl)* /ˈɡɑːlɪk/ Knoblauch 1/2
gave /ɡeɪv/ *Vergangenheitsform von „give"*
geography /dʒiːˈɒɡrəfi/ Erdkunde, Geografie I
German /ˈdʒɜːmən/ Deutsch I
German /ˈdʒɜːmən/ deutsch I
in German /ɪn ˈdʒɜːmən/ auf Deutsch I
Germany /ˈdʒɜːməni/ Deutschland I
get *(irr)* /ɡet/ erhalten, bekommen I; holen I; werden II
get *(irr)* /ɡet/ steigen II
get *(irr)* /ɡet/ verstehen 1/CC; (an)kommen 3/10
get dressed /ɡet‿ˈdrest/ sich anziehen 5/5
get married /ɡet ˈmærid/ heiraten II
get off the ground /ˌɡet‿ˌɒf ðə ˈɡraʊnd/ abheben; verwirklicht werden 5/M6
get over sth/sb /ɡet‿ˈəʊvə ˌsʌmθɪŋ/ˌsʌmbədi/ hinwegkommen über etw/jdn 4/7
get up /ɡet‿ˈʌp/ aufstehen I
get well /ɡet ˈwel/ gesund werden II
get well card /ɡet ˈwel kɑːd/ Genesungskarte II
Get well soon. /ɡet wel ˈsuːn/ Gute Besserung! II
ghost /ɡəʊst/ Geist, Gespenst II
giant /ˈdʒaɪənt/ Riese 6/13
girl /ɡɜːl/ Mädchen I
girlfriend /ˈɡɜːlˌfrend/ (feste) Freundin 4/M9
give *(irr)* /ɡɪv/ geben I
give a talk /ˌɡɪv‿ə ˈtɔːk/ einen Vortrag halten 4/M2
give directions /ˌɡɪv dɪˈrekʃnz/ den Weg beschreiben 6/M7
give in /ˌɡɪv‿ˈɪn/ nachgeben 2/7
give reasons /ɡɪv ˈriːznz/ begründen, Gründe angeben 5/14
give up /ˌɡɪv‿ˈʌp/ aufgeben 2/7
glad /ɡlæd/ glücklich, froh I
glass /ɡlɑːs/ Glas II
glasses *(only pl!)* /ˈɡlɑːsɪz/ Brille I
glimpse /ɡlɪmps/ (kurzer) (Ein)blick 5/8
glove /ɡlʌv/ Handschuh I
go *(irr)* /ɡəʊ/ gehen I; fahren II
go crazy *(informal)* /ɡəʊ ˈkreɪzi/ durchdrehen, ausflippen I
go for a walk /ˌɡəʊ fər‿ə ˈwɔːk/ spazieren gehen I
go out /ɡəʊ‿ˈaʊt/ (hinaus) gehen; ausgehen 5/6
go shopping /ɡəʊ ˈʃɒpɪŋ/ einkaufen gehen I
go wild *(informal)* /ɡəʊ ˈwaɪld/ außer sich geraten, aus dem Häuschen geraten 2/8
go with /ˈɡəʊ wɪð/ gehören zu, passen zu 1/14
goal /ɡəʊl/ Tor 2/8
score a goal /skɔːr‿ə ˈɡəʊl/ ein Tor schießen 2/8
goalkeeper /ˈɡəʊlˌkiːpə/ Tormann/Torfrau 2/6
goat /ɡəʊt/ Ziege I
god /ɡɒd/ Gott II
going to /ˈɡəʊɪŋ tə/ werden II
goldfish *(pl -)* /ˈɡəʊldˌfɪʃ/ Goldfisch I
gone /ɡɒn/ *siehe „go"*
good /ɡʊd/ gut I
be good at sth /bi ˈɡʊd‿æt ˌsʌmθɪŋ/ gut in etw sein; etw gut können I
Good luck! /ɡʊd ˈlʌk/ Viel Glück! 6/11
good-looking /ˌɡʊdˈlʊkɪŋ/ gut aussehend I
got /ɡɒt/ *Vergangenheitsform von „get"*
grammar /ˈɡræmə/ Grammatik 2/P6
grandfather /ˈɡrænˌfɑːðə/ Großvater I
grandma *(informal)* /ˈɡrænˌmɑː/ Oma, Omi I
grandmother /ˈɡrænˌmʌðə/ Großmutter I
grandparents *(only pl)* /ˈɡrænˌpeərənts/ Großeltern I
grass *(no pl)* /ɡrɑːs/ Gras; Wiese, Rasen II
great /ɡreɪt/ groß, riesig; großartig, wunderbar I
Great Britain /ˌɡreɪt ˈbrɪtn/ Großbritannien II
Greece /ɡriːs/ Griechenland I
Greek /ɡriːk/ griechisch 1/7
green /ɡriːn/ grün I
grey /ɡreɪ/ grau I
grid /ɡrɪd/ Gitter; Tabelle 1/5
mixed grill /mɪkst ˈɡrɪl/ Grillteller, Grillplatte 1/4
get off the ground /ˌɡet‿ˌɒf ðə ˈɡraʊnd/ abheben; verwirklicht werden 5/M6
ground floor /ˌɡraʊnd ˈflɔː/ Erdgeschoss, Parterre 5/8
group /ɡruːp/ Gruppe I
group of three /ɡruːp‿əv ˈθriː/ Dreiergruppe 1/3
grow *(irr)* /ɡrəʊ/ wachsen; werden 5/CC
grow up /ɡrəʊ‿ˈʌp/ erwachsen werden II
guard /ɡɑːd/ bewachen 2/P6
guardian /ˈɡɑːdiən/ Erziehungsberechtigte/r 6/5
guess /ɡes/ Vermutung 2/1
guess /ɡes/ (er)raten; vermuten, schätzen II
have a guess /ˌhæv‿ə ˈɡes/ raten, schätzen; vermuten 2/11
guest /ɡest/ Gast 1/6
guinea pig /ˈɡɪni ˌpɪɡ/ Meerschweinchen I
guitar /ɡɪˈtɑː/ Gitarre I
guys *(only pl)* *(informal)* /ɡaɪz/ Leute 3/M5
gym (= gymnasium) /dʒɪm, dʒɪmˈneɪziəm/ Turnhalle II
gypsy /ˈdʒɪpsi/ Zigeuner/in 3/P3

H

eating habits *(only pl)* / ˌiːtɪŋ ˈhæbɪts / Essgewohnheiten 1/14
had / hæd / *Vergangenheitsform von „have"*
hair *(no pl)* / heə / Haar(e) I
hairdresser / ˈheəˌdresə / Friseur/in II
half *(pl* **halves***)* / hɑːf, hɑːvz / Hälfte 2/8
half / hɑːf / halb 4/M3
half past (eight) / ˈhɑːf ˌpɑːst / halb (neun) I
half time / ˌhɑːf ˈtaɪm / Halbzeit 2/8
hall / hɔːl / Flur 5/5
hall / hɔːl / Halle; Saal II
ham *(no pl)* / hæm / Schinken 1/2
Hands up! / ˌhændz‿ˈʌp / Hände hoch!; Meldet euch! 1/9
hang *(irr)* / hæŋ / (auf)hängen I
happen / ˈhæpən / geschehen, passieren I
happy / ˈhæpi / glücklich; zufrieden; fröhlich II
Happy birthday! / ˌhæpi ˈbɜːθdeɪ / Alles Gute zum Geburtstag! I
hard / hɑːd / hart; schwer II
try hard to do sth / ˌtraɪ ˈhɑːd‿tə duː sʌmθɪŋ / sich sehr bemühen, etw zu tun II
hard-working / ˌhɑːdˈwɜːkɪŋ / fleißig II
hat / hæt / Hut; Mütze I
hate / heɪt / hassen, nicht ausstehen können I
have *(irr)* / hæv / haben; essen I
have a guess / ˌhəv‿ə ˈges / raten, schätzen; vermuten 2/11
have got / hæv ˈgɒt / haben I
have to / ˈhæv tə / müssen I
he / hi / er I
head / hed / Kopf I
headache / ˈhedeɪk / Kopfschmerzen, Kopfweh 2/P8
headdress / ˈhedˌdres / Kopfschmuck 3/12
heading / ˈhedɪŋ / Überschrift, Titel 4/7
headphones *(only pl)* / ˈhedˌfəʊnz / Kopfhörer 5/CC
headteacher / ˌhedˈtiːtʃə / Schulleiter/in, Rektor/in II
health *(no pl)* / helθ / Gesundheit 1/10
healthy / ˈhelθi / gesund II
hear *(irr)* / hɪə / hören I
heard / hɜːd / *Vergangenheitsform von „hear"*
heart / hɑːt / Herz 4/5
by heart / baɪ ˈhɑːt / auswendig 1/P9
heat *(no pl)* / hiːt / Wärme; Hitze 1/CC
heat / hiːt / erhitzen 1/12
heavy / ˈhevi / schwer 6/13
hedge / hedʒ / Hecke 6/14
like hell / laɪk ˈhel / wie verrückt, höllisch 2/M7
hello / həˈləʊ / hallo I
helmet / ˈhelmɪt / Helm 2/3
help / help / Hilfe I
help / help / helfen I
help out / ˌhelp‿ˈaʊt / (aus)helfen, unterstützen 1/P7
helpful / ˈhelpfl / hilfsbereit; hilfreich, nützlich 4/8
helpless / ˈhelpləs / hilflos 4/1
her / hɜː / sie; ihr(e, n) I
here / hɪə / hier(her) I
Here you are. / ˌhɪə ju‿ˈɑː / Hier, bitte!, Bitte schön! I
hero *(pl* **-es***)* / ˈhɪərəʊ, ˈhɪərəʊz / Held/in II
herself / həˈself / sich (selbst); selbst 5/P13
hi / haɪ / hallo, hi I
hide *(irr)* / haɪd / (sich) verstecken II
hieroglyphics *(only pl)* / ˌhaɪərəˈglɪfɪks / Hieroglyphen 5/M1
high / haɪ / hoch II
give sb a high five / gɪv ˌsʌmbədi ə ˌhaɪ ˈfaɪv / jdn abklatschen 3/3
high heels *(only pl)* / haɪ ˈhiːlz / hochhackige Schuhe, High Heels 3/M6
highlight / ˈhaɪˌlaɪt / Höhepunkt, Highlight II
hiking *(no pl)* / ˈhaɪkɪŋ / Wandern II
hill / hɪl / Hügel II
him / hɪm / ihm, ihn I
hippo (= hippopotamus) / ˈhɪpəʊ, ˌhɪpəˈpɒtəməs / Nilpferd II
his / hɪz / sein(e, r) I
history / ˈhɪstri / Geschichte I
hit *(irr)* / hɪt / schlagen; treffen; stoßen (gegen) 4/1
hold *(irr)* / həʊld / halten 1/14
hole / həʊl / Loch II
holiday / ˈhɒlɪdeɪ / Urlaub, Ferien I
go on holiday / ˌgəʊ‿ɒn ˈhɒlɪdeɪ / Urlaub machen, in den Urlaub fahren II
home / həʊm / Zuhause, Heim 4/I
home / həʊm / zu Hause; nach Hause II
at home / ət ˈhəʊm / zu Hause I
Home, sweet home! / həʊm swiːt ˈhəʊm / Trautes Heim, Glück allein! 4/1
home town / ˌhəʊm ˈtaʊn / Heimatort II
feel homesick / fiːl ˈhəʊmsɪk / Heimweh haben 4/1
homework *(no pl)* / ˈhəʊmˌwɜːk / Hausaufgaben I
honest / ˈɒnɪst / ehrlich II
honey *(no pl)* / ˈhʌni / Honig I
hoover / ˈhuːvə / staubsaugen I
hope / həʊp / hoffen I
horoscope / ˈhɒrəˌskəʊp / Horoskop II
horrible / ˈhɒrəbl / schrecklich 4/7
horse / hɔːs / Pferd I
hospital / ˈhɒspɪtl / Krankenhaus 4/9

hot /hɒt/ heiß I; scharf 1/3
hot-air balloon /ˌhɒt ˈeə bəˌluːn/ Heißluftballon 5/M6
hour /ˈaʊə/ Stunde I
house /haʊs/ Haus I
housework *(no pl)* /ˈhaʊsˌwɜːk/ Hausarbeit 4/9
how /haʊ/ wie I
How are you? /haʊ‿ˈɑː juː/ Wie geht es dir/Ihnen/euch? I
How much is/are ... ? /ˌhaʊ ˈmʌtʃ‿ɪz/ɑː/ Was kostet/kosten ... ? I
How old are you? /haʊ‿ˈəʊld‿ə jʊ/ Wie alt bist du/seid ihr? I
how to /haʊ tə/ wie man 1/1
hug /hʌɡ/ Umarmung 3/12
huge /hjuːdʒ/ riesig, riesengroß II
huh /hʌ/ häh? 2/12
hungry /ˈhʌŋɡri/ hungrig I
hunter /ˈhʌntə/ Jäger/in I
hurry /ˈhʌri/ sich beeilen 6/7
hurry up /ˌhʌri‿ˈʌp/ sich beeilen I
hurt *(irr)* /hɜːt/ wehtun, schmerzen 2/11
hurt sb /ˈhɜːt ˌsʌmbədi/ jdn verletzen, jdm wehtun I
hurt /hɜːt/ verletzt, verwundet 4/11
hurt /hɜːt/ *Vergangenheitsform von „hurt"*
husband /ˈhʌzbənd/ Ehemann I
hyena /haɪˈiːnə/ Hyäne 3/8

I

I /aɪ/ ich I
I see. /aɪ siː/ Aha!, Ich verstehe. 2/12
I'm fine. /aɪm ˈfaɪn/ Es geht mir gut. II
ice cream /ˈaɪs ˌkriːm/ Eiskrem I
ice hockey /ˈaɪs ˌhɒki/ Eishockey 2/3
ice skate /ˈaɪsskeɪt/ Schlittschuh 4/M3
ICT (= information and communication technology) /ˌaɪ siː ˈtiː, ˌɪnfəˌmeɪʃn‿ən kəˌmjuːnɪˌkeɪʃn tekˈnɒlədʒi/ Informatik I
idea /aɪˈdɪə/ Idee I
if /ɪf/ wenn, falls 4/9
if /ɪf/ ob 3/M5
what if /wɒt‿ɪf/ was ist/wäre, wenn 4/M10
ignore /ɪɡˈnɔː/ ignorieren 4/8
ill /ɪl/ krank I
imagination /ɪˌmædʒɪˈneɪʃn/ Fantasie, Vorstellungskraft; Einbildung 5/P10
imagine /ɪˈmædʒɪn/ sich vorstellen 2/14
immediately /ɪˈmiːdiətli/ sofort 6/P6
important /ɪmˈpɔːtnt/ wichtig I
impossible /ɪmˈpɒsəbl/ unmöglich 6/M2
in /ɪn/ in I
in a minute /ˌɪn‿ə ˈmɪnɪt/ gleich, sofort I
in front of /ɪn ˈfrʌnt‿əv/ vor I
in the end /ˌɪn ðiˈend/ letzten Endes; schließlich 3/6
incident /ˈɪnsɪdnt/ Vorfall 3/M8
incredible /ɪnˈkredəbl/ unglaublich II
India /ˈɪndiə/ Indien II
Indian /ˈɪndiən/ indisch; indianisch II
information *(no pl)* /ˌɪnfəˈmeɪʃn/ Information I
information desk /ˌɪnfəˈmeɪʃn desk/ Information(stheke) 5/8
information point /ˌɪnfəˈmeɪʃn pɔɪnt/ Informationsstelle 6/6
ingredient /ɪnˈɡriːdiənt/ Zutat 1/CC
injured /ˈɪndʒəd/ verletzt 2/8
injury /ˈɪndʒəri/ Verletzung 2/M7
insect /ˈɪnsekt/ Insekt II
insert /ɪnˈsɜːt/ einwerfen, (hinein)stecken 6/P6
inside /ɪnˈsaɪd/ drinnen; innen 1/3
instead (of) /ɪnˈsted (‿əv)/ stattdessen; (an)statt II
instruction /ɪnˈstrʌkʃn/ Anweisung, Anleitung 5/13
instructor /ɪnˈstrʌktə/ Betreuer/in 6/5
interested (in sth) /ˈɪntrəstɪd/ interessiert (an etw) II
interesting /ˈɪntrəstɪŋ/ interessant I
interview /ˈɪntəˌvjuː/ Interview; Befragung 3/16
interview /ˈɪntəˌvjuː/ befragen 3/10; interviewen 1/11
into /ˈɪntʊ/ in 1/12
invent /ɪnˈvent/ erfinden 5/11
invention /ɪnˈvenʃn/ Erfindung 5/10
inventor /ɪnˈventə/ Erfinder/in 5/11
invitation /ˌɪnvɪˈteɪʃn/ Einladung I
invite /ɪnˈvaɪt/ einladen I
Ireland /ˈaɪələnd/ Irland II
Irish /ˈaɪrɪʃ/ Irisch II
Irish /ˈaɪrɪʃ/ irisch II
the Irish Sea /ði‿ˌaɪrɪʃ ˈsiː/ die Irische See 6/13
iron /ˈaɪən/ bügeln I
island /ˈaɪlənd/ Insel 4/1
it /ɪt/ es I
(it's) your turn /ˈjɔː ˌtɜːn/ du bist dran I
Italian /ɪˈtæliən/ Italienisch II
Italian /ɪˈtæliən/ italienisch II
Italy /ˈɪtəli/ Italien II
item /ˈaɪtəm/ Artikel, Ding 1/10
its /ɪts/ sein(e), ihr(e) II

J

jacket /ˈdʒækɪt/ Jacke I
jam /dʒæm/ Marmelade I
Jamaican /dʒəˈmeɪkən/ jamaikanisch 3/CC
January /ˈdʒænjuəri/ Januar I
jealous /ˈdʒeləs/ eifersüchtig 3/8

jewellery *(no pl)* /ˈdʒuːəlri/ Schmuck 3/P13
join /dʒɔɪn/ mitmachen bei; beitreten I
joke /dʒəʊk/ Witz 4/CC
journey /ˈdʒɜːni/ Reise; Fahrt 6/P6
juggler /ˈdʒʌɡlə/ Jongleur/in II
juice /dʒuːs/ Saft I
July /dʒʊˈlaɪ/ Juli I
jump /dʒʌmp/ springen I
June /dʒuːn/ Juni I
jungle /ˈdʒʌŋɡl/ Dschungel, Urwald II
just /dʒʌst/ gleich; einfach II; nur 2/1
just /dʒʌst/ gerade 2/M7
just a minute /ˌdʒʌst‿ə ˈmɪnɪt/ einen Moment/Augenblick bitte 6/11

K

kangaroo /ˌkæŋɡəˈruː/ Känguru I
kayaking /ˈkaɪækɪŋ/ Kajakfahren, Kajaken 6/14
keep *(irr)* /kiːp/ (be)halten; aufbewahren I
keep doing sth /kiːp ˈduːɪŋ sʌmθɪŋ/ etw weiter tun 2/8
keep fit /ˌkiːp ˈfɪt/ sich fit halten 2/9
keep up sth /ˌkiːp‿ˈʌp ˌsʌmθɪŋ/ etw fortführen, etw weiterhin tun 2/1
keeper /ˈkiːpə/ Tierpfleger/in II
kept /kept/ *Vergangenheitsform von „keep"*
kettle /ketl/ Wasserkocher 5/12
key /kiː/ Schlüssel I
key /kiː/ Legende 5/8
keyword /ˈkiːˌwɜːd/ Schlüsselwort 5/M1
kick /kɪk/ treten, schießen, kicken 4/11
kickboxing /ˈkɪkˌbɒksɪŋ/ Kickboxen 2/CC
kill /kɪl/ töten 3/8
kilometre /ˈkɪləˌmiːtə/ Kilometer 2/M1
kind /kaɪnd/ Art, Sorte II
king /kɪŋ/ König II
kiss /kɪs/ Kuss II
kiss /kɪs/ küssen II
kitchen /ˈkɪtʃən/ Küche I
knee /niː/ Knie II
knew /njuː/ *Vergangenheitsform von „know"*
knife *(pl* **knives***)* /naɪf, naɪvz/ Messer I
knock sb /ˈnɒk ˌsʌmbədi/ jdn stoßen 3/15
knock down sb/sth /nɒk ˈdaʊn ˌsʌmbədi/ˌsʌmθɪŋ/ jdn/etw umstoßen 2/8
know *(irr)* /nəʊ/ wissen; kennen I
kph /ˌkeɪ pi‿ˈeɪtʃ/ km/h 5/M6

L

label /ˈleɪbl/ beschriften 1/15
lady /ˈleɪdi/ Frau; Dame II
lake /leɪk/ See II
lamb /læm/ Lamm I
lamp /læmp/ Lampe I
land /lænd/ (Fest)land 5/M6
land /lænd/ landen 6/11
language /ˈlæŋɡwɪdʒ/ Sprache II
large /lɑːdʒ/ groß I
last /lɑːst/ letzte(r, s) I
last /lɑːst/ (an)dauern 3/11
at last /ət ˈlɑːst/ endlich, schließlich 6/11
late /leɪt/ (zu) spät I
be late /biː ˈleɪt/ (zu) spät kommen, sich verspäten I
later /ˈleɪtə/ später II
laugh /lɑːf/ lachen I
laugh at sb /ˈlɑːf‿ət ˌsʌmbədi/ jdn auslachen 6/13
laughter *(no pl)* /ˈlɑːftə/ Lachen, Gelächter 6/1
launchpad /ˈlɔːntʃpæd/ Startrampe, Abschussrampe 5/8
lawn /lɔːn/ Rasen 3/M2
lead *(irr)* /liːd/ (an)führen, leiten 2/P3
leaf *(pl* **leaves***)* /liːf, liːvz/ Blatt II
leaflet /ˈliːflət/ Prospekt, Broschüre 2/M1
learn *(irr)* /lɜːn/ lernen I
at least /ət ˈliːst/ mindestens, wenigstens 2/M7
leave *(irr)* /liːv/ verlassen II; lassen 4/7; abfahren 6/6
leave sb alone /ˌliːv ˌsʌmbədi‿əˈləʊn/ jdn in Ruhe lassen 4/M9
leave sb out /ˌliːv ˌsʌmbədi‿ˈaʊt/ jdn ausschließen 4/11
leek /liːk/ Lauch 1/12
left /left/ (nach) links II; übrig 2/8
on the/your left /ˌɒn ðə/jɔː ˈleft/ links, auf der linken Seite II
left /left/ *Vergangenheitsform von „leave"*
leg /leg/ Bein I
legend /ˈledʒ(ə)nd/ Sage, Legende 6/13
lemon /ˈlemən/ Zitrone 1/CC
lemon curd *(no pl)* /ˌlemən ˈkɜːd/ *Creme aus Eiern, Zucker und Zitronensaft* 1/CC
lemon meringue pie /ˌlemən məˌræŋ ˈpaɪ/ *Zitronen-Baiser-Torte* 1/CC
lemonade /ˌleməˈneɪd/ Limonade I
lentil /ˈlentɪl/ Linse 1/M1
less /les/ weniger 4/10
lesson /ˈlesn/ Stunde I
let *(irr)* /let/ lassen II
let's (= let us) /lets, ˈlet‿əs/ lass(t) uns I
Let's go! /lets ˈɡəʊ/ Los!, Auf geht's! II
letter /ˈletə/ Brief; Buchstabe 4/7
lettuce /ˈletɪs/ Blattsalat; Kopfsalat 1/2

library /ˈlaɪbrəri/ Bibliothek, Bücherei I
lie *(irr)* /laɪ/ liegen 6/13
life *(pl **lives**)* /laɪf, laɪvz/ Leben II
life-sized /ˈlaɪfsaɪzd/ in Lebensgröße, lebensgroß 6/P13
lift /lɪft/ Aufzug, Lift 5/8
light /laɪt/ Licht I
light /laɪt/ erhellen, erleuchten 5/11
light /laɪt/ leicht 2/M7
light bulb /ˈlaɪt ˌbʌlb/ Glühbirne 5/10
like /laɪk/ mögen I
like /laɪk/ wie II
like hell /laɪk ˈhel/ wie verrückt, höllisch 2/M7
like this /laɪk ˈðɪs/ so 1/5
What's … like? /wɒts ˈlaɪk/ Wie ist … ? II
limited /ˈlɪmɪtɪd/ begrenzt, eingeschränkt 5/M4
line /laɪn/ Linie 5/13
centre line /ˌsentə ˈlaɪn/ Mittellinie 5/13
linking word /ˈlɪŋkɪŋ wɜːd/ Bindewort 2/M4
lion /ˈlaɪən/ Löwe I
list /lɪst/ Liste I
listen (to) /ˈlɪsn/ (zu)hören I
litre /ˈliːtə/ Liter 3/CC
little /ˈlɪtl/ klein I
little /ˈlɪtl/ wenig 5/M4
a little /ə ˈlɪtl/ ein bisschen II
live /lɪv/ leben, wohnen I
living room /ˈlɪvɪŋ ˌruːm/ Wohnzimmer I
local /ˈləʊkl/ örtlich 2/M7
location /ləʊˈkeɪʃn/ Lage; (Stand)ort 4/P6
loch /lɒk/ See 6/13
lock /lɒk/ (ein)schließen 4/11
locker /ˈlɒkə/ Schließfach, Spind 5/M4
logo /ˈləʊgəʊ/ Abzeichen, Logo II

LOL (= Laugh(ing) out loud) /ˌel‿əʊ‿ˈel/ *Abkürzung für:* laut lachen(d) 5/3
the London Eye /ðə ˌlʌndən‿ˈaɪ/ *Riesenrad in London* 5/P12
lonely /ˈləʊnli/ einsam II
long /lɒŋ/ lang I
it's been much too long /ɪts biːn ˌmʌtʃ tuː ˈlɒŋ/ es ist viel zu lange her 6/11
long-sleeved /ˌlɒŋˌsliːvd/ langärm(e)lig 6/P13
look /lʊk/ sehen, schauen I; aussehen II
have a look (at sth) /hæv‿ə ˈlʊk/ (sich) (etw) (an)schauen 1/3
look after /ˌlʊk‿ˈɑːftə/ sich kümmern um I
look at /ˈlʊk‿ət/ betrachten, sehen, anschauen I
look for /ˈlʊk fɔː/ suchen (nach) I
look forward to sth /ˌlʊk ˈfɔːwəd‿tə ˌsʌmθɪŋ/ sich auf etw freuen I
look up /lʊk‿ˈʌp/ nachschlagen 3/9
look up to /lʊk‿ˈʌp tə/ aufblicken zu 3/8
lose *(irr)* /luːz/ verlieren II
lose consciousness /luːz ˈkɒnʃəsnəs/ bewusstlos werden, das Bewusstsein verlieren 4/M3
lost /lɒst/ verloren 4/11
lost /lɒst/ *Vergangenheitsform von „lose"*
a lot (of) /ə ˈlɒt/ sehr; viel(e) I
lots (= a lot) *(informal)* /lɒts/ viel, jede Menge 3/13
lots of /ˈlɒts‿əv/ viel, jede Menge I
loud /laʊd/ laut II
love /lʌv/ Liebe; herzliche Grüße, alles Liebe II
love /lʌv/ lieben; sehr gern mögen I

sb would love (to) /ˌsʌmbədi wʊd ˈlʌv/ jmd möchte sehr gern 3/4
be in love (with) /bi ɪn lʌv/ verliebt sein (in) 4/7
lovely /ˈlʌvli/ schön, hübsch I
low /ləʊ/ niedrig 1/12
luck *(no pl)* /lʌk/ Glück 2/M7
Good luck! /gʊd ˈlʌk/ Viel Glück! 6/11
lucky /ˈlʌki/ glücklich, glücksbringend, Glücks- II
be lucky /biː ˈlʌki/ Glück haben I
lunch /lʌntʃ/ Mittagessen I
lunchtime /ˈlʌntʃˌtaɪm/ Mittagszeit; Mittagspause II
luxury /ˈlʌkʃəri/ Luxus 1/CC
lyrics *(only pl)* /ˈlɪrɪks/ (Lied)text 4/11

M

macaroni *(no pl)* /ˌmækəˈrəʊni/ Makkaroni 1/12
machine /məˈʃiːn/ Maschine I
made /meɪd/ *Vergangenheitsform von „make"*
magazine /ˌmægəˈziːn/ Zeitschrift, Magazin I
magic *(no pl)* /ˈmædʒɪk/ Magie, Zauber 6/13
magical /ˈmædʒɪkl/ magisch 3/M4
magician /məˈdʒɪʃn/ Zauberer/ Zauberin 6/13
main /meɪn/ Haupt- 3/11
main course /ˌmeɪn ˈkɔːs/ Hauptgericht, Hauptgang 1/2
main dish /meɪn ˈdɪʃ/ Hauptgericht 1/4
major /ˈmeɪdʒə/ bedeutend, wichtig 2/M3
make *(irr)* /meɪk/ machen I
make fun of sb /meɪk ˈfʌn‿əv ˌsʌmbədi/ sich über jdn lustig machen I
make money /meɪk ˈmʌni/ Geld verdienen II

make notes /meɪk ˈnəʊts/ (sich) Notizen machen 1/2
make sb believe sth /meɪk ˌsʌmbədi bɪˈliːv ˌsʌmθɪŋ/ jdn etw glauben machen, jdm etw weismachen 3/8
make sure /ˌmeɪk ˈʃɔː/ sich versichern, darauf achten 2/P3
make up sth /ˌmeɪk‿ˈʌp ˌsʌmθɪŋ/ (sich) etw ausdenken, etw erfinden 1/6
put on make-up /pʊt‿ˌɒn ˈmeɪkˌʌp/ sich schminken II
male /meɪl/ männlich 6/5
stick man /ˈstɪk ˌmæn/ Strichmännchen 2/16
man *(pl* **men***)* /mæn, men/ Mann I
manage /ˈmænɪdʒ/ es schaffen 3/15
many /ˈmeni/ viele I
map /mæp/ (Land)karte I
March /mɑːtʃ/ März I
marine engineering *(no pl)* /məˌriːn‿ˌendʒɪˈnɪərɪŋ/ Schiffsmaschinenbau 5/8
mark /mɑːk/ (Schul)note II
mark /mɑːk/ Markierung 5/13
mark /mɑːk/ markieren, kennzeichnen 5/P10
market /ˈmɑːkɪt/ Markt I
get married /get ˈmærid/ heiraten II
marry /ˈmæri/ heiraten II
masala /məˈsɑːlə/ *würzige indische Soße* 1/M1
mass /mæs/ Masse 2/M1
match /mætʃ/ Spiel I; Streichholz, Zündholz 4/3
match /mætʃ/ passen (zu) 3/10
match (with) /mætʃ/ zuordnen 1/14
mathematics *(only pl)* /ˌmæθəˈmætɪks/ Mathematik 5/8
maths /mæθs/ Mathe I
matter /ˈmætə/ Angelegenheit, Sache 5/8
What's the matter? /ˌwɒts ðə ˈmætə/ Was ist (denn) los? II
May /meɪ/ Mai I
may *(irr)* /meɪ/ können; dürfen II
may not /meɪ ˈnɒt/ nicht dürfen II
maybe /ˈmeɪbi/ vielleicht, möglicherweise I
maze /meɪz/ Labyrinth, Irrgarten 6/14
me /miː/ mir, mich I
Me too. /mi ˈtuː/ Ich auch. 4/12
meal /miːl/ Mahlzeit, Essen II
mean *(irr)* /miːn/ bedeuten; meinen 1/8
mean /miːn/ gemein, fies II
meaning /ˈmiːnɪŋ/ Bedeutung 1/M3
measure /ˈmeʒə/ messen 5/8
meat *(no pl)* /miːt/ Fleisch I
medal /ˈmedl/ Medaille II
medical /ˈmedɪkl/ medizinisch, ärztlich 5/8
medicine *(no pl)* /ˈmedsn/ Medizin, Medikament(e) 2/14
meet *(irr)* /miːt/ (sich) treffen; kennenlernen I
Nice to meet you. /ˌnaɪs tə ˈmiːt jə/ Es freut mich, Sie/dich kennenzulernen. I
melody /ˈmelədi/ Melodie 4/11
melon /ˈmelən/ Melone 1/2
member /ˈmembə/ Mitglied I
mention /ˈmenʃn/ erwähnen 1/M1
menu /ˈmenjuː/ Speisekarte 1/2
message /ˈmesɪdʒ/ Nachricht II
message in a bottle /ˌmesɪdʒ‿ɪn‿ə ˈbɒtl/ Flaschenpost 4/6
met /met/ *Vergangenheitsform von „meet"*
metal /ˈmetl/ Metall 5/M6
metre /ˈmiːtə/ Meter II
microwave /ˈmaɪkrəˌweɪv/ Mikrowelle(nherd) 5/10
middle /ˈmɪdl/ Mitte 1/12
in the middle /ˌɪn ðə ˈmɪdl/ in der Mitte; mitten in/auf II
mild /maɪld/ sanft; mild 1/M1
mile /maɪl/ Meile 2/M1
milk *(no pl)* /mɪlk/ Milch I
milkshake /ˈmɪlkˌʃeɪk/ Milchshake II
mill around /mɪl‿əˈraʊnd/ umherlaufen 4/14
millionaire /ˌmɪljəˈneə/ Millionär/in 1/CC
miniskirt /ˈmɪniˌskɜːt/ Minirock II
mint *(no pl)* /mɪnt/ Minze 1/2
minute /ˈmɪnɪt/ Minute I
in a minute /ˌɪn‿ə ˈmɪnɪt/ gleich, sofort I
just a minute /ˌdʒʌst‿ə ˈmɪnɪt/ einen Moment/Augenblick bitte 6/11
mirror /ˈmɪrə/ Spiegel 5/M1
miss /mɪs/ verpassen I; vermissen
missing /ˈmɪsɪŋ/ fehlend 1/P2
mission /ˈmɪʃn/ Auftrag, Mission 6/M2
mistake /mɪˈsteɪk/ Fehler, Irrtum 3/P3
mix /mɪks/ (ver)mischen, anrühren 1/12
mix up /mɪks‿ˈʌp/ verwechseln 6/11
mixed /mɪkst/ gemischt 1/2
mixed grill /mɪkst ˈgrɪl/ Grillteller, Grillplatte 1/4
mixture /ˈmɪkstʃə/ Mischung 1/P12
mobile (= mobile phone) /ˈməʊbaɪl, ˌməʊbaɪl ˈfəʊn/ Mobiltelefon, Handy I
mobile /ˈməʊbaɪl/ mobil 3/11
model /ˈmɒdl/ Modell 6/P13
mom *(AE)* = mum *(BE)* *(informal)* /mɒm/ Mama 6/11
moment /ˈməʊmənt/ Moment, Augenblick II
at the moment /æt ðə ˈməʊmənt/ im Moment II
Monday /ˈmʌndeɪ/ Montag I

money *(no pl)* /ˈmʌni/ Geld I
make money /meɪk ˈmʌni/ Geld verdienen II
raise money /reɪz ˈmʌni/ Geld aufbringen/auftreiben 2/P7
monkey /ˈmʌŋki/ Affe I
month /mʌnθ/ Monat I
monument /ˈmɒnjʊmənt/ Denkmal, Monument 6/13
moon /muːn/ Mond II
moonlight /ˈmuːnˌlaɪt/ Mondlicht II
moor /mʊə/ Heideland, (Hoch)moor 6/13
more /mɔː/ (noch) mehr I
morning /ˈmɔːnɪŋ/ Morgen I
in the morning /ˌɪn ðə ˈmɔːnɪŋ/ morgens, am Morgen, vormittags I
this morning /ðɪs ˈmɔːnɪŋ/ heute Morgen 3/M8
morning break /ˈmɔːnɪŋ ˌbreɪk/ Frühstückspause II
most /məʊst/ die meisten II
most /məʊst/ am meisten 4/M1
most (of) /məʊst/ das meiste (von), ein Großteil 3/4
most of all /ˌməʊst‿əv‿ˈɔːl/ am (aller)meisten 4/M1
mostly /ˈməʊstli/ größtenteils; hauptsächlich; meistens 2/1
mother /ˈmʌðə/ Mutter I
motorbike /ˈməʊtəˌbaɪk/ Motorrad II
mountain /ˈmaʊntɪn/ Berg II
mouse *(pl* **mice***)* /maʊs, maɪs/ Maus I
mouth /maʊθ/ Mund I
move /muːv/ Bewegung; Schritt 6/8
move /muːv/ umziehen II
move /muːv/ sich bewegen II
move /muːv/ bewegen, verschieben 6/13
movie *(AE)* = film *(BE)* /ˈmuːvi/ (Kino-, Spiel)film 6/1
mow *(irr)* /məʊ/ mähen 3/M2
Mr /ˈmɪstə/ Herr *(Anrede)* I
Mrs /ˈmɪsɪz/ Frau *(Anrede)* I
much /mʌtʃ/ viel; sehr I
muesli *(no pl)* /ˈmjuːzli/ Müsli I
multiply by /ˈmʌltɪplaɪ baɪ/ multiplizieren mit; sich vermehren/vervielfachen um 5/CC
mum *(informal)* /mʌm/ Mama, Mutti I
Munich /ˈmjuːnɪk/ München II
muscle /ˈmʌsl/ Muskel 2/M7
mushroom /ˈmʌʃruːm/ Pilz 1/2
music *(no pl)* /ˈmjuːzɪk/ Musik I
musical instrument /ˌmjuːzɪkl‿ˈɪnstrʊmənt/ Musikinstrument 3/P3
must /mʌst/ müssen II
must not /mʌst ˈnɒt/ nicht dürfen II
my /maɪ/ mein(e) I
my name is /maɪ ˈneɪm‿ˌɪz/ ich heiße I
myself /maɪˈself/ mich, mir; selbst 5/F13

N

naaah *(informal)* /nɑː/ ne(e) 6/11
name /neɪm/ Name I
name /neɪm/ *(BE)* nennen 1/M5
my name is /maɪ ˈneɪm‿ˌɪz/ ich heiße I
What's your name? /ˌwɒts jə ˈneɪm/ Wie heißt du?, Wie heißen Sie? I
narrow /ˈnærəʊ/ eng, schmal II
narrow /ˈnærəʊ/ knapp 3/15
the Nationals /ðə ˈnæʃnəlz/ *nationaler Wettkampf* 2/M7
natural /ˈnætʃrəl/ natürlich 6/P13
nature *(no pl)* /ˈneɪtʃə/ Natur II
naughty /ˈnɔːti/ ungezogen, frech II
near /nɪə/ nah(e) I
nearby /ˌnɪəˈbaɪ/ nahe/in der Nähe gelegen, benachbart 6/11
nearly /ˈnɪəli/ fast, beinahe II
need /niːd/ brauchen I
need to /ˈniːd tə/ müssen 2/11
negative /ˈnegətɪv/ negativ 3/M4
neighbour /ˈneɪbə/ Nachbar/in I
never /ˈnevə/ nie(mals) I
new /njuː/ neu I
New Year /ˌnjuː ˈjɪə/ Neujahr II
New Year's Eve /ˌnjuː jɪəz‿ˈiːv/ Silvester II
New Zealand /nju ˈziːlənd/ Neuseeland 2/M3
news *(no pl)* /njuːz/ Neuigkeit; Nachrichten II
newspaper /ˈnjuːzˌpeɪpə/ Zeitung 4/9
next /nekst/ nächste(r, s) I
the next day /ðə ˌnekst ˈdeɪ/ am nächsten Tag 2/M4
next to /ˈnekst‿tə/ neben I
nice /naɪs/ schön, angenehm; nett, freundlich I
Nice to meet you. /ˌnaɪs tə ˈmiːt jə/ Es freut mich, Sie/dich kennenzulernen. I
night /naɪt/ Nacht I
night /naɪt/ Abend 2/M3
at night /æt ˈnaɪt/ nachts II
no /nəʊ/ nein I
no /nəʊ/ kein(e) I
no one /ˈnəʊ wʌn/ keiner, niemand II
nobody else /ˌnəʊˌbɒdi‿ˈels/ niemand anders 5/P12
noise /nɔɪz/ Lärm, Krach; Geräusch II
noisy /ˈnɔɪzi/ laut 1/3
normally /ˈnɔːmli/ normalerweise I
north /nɔːθ/ Norden 6/12; Nord- 3/4
north /nɔːθ/ nördlich 3/4
Northern Ireland /ˌnɔːðn‿ˈaɪələnd/ Nordirland 6/12
nose /nəʊz/ Nase I
not /nɒt/ nicht I
not any /nɒt‿ˈeni/ kein(e) I
not anymore /ˌnɒt eniˈmɔː/ nicht mehr II

not at all /nɒt‿ət‿'ɔ:l/ überhaupt nicht 2/1
not exactly /nɒt‿ɪg'zæktli/ nicht gerade 5/M6
not quite /nɒt 'kwaɪt/ nicht ganz 2/1
not yet /nɒt 'jet/ noch nicht II
note /nəʊt/ Notiz 1/11
make notes /meɪk 'nəʊts/ (sich) Notizen machen 1/2
take notes /teɪk 'nəʊts/ (sich) Notizen machen II
nothing /'nʌθɪŋ/ nichts II
notice /'nəʊtɪs/ bemerken I
noun /naʊn/ Substantiv 4/P2
November /nəʊ'vembə/ November I
now /naʊ/ jetzt I
number /'nʌmbə/ Zahl; Ziffer, Nummer I
nurse /nɜ:s/ (Kranken) schwester, (Kranken)pfleger II

O

(seven) o'clock /ə'klɒk/ (sieben) Uhr I
object /'ɒbdʒekt/ Objekt, Gegenstand, Sache 5/9
ocean /'əʊʃn/ Meer; Ozean 4/M3
October /ɒk'təʊbə/ Oktober I
be the odd one out /bi: ði‿ˌɒd wʌn‿'aʊt/ aus der Reihe fallen, nicht dazugehören 5/P1
of /əv/ von I
of course /əv 'kɔ:s/ natürlich I
off /ɒf/ weg von 1/12
offer /'ɒfə/ Angebot 3/M3
offer /'ɒfə/ (an)bieten II
office /'ɒfɪs/ Büro I
official /ə'fɪʃl/ offiziell 3/11
often /'ɒfn/ oft, häufig I
Oh dear! /əʊ 'dɪə/ Du meine Güte! 2/1
oil /ɔɪl/ Öl 1/12
OK then *(informal)* /ˌəʊ'keɪ ðen/ na gut, also gut 1/3
old /əʊld/ alt I
How old are you? /haʊ‿'əʊld‿ə jʊ/ Wie alt bist du/seid ihr? I
Olympic Games /əˌlɪmpɪk 'geɪmz/ Olympische Spiele II
OMG (= Oh my god) /ˌəʊ‿em 'dʒi:/ *Abkürzung für:* Oh mein Gott! 5/3
on /ɒn/ auf, an; in; am I
on /ɒn/ im I
on one's own /ɒn wʌnz‿'əʊn/ allein(e) 6/11
once /wʌns/ einmal II
one /wʌn/ eins; ein(e) I
one day /'wʌn deɪ/ eines Tages II
onion /'ʌnjən/ Zwiebel 1/2
onion rings /'ʌnjən ˌrɪŋz/ Zwiebelringe 1/2
only /'əʊnli/ nur I
only /'əʊnli/ einzige(r, s) 3/M4
only /'əʊnli/ erst 6/CC
onto /'ɒntə/ auf 1/14
open /'əʊpən/ (sich) öffnen I
open /'əʊpən/ offen, geöffnet I
cut sth open /kʌt ˌsʌmθɪŋ‿'əʊpən/ etw aufschneiden 1/12
Open Day /'əʊpən ˌdeɪ/ Tag der offenen Tür 3/10
opening times *(only pl)* /'əʊpnɪŋ ˌtaɪmz/ Öffnungszeiten 3/10
opinion /ə'pɪnjən/ Meinung, Ansicht II
opposite /'ɒpəzɪt/ gegenüber(liegend) 6/6
opposite /'ɒpəzɪt/ Gegenteil 4/P2
optimistic /ˌɒptɪ'mɪstɪk/ optimistisch, zuversichtlich II
or /ɔ:/ oder I
orange /'ɒrɪndʒ/ Orange, Apfelsine I
orange /'ɒrɪndʒ/ orange(farben) I
order /'ɔ:də/ Ordnung, Reihenfolge 1/12
order /'ɔ:də/ bestellen 1/3
original /ə'rɪdʒnəl/ ursprünglich 1/M1
other /'ʌðər/ andere(r, s) I
ouch /aʊtʃ/ aua, autsch 1/M6
our /aʊə/ unser(e) I
out /aʊt/ draußen 2/14
go out /gəʊ‿'aʊt/ (hinaus) gehen; ausgehen 2/P10
out of /'aʊt‿əv/ (her)aus II
out of place /aʊt‿əv 'pleɪs/ fehl am Platz(e) 4/11
out of work /aʊt‿əv 'wɜ:k/ arbeitslos 4/9
outside /ˌaʊt'saɪd/ im Freien, draußen I
outside /ˌaʊt'saɪd/ nach draußen, raus II
over /'əʊvə/ über I; vorbei 4/7
over /'əʊvə/ hinüber, herüber 3/12
over here /ˌəʊvə 'hɪə/ hier drüben 3/M5
over there /ˌəʊvə 'ðeə/ dort (drüben) I
overcome *(irr)* /ˌəʊvə'kʌm/ überwinden, bewältigen 4/M3
overweight /ˌəʊvə'weɪt/ übergewichtig 1/12
ow /aʊ/ au 1/M6
own /əʊn/ eigene(r, s) II
on one's own /ɒn wʌnz‿'əʊn/ allein(e) 6/11

P

p (= penny, pence) /pi:, 'penni, pens/ Penny, Centstück II
the Pacific (Ocean) /ðə pəˌsɪfɪk(‿'əʊʃn)/ der Pazifische Ozean 4/M3
pack /pæk/ packen I
package /'pækɪdʒ/ Paket 4/M3
packed /pækt/ voll 3/M5
packet /'pækɪt/ Packung, Schachtel 4/3
page /peɪdʒ/ Seite 4/7
paid /peɪd/ *Vergangenheitsform von „pay"*
paint /peɪnt/ Farbe 3/CC
paint /peɪnt/ (an)malen II

painting /ˈpeɪntɪŋ/ Bild, Gemälde 3/P3
pair /peə/ Paar 3/6
palace /ˈpæləs/ Palast II
pan /pæn/ Pfanne 1/12
panic /ˈpænɪk/ Panik 3/8
paper *(no pl)* /ˈpeɪpə/ Papier I
piece of paper /ˌpiːs‿əv ˈpeɪpə/ Blatt Papier, Zettel 1/M7
parachute jump /ˈpærəʃuːt dʒʌmp/ Fallschirmsprung 5/M6
parade /pəˈreɪd/ Parade, Umzug 3/11
parade /pəˈreɪd/ einen Umzug machen, durch die Straßen ziehen 3/11
paragraph /ˈpærəˌɡrɑːf/ Absatz, Abschnitt 5/M1
Paralympic /ˌpærəˈlɪmpɪk/ paralympisch 2/M3
The Paralympic World Championships /ðə ˌpærəˌlɪmpɪk ˌwɜːld ˈtʃæmpiənʃɪps/ *Leichtathletik-Weltmeisterschaften der Behinderten* 2/M3
parent /ˈpeərənt/ Elternteil, Erziehungsberechtigte/r 6/5
parents *(only pl)* /ˈpeərənts/ Eltern I
parking /ˈpɑːkɪŋ/ Parken; Parkmöglichkeit, Parkplatz 3/P6
parrot /ˈpærət/ Papagei I
parsley *(no pl)* /ˈpɑːsli/ Petersilie 1/12
part /pɑːt/ Teil 1/P4
take part (in) /ˌteɪk ˈpɑːt/ teilnehmen (an) 6/8
participant /pɑːˈtɪsɪpənt/ Teilnehmer/in 6/5
pass /pɑːs/ Pass; Karte 6/P6
pass /pɑːs/ vorbeikommen; abgeben, abspielen 2/7
pass by /pɑːs baɪ/ vorbeifahren, vorbeigehen 3/M5
past /pɑːst/ vorbei/vorüber an II
pasta *(no pl)* /ˈpæstə/ Nudeln 1/11
patient /ˈpeɪʃnt/ Patient/in 2/14
pattern pod /ˈpætən pɒd/ *Erfahrungsraum zum Begreifen von Formen und Mustern* 5/8
patty /ˈpæti/ Fastetchen 3/CC
paw /pɔː/ Pfote, Tatze II
pay *(irr)* /peɪ/ (be)zahlen I
PE (= physical education) /ˌpiː‿ˈiː, ˌfɪzɪkl‿ˌedjʊˈkeɪʃn/ Sport(unterricht) I
pea /piː/ Erbse 1/10
peanut /ˈpiːnʌt/ Erdnuss 1/9
pedal /ˈpedl/ in die Pedale treten, strampeln 5/M6
pedal power /ˈpedl ˌpaʊə/ Pedalkraft 5/M6
pen /pen/ Stift I
pencil /ˈpensl/ Bleistift I
pencil case /ˈpensl ˌkeɪs/ (Feder)mäppchen I
pencil sharpener /ˈpensl ʃɑːpnə/ (Bleistift)spitzer I
pendulum /ˈpendjʊləm/ Pendel 5/8
penguin /ˈpeŋɡwɪn/ Pinguin I
people *(no pl)* /ˈpiːpl/ Leute, Menschen I
pepper *(no pl)* /ˈpepə/ Pfeffer 1/12
perfect /ˈpɜːfɪkt/ perfekt II
perform /pəˈfɔːm/ vorführen; aufführen 3/M5
performance /pəˈfɔːməns/ Vorführung, Darbietung 3/M4; Aufführung 6/8
perfume /ˈpɜːfjuːm/ Parfüm II
perhaps /pəˈhæps/ vielleicht II
person /ˈpɜːsn/ Person, Mensch II
pet /pet/ Haustier I
pet /pet/ streicheln I
phew /fjuː/ puh 1/M6
phone /fəʊn/ anrufen I
(phone) call /(ˈfəʊn) kɔːl/ (Telefon)anruf II
(tele)phone /fəʊn/ Telefon I
photo /ˈfəʊtəʊ/ Foto I
take photos /ˌteɪk ˈfəʊtəʊz/ Bilder machen, fotografieren II
phrase /freɪz/ Satz; Ausdruck, (Rede)wendung 1/6
phrase book /ˈfreɪz bʊk/ Sprachführer 6/M7
physiotherapist /ˌfɪziəʊˈθerəpɪst/ Physiotherapeut/in, Krankengymnast/in 2/M7
piano /piˈænəʊ/ Klavier II
pick /pɪk/ aussuchen, auswählen 4/P12
pick pockets /pɪk ˈpɒkɪts/ Taschendiebstahl begehen 3/CC
pick up /ˌpɪk‿ˈʌp/ aufheben, aufnehmen 1/14; abholen 6/11
pickpocket /ˈpɪkˌpɒkɪt/ Taschendieb/in 3/12
picnic /ˈpɪknɪk/ Picknick 5/8
picture /ˈpɪktʃə/ Bild, Foto I
pie /paɪ/ Pastete 1/2
piece /piːs/ Stück 1/10
piece of paper /ˌpiːs‿əv ˈpeɪpə/ Blatt Papier, Zettel 1/M7
pier /pɪə/ Pier; Landungsbrücke 6/14
pig /pɪɡ/ Schwein I
pilot /ˈpaɪlət/ Pilot/in II
pink /pɪŋk/ rosa, pink I
pirate /ˈpaɪrət/ Pirat, Seeräuber I
place /pleɪs/ Ort; Platz I
place /pleɪs/ stellen, legen 2/P6
out of place /aʊt‿əv ˈpleɪs/ fehl am Platz(e) 4/11
take place /teɪk ˈpleɪs/ stattfinden 2/M1
placemat /ˈpleɪsˌmæt/ Set, Platzdeckchen 3/M2
plan /plæn/ planen 3/10
plane /pleɪn/ Flugzeug II
plant /plɑːnt/ Pflanze II
plastic /ˈplæstɪk/ Plastik, Kunststoff 4/3
plate /pleɪt/ Teller I
a plateful of /ə ˈpleɪtfʊl‿əv/ ein Teller (voll) 1/CC

platform /ˈplætˌfɔːm/ Plattform; Bahnsteig, Gleis 6/6
play /pleɪ/ Spiel; (Theater)stück I
play /pleɪ/ spielen I
player /ˈpleɪə/ Spieler/in I
playground /ˈpleɪˌgraʊnd/ Spielplatz I
please /pliːz/ bitte I
pm (= post meridiem) /ˌpiːˈem, ˌpəʊst məˈrɪdiəm/ *nachmittags, abends (nur hinter Uhrzeit zwischen 12 Uhr mittags und Mitternacht)* 2/8
pocket /ˈpɒkɪt/ Tasche 3/4
pocket money *(no pl)* /ˈpɒkɪt ˌmʌni/ Taschengeld 3/4
pick pockets /pɪk ˈpɒkɪts/ Taschendiebstahl begehen 3/CC
poem /ˈpəʊɪm/ Gedicht 1/P9
point /pɔɪnt/ Punkt 2/M1
point (to) /pɔɪnt/ deuten/zeigen (auf) 3/M5
Poland /ˈpəʊlənd/ Polen II
police *(no pl)* /pəˈliːs/ Polizei II
police officer /pəˈliːs ˌɒfɪsə/ Polizeibeamter/-beamtin II
polite /pəˈlaɪt/ höflich II
poor /pɔː/ arm I
poor you /pɔː ˈjuː/ du Arme(r) 1/M6
popular /ˈpɒpjʊlə/ beliebt 1/M1
pork *(no pl)* /pɔːk/ Schweinefleisch 1/P9
portfolio /pɔːtˈfəʊliəʊ/ (Akten)mappe 1/7
possible /ˈpɒsəbəl/ möglich 2/M7
post sth /ˈpəʊst ˌsʌmθɪŋ/ etw schicken; etw ins Internet stellen 3/M4
postcard /ˈpəʊstˌkɑːd/ Postkarte II
postcode /ˈpəʊstˌkəʊd/ Postleitzahl 6/5
potato *(pl* **-es***)* /pəˈteɪtəʊ, pəˈteɪtəʊz/ Kartoffel II
pound /paʊnd/ Pfund *(brit. Währung)* II
pour /pɔː/ gießen, schütten 1/12
powder *(no pl)* /ˈpaʊdə/ Pulver 1/12
powerful /ˈpaʊəfl/ mächtig 3/8
powerful /ˈpaʊəfl/ stark, heftig 4/M3
practise /ˈpræktɪs/ üben 2/3
prebooked /ˌpriːˈbʊkt/ im Voraus gebucht 3/P6
prefer /prɪˈfɜː/ vorziehen, bevorzugen, lieber mögen 4/7
pregnant /ˈpregnənt/ schwanger 4/M9
prepare /prɪˈpeə/ (sich) vorbereiten 2/M2
prescription /prɪˈskrɪpʃən/ Rezept, Verschreibung 2/12
present /ˈpreznt/ Geschenk I
present /prɪˈzent/ präsentieren 1/7
presentation /ˌpreznˈteɪʃn/ Präsentation 5/P10
press /pres/ drücken, pressen 2/1
press-up /ˈpres ʌp/ Liegestütz 2/9
pretty /ˈprɪti/ hübsch II
price /praɪs/ Preis I
primary school /ˈpraɪməri ˌskuːl/ Grundschule II
prisoner /ˈprɪznə/ Gefangene/r 4/1
prize /praɪz/ Preis, Gewinn II
probably /ˈprɒbəbli/ wahrscheinlich II
product /ˈprɒdʌkt/ Produkt, Erzeugnis 5/11
programme /ˈprəʊgræm/ Programm; Sendung II
project /ˈprɒdʒekt/ Projekt 3/10
promise /ˈprɒmɪs/ versprechen II
proper /ˈprɒpə/ richtig 6/P13
protect /prəˈtekt/ (be)schützen II
proud (of sb) /praʊd/ stolz (auf jmd) II
prove /pruːv/ beweisen 2/M3
provide /prəˈvaɪd/ zur Verfügung stellen, sorgen für 5/M4
pub /pʌb/ Kneipe, Gaststätte 1/3
public /ˈpʌblɪk/ öffentlich 5/8
pull /pʊl/ ziehen 3/15
pump /pʌmp/ pumpen 5/M6
punchbag /ˈpʌntʃˌbæg/ Sandsack, Boxsack 2/4
purple /ˈpɜːpl/ violett, lila(farben) I
purse /pɜːs/ Portemonnaie 3/CC
push /pʊʃ/ drücken; schubsen, stoßen 4/11
put *(irr)* /pʊt/ setzen, legen, stellen I
put in /pʊt‿ˈɪn/ hineinsetzen/-legen/-stellen; hineintun 1/M6
put on /pʊt‿ˈɒn/ anziehen; auftragen 2/13
put on make-up /pʊt‿ˌɒn ˈmeɪkˌʌp/ sich schminken II
put together /pʊt təˈgeðə/ zusammensetzen, zusammenstellen 1/M5
put up /pʊt‿ˈʌp/ aufhängen 3/12
put up /pʊt‿ˈʌp/ aufstellen 3/17
crossword puzzle /ˈkrɒswɜːd ˌpʌzl/ Kreuzworträtsel 1/7

Q

quality /ˈkwɒləti/ Qualität 3/M4
quarter (to/past) /ˈkwɔːtə/ Viertel (vor/nach) I
queen /kwiːn/ Königin II
question /ˈkwestʃn/ Frage I
question sb /ˈkwestʃn ˌsʌmbədi/ jdn befragen 3/15
question tag /ˈkwestʃn ˌtæg/ Bestätigungsfrage 1/8
queue /kjuː/ Schlange, Reihe II
quick /kwɪk/ schnell II
quiet /ˈkwaɪət/ leise, ruhig I
quite /kwaɪt/ ziemlich 1/3
not quite /nɒt ˈkwaɪt/ nicht ganz 2/1
quiz sb /ˈkwɪz‿ˌsʌmbədi/ jdn befragen/prüfen 4/P4

R

rabbit /ˈræbɪt/ Kaninchen I
race /reɪs/ Rennen 2/3
radio station /ˈreɪdiəʊ ˌsteɪʃn/ Radiosender II
raft /rɑːft/ Floß 4/1
rain /reɪn/ Regen 2/14
rain /reɪn/ regnen II
rainbow /ˈreɪnˌbəʊ/ Regenbogen II
raincoat /ˈreɪnˌkəʊt/ Regenmantel 6/P13
rainforest /ˈreɪnˌfɒrɪst/ Regenwald II
rainy /ˈreɪni/ regnerisch I
raise money /reɪz ˈmʌni/ Geld aufbringen/auftreiben 2/8
raita /ˈraɪtə/ *Joghurt mit Gurke und Minze* 1/4
ran /ræn/ *Vergangenheitsform von „run"*
rang /ræŋ/ *Vergangenheitsform von „ring"*
rat /ræt/ Ratte II
rather /ˈrɑːðə/ ziemlich; lieber 3/4
RE (= religious education) /ˌɑː(r)‿ˈiː, rəˌlɪdʒəs‿ˌedjʊˈkeɪʃn/ Religion(sunterricht) I
reach /riːtʃ/ erreichen 4/M3
read *(irr)* /riːd/ lesen I
read along /ˌriːd‿əˈlɒŋ/ mitlesen 1/3
read out loud /ˌriːd‿ˌaʊt ˈlaʊd/ laut vorlesen 4/M6
reading /ˈriːdɪŋ/ Lesen; Lesung 2/16
ready /ˈredi/ fertig, bereit I
real /rɪəl/ wirklich; echt II
really /ˈrɪəli/ wirklich I
reason /ˈriːzn/ Grund 2/14
give reasons /gɪv ˈriːznz/ begründen, Gründe angeben 5/14
receive /rɪˈsiːv/ empfangen, erhalten 4/7
receptionist /rɪˈsepʃnɪst/ Sprechstundenhilfe 2/12; Empfangschef/in 6/11
recipe /ˈresəpi/ Rezept 1/12
recommend /ˌrekəˈmend/ empfehlen 3/M4
record /rɪˈkɔːd/ aufnehmen, aufzeichnen 2/16
record player /ˈrekɔːd ˌpleɪə/ (Schall)plattenspieler 5/M1
recording /rɪˈkɔːdɪŋ/ Aufnahme 6/P3
recover /rɪˈkʌvə/ sich erholen 2/M7
red /red/ rot I
referee /ˌrefəˈriː/ Schiedsrichter/in 2/8
regular /ˈregjʊlə/ regelmäßig; normal 1/2
relative /ˈrelətɪv/ Verwandte(r), Angehörige(r) II
relax /rɪˈlæks/ sich entspannen II
relaxed /rɪˈlækst/ entspannt; locker, gelassen II
remember /rɪˈmembə/ (an etw) denken II
remember /rɪˈmembə/ sich erinnern (an) I
repair /rɪˈpeə/ reparieren II
repeat /rɪˈpiːt/ wiederholen II
report /rɪˈpɔːt/ Bericht I
report /rɪˈpɔːt/ Zeugnis 4/9
report /rɪˈpɔːt/ berichten 1/9
require /rɪˈkwaɪə/ brauchen; erfordern 5/M4
rescue /ˈreskjuː/ retten 4/1
reservation /ˌrezəˈveɪʃn/ Reservierung 6/M6
respect *(no pl)* /rɪˈspekt/ Respekt, Achtung II
result /rɪˈzʌlt/ Ergebnis; Folge 2/M2
return (ticket) /rɪˈtɜːn/ Hin- und Rückfahrkarte 6/7
return /rɪˈtɜːn/ zurückkehren 3/8
review /rɪˈvjuː/ Kritik, Rezension 3/M4
rhyming pair /ˈraɪmɪŋ peə/ Reimpaar 3/P8
rhythm /ˈrɪðəm/ Rhythmus, Takt 3/M5
rice *(no pl)* /raɪs/ Reis II
rich /rɪtʃ/ reich II
ride *(irr)* /raɪd/ fahren; reiten I
ride a bike /ˌraɪd‿ə ˈbaɪk/ (Fahr)rad fahren I
rider /ˈraɪdə/ Reiter/in 5/P10
riding /ˈraɪdɪŋ/ Reiten I
right /raɪt/ richtig I; (nach) rechts II
right /raɪt/ oder 3/4
be right /biː ˈraɪt/ Recht haben I
on the/your right /ˌɒn ðə/jɔː ˈraɪt/ rechts, auf der rechten Seite II
ring *(irr)* /rɪŋ/ klingeln, läuten 5/5
river /ˈrɪvə/ Fluss I
road /rəʊd/ Straße 5/11
roar /rɔː/ brüllen II
roast lamb /ˌrəʊst ˈlæm/ Lammbraten 1/2
robot /ˈrəʊbɒt/ Roboter II
robotics *(only pl)* /rəʊˈbɒtɪks/ Robotik, Robotertechnik 6/M2
rock /rɒk/ Stein, Fels(en) 4/1
role /rəʊl/ Rolle 2/12
roll /rəʊl/ rollen 1/14
room /ruːm/ Zimmer I
rope /rəʊp/ Seil 4/3
rubber *(BE)* /ˈrʌbə/ Radiergummi I
rubbish *(no pl)* /ˈrʌbɪʃ/ Müll I
ruined /ˈruːɪnd/ zerstört, ruiniert 2/M7
rule /ruːl/ Regel II
ruler /ˈruːlə/ Lineal I
run *(irr)* /rʌn/ laufen, rennen I
run into sb/sth /rʌn‿ˈɪntʊ ˌsʌmbədi/ˌsʌmθɪŋ/ in jdn/etw hineinrennen 2/8
run over sb /rʌn‿ˈəʊvə ˌsʌmbədi/ jdn überfahren 3/15
runner /ˈrʌnə/ Läufer/in I
running /ˈrʌnɪŋ/ Laufen, Rennen 2/3
Russia /ˈrʌʃə/ Russland I

Russian /ˈrʌʃn/ Russisch II
Russian /ˈrʌʃn/ russisch II

S

sacrifice /ˈsækrɪfaɪs/ Opfer 2/M3
sad /sæd/ traurig II
safe /seɪf/ sicher II
safety *(no pl)* /ˈseɪftɪ/ Sicherheit 3/P13
said /sed/ *Vergangenheitsform von „say"*
sail /seɪl/ Segel 4/M3
sail /seɪl/ segeln 4/1
salad /ˈsæləd/ Salat II
sale /seɪl/ (Aus)verkauf 3/P6
salt *(no pl)* /sɔːlt/ Salz 1/12
salted /ˈsɔːltɪd/ gesalzen 1/12
the same /ðə ˈseɪm/ der-/die-/dasselbe II
the same /ðə ˈseɪm/ gleich 3/3
at the same time /æt ðə seɪm ˈtaɪm/ gleichzeitig 2/M3
samosa /səˈməʊsə/ *gefüllte Teigtasche* 3/CC
sat /sæt/ *Vergangenheitsform von „sit"*
Saturday /ˈsætədeɪ/ Samstag I
sauce /sɔːs/ Soße II
sausage /ˈsɒsɪdʒ/ Wurst, Würstchen I
save /seɪv/ retten 3/8; speichern, sichern 5/5
save /seɪv/ aufheben 1/CC; sparen 3/P4
saw /sɔː/ *Vergangenheitsform von „see"*
say *(irr)* /seɪ/ sagen I
say out loud /ˌseɪ‿ˌaʊt ˈlaʊd/ laut sagen 4/M7
saying /ˈseɪɪŋ/ Sprichwort 4/5
scare /skeə/ Angst machen, erschrecken 3/8
be scared (of sth) /biː ˈskeəd/ (vor etw) Angst haben II
scarf *(pl* **-s** *or* **scarves***)* /skɑːf, skɑːvz/ Schal I
scary /ˈskeəri/ Furcht erregend; unheimlich II

scene /siːn/ Szene 1/3
scheduled /ˈʃedjuːld/ geplant, planmäßig 5/M4
school /skuːl/ Schule I
schoolbag /ˈskuːlbæg/ Schultasche I
science /ˈsaɪəns/ (Natur)wissenschaft I
(pair of) scissors *(only pl)* /ˈsɪzəz/ Schere I
score /skɔː/ Punktestand; Spielstand 2/8
score a goal /skɔːr‿ə ˈgəʊl/ ein Tor schießen 2/8
Scotland /ˈskɒtlənd/ Schottland II
Scottish /ˈskɒtɪʃ/ schottisch 6/13
scream /skriːm/ schreien; kreischen II
the sea *(no pl)* /ðə ˈsiː/ das Meer, die See II
search /sɜːtʃ/ Suche 4/P4
search /sɜːtʃ/ (durch)suchen 5/2
seasick /ˈsiːˌsɪk/ seekrank 4/1
second /ˈsekənd/ Sekunde 2/1
second /ˈsekənd/ zweite(r, s) I
secret /ˈsiːkrət/ geheim 5/5
secretary /ˈsekrətri/ Sekretär/in I
see *(irr)* /siː/ sehen I
see you /ˈsiː juː/ bis dann, bis bald II
I see. /aɪ siː/ Aha!, Ich verstehe. 2/12
seed /siːd/ Same(n), Korn 1/12
seen /siːn/ *siehe „see"*
select /sɪˈlekt/ (aus)wählen, aussuchen 6/P6
self-confident /ˌselfˈkɒnfɪdnt/ selbstbewusst, selbstsicher II
sell *(irr)* /sel/ verkaufen I
seller /ˈselə/ Verkäufer/in II
send *(irr)* /send/ (zu)schicken II
sentence /ˈsentəns/ Satz I
September /sepˈtembə/ September I
sequin /ˈsiːkwɪn/ Paillette 3/CC

servant /ˈsɜːvnt/ Bedienstete/r 5/P13
serve /sɜːv/ servieren 1/14
set the table /ˌset ðə ˈteɪbl/ den Tisch decken II
set-up /ˈsetʌp/ Aufbau 3/P6
sex /seks/ Geschlecht 6/5
shadow /ˈʃædəʊ/ Schatten II
share /ʃeə/ teilen 1/1
she /ʃiː/ sie I
sheep *(pl -)* /ʃiːp/ Schaf I
shelf *(pl* **shelves***)* /ʃelf, ʃelvz/ Regal I
shine *(irr)* /ʃaɪn/ scheinen (Sonne) 6/1
ship /ʃɪp/ Schiff I
shirt /ʃɜːt/ Hemd; Bluse I
shocked /ˈʃɒkt/ schockiert, entsetzt 4/1
shoe /ʃuː/ Schuh I
shop /ʃɒp/ Geschäft, Laden I
shop assistant /ˈʃɒp‿əˌsɪstənt/ Verkäufer/in II
do the shopping /ˌduː ðə ˈʃɒpɪŋ/ einkaufen (gehen) I
go shopping /gəʊ ˈʃɒpɪŋ/ einkaufen gehen I
short /ʃɔːt/ kurz 2/3
in short /ɪn ˈʃɔːt/ in Kürze, kurz gefasst 4/P5
should /ʃʊd/ sollte/müsste I
shoulder /ˈʃəʊldə/ Schulter 2/M7
shout /ʃaʊt/ schreien, rufen I
show *(irr)* /ʃəʊ/ zeigen II
showcave /ˈʃəʊkeɪv/ Schauhöhle 6/P13
shower /ˈʃaʊə/ Dusche 5/M6
shown /ʃəʊn/ *siehe „show"*
sb is sick /ˌsʌmbədi ɪz‿ˈsɪk/ jdm ist schlecht/übel 5/M6
side /saɪd/ Seite II
side order /ˈsaɪd‿ˌɔːdə/ Beilage 1/4
sight /saɪt/ Sehenswürdigkeit II
sign /saɪn/ Zeichen; (Straßen-/Verkehrs)schild II
signature /ˈsɪgnətʃə/ Unterschrift 6/5

silly /ˈsɪli/ dumm; albern 4/8
silver /ˈsɪlvə/ silbern II
similar /ˈsɪmɪlə/ ähnlich 1/P1
simple past /ˌsɪmpl ˈpɑːst/ einfache Vergangenheit 4/P4
since /sɪns/ seit 4/7
since then /ˌsɪns ˈðen/ seitdem, seither 2/M3
sing *(irr)* /sɪŋ/ singen I
sing along /ˌsɪŋ‿əˈlɒŋ/ mitsingen 4/11
singer /ˈsɪŋə/ Sänger/in II
single (ticket) /ˈsɪŋgl/ Einzelfahrkarte 6/7
single journey /ˌsɪŋgl ˈdʒɜːni/ Einzelfahrt 6/P5
sinking /ˈsɪŋkɪŋ/ sinkend 4/M3
sister /ˈsɪstə/ Schwester I
brothers and sisters /ˌbrʌðəz‿ænd ˈsɪstəz/ Geschwister II
sit *(irr)* /sɪt/ sitzen I
situation /ˌsɪtʃuˈeɪʃn/ Situation, Lage 4/1
size /saɪz/ Größe 3/7
skate park /ˈskeɪt pɑːk/ Skatepark 2/3
skateboarding /ˈskeɪtˌbɔːdɪŋ/ Skateboardfahren 2/3
skiing /ˈskiːɪŋ/ Skifahren, Skilaufen 2/CC
skirt /skɜːt/ Rock I
sky /skaɪ/ Himmel 3/P3
sleep *(no pl)* /sliːp/ Schlaf 2/9
sleep *(irr)* /sliːp/ schlafen I
sleep late /ˌsliːp ˈleɪt/ ausschlafen, lange schlafen 6/8
sleep over /sliːp‿ˈəʊvə/ übernachten, über Nacht bleiben II
slice /slaɪs/ Scheibe 1/P12
slide show /ˈslaɪd ʃəʊ/ Diashow 4/1
slim /slɪm/ schlank, schmal, dünn 2/5
slow /sləʊ/ langsam II
small /smɔːl/ klein I
smell /smel/ Geruch; Duft; Gestank I
smell (of) /smel/ riechen (nach) II
smile /smaɪl/ lächeln II
smoke signal /ˈsməʊk ˌsɪgnl/ Rauchzeichen 5/M1
snake /sneɪk/ Schlange I
snow *(no pl)* /snəʊ/ Schnee II
snowy /ˈsnəʊi/ schneereich; verschneit I
so /səʊ/ so I; deshalb; also II
so /səʊ/ damit, sodass 2/12
soap *(no pl)* /səʊp/ Seife 4/3
soap (opera) /ˈsəʊp (‿ˌɒprə)/ Seifenoper, Soap II
social /ˈsəʊʃl/ sozial 2/M3; gesellschaftlich 5/3
sock /sɒk/ Socke I
soft /sɒft/ weich 1/11
some /sʌm/ einige; etwas I
some of which /ˈsʌm‿əv wɪtʃ/ von denen einige 1/M1
somebody /ˈsʌmbədi/ jemand II
somehow /ˈsʌmhaʊ/ irgendwie 4/11
someone /ˈsʌmwʌn/ jemand II
something /ˈsʌmθɪŋ/ etwas I
something else /ˌsʌmθɪŋ‿ˈels/ (noch) etwas anderes 4/M9
sometimes /ˈsʌmtaɪmz/ manchmal I
somewhere /ˈsʌmweə/ irgendwo II
son /sʌn/ Sohn I
soon /suːn/ bald I
sore /sɔː/ wund, entzündet 2/14
sorry /ˈsɒri/ Verzeihung!, Entschuldigung!; Wie bitte? I
(I'm) sorry. /ˈsɒri/ Entschuldigung, das tut mir leid. II
feel sorry for sb /ˌfiːl ˈsɒri fə sʌmbədi/ Mitleid mit jdm haben 4/M9
sort /sɔːt/ Art, Sorte I
sort /sɔːt/ sortieren 3/9
sound /saʊnd/ Geräusch, Klang, Ton II
sound /saʊnd/ klingen, sich anhören I
sound system /ˈsaʊnd ˌsɪstəm/ Stereoanlage, Hi-Fi-Anlage 3/11
soup /suːp/ Suppe 1/2
south /saʊθ/ Süden 6/11
South Africa /saʊθ‿ˈæfrɪkə/ Südafrika II
space /speɪs/ Platz, Raum 5/M4; Weltraum 5/8
spaceship /ˈspeɪsˌʃɪp/ Raumschiff II
spade /speɪd/ Spaten, Schaufel 4/3
Spain /speɪn/ Spanien I
Spanish /ˈspænɪʃ/ Spanisch I
Spanish /ˈspænɪʃ/ spanisch I
speak *(irr)* /spiːk/ sprechen, reden II
special /ˈspeʃl/ besondere(r, s), speziell I
special feature /ˌspeʃl ˈfiːtʃə/ Besonderheit 5/M7
special offer /ˌspeʃl‿ˈɒfə/ Sonderangebot 3/7
speciality /ˌspeʃiˈæləti/ Spezialität 1/CC
spectacular /spekˈtækjʊlə/ atemberaubend, spektakulär 6/P13
speech bubble /ˈspiːtʃ ˌbʌbl/ Sprechblase 1/8
spell *(irr)* /spel/ buchstabieren I
spelling /ˈspelɪŋ/ Rechtschreibung 3/17
spend *(irr)* /spend/ ausgeben *(Geld)*; verbringen *(Zeit)* II
spent /spent/ *Vergangenheitsform von „spend"*
spice /spaɪs/ Gewürz 1/M1
spicy /ˈspaɪsi/ würzig; scharf 1/3
spider /ˈspaɪdə/ Spinne II
spinach *(no pl)* /ˈspɪnɪdʒ/ Spinat 1/10
spit *(irr)* /spɪt/ spucken I
split up /splɪt‿ˈʌp/ sich teilen; sich trennen 4/7
spoke /spəʊk/ *Vergangenheitsform von „speak"*

spoken /ˈspəʊkən/ *siehe „speak"*
spooky *(informal)* /ˈspuːki/ unheimlich; schaurig II
spoon /spuːn/ Löffel I
sports *(only pl)* /spɔːts/ Sport; Sportart I
sports field /ˈspɔːts fiːld/ Sportplatz, Spielfeld 2/8
sports ground /ˈspɔːts ˌgraʊnd/ Sportplatz I
sports hall /ˈspɔːts hɔːl/ Sporthalle 2/3
sportsmanship *(no pl)* /ˈspɔːtsmənʃɪp/ Fairness 2/8
sportsperson /ˈspɔːtsˌpɜːsn/ Sportler/in 2/6
spring /sprɪŋ/ Frühling I
stadium /ˈsteɪdiəm/ Stadion II
stage /steɪdʒ/ Bühne II
stair /steə/ (Treppen)stufe 2/1
stairs *(only pl)* /steəz/ Treppe 5/5
stall /stɔːl/ (Verkaufs)stand II
stamp /stæmp/ Briefmarke I
stand *(irr)* /stænd/ stehen; ertragen, ausstehen, aushalten I
stand for sth /ˈstænd fə ˌsʌmθɪŋ/ für etw stehen, etw bedeuten 2/4
star /stɑː/ Stern II
star sign /ˈstɑː saɪn/ Sternzeichen II
start /stɑːt/ Anfang, Beginn 2/P6
start /stɑːt/ anfangen, beginnen I
starter /ˈstɑːtə/ Vorspeise 1/2
starting point /ˈstɑːtɪŋ ˌpɔɪnt/ Start, Startpunkt 2/M1
statement /ˈsteɪtmənt/ Aussage; Äußerung 1/11
radio station /ˈreɪdiəʊ ˌsteɪʃn/ Radiosender II
station /ˈsteɪʃn/ Bahnhof; Station II
stay /steɪ/ bleiben I; untergebracht sein, wohnen II
stay up /ˌsteɪ‿ˈʌp/ aufbleiben, wach bleiben I
steal *(irr)* /stiːl/ stehlen, klauen II
steel *(no pl)* /stiːl/ Stahl 3/11
step on sth /ˈstep‿ɒn ˌsʌmθɪŋ/ auf etw treten 2/14
stereo /ˈsteriəʊ/ (Stereo)anlage II
stick /stɪk/ Stock I
stick *(irr)* /stɪk/ kleben 3/10
stick man /ˈstɪk ˌmæn/ Strichmännchen 2/16
still /stɪl/ (immer) noch, noch immer 2/11
still /stɪl/ trotzdem, dennoch 2/3
stir /stɜː/ rühren 1/12
stole /stəʊl/ *Vergangenheitsform von „steal"*
stomach ache /ˈstʌmək ‿ˌeɪk/ Magenschmerzen, Bauchschmerzen 2/14
stone /stəʊn/ Stein 6/13
the Stone Age /ðə ˈstəʊn eɪdʒ/ die Steinzeit 5/M1
stop /stɒp/ aufhören; beenden; anhalten I
stop /stɒp/ aufhalten 2/M3
storm /stɔːm/ Sturm 4/1
story /ˈstɔːri/ Geschichte, Erzählung I
stove /stəʊv/ Herd 1/12
straight (on) /streɪt/ gerade(aus) II
stranded /ˈstrændɪd/ gestrandet 4/6
strange /streɪndʒ/ sonderbar, komisch II
strawberry /ˈstrɔːbri/ Erdbeere 1/2
street /striːt/ Straße I
stretch /stretʃ/ (sich) dehnen 2/4
strict /strɪkt/ streng II
strip /strɪp/ Streifen 1/12
strong /strɒŋ/ stark I
student /ˈstjuːdnt/ Student/in, Studierende/r; Schüler/in I
study /ˈstʌdi/ studieren; lernen II
study /ˈstʌdi/ erforschen 4/P6
stupid /ˈstjuːpɪd/ dumm, blöd I
style /staɪl/ Stil 4/14
style /staɪl/ frisieren II
subject /ˈsʌbdʒɪkt/ Thema; (Schul)fach I
success *(no pl)* /səkˈses/ Erfolg 2/M7
successful /səkˈsesfl/ erfolgreich 2/6
such /sʌtʃ/ solche(r,s) 6/CC
suddenly /ˈsʌdnli/ plötzlich, auf einmal I
sugar *(no pl)* /ˈʃʊgə/ Zucker II
sugary /ˈʃʊgəri/ zuckerhaltig 1/9
suitcase /ˈsuːtˌkeɪs/ Koffer II
summer /ˈsʌmə/ Sommer I
summer camp /ˈsʌmə ˌkæmp/ Ferienlager 6/4
sun /sʌn/ Sonne II
Sunday /ˈsʌndeɪ/ Sonntag I
sunglasses *(only pl)* /ˈsʌnˌglɑːsɪz/ Sonnenbrille I
sunlight /ˈsʌnˌlaɪt/ Sonnenlicht 5/CC
sunny /ˈsʌni/ sonnig I
sunrise /ˈsʌnˌraɪz/ Sonnenaufgang II
sunshine *(no pl)* /ˈsʌnˌʃaɪn/ Sonnenschein 3/M5
superlative (form) /sʊˈpɜːlətɪv/ Superlativ 2/P5
supermarket /ˈsuːpəˌmɑːkɪt/ Supermarkt I
sure /ʃɔː/ sicher I
make sure /ˌmeɪk ˈʃɔː/ sich versichern, darauf achten 2/P3
surgery /ˈsɜːdʒəri/ (Arzt)praxis 2/12
surname /ˈsɜːˌneɪm/ Familienname, Nachname 6/5
surprise /səˈpraɪz/ Überraschung II
surprised /səˈpraɪzd/ überrascht II

surprising /sə'praɪzɪŋ/ überraschend 1/10
survey /'sɜːveɪ/ Untersuchung, Umfrage 1/9
survival kit /sə'vaɪvl kɪt/ Überlebensausrüstung 4/3
survive /sə'vaɪv/ überleben II
swam /swæm/ *Vergangenheitsform von „swim"*
swap /swɒp/ tauschen 3/17
sweet /swiːt/ Süßigkeit I
sweet /swiːt/ süß I
have a sweet tooth /hæv‿ə swiːt 'tuːθ/ gerne Süßigkeiten essen, eine Naschkatze sein 1/11
swim *(irr)* /swɪm/ schwimmen I
swimmer /'swɪmə/ Schwimmer/in 2/3
swimming /'swɪmɪŋ/ Schwimmen I
swimming pool /'swɪmɪŋ puːl/ Schwimmbecken, -bad I
swing *(irr)* /swɪŋ/ schwingen, schaukeln 5/M6
swollen /'swəʊlən/ geschwollen 2/12
swung /swʌŋ/ *Vergangenheitsform von „swing"*

T

table /'teɪbl/ Tisch I
set the table /ˌset ðə 'teɪbl/ den Tisch decken II
table tennis *(no pl)* /'teɪbl ˌtenɪs/ Tischtennis I
tablespoon /'teɪblˌspuːn/ Esslöffel 1/12
tail /teɪl/ Schwanz II
take *(irr)* /teɪk/ (mit)nehmen; bringen I
take *(irr)* /teɪk/ brauchen 3/CC
take care of /teɪk 'keər‿əv/ sich kümmern um, versorgen II
take notes /teɪk 'nəʊts/ (sich) Notizen machen II
take out /ˌteɪk‿'aʊt/ hinausbringen I
take out /ˌteɪk‿'aʊt/ herausnehmen II
take part (in) /ˌteɪk 'pɑːt/ teilnehmen (an) II
take photos /ˌteɪk 'fəʊtəʊz/ Bilder machen, fotografieren II
take place /teɪk 'pleɪs/ stattfinden 2/M1
take sb out /teɪk 'sʌmbədi‿aʊt/ jdn (zum Essen) einladen 5/5
take turns /ˌteɪk 'tɜːnz/ sich abwechseln 1/M7
takeaway /'teɪkəˌweɪ/ Imbiss 1/M1
takeaway (food) /'teɪkəˌweɪ/ Essen zum Mitnehmen 1/3
taken /'teɪkən/ *siehe „take"*
talented /'tæləntɪd/ talentiert, begabt 2/M3
talk /tɔːk/ Gespräch; Unterhaltung; Vortrag 4/M2
talk (to) /tɔːk/ sprechen, reden, sich unterhalten (mit) I
give a talk /ˌgɪv‿ə 'tɔːk/ einen Vortrag halten 4/6
tall /tɔːl/ hoch; groß I
tap /tæp/ Wasserhahn 1/M6
taste /teɪst/ schmecken 1/3
taught /tɔːt/ *Vergangenheitsform von „teach"*
tea /tiː/ Tee I
teach *(irr)* /tiːtʃ/ unterrichten I; beibringen 4/1
teacher /'tiːtʃə/ Lehrer/in I
tear /tɪə/ Träne I
tear *(irr)* /teə/ (zer)reißen 2/M7
technician /tek'nɪʃn/ Techniker/in II
technology /tek'nɒlədʒi/ Technik, Technologie 5/2
teddy bear /'tedi ˌbeə/ Teddybär 5/P12
telecommunications *(only pl)* /ˌtelikəˌmjuːnɪ'keɪʃnz/ Telekommunikation 5/8
(tele)phone /fəʊn/ Telefon I
telephone box /'telɪfəʊn bɒks/ Telefonzelle 6/6
tell *(irr)* /tel/ erzählen; sagen I
temperature /'temprɪtʃə/ Temperatur 1/12
temple /'templ/ Tempel II
terrible /'terəbl/ schrecklich, furchtbar II
test /test/ Prüfung, Test; Klassenarbeit II
test /test/ prüfen, testen 2/1
test of courage /test‿əv 'kʌrɪdʒ/ Mutprobe 1/M1
text /tekst/ SMS schicken 5/P6
text message /'tekst ˌmesɪdʒ/ SMS, Kurznachricht 5/4
Thai /taɪ/ thailändisch 1/13
the (River) Thames /ðə 'temz/ die Themse II
than /ðæn/ als II
thank you /'θæŋk juː/ danke I
thank you /'θæŋk juː/ Dankeschön, Danke 2/P7
thanks /θæŋks/ danke I
thanks a lot /ˌθæŋks‿ə 'lɒt/ vielen Dank II
that /ðæt/ das; der/die/das I
that /ðæt/ dass 1/M1
that's why /'ðæts waɪ/ deshalb; das ist der Grund, warum I
the /ðə/ der/die/das I
the ... way /ðə 'weɪ/ auf die ... Art 1/CC
theatre /'θɪətə/ Theater 3/P1
their /ðeə/ ihr(e) I
them /ðem/ sie, ihnen I
theme /θiːm/ Thema; Lektion, Kapitel 1/I
then /ðen/ dann I
then /ðen/ danach I
then /ðen/ damals 5/6
there /ðeə/ dort, da I
over there /ˌəʊvə 'ðeə/ dort (drüben) I
there are /ðear‿'ɑː/ es gibt, da sind I
there is /ðear‿'ɪz/ es gibt, da ist I

these *(pl of* **this***)* /ðiːz/ diese I
they /ðeɪ/ sie I
thick /θɪk/ dick 1/CC
thin /θɪn/ dünn II
thing /θɪŋ/ Ding, Gegenstand, Sache I
think *(irr)* /θɪŋk/ denken, glauben, meinen I
think about (sb/sth) /ˈθɪŋk‿əˌbaʊt/ an (jdn/etw) denken; über (jdn/etw) nachdenken 2/15; sich (etw) überlegen 3/10
think of /ˈθɪŋk‿əv/ denken an; sich ausdenken 4/3
this /ðɪs/ diese(r, s); das I
this afternoon /ðɪs‿ˌɑːftəˈnuːn/ heute Nachmittag 6/P4
this evening /ðɪs‿ˈiːvnɪŋ/ heute Abend 6/P4
this morning /ðɪs ˈmɔːnɪŋ/ heute Morgen 3/M8
this way /ˈðɪs weɪ/ so, auf diese Art und Weise 3/3
those *(pl of* **that***)* /ðəʊz/ diese; jene I
thought /θɔːt/ *Vergangenheitsform von „think"*
thought bubble /ˈθɔːt ˌbʌbl/ Denkblase, Gedankenblase 1/M4
thriller /ˈθrɪlə/ Krimi, Thriller I
through /θruː/ durch II
throw *(irr)* /θrəʊ/ werfen 4/8
thumb /θʌm/ Daumen 1/14
Thursday /ˈθɜːzdeɪ/ Donnerstag I
ticket counter /ˈtɪkɪt ˌkaʊntə/ Fahrkartenschalter 6/6
ticket machine /ˈtɪkɪt məˌʃiːn/ Fahrkartenautomat 6/P6
tidy up /ˌtaɪdi‿ˈʌp/ aufräumen I
tie /taɪ/ Krawatte II
tikka /ˈtiːkə/ *indisches Gericht* 1/M1
time /taɪm/ (Uhr)zeit I; Mal II
at the same time /æt ðə seɪm ˈtaɪm/ gleichzeitig 2/M3

What time is it? /wɒt‿ˈtaɪm ˌɪz‿ɪt/ Wie spät/ Wie viel Uhr ist es? I
timeline /ˈtaɪmˌlaɪn/ Zeitstrahl 5/M1
timetable /ˈtaɪmteɪbl/ Stundenplan I; Fahrplan 6/6
tip /tɪp/ Tipp II
tip /tɪp/ Spitze 5/13
tired /ˈtaɪəd/ müde I
title /ˈtaɪtl/ Titel 3/11
to /tə/ in, nach, zu, an; vor; bis I
today /təˈdeɪ/ heute I
together /təˈgeðə/ zusammen, gemeinsam I
toilet /ˈtɔɪlət/ Toilette, Klo 5/8
told /təʊld/ *Vergangenheitsform von „tell"*
tomato *(pl* **-es***)* /təˈmɑːtəʊ, təˈmɑːtəʊz/ Tomate I
tomorrow /təˈmɒrəʊ/ morgen I
ton *(pl - or -s)* /tʌn, tʌnz/ Tonne 3/CC
tongue twister /ˈtʌŋ ˌtwɪstə/ Zungenbrecher 3/CC
tonight /təˈnaɪt/ heute Abend 1/3
tonight /təˈnaɪt/ heute Nacht 2/M7
too /tuː/ zu; auch I
too bad /ˌtuː ˈbæd/ wirklich schade 6/11
too bad /ˌtuː ˈbæd/ so ein Pech 2/15
took /tʊk/ *Vergangenheitsform von „take"*
tooth *(pl* **teeth***)* /tuːθ, tiːθ/ Zahn I
toothache /ˈtuːθeɪk/ Zahnschmerzen 2/P8
toothbrush /ˈtuːθˌbrʌʃ/ Zahnbürste 4/3
top /tɒp/ oberes Ende, Spitze; Gipfel II; Top-, Spitzen- 3/11
at the top (of) /æt ðə ˈtɒp/ oben, am oberen Ende (von), an der Spitze (von) 3/2

tortoise /ˈtɔːtəs/ (Land)schildkröte II
touch /tʌtʃ/ berühren I
tough /tʌf/ robust, zäh, tough; hart 2/M3
toward(s) /təˈwɔːd(z)/ in Richtung 2/8
towel /ˈtaʊəl/ Handtuch I
tower /ˈtaʊə/ Turm II
town /taʊn/ Stadt I
toy /tɔɪ/ Spielzeug 3/7
tractor /ˈtræktə/ Traktor I
traditional /trəˈdɪʃnəl/ traditionell II
traditionally /trəˈdɪʃnəli/ traditionell; üblicherweise, normalerweise 1/M1
traffic light /ˈtræfɪk laɪt/ Ampel II
train /treɪn/ Zug, Eisenbahn II
train /treɪn/ trainieren 2/3
trainer *(BE)* /ˈtreɪnə/ Turnschuh 6/P13
trample down /ˌtræmpl ˈdaʊn/ niedertrampeln, zertrampeln 3/8
translation /trænsˈleɪʃn/ Übersetzung 1/8
trap /træp/ Falle II
travel /ˈtrævl/ Reise- 6/14
travel /ˈtrævl/ reisen II
travel agency /ˈtrævl‿ˌeɪdʒnsi/ Reisebüro 6/14
traveller /ˈtrævlə/ Reisende/r 6/M8
travelling *(no pl)* /ˈtrævlɪŋ/ Reisen 6/2
tree /triː/ Baum I
trip /trɪp/ Ausflug; Reise, Fahrt II
tropical /ˈtrɒpɪkl/ tropisch, Tropen- 3/12
trouble *(no pl)* /ˈtrʌbl/ Schwierigkeiten 2/8
get into trouble /get‿ɪntə ˈtrʌbl/ Schwierigkeiten bekommen II
trousers *(only pl)* /ˈtraʊzəz/ Hose I

true /truː/ wahr; richtig II
come true /ˌkʌm ˈtruː/ wahr werden 5/1
truly /ˈtruːli/ wirklich 3/M4
trumpet /ˈtrʌmpɪt/ Trompete 4/3
truth /truːθ/ Wahrheit 1/P9
try /traɪ/ (aus)probieren; versuchen II
try hard to do sth /ˌtraɪ ˈhɑːd‿tə duː sʌmθɪŋ/ sich sehr bemühen, etw zu tun II
tube *(no pl)* /tjuːb/ Londoner U-Bahn II
Tuesday /ˈtjuːzdeɪ/ Dienstag I
Turkey /ˈtɜːki/ Türkei I
turkey /ˈtɜːki/ Truthahn/-henne, Pute/r II
Turkish /ˈtɜːkɪʃ/ Türkisch II
Turkish /ˈtɜːkɪʃ/ türkisch II
turn /tɜːn/ sich drehen; abbiegen II
(it's) your turn /ˈjɔː ˌtɜːn/ du bist dran I
turn into /ˌtɜːn‿ˈɪntʊ/ umwandeln in, verändern in 4/P1
turn off /ˌtɜːn‿ˈɒf/ ausmachen, ausschalten 5/5
turn on /ˌtɜːn‿ˈɒn/ einschalten 5/5
turn over /tɜːn‿ˈəʊvə/ (sich) umdrehen 5/13
turn round /tɜːn ˈraʊnd/ (sich) umdrehen 3/M8
turn up /ˌtɜːn‿ˈʌp/ aufdrehen, lauter stellen 4/11
take turns /ˌteɪk ˈtɜːnz/ sich abwechseln 1/M7
turtle /ˈtɜːtl/ Schildkröte I
TV (= television) /ˌtiːˈviː, ˈtelɪˌvɪʒn/ Fernseher; Fernsehen I
watch TV /ˌwɒtʃ ˌtiː ˈviː/ fernsehen I
TV series *(only pl)* /ˌtiːˈviː ˌsɪəriːz/ Fernsehserie II
twice /twaɪs/ zweimal 2/3
twin /twɪn/ Zwilling, Zwillings- II

type /taɪp/ Art; Typ, Sorte 1/M1
typical /ˈtɪpɪkl/ typisch 1/14

U

ugly /ˈʌgli/ hässlich I
UK (= United Kingdom) /ˌjuːˈkeɪ, juːˌnaɪtɪd ˈkɪŋdəm/ Vereinigtes Königreich II
uncle /ˈʌŋkl/ Onkel I
under /ˈʌndə/ unter I
underground /ˈʌndəˌgraʊnd/ U-Bahn II
underline /ˌʌndəˈlaɪn/ unterstreichen 1/6
understand *(irr)* /ˌʌndəˈstænd/ verstehen I
understanding *(no pl)* /ˌʌndəˈstændɪŋ/ Verständnis 6/P13
unfortunately /ʌnˈfɔːtʃnətli/ leider, unglücklicherweise II
unfriendly /ʌnˈfrendli/ unfreundlich II
unhappy /ʌnˈhæpi/ unglücklich 4/1
unhealthy /ʌnˈhelθi/ ungesund 1/10
unique /juːˈniːk/ einzigartig 6/M2
universe /ˈjuːnɪˌvɜːs/ Universum II
university /juːnɪˈvɜːsəti/ Universität 2/M3
unsweetened /ˌʌnˈswiːtənd/ ungesüßt 1/10
until /ənˈtɪl/ bis II
up /ʌp/ (nach) oben; hinauf 5/13
up and away /ˌʌp‿ən‿əˈweɪ/ auf und davon 5/I
up and down /ˌʌp‿ən ˈdaʊn/ auf und ab 2/1
up to /ˈʌp tuː/ bis (zu) 6/M2
get up /get‿ˈʌp/ aufstehen I
upstairs /ʌpˈsteəz/ (nach) oben II
us /ʌs/ uns I
use /juːz/ benutzen II

useful /ˈjuːsfl/ nützlich, hilfreich 4/3
usually /ˈjuːʒʊəli/ gewöhnlich, normalerweise I

V

vacation *(AE)* = holiday *(BE)* /vəˈkeɪʃn/ Ferien, Urlaub 6/11
valid /ˈvælɪd/ gültig 6/P6
valley /ˈvæli/ Tal 3/8
vegetable /ˈvedʒtəbl/ Gemüse I
vegetarian /ˌvedʒəˈteəriən/ Vegetarier/in 1/2
vegetarian /ˌvedʒəˈteəriən/ vegetarisch 1/2
verse /vɜːs/ Strophe 3/3
version /ˈvɜːʃn/ Version, Fassung 4/1
very /ˈveri/ sehr I
vet (= veterinarian) /vet, ˌvetrɪˈneəriən/ Tierarzt/-ärztin II
veterinary /ˈvetnri/ tierärztlich 5/8
view /vjuː/ Sicht; (Aus)blick, Aussicht II
village /ˈvɪlɪdʒ/ Dorf II
vindaloo /ˌvɪndəˈluː/ *sehr scharfes indisches Gericht* 1/M1
visit /ˈvɪzɪt/ Besuch 2/9
visit /ˈvɪzɪt/ besuchen I
visitor /ˈvɪzɪtə/ Besucher/in 3/10
voice /vɔɪs/ Stimme II
volcano *(pl* **-oes** *or* **-os***)* /vɒlˈkeɪnəʊ, vɒlˈkeɪnəʊz/ Vulkan 6/11
volunteer /ˌvɒlənˈtɪə/ Freiwillige/r I

W

wait (for) /weɪt/ warten (auf) II
sb cannot wait (to do sth) /ˌsʌmbədi ˌkænɒt ˈweɪt (‿tə duː ˌsʌmθɪŋ)/ jmd kann es kaum erwarten (, etw zu tun) 3/M4
waiter/waitress /ˈweɪtə, ˈweɪtrəs/ Bedienung, Kellner/in II

waiting room /ˈweɪtɪŋ ˌruːm/ Wartezimmer 2/12
wake up /weɪk‿ˈʌp/ aufwecken; aufwachen I
walk /wɔːk/ Spaziergang II
walk /wɔːk/ (zu Fuß) gehen, laufen I
go for a walk /ˌɡəʊ fər‿ə ˈwɔːk/ spazieren gehen I
walk the dog /ˌwɔːk ðə ˈdɒɡ/ den Hund ausführen 4/7
wall /wɔːl/ Wand I
wall climbing /ˈwɔːl ˌklaɪmɪŋ/ Klettern an der Kletterwand II
wallet /ˈwɒlɪt/ Portemonnaie, Brieftasche 3/12
want /wɒnt/ wollen I
want to do sth /ˌwɒnt‿tə ˈduː ˌsʌmθɪŋ/ etw tun wollen I
wardrobe /ˈwɔːdrəʊb/ Kleiderschrank I
warm-up /ˈwɔːmˌʌp/ Warm-up, Aufwärmen 2/4
warning /ˈwɔːnɪŋ/ Warnung II
was /wɒz/ *Vergangenheitsform von „be"*
wash /wɒʃ/ (sich) waschen I
wash up /wɒʃ‿ˈʌp/ anspülen, anschwemmen 4/M3
watch /wɒtʃ/ (Armband)uhr 3/12
watch /wɒtʃ/ beobachten; anschauen; zusehen I
watch out (for) /wɒtʃ‿ˈaʊt/ aufpassen (auf), sich in Acht nehmen (vor) 3/M5
watch TV /ˌwɒtʃ ˌtiː ˈviː/ fernsehen I
water *(no pl)* /ˈwɔːtə/ Wasser I
water /ˈwɔːtə/ gießen II
water /ˈwɔːtə/ tränen 1/M6
waterfall /ˈwɔːtəˌfɔːl/ Wasserfall 4/4
wave /weɪv/ Welle 4/M3
wave /weɪv/ winken 3/M5
way /weɪ/ Weg II
way /weɪ/ Art, Weise 1/14
the … way /ðə ˈweɪ/ auf die … Art 1/CC

this way /ˈðɪs weɪ/ so, auf diese Art und Weise 3/3
we /wiː/ wir I
weapon /ˈwepən/ Waffe II
wear *(irr)* /weə/ tragen I
weather /ˈweðə/ Wetter I
wedding /ˈwedɪŋ/ Hochzeit II
Wednesday /ˈwenzdeɪ/ Mittwoch I
week /wiːk/ Woche I
a week /ə ˈwiːk/ pro/ in der Woche 1/9
weekend /ˌwiːkˈend/ Wochenende II
at the weekend /æt ðə ˈwiːkˌend/ am Wochenende I
welcome /ˈwelkəm/ willkommen heißen, begrüßen 6/M2
welcome (to) /ˈwelkəm/ willkommen (in) II
You're welcome. /ˌjɔː ˈwelkəm/ Gern geschehen., Bitte. 6/11
well /wel/ gut II
well /wel/ nun (ja), tja 1/M6
Welsh /welʃ/ Walisisch 6/12
Welsh /welʃ/ walisisch 6/12
went /went/ *Vergangenheitsform von „go"*
were /wɜː/ *Vergangenheitsform von „be"*
west /west/ Westen 4/5
wet /wet/ nass II
what /wɒt/ was; welche(r, s) I
What about … ? *(informal)* /ˈwɒt‿əˌbaʊt/ Was ist mit … ?, Wie wäre es mit … ? I
what else /wɒt‿ˈels/ was noch, was sonst 1/P11
what if /wɒt‿ɪf/ was ist/wäre, wenn 4/M10
What time is it? /wɒt‿ˈtaɪm ˌɪz‿ɪt/ Wie viel Uhr ist es? I
What's … like? /wɒts ˈlaɪk/ Wie ist … ? II
What's on? /wɒts‿ˈɒn/ Was ist los? 3/I
What's the matter? /ˌwɒts ðə ˈmætə/ Was ist (denn) los? II

What's wrong? /wɒts ˈrɒŋ/ Was ist los? 1/8
What's your name? /ˌwɒts jə ˈneɪm/ Wie heißt du?, Wie heißen Sie? I
wheel /wiːl/ Rad II
wheelchair /ˈwiːlˌtʃeə/ Rollstuhl II
when /wen/ wann; wenn I; als II
whenever /wenˈevə/ immer wenn, wann (auch) immer 2/3
where /weə/ wo(hin) I
Where are you from? /ˌweər‿ɑː jə ˈfrɒm/ Wo kommst du her? I
which /wɪtʃ/ welche(r, s); der/ die/das 3/12
which /wɪtʃ/ welche(r, s) 1/3
which one /ˈwɪtʃ wʌn/ welche(r, s) 4/8
some of which /ˈsʌm‿əv wɪtʃ/ von denen einige 1/M1
while /waɪl/ während 3/15
whisper /ˈwɪspə/ flüstern II
white /waɪt/ weiß I
who /huː/ wer I; der/die/das 2/5
who /huː/ wen, wem 3/16
who else /hu‿ˈels/ wer noch, wer sonst 4/M8
whole /həʊl/ ganz, gesamt II
whose /huːz/ wessen; dessen 4/7
why /waɪ/ warum I
that's why /ˈðæts waɪ/ deshalb; das ist der Grund, warum I
wide /waɪd/ breit 5/M6
wife *(pl* **wives***)* /waɪf, waɪvz/ Ehefrau I
will *(irr)* /wɪl/ werden II
win *(irr)* /wɪn/ gewinnen II
window /ˈwɪndəʊ/ Fenster I
windy /ˈwɪndi/ windig I
wine /waɪn/ Wein 1/2
wing /wɪŋ/ Flügel 5/13
winner /ˈwɪnə/ Gewinner/in, Sieger/in II

wire /ˈwaɪə/ Draht; Leitung, Kabel II
wish /wɪʃ/ (sich) wünschen II
best wishes /ˌbest ˈwɪʃɪz/ viele Grüße II
with /wɪð/ mit I
within /wɪðˈɪn/ innerhalb 6/P6
without /wɪðˈaʊt/ ohne 1/10
woman *(pl* **women***)* /ˈwʊmən, ˈwɪmɪn/ Frau I
won /wʌn/ *Vergangenheitsform von „win"*
wonder /ˈwʌndə/ Wunder 6/P13
wonderful /ˈwʌndəfl/ wunderbar, wundervoll II
wood /wʊd/ Holz 5/P8
word /wɜːd/ Wort I
word web /ˈwɜːd web/ Wortnetz 2/P1
wordbank /ˈwɜːdbæŋk/ Wortfeld 1/6
wordsearch /ˈwɜːdsɜːtʃ/ Wortsuchrätsel 1/7
wore /wɔː/ *Vergangenheitsform von „wear"*
work /wɜːk/ Arbeit 3/4
work /wɜːk/ arbeiten I; funktionieren 3/7
out of work /aʊt‿əv ˈwɜːk/ arbeitslos 4/9
workbook /ˈwɜːkˌbʊk/ Arbeitsbuch 6/M7
worker /ˈwɜːkə/ Arbeiter/in 5/P10
world /wɜːld/ Welt, Erde II
all over the world /ˌɔːl‿ˌəʊvə ðə ˈwɜːld/ auf der ganzen Welt 5/P11
around the world /əˌraʊnd ðə ˈwɜːld/ weltweit, auf der ganzen Welt 1/14
from all over the world /frəm‿ɔːl‿ˌəʊvə ðə ˈwɜːld/ aus der ganzen Welt 2/M1
World Cup /ˌwɜːld ˈkʌp/ Weltmeisterschaft 1/M1
world-famous /ˈwɜːldˌfeɪməs/ weltberühmt, weltbekannt 3/M4
worried /ˈwʌrid/ beunruhigt, besorgt 4/1
worry /ˈwʌri/ Sorge 4/M9
worry /ˈwʌri/ sich Sorgen machen II
worry sb /ˈwʌri ˌsʌmbədi/ jdn beunruhigen, jdm Sorgen bereiten 4/7
worse /wɜːs/ schlimmer, schlechter II
worst /wɜːst/ schlechteste(r, s), schlimmste(r, s) I
would /wʊd/ würde(st, n, t) I
sb would like (to) /wʊd ˈlaɪk/ jmd möchte (gern) I
sb would love (to) /ˌsʌmbədi wʊd ˈlʌv/ jmd möchte sehr gern 3/4
wreck /rek/ Wrack 4/1
wrestling /ˈreslɪŋ/ Ringen, Ringkampf 2/CC
write down /raɪt ˈdaʊn/ aufschreiben 1/1
write *(irr)* /raɪt/ schreiben I
writer /ˈraɪtə/ Schriftsteller/in, Autor/in II
written /ˈrɪtn/ *siehe „write"*
wrong /rɒŋ/ falsch I
What's wrong? /wɒts ˈrɒŋ/ Was ist los? 1/8
wrote /rəʊt/ *Vergangenheitsform von „write"*

X

X-ray /ˈeksˌreɪ/ Röntgenstrahl(en); Röntgenbild 2/12; Röntgen- 5/M7

Y

yeah *(informal)* /jeə/ ja 3/3
year /jɪə/ Jahr I
a year /ə ˈjɪə/ pro/im Jahr II
yellow /ˈjeləʊ/ gelb I
yes /jes/ ja I
yesterday /ˈjestədeɪ/ gestern I
yet /jet/ schon; bis jetzt 3/4
not yet /nɒt ˈjet/ noch nicht II
yoghurt *(no pl)* /ˈjɒgət/ Joghurt 1/10
Yorkshire pudding /ˌjɔːkʃə ˈpʊdɪŋ/ *eine Art Gebäck als Beilage zu Fleischgerichten* 1/2
you /juː/ du, dich, dir, Sie, Ihnen; ihr, euch I
You're welcome. /ˌjɔː ˈwelkəm/ Gern geschehen., Bitte. 6/11
young /jʌŋ/ jung I
your /jɔː/ dein(e); euer/eure; Ihr(e) I
yours /jɔːz/ deine(r, s); eure(r, s); Ihre(r, s) 4/M6
yourself *(pl* yourselves*)* /jəˈself, jəˈselvz/ dich, dir; selbst/ihr, euch; selbst 1/P9
youth club /ˈjuːθ ˌklʌb/ Jugendzentrum II
yummy *(informal)* /ˈjʌmi/ lecker II

Z

zip /zɪp/ Reißverschluss 5/10

A

abbiegen turn
Abend evening; night
am Abend in the evening
heute Abend tonight
Abendessen dinner
abends in the evening; pm (= post meridiem) *(nur hinter Uhrzeit)*
Abenteuer adventure
aber but
abfahren leave *(irr)*
Abzeichen logo
sich in Acht nehmen (vor) watch out (for)
Achtung respect *(no pl)*
Adler eagle
Adresse address
Affe monkey
Afrika Africa
aktiv active
Aktivität activity
albern silly
alle everyone; everybody
alle(s) all
allein alone
allein(e) on one's own
alles everything
als as; than; when
also so
alt old
Alter age
am on
amerikanisch American
Ampel traffic light
an on; at; to
(an)bieten offer
andere(r, s) other; different
ein(e) andere(r, s) another
(sich) (ver)ändern change
anders different
(Ver)änderung change
Anfang beginning
am Anfang in the beginning
anfangen start; begin *(irr)*
anfangs at first
Angebot offer
Angehörige(r) relative
angeln fish
angenehm nice
angreifen attack
Angst haben (vor) be frightened (of sth), be scared (of sth/sb), be afraid (of sth/sb)
Angst machen scare
anhalten stop
sich anhören sound
(an)klicken click
ankommen arrive
(Stereo)anlage stereo
(an)malen paint
(Telefon)anruf (phone) call
anrufen phone; call
anrühren mix
anschauen look at; watch
anschließend after that; afterwards
Ansicht opinion
(an)statt instead (of)
Antwort answer
(be)antworten answer
Anzeige advert (= advertisement)
anziehen put on
Apfel apple
Apfelsine orange
April April
Aquarium fish tank
Arbeit work
arbeiten work
arbeitslos out of work
arbeitsreich busy
arm poor
(Armband)uhr watch
Art sort; kind; type
Arzt/Ärztin doctor
Astronaut/in astronaut
Athlet/in athlete
der Atlantische Ozean the Atlantic (Ocean)
auch also; too
auf on; at
auf einmal suddenly
aufbewahren keep *(irr)*
aufbleiben stay up
aufgeben give up
aufgeregt excited
aufhalten stop
(auf)hängen hang *(irr)*
aufhängen put up
aufhören stop; finish
aufpassen (auf) watch out (for)
aufräumen tidy up
aufregend exciting
aufstehen get up
auftragen put on
aufwachen wake up
aufwecken wake up
Aufzug lift
Auge eye
Augenblick moment
August August
aus from
(her)aus out of
(Aus)bildung education *(no pl)*
(Aus)blick view
ausbrechen escape
Außerirdische(r) alien
ausflippen go crazy *(informal)*
Ausflug trip
Ausgang exit
ausgeben *(Geld)* spend *(irr)*
ausgehen go out
aushalten stand *(irr)*
ausmachen turn off
(aus)probieren try
ausräumen empty
Ausrede excuse
ausreichend enough
ausschalten turn off
aussehen look
Aussicht view
ausstehen stand *(irr)*
Australien Australia
auswählen choose *(irr)*
Auto car
Autogramm autograph
Autor/in writer author

B

backen bake
Bad(ezimmer) bathroom

Bahnhof station
Bahnsteig platform
bald soon
bis bald bye for now
Ballon balloon
Banane banana
Bart beard
Bauarbeiter/in builder
Bauchschmerzen stomach ache
bauen build *(irr)*
Bauer/Bäuerin farmer
Bauernhof farm
Baum tree
(be)antworten answer
bedeckt cloudy
bedeuten mean *(irr)*
Bedienung waiter/waitress
sich beeilen hurry (up)
beenden finish; stop
jdn befragen question sb
begabt talented
begeistert excited
zu Beginn in the beginning
beginnen start; begin *(irr)*
(be)halten keep *(irr)*
behindert disabled
bei at; by
beibringen teach *(irr)*
beide(s) both
Bein leg
beinahe nearly, almost
beißen bite *(irr)*
Beispiel example
zum Beispiel for example
beitreten join
(be)kämpfen fight *(irr)*
bekommen get *(irr)*
beliebt popular
bellen bark
bemerken notice
Bemerkung comment
sich sehr bemühen, etw zu tun try hard to do sth
benutzen use
beobachten watch
bequem comfortable
bereit ready
Berg mountain
Bergsteigen climbing
Bericht report
sich beruhigen cool down
berühmt famous
berühren touch
beschäftigt busy
beschließen decide
(be)schützen protect
besondere(r, s) special
besorgt worried
besser better
bestellen order
beste(r, s) best
am besten best
besuchen visit
betrachten look at
Bett bed
beunruhigt worried
bevor before
bevorzugen prefer
sich bewegen move
Bewegung exercise
beweisen prove
bewölkt cloudy
(be)zahlen pay *(irr)*
bezaubernd charming
Bibliothek library
(an)bieten offer
Bild picture
Bilder machen take photos
(Aus)bildung education *(no pl)*
billig cheap
Biologie biology
bis to; until
(spätestens) bis (acht Uhr) by (eight o'clock)
bis (zu) up to
bis dann see you
ein bisschen a bit; a little
bitte please
bitten ask
Blatt leaf *(pl leaves)*
blau blue
bleiben stay
Bleistift pencil
(Bleistift)spitzer pencil sharpener
(Aus)blick view
blöd stupid
Blume flower
Bluse shirt
Boden floor
Bohne bean
Boot boat
brauchen need
braun brown
(zer)brechen break *(irr)*
breit wide
(ver)brennen burn *(irr)*
Brett board
Brettspiel board game
Brief letter
Briefmarke stamp
Brieftasche wallet
Briefumschlag envelope
Brille glasses *(only pl)*
bringen take *(irr)*
die Briten the British *(only pl)*
britische(r, s) British
Bronze bronze
Brot bread *(no pl)*
Brötchen bread roll
Brücke bridge
Bruder brother
brüllen roar
Buch book
Bücherei library
Bücherregal bookcase
Bücherschrank bookcase
Buchstabe letter
buchstabieren spell *(irr)*
bügeln iron
Bühne stage
Burg castle
Büro office
bürsten brush
Bushaltestelle bus stop

C

Campingplatz campsite
charmant charming
chatten chat
Chef/in boss
Chemie chemistry
Chinesisch Chinese

chinesisch Chinese
Chips crisps *(only pl) (BE)*
Cousin/e cousin
Creme cream
Curry(gericht) curry

D

da there
Dame lady
danach afterwards; after that; then
danke thanks; thank you
dann then
das the; that; this; who; which
dass that
dasselbe the same
Datum date
(Zimmer)decke ceiling
den Tisch decken set the table
dein(e) your
deine(r, s) yours
dekorieren decorate
denken think *(irr)*
(an etw) denken remember
deprimiert depressed
der the; that; who; which
derselbe the same
deshalb so; that's why
(Privat)detektiv/in detective
Deutsch German
deutsch German
Deutsche/r German
Deutschland Germany
Dezember December
dich you
die the; that; who; which
Dienstag Tuesday
diese these *(pl of* this*)*; those *(pl of* that*)*
diese(r, s) this
dieselbe the same
Ding thing
dir you
Direktor/in director
Donnerstag Thursday
Dorf village
dort there
dort (drüben) over there
downloaden download
Drache dragon
Draht wire
draußen outside
nach draußen outside
dreckig dirty
sich drehen turn
drinnen inside
dort (drüben) over there
drücken click
Dschungel jungle
du you
Duft smell
dumm stupid; silly
dunkel dark
Dunkelheit darkness
dünn thin; slim
durch through; by
durchdrehen go crazy *(informal)*
durchqueren cross
(durch)suchen search
dürfen may
etw tun dürfen be allowed to do sth
Dusche shower

E

echt real
Ecke corner
Ehefrau wife *(pl* wives*)*
Ehemann husband
ehrlich honest
Ei egg
eifersüchtig jealous
eigene(r, s) own
ein bisschen a bit; a little
ein(e) a/an; one
eines Tages one day
einfach easy; just
einige a few; some
einkaufen (gehen) do the shopping
einkaufen gehen go shopping
einladen invite
Einladung invitation
einmal once
auf einmal suddenly
noch (ein)mal again
einsam lonely
einschalten turn on
Einzelfahrkarte single (ticket)
einzige(r, s) only
Eisenbahn train
Eiskrem ice cream
Elefant elephant
Elektrizität electricity *(no pl)*
Ellbogen elbow
Eltern parents *(only pl)*
Ende end
enden end
endlich finally
Energie energy
eng narrow
Englisch English
englisch English
entdecken discover
Ente duck
(ent)fliehen escape
entkommen escape
(ent)leeren empty
(sich) entscheiden decide
Entschuldigung excuse
entsetzt shocked
sich entspannen relax
entspannt relaxed
enttäuscht disappointed; frustrated
entzündet sore
er he
Erbse pea
Erdbeere strawberry
Erde world
Erdkunde geography
Erfahrung experience
erfinden invent
Erfindung invention
Erfolg success *(no pl)*
erfolgreich successful
erforschen explore
Ergebnis result
erhalten get *(irr)*
erhitzen heat
sich erinnern (an) remember
Erkältung cold

erklären explain
erlaubt allowed
Erlebnis adventure; experience
(er)raten guess
erreichen reach
erschaffen create
erschrecken scare
erste(r, s) first
erstens first of all
ertragen stand
erwachsen werden grow up
jmd kann es kaum erwarten (, etw zu tun) sb cannot wait (to do sth)
erzählen tell *(irr)*
Erzählung story
es it
Essen food *(no pl)*; meal
essen eat *(irr)*; have *(irr)*
etwas something; any; some
(irgend) (et)was anything
euch you
euer your
eure your
eure(r, s) yours
Europa Europe
extrem extreme

F

Fabrik factory
(Schul)fach subject
Fahne flag
Fähre ferry
fahren drive *(irr)*; ride *(irr)*; go *(irr)*
Fahrer/in driver
Fahrkartenschalter ticket counter
Fahrplan timetable
(Fahr)rad bike
(Fahr)rad fahren ride a bike
Fahrt trip
Falle trap
fallen fall *(irr)*
fallen lassen drop
falls if
falsch wrong
Familie family
Familienname surname
fangen catch *(irr)*
fantastisch fantastic *(informal)*
Farbe colour
farbenfroh colourful
farbenprächtig colourful
fast nearly; almost
Februar February
Feder feather
(Feder)mäppchen pencil case
Fehler fault
Feier celebration
feiern celebrate
Fell fur
Fels(en) rock
Fenster window
Ferien holiday
Ferienlager summer camp
Fernsehen TV (= television)
fernsehen watch TV
Fernseher TV (= television)
Fernsehserie TV series *(only pl)*
fertig ready
Fest celebration; festival
(Fest)land land
festnehmen catch *(irr)*
Feuer fire
Feuerwehrmann/-frau firefighter
fies mean
Filzstift felt tip
finden find *(irr)*
Finsternis darkness
Fisch fish *(pl - or -es)*
fischen fish
flach flat
Flagge flag
Flasche bottle
Fleisch meat *(no pl)*
fleißig hard-working
(ent)fliehen escape
fliegen fly *(irr)*
Flucht escape
Flughafen airport
Flugzeug plane
Flur hall
Fluss river
flüstern whisper
Folge result
folgen follow
Foto photo; picture
fotografieren take photos
Frage question
fragen ask
Frankreich France
Französisch French
französisch French
Frau woman *(pl women)*; lady
Frau *(Anrede)* Mrs
frech naughty
frei free
im Freien outside
Freiheit freedom *(no pl)*
Freitag Friday
Freiwillige/r volunteer
sich auf etw freuen look forward to sth
Freund/in friend
(fester) Freund boyfriend
(feste) Freundin girlfriend
freundlich friendly; nice
frisch fresh
Friseur/in hairdresser
frisieren style
froh glad
fröhlich happy
Frucht fruit
früh early
Frühling spring
Frühstück breakfast
Frühstückspause morning break
frustriert frustrated
(sich) fühlen feel *(irr)*
funktionieren work
für for
Furcht erregend scary
furchtbar terrible
sich fürchten (vor) be frightened (of)
Fuß foot *(pl feet)*
zu Fuß on foot
(zu Fuß) gehen walk

Fußball football
füttern feed *(irr)*

G

Gabel fork
ganz whole; completely; altogether
Garten garden
Gärtner/in gardener
Gast guest
Gaststätte pub
Gebäude building
geben give *(irr)*
Gebiet area
geboren born
Geburtsdatum date of birth
Geburtstag birthday
Gefahr danger
gefährlich dangerous
Gefangene/r prisoner
Gefühl feeling
gegen against
Gegend area
Gegenstand thing
gegenüber(liegend) opposite
geheim secret
gehen go *(irr)*
(hinaus)gehen go out
(zu Fuß) gehen walk
jdm/zu etw gehören belong to sb/sth
Geist ghost
gelangweilt bored
gelassen relaxed
gelb yellow
Geld money *(no pl)*
Geld verdienen make money
Geldautomat cash machine
gemein mean
gemeinsam together
Gemüse vegetable
(genau)so ... wie ... as ... as
Genesungskarte get well card
genießen enjoy
genug enough
genügend enough
geöffnet open
Geografie geography
gerade just
gerade(aus) straight (on)
Geräusch sound; noise
Gericht dish *(pl -es)*
sehr gern mögen love
Geruch smell
gesamt whole
Gesamtschule comprehensive school
Geschäft shop
geschehen happen
gescheit clever
Geschenk present
Geschichte history; story
Geschirrspülmaschine dishwasher
Geschwister brothers and sisters
Gesicht face
Gespenst ghost
gestalten create
Gestank smell
gestern yesterday
gesund healthy
gesund werden get well
Gesundheit health *(no pl)*
Getränk drink
Gewinn prize
gewinnen win *(irr)*
Gewinner/in winner
gewöhnlich usually
Gewürz spice
gießen water
Gipfel top
Gitarre guitar
Glas glass
glauben think *(irr)*
glauben (an) believe (in)
gleich in a minute; just
Gleis platform
Glück luck *(no pl)*
Glück haben be lucky
glücklich glad; lucky; happy
Glücks- lucky
glücksbringend lucky
Glühbirne light bulb
Goldfisch goldfish *(pl -)*
Gott god
Gras grass *(no pl)*
gratis for free
grau grey
Griechenland Greece
grillen have a barbecue
groß large; big; great; tall
großartig great
Großbritannien Great Britain
Größe size
Großeltern grandparents *(only pl)*
Großmutter grandmother
(Groß)stadt city
ein Großteil most (of)
Großvater grandfather
grün green
Grundschule primary school
Gruppe group
(Salat)gurke cucumber
gut good; well; fine
gut aussehend good-looking
gut in etw sein be good at sth
etw gut können be good at sth

H

Haar(e) hair *(no pl)*
haben have got *(irr)*; have *(irr)*
Hähnchen chicken
halb half
halb (neun) half past (eight)
Hälfte half *(pl halves)*
Halle hall
halten hold *(irr)*
(be)halten keep *(irr)*
Handschuh glove
Handtuch towel
Handy mobile (= mobile phone)
(auf)hängen hang *(irr)*
hart hard
hassen hate
hässlich ugly
häufig often
Haus house
Hausaufgaben homework *(no pl)*

nach Hause home
zu Hause (at) home
Haustier pet
Heft exercise book
heftig powerful
Heiligabend Christmas Eve
Heim home
Heimatort home town
heiraten get married; marry
heiß hot
heißen be called
Held/in hero *(pl -es)*
helfen help
Helm helmet
Hemd shirt
(her)aus out of
herausnehmen take out
Herbst autumn
hereinkommen come in
Herr *(Anrede)* Mr
herum around
herunterladen download
hervorragend brilliant *(informal)*
Herz heart
heute today
heute Abend tonight
heute Nacht tonight
heute Morgen this morning
heute Nachmittag this afternoon
hier(her) here
Hilfe help
hilfreich helpful
hilfsbereit helpful
Hin- und Rückfahrkarte return (ticket)
hinab down
(hinauf)klettern climb
(hinauf)steigen climb
hinausbringen take out
(hinaus)gehen go out
hinfallen fall down
hinter behind
hinüber over
hinunter down
hinzufügen add
hoch high; tall
Hochzeit wedding
hoffen hope
höflich polite
Höhepunkt highlight
Höhle cave
holen get *(irr)*
Honig honey *(no pl)*
hören hear *(irr)*
(zu)hören listen (to)
Horoskop horoscope
Hose trousers *(only pl)*
hübsch pretty; lovely
Hügel hill
Huhn chicken
Hund dog
hungrig hungry
Hut hat

I

ich I
Idee idea
ihm him
ihn him
ihnen them
Ihnen you
ihr her; you
ihr(e) their; her; its
Ihr(e) your
ihr(e, n) her
Ihre(r, s) yours
im on
im Freien outside
im Moment at the moment
immer always
(immer) noch still
in in; into; at; on; to
in Ordnung fine
indianisch Indian
Indien India
indisch Indian
Informatik ICT (= information and communication technology)
Information information *(no pl)*
innen inside
Insekt insect
Insel island
Inserat advert (= advertisement)
insgesamt altogether
interessant interesting
interessiert (an etw) interested (in sth)
irgendein(e) any
(irgend)(et)was anything
irgendwelche any
irgendwo somewhere
Irisch Irish
irisch Irish
Irland Ireland
Italien Italy
Italienisch Italian
italienisch Italian

J

ja yes
Jacke jacket
Jäger/in hunter
Jahr year
pro/im Jahr a year
Jahrhundert century
Januar January
jede(r) everyone; everybody
jede(r, s) every; each
jemals ever
jemand somebody; someone
jene those *(pl of that)*
jetzt now
Joghurt yoghurt *(no pl)*
Jongleur/in juggler
jubeln cheer
Jugendzentrum youth club
Juli July
jung young
Junge boy
Juni June

K

Kabel wire
Käfig cage
Kalender calendar
kalt cold
Kälte cold
Kamin chimney
(be)kämpfen fight *(irr)*

Kämpfer(in) fighter
Känguru kangaroo
Kaninchen rabbit
Kapitän/in captain
Kappe cap
kaputt broken
Karikatur cartoon
Karneval carnival
Karotte carrot
Karriere career
Karte card
(Land)karte map
Kartoffel potato *(pl -es)*
Karton card
Käse cheese *(no pl)*
Katze cat
kauen chew
kaufen buy *(irr)*
Kaufhaus department store
Kaugummi (chewing) gum *(no pl)*
kein(e) no; not any
keiner no one
Kellner/in waiter/waitress
kennen know *(irr)*
(sich) kennenlernen meet *(irr)*
Kerze candle
Kilometer kilometre
Kind child *(pl* children*)*
Kinn chin
Kino cinema
Kirche church
Kissen cushion
Klang sound
(Schul)klasse class
Klassenarbeit test
Klassenkamerad/in classmate
Klassenzimmer classroom
klauen steal
Klavier piano
Kleid dress
Kleider clothes *(only pl)*
Kleiderschrank wardrobe
Kleidung clothes *(only pl)*
klein small; little
Kletter- climbing
Klettern climbing
(hinauf)klettern climb
(an)klicken click
klingeln ring *(irr)*
klingen sound
Klo toilet
Klub club
klug clever
Kneipe pub
Knie knee
Knochen bone
Koch/Köchin cook
kochen do the cooking; cook
Koffer suitcase
Kollege/Kollegin colleague
komisch strange; funny
kommen come *(irr)*
Kommentar comment
Komödie comedy
König king
Königin queen
können can; may
etw gut können be good at sth
etw tun können be able to do sth
könnte(st, n, t) could
kontrollieren check
sich konzentrieren concentrate
Konzert concert
Kopf head
Korb basket
Körper body
korrekt correct
kosten cost *(irr)*
köstlich delicious
Kostüm costume
Krach noise
Kraft energy
krank ill
Krankenhaus hospital
(Kranken)pfleger nurse
(Kranken)schwester nurse
Krawatte tie
kreativ creative
Kreis circle
kreischen scream
Krimi thriller
Kriminelle/r criminal
Krokodil crocodile
Krone crown
Küche kitchen
Kuchen cake
Kuh cow
Kühlschrank fridge *(informal)*
sich kümmern um look after; take care of
Kunde/Kundin customer
Kunst art
Kunststoff plastic
Kurs course
kurz short
Kuss kiss
küssen kiss
Küste coast
Kuvert envelope

L

lächeln smile
lachen laugh
Laden shop
Lamm lamb
Lampe lamp
Land country
(Fest)land land
landen land
(Land)karte map
(Land)schildkröte tortoise
lang long
langsam slow
langweilig boring
Lärm noise
lassen let *(irr)*; leave *(irr)*
laufen run *(irr)*; walk
Laufen running
Läufer/in runner
laut loud; noisy
läuten ring *(irr)*
Leben life *(pl* lives*)*
leben live
lecker delicious; yummy *(informal)*
(ent)leeren empty
legen put *(irr)*
Lehnstuhl armchair
Lehrer/in teacher

leicht easy
leider unfortunately
leise quiet
Leiter/in director
Leitung wire
lernen learn *(irr)*; study
lesen read *(irr)*
letzte(r, s) last
Leute people *(no pl)*
Licht light
Liebe love
lieben love
lieber better
lieber mögen prefer
Lieblings- favourite
am liebsten best
lila(farben) purple
Limonade lemonade
Lineal ruler
links on the/your left
(nach) links left
Liste list
Loch hole
locker relaxed
Löffel spoon
Löwe lion
Luft air *(no pl)*
lustig funny; fun
sich über jdn lustig machen make fun of sb

M

machen make *(irr)*; do *(irr)*
mächtig powerful
Mädchen girl
Magazin magazine
Magenschmerzen stomach ache
Magie magic *(no pl)*
mähen mow *(irr)*
Mahlzeit meal
Mai May
Mal time
(an)malen paint
manchmal sometimes
Mann man *(pl men)*
(Feder)mäppchen pencil case
Mappe folder
Markt market
Marmelade jam
März March
Maschine machine
Mathe maths
Maus mouse *(pl mice)*
Medaille medal
Medikament(e) medicine *(no pl)*
Medizin medicine *(no pl)*
Meer ocean
das Meer the sea *(no pl)*
Meerschweinchen guinea pig
Mehl flour *(no pl)*
mehr better
(noch) mehr more
Meile mile
mein(e) my
meinen mean *(irr)*; think *(irr)*
Meinung opinion
das meiste (von) most (of)
am meisten most; best
die meisten most
(Menschen)menge crowd
jede Menge lots of
Mensch person
Menschen people *(no pl)*
(Menschen)menge crowd
Messer knife *(pl knives)*
Metall metal
Meter metre
mich me
Mikrowelle(nherd) microwave
Milch milk
Milchshake milkshake
mindestens at least
Minirock miniskirt
Minute minute
mir me
(ver)mischen mix
mit with; by
Mitarbeiter/in colleague
(mit)bringen bring *(irr)*
Mitglied member
Mitleid mit jdm haben feel sorry for sb
mitmachen bei join
(mit)nehmen take *(irr)*
Mitschüler/in classmate
Mittagessen lunch; dinner
Mittagspause lunchtime
Mittagszeit lunchtime
Mitte middle
Mittwoch Wednesday
mobben bully
Mobbing bullying *(no pl)*
Mobiltelefon mobile (= mobile phone)
jmd möchte (gern) sb would like (to)
jmd möchte sehr gern sb would love (to)
mögen like; enjoy
lieber mögen prefer
sehr gern mögen love
möglicherweise maybe
Möglichkeit chance
Möhre carrot
Mohrrübe carrot
Moment moment
Monat month
Mond moon
Mondlicht moonlight
Montag Monday
morgen tomorrow
Morgen morning
am Morgen in the morning
heute Morgen this morning
morgens in the morning; am (= ante meridiem) *(nur hinter Uhrzeit)*
Motorrad motorbike
müde tired
Müll rubbish *(no pl)*
Mülleimer bin
Mülltonne bin
München Munich
Mund mouth
Musik music
Muskel muscle
Müsli muesli *(no pl)*
müssen have to; must
müsste should
mutig brave
Mutter mother
Mütze hat

N

nach after; to
nach dem Weg fragen ask for directions
nach Hause home
(nach) links left
(nach) oben upstairs
(nach) rechts right
(nach) unten down
Nachbar/in neighbour
nachdem after
Nachmittag afternoon
am Nachmittag in the afternoon
heute Nachmittag this afternoon
nachmittags in the afternoon; pm (= post meridiem) *(nur hinter Uhrzeit)*
Nachname surname
Nachricht message
Nachrichten news
nächste(r, s) next
Nacht night
heute Nacht tonight
über Nacht bleiben sleep over
Nachtisch dessert
nachts at night
nah(e) near
in der Nähe by
Name name
Nase nose
nass wet
Natur nature
natürlich of course
(Natur)wissenschaft science
Nebel fog
neben next to
neblig foggy
negativ negative
(mit)nehmen take *(irr)*
nein no
nennen call
nett nice
neu new
Neuigkeit news
Neujahr New Year
Neuseeland New Zealand
nicht not
nicht dürfen must not; may not
nicht mehr not anymore
nichts nothing; not anything
nie(mals) never
niedlich cute
niemand no one
Nilpferd hippo (= hippopotamus)
(immer) noch, noch immer still
noch ein(e, r, s) another
noch (ein)mal again
(noch) mehr more
noch nicht not yet
Nord- north
Norden north
Nordirland Northern Ireland
nördlich north
normalerweise normally; usually
(Schul)note mark
(sich) Notizen machen take notes
November November
Nudeln pasta *(no pl)*
Nummer number
nun (ja) well
nur only; just
nützlich helpful

O

oben at the top (of)
(nach) oben upstairs
oberes Ende top
Obst fruit
oder or
offen open
(sich) öffnen open
oft often
ohne without
Ohr ear
Ohrring earring
Oktober October
Öl oil
Olympische Spiele Olympic Games
Oma grandma *(informal)*
Omi grandma *(informal)*
Onkel uncle
optimistisch optimistic
Orange orange
orange(farben) orange
in Ordnung fine
Ort place
Osten east
Osterfest Easter
Ostern Easter
Ozean ocean

P

Paar pair
packen pack
Paket package
Palast palace
Panik panic
Papagei parrot
Papier paper *(no pl)*
Pappe card
Parade parade
Parfüm perfume
Patient/in patient
passieren happen
Pause break
der Pazifische Ozean the Pacific (Ocean)
peinlich berührt embarrassed
Pelz fur
Penny p (= penny, pence)
perfekt perfect
Person person
Pfeffer pepper
Pferd horse
Pflanze plant
(Kranken)pfleger/in nurse
Pfote paw
Pfund *(brit. Währung)* pound
Pilot/in pilot
Pilz mushroom
Pinguin penguin
Pirat pirate
Plastik plastic
platt flat
Plattform platform
Platz place

plötzlich suddenly
Polen Poland
Polizei police
Polizeibeamter/-beamtin police officer
Pommes frites chips *(only pl) (BE)*
Portemonnaie wallet
Postkarte postcard
Preis price; prize
preiswert cheap
(Privat)detektiv/in detective
pro/am Tag a day
pro/im Jahr a year
pro/in der Woche a week
(aus)probieren try
Programm programme
prüfen test
Prüfung test
Punkt point
Pute/r turkey
putzen clean; brush

Q

Qualität quality

R

Rabauke bully
Rad wheel
(Fahr)rad bike
(Fahr)rad fahren ride a bike, cycle
Radfahren cycling
Radfahrer/in cyclist
Radiergummi rubber *(BE)*
Radiosender radio station
Rasen lawn; grass *(no pl)*
(er)raten guess
Ratte rat
Raumschiff spaceship
raus outside
(Taschen)rechner calculator
Rechnung bill
Recht haben be right
rechts on the/your right
(nach) rechts right
reden speak *(irr)*
reden (mit) talk (to)
Regal shelf *(pl shelves)*
Regel rule
Regen rain
Regenbogen rainbow
Regenwald rainforest
Region area
regnen rain
regnerisch rainy
reich rich
Reihe queue
reinigen clean
Reis rice
Reise trip
reisen travel
Reisende/r traveller
Reißverschluss zip
reiten ride *(irr)*
Reiten riding
Rektor/in headteacher
Religion(sunterricht) RE (= religious education)
rennen run *(irr)*
Rennen race; running
reparieren repair
Reservierung reservation
Respekt respect *(no pl)*
retten save; rescue
Rezept recipe
Rhythmus rhythm
richtig right; true; correct
Richtung direction
riechen (nach) smell (of)
Riese giant
riesengroß huge
riesig huge; great
Roboter robot
Rock skirt
rollen roll
Rollstuhl wheelchair
Rolltreppe escalator
rosa pink
rot red
Rücken back
Rückenschmerzen backache
Hin- und Rückfahrkarte return (ticket)
Rückseite back
rufen shout
ruhig quiet
Rüpel bully
Russe/Russin Russian
Russisch Russian
russisch Russian
Russland Russia

S

Saal hall
Sache thing
Saft juice
sagen say *(irr)*; tell *(irr)*
Sahne cream
Salat salad
(Salat)gurke cucumber
Salbe cream
Salz salt
sammeln collect
Samstag Saturday
Sänger/in singer
Sarg coffin
Satz sentence
sauber clean
sauber machen clean
Schach(spiel) chess *(no pl)*
Schaf sheep *(pl -)*
es schaffen manage
Schal scarf *(pl -s or* scarves*)*
scharf hot
Schatten shadow
schätzen guess
schauen look
schaurig spooky *(informal)*
Schauspieler/in actor/actress
Schauspielerei drama
Schere (pair of) scissors *(only pl)*
Scheune barn
(zu)schicken send *(irr)*
Schiedsrichter/in referee
ein Tor schießen score a goal
Schiff ship; boat
(Straßen)schild sign
(Verkehrs)schild sign
Schildkröte turtle
(Land)schildkröte tortoise
Schinken ham
schlafen sleep *(irr)*

Schlafzimmer bedroom
schlagen hit *(irr)*
Schlange snake; queue
schlank slim
schlau clever
schlecht bad
schlechter worse
schlechteste(r, s) worst
schließen close
schließlich finally
schlimm bad
schlimmer worse
schlimmste(r, s) worst
Schloss castle
zum Schluss finally
Schlüssel key
schmal narrow; slim
schmecken taste
schmerzen hurt *(irr)*
sich schminken put on make-up
schmücken decorate
schmutzig dirty
Schnee snow
schneereich snowy
schneiden cut *(irr)*
schnell fast; quick
Schnellhefter folder
Schnupfen cold
schockiert shocked
Schokolade chocolate *(no pl)*
schon already
schön beautiful; nice; lovely
Schornstein chimney
schottisch Scottish
Schottland Scotland
Schrank cupboard
schrecklich horrible; terrible
schreiben write *(irr)*
Schreibtisch desk
schreien shout; scream; cry
Schriftsteller/in writer; author
Schuh shoe
Schuld fault
Schule school
Schüler/in student
(Schul)fach subject
(Schul)klasse class
Schulleiter/in headteacher
(Schul)note mark
Schultasche schoolbag
Schulter shoulder
(be)schützen protect
schwanger pregnant
Schwanz tail
schwarz black
Schwein pig
schwer heavy; hard; difficult
Schwester sister
(Kranken)schwester nurse
schwierig difficult
Schwierigkeiten trouble *(no pl)*
Schwierigkeiten bekommen get into trouble
Schwimmbad swimming pool
Schwimmbecken swimming pool
Schwimmen swimming
schwimmen swim *(irr)*
Schwimmer/in swimmer
See lake
die See the sea *(no pl)*
Seeräuber pirate
Segel sail
segeln sail
sehen see *(irr)*; look (at)
Sehenswürdigkeit sight
sehr very; a lot; much
viel(e) a lot (of)
Seife soap *(no pl)*
Seifenoper soap (opera)
Seil rope
sein be *(irr)*
sein(e) its
sein(e, r) his
seit since
Seite side; page
Sekretär/in secretary
Sekunde second
selbst even
selbstbewusst self-confident
selbstsicher self-confident
Sendung programme
September September
Sessel armchair
setzen put *(irr)*
sicher sure; safe
sichern save
Sicht view
sie she; they; her; them
Sie you
Sieger/in winner
silbern silver
Silvester New Year's Eve
singen sing *(irr)*
sitzen sit *(irr)*
SMS text message
so so
(genau)so ... wie ... as ... as
Socke sock
Sofa couch
sofort in a minute
sogar even
Sohn son
sollte should
Sommer summer
Sonderangebot special offer
sonderbar strange
Sonne sun
Sonnenaufgang sunrise
Sonnenbrille sunglasses
Sonnenschein sunshine
sonnig sunny
Sonntag Sunday
sich Sorgen machen worry
sorgfältig careful
Sorte sort; kind; type
Soße sauce
Spanien Spain
Spanisch Spanish
spanisch Spanish
spannend exciting
Spaß fun *(no pl)*
(viel) Spaß machen be (great) fun
spaßig fun
(zu) spät late
(zu) spät kommen be late
später afterwards; later
spazieren gehen go for a walk
Spaziergang walk
speichern save

Speisekarte menu
speziell special
Spiegel mirror
Spiel game; match; play
spielen play
Spieler/in player
Spielfeld sports field
Spielplatz playground
Spielzeug toy
Spinne spider
Spitze top
Spitzen- top
(Bleistift)spitzer pencil sharpener
Sport sports
Sportart sports
Sporthalle sports hall
Sportler/in sportsperson
Sportplatz sports ground, sports field
Sport(unterricht) PE (= physical education)
Sprache language
sprechen speak *(irr)*; talk (to)
springen jump
spucken spit *(irr)*
Stadion stadium
Stadt town
(Groß)stadt city
(Vieh)stall barn
(Verkaufs)stand stall
stark strong; powerful
Station station
(an)statt instead (of)
stattdessen instead (of)
stattfinden take place
staubsaugen hoover
stehen stand *(irr)*
stehlen steal *(irr)*
(hinauf)steigen climb
Stein stone; rock
stellen put *(irr)*
sterben die
(Stereo)anlage stereo
Stern star
Sternzeichen star sign
Stift pen
Stimme voice
Stock stick
Stockwerk floor
stolz (auf jmd) proud (of sb)
jdn stoßen knock sb
stoßen (gegen) hit *(irr)*
Strand beach
Straße street; road
streicheln pet
Streichholz match
streng strict
Strom electricity *(no pl)*
Student/in student
studieren study
Stück piece
(Theater)stück play
Stuhl chair
Stunde lesson; hour
Stundenplan timetable
Sturm storm
stürzen crash
suchen (nach) look for
(durch)suchen search
Südafrika South Africa
Süden south
Supermarkt supermarket
Suppe soup
süß sweet; cute
Süßigkeit sweet

T

Tafel board
Tag day
pro/am Tag a day
Tagebuch diary
eines Tages one day
Takt rhythm
Tal valley
talentiert talented
Tante aunt
Tanz dance
Tanzen dancing
tanzen dance
Tänzer/in dancer
Tasche bag; pocket
Taschendieb/in pickpocket
Taschengeld pocket money *(no pl)*
(Taschen)rechner calculator
Tasse cup
Tatze paw
Techniker/in technician
Tee tea
sich teilen split up
teilnehmen (an) take part (in)
Telefon (tele)phone
(Telefon)anruf (phone) call
Telefonzelle telephone box
Teller plate
Tempel temple
Teppich carpet
testen test
teuer expensive
Teufel devil
(Theater)stück play
Thema subject
die Themse the (River) Thames
Tier animal
Tierarzt/-ärztin vet (= veterinarian)
Tierpfleger/in keeper
Tipp tip
Tisch table
den Tisch decken set the table
Tischtennis table tennis
Titel title
tja well
Tochter daughter
Toilette toilet
toll brilliant *(informal)*; amazing *(informal)*
Tomate tomato *(pl -es)*
Ton sound
Tor goal
ein Tor schießen score a goal
Tormann/Torfrau goalkeeper
tot dead
töten kill
Tracht costume
traditionell traditional
tragen wear *(irr)* *(Kleidung)*; carry
Trainer(in) coach
trainieren train
Traktor tractor
Träne tear
tränen water

Traum dream
traurig sad
treffen hit *(irr)*
(sich) treffen meet *(irr)*
sich trennen split up
Treppe stairs *(only pl)*
trinken drink *(irr)*
Trommel drum
Truthahn/-henne turkey
tschüss bye *(informal)*
tun do *(irr)*
Türkei Turkey
Türkisch Turkish
türkisch Turkish
Türklingel doorbell
Turm tower
Turnhalle gym (= gymnasium)
Typ type
tyrannisieren bully

U

U-Bahn underground
üben practise
über about; over; across
überall everywhere
überleben survive
übernachten sleep over
überprüfen check
überqueren cross
überrascht surprised
Überraschung surprise
übrig left
Übung exercise
Uhr clock
(sieben) Uhr (seven) o'clock
(Armband)uhr watch
(Uhr)zeit time
um at *(Uhrzeit)*; around
(sich) umdrehen turn round
umher around
umsonst for free
umziehen move
Umzug parade
und and
unerschrocken brave
Unfall accident
unfreundlich unfriendly
ungefähr about
ungesund unhealthy
ungezogen naughty
unglaublich incredible; amazing *(informal)*
unglücklich unhappy
unglücklicherweise unfortunately
unheimlich scary; spooky *(informal)*
Universum universe
uns us
unser(e) our
unten at the bottom (of)
(nach) unten down
unter under
untergebracht sein stay
sich unterhalten chat
sich unterhalten (mit) talk (to)
unterrichten teach *(irr)*
Unterschied difference
unterschiedlich different
Unterschrift signature
untersuchen explore
Urlaub holiday
Urlaub machen go on holiday
in den Urlaub fahren go on holiday
Urwald jungle

V

Vater father
Vegetarier/in vegetarian
vegetarisch vegetarian
(sich) (ver)ändern change
(Ver)änderung change
verärgert angry
Verband bandage
Verbrecher/in criminal
(ver)brennen burn *(irr)*
verbringen *(Zeit)* spend *(irr)*
verdienen earn
Geld verdienen make money
Verein club
Vereinigtes Königreich UK (= United Kingdom)
vergessen forget *(irr)*
Verkäufer/in shop assistant; seller
verkaufen sell *(irr)*
(Verkaufs)stand stall
(Verkehrs)schild sign
sich verkleiden (als) dress up (as)
verlassen leave *(irr)*
verlegen embarrassed
jdn verletzen hurt sb
verletzt injured
Verletzung injury
verlieren lose *(irr)*
(ver)mischen mix
vermissen miss
vermuten guess
verpassen miss
verrückt crazy
verschieden different
verschneit snowy
versorgen take care of
sich verspäten be late
versprechen promise
(sich) verstecken hide *(irr)*
verstehen understand *(irr)*
versuchen try
Verwandte(r) relative
verwechseln mix up
(Vieh)stall barn
(viel) Spaß machen be (great) fun
viel lots of; much
viel(e) a lot (of)
viele many
vielleicht perhaps; maybe
Viertel area
Viertel (vor/nach) quarter (to/past)
violett purple
Vogel bird
voll full; packed
völlig completely; altogether
von of; by; from
vor before; in front of
vor (drei Tagen) (three days) ago
vorbei over
vorbei an past

vorbeifahren pass by
vorbeigehen pass by
(sich) vorbereiten prepare
Vorhang curtain
vormittags in the morning; am (= ante meridiem) *(nur hinter Uhrzeit)*
Vorname first name
vorsichtig careful
vorüber an past
vorziehen prefer
Vulkan volcano *(pl -oes or -os)*

W

wach bleiben stay up
Waffe weapon
wahr true
während during; while
wahrscheinlich probably
Wald forest
Walisisch Welsh
walisisch Welsh
Wand wall
Wandern hiking
wann when
Warnung warning
warten (auf) wait (for)
warum why
was what
(irgend)(et)was anything
(sich) waschen wash
Wasser water
Wasserhahn tap
Wasserkocher kettle
Wechselgeld change
wechseln change
Wecker alarm clock
weg away
Weg way
den Weg beschreiben give directions
nach dem Weg fragen ask for directions
wehtun hurt *(irr)*
jdm wehtun hurt sb
weich soft
Weihnachten Christmas
erster Weihnachtsfeiertag Christmas Day
Weihnachtsmann Father Christmas
weil because
weinen cry
weiß white
weit far
welche(r, s) what; which
Welle wave
Wellensittich budgie (= budgerigar)
Welt world
wenige few
wenigstens at least
wenn when; if
wer who
werden become *(irr)*; get *(irr)*; will; going to
werfen throw *(irr)*
Werk factory
Westen west
Wettbewerb competition
Wetter weather
wichtig important
widerlich disgusting
wie how; like
(genau)so ... wie ... as ... as
wieder again
wiederholen repeat
Wiese grass
willkommen (in) welcome (to)
windig windy
Windpocken chickenpox *(no pl)*
winken wave
wir we
wirklich really
wirklich real
wissen know *(irr)*
(Natur)wissenschaft science
witzig funny; fun
Woche week
pro/in der Woche a week
Wochenende weekend
am Wochenende at the weekend
wo(hin) where
wohnen live; stay
Wohnung flat, apartment
Wohnwagen caravan
Wohnzimmer living room
wollen want
etw tun wollen want to do sth
Wort word
Wörterbuch dictionary
wund sore
wunderbar wonderful; fantastic *(informal)*; great
wundervoll wonderful
(sich) wünschen wish
würde(st, n, t) would
Wurst sausage
Würstchen sausage
wütend angry

Z

Zahl number
(be)zahlen pay *(irr)*
Zahn tooth *(pl teeth)*
Zahnbürste toothbrush
Zauber magic
Zauberer/Zauberin magician
Zeichen sign
Zeichentrickfilm cartoon
zeichnen draw *(irr)*
zeigen show *(irr)*
(Uhr)zeit time
zeitig early
Zeitschrift magazine
Zeitung newspaper
Zeltplatz campsite
Zentrum centre
(zer)brechen break *(irr)*
zerbrochen broken
zerstören destroy
Ziege goat
ziehen pull
ziemlich quite
Ziffer number
Zimmer room
(Zimmer)decke ceiling
zornig angry
zu to; too
zu Fuß on foot

(zu Fuß) gehen walk
zu Hause at home
(zu) spät late
(zu) spät kommen be late
Zucker sugar
zuerst (at) first
zufrieden happy
Zug train
Zuhause home
(zu)hören listen (to)
Zukunft future
zumachen close
zum Beispiel for example
Zündholz match
zurück back
zurückkehren return
zusammen together
Zuschauermenge crowd
(zu)schicken send *(irr)*
zusehen watch
(jdm) zustimmen agree (with sb)
zuversichtlich optimistic
zweimal twice
zweite(r, s) second
Zwiebel onion
Zwilling twin
Zwillings- twin
zwischen between

Girls/Women

Anna /ˈænə/
Barbara /ˈbɑːbrə/
Caitlin /ˈkeɪtlɪn/
Caroline /ˈkærəlaɪn/
Cheryl /ˈtʃerəl/
Daisy /ˈdeɪzi/
Ella /ˈelə/
Fiona /fiˈəʊnə/
Gill /gɪl/
Gillian /ˈdʒɪliən/
Gina /ˈdʒiːnə/
Gloria /ˈglɔːriə/
Gwen /gwen/
Jessica /ˈdʒesɪkə/
Karen /ˈkærən/
Karla /ˈkɑːlə/
Katie /ˈkeɪti/
Lena /ˈliːnə/
Lilly /ˈlɪli/
Pam /pæm/
Patty /ˈpæti/
Paula /ˈpɔːlə/
Penny /ˈpeni/
Ronda /ˈrɒndə/
Safia /ˈsɑːfiə/
Sally /ˈsæli/
Sarah /ˈseərə/
Sharon /ˈʃærən/
Sheila /ˈʃiːlə/
Shima /ˈʃiːmə/
Sue /suː/
Susan /ˈsuːzn/
Telisha /təˈliːʃə/

Boys/Men

Adam /ˈædəm/
Alex /ˈælɪks/
Amar /əˈmɑː/
Andrew /ˈændruː/
Arthur /ˈɑːθə/
Ben /ben/
Bill /bɪl/
Brian /ˈbraɪən/
Charlie /ˈtʃɑːli/
Chuck /tʃʌk/
Ciaran /ˈkɪərən/
Daniel /ˈdænjəl/
Dave /deɪv/
George /dʒɔːdʒ/
Henry /ˈhenri/
Jack /dʒæk/
Jason /ˈdʒeɪsən/
Jeff /dʒef/
Joe /dʒəʊ/
John /dʒɒn/
Josh /dʒɒʃ/
Kay /keɪ/
Leroy /ˈliːrɔɪ/
Liam /ˈliːəm/
Marcus /ˈmɑːkəs/
Mark /mɑːk/
Michael /ˈmaɪkəl/
Nick /nɪk/
Oliver /ˈɒlɪvə/
Peter /ˈpiːtə/
Rajiv /rɑːˈdʒiːv/
Robert /ˈrɒbət/
Roger /ˈrɒdʒə/
Sunit /ˈsʊnit/
Taylor /ˈteɪlə/
Thomas /ˈtɒməs/
Tim /tɪm/
Tom /tɒm/
Tommy /ˈtɒmi/
Wilson /ˈwɪlsən/
Yusuf /ˈjʊsʊf/

Families

Baker /ˈbeɪkə/
Batson /ˈbætsən/
Bell /bel/
Chang /tʃæŋ/
Collins /ˈkɒlɪnz/
Davis /ˈdeɪvɪs/
Dickins /ˈdɪkɪnz/
Dixon /ˈdɪksən/
Donalds /ˈdɒnəldz/
Edwards /ˈedwədz/
Fallon /ˈfælən/
Haffner /ˈhæfnə/
Harley /ˈhɑːli/
Harmer /ˈhɑːmə/
Henry /ˈhenri/
Hill /hɪl/
Hull /hʌl/
Jackson /ˈdʒæksən/
Killmouskey /kɪlˈmaʊski/
Knight /naɪt/
Kumalo /ˌkʊˈmɑːləʊ/
Lambraki /læmˈbrɑːki/
Monkhouse /ˈmʌŋkhaʊs/
Murphy /ˈmɜːfi/
Nandi /ˈnændi/
Noland /ˈnəʊlənd/
Patel /pəˈtel/
Perry /ˈperi/
Pritchett /ˈprɪtʃɪt/
Scott /skɒt/
Taylor /ˈteɪlə/
Thompson /ˈtɒmpsən/
Waterman /ˈwɔːtəmən/
West /west/

Other Names

Adele /əˈdel/
Alexander Graham Bell
/ˌælɪgˌzɑːndə ˌgreɪəm ˈbel/
Amphicar /ˌæmpfikɑː/
Amy Winehouse
/ˌeɪmi ˈwaɪnhaʊs/
André Garnerin
/ˌɒndreɪ ˌgɑːnərˈæn/
Apollo 10 /əˌpɒləʊ ˈten/
Arsenal /ˈɑːsnl/
Arthur's Seat /ˌɑːθəz ˈsiːt/
BBC (= British Broadcasting Corporation) /ˌbiː biː ˈsiː, ˌbrɪtɪʃ ˈbrɔːdkɑːstɪŋ ˌkɔːpəˌreɪʃn/
Bengal Tiger
/ˌbenˌgɔːl ˈtaɪgə/
Boom Trader /ˈbuːm ˌtreɪdə/
the British Heart Foundation
/ðə ˌbrɪtɪʃ ˈhɑːt faʊnˌdeɪʃn/
Buckingham Palace
/ˌbʌkɪŋəm ˈpælɪs/
Burger Queen /ˈbɜːgə kwiːn/
Camden Chronicle
/ˌkæmdən ˈkrɒnɪkl/
Camden Market
/ˌkæmdən ˈmɑːkɪt/
the Canal Café
/ðə kəˌnæl ˈkæfeɪ/

the Children's Trust
/ðə ˌtʃɪldrənz ˈtrʌst/
Christy Brown /ˌkrɪsti ˈbraʊn/
Cliff Richard /ˌklɪf ˈrɪtʃəd/
Daniel Defoe /ˌdænjəl diˈfəʊ/
Ed Sheeran /ed ˈʃiːrən/
Eugene Meyer /ˌjuːdʒiːn ˈmaɪə/
Foucault /fuːˈkəʊ/
Harry Potter /ˌhæri ˈpɒtə/
Haverstock /ˈhævəstɒk/
Haverstock School
/ˈhævəstɒk skuːl/
Hendon School
/ˈhendən skuːl/
Henry Ford /ˌhenri ˈfɔːd/
the Highland Games
/ðə ˈhaɪlənd geɪmz/
Hotel Alexandra
/həʊˌtel ˌælɪgˈzɑːndrə/
J.K. Rowling /ˌdʒeɪ keɪ ˈrəʊlɪŋ/
James Chalmer
/ˌdʒeɪmz ˈtʃɑːmə/
James Watt /ˌdʒeɪmz ˈwɒt/
Jessie J /ˌdʒesi ˈdʒeɪ/
John Eckert /ˌdʒɒn‿ˈekət/
John Kemp Starley
/ˌdʒɒn kemp ˈstɑːli/
John Mauchly /ˌdʒɒn ˈmɔːtʃli/
John Walker /ˌdʒɒn ˈwɔːkə/
Josephine Cochrane
/ˌdʒəʊzɪfiːn kɒʃreɪn/
King Arthur /kɪŋ‿ˈɑːθə/
Leona Lewis /liˌəʊnə ˈluːɪs/
the Lion King /ðə ˈlaɪən kɪŋ/
Lord Charles Beresford
/ˌlɔːd tʃɑːlz ˈberɪsfəd/
the Mall /ðə ˈmɔːl/
Man Friday /mæn ˈfraɪdeɪ/
Merlin /ˈmɜːlɪn/
Mufasa /muˈfɑːsə/
Nala /ˈnɑːlə/
Patch /pætʃ/
Percy Spencer /ˌpɜːsi ˈspentsə/
Philo Farnsworth
/ˌfaɪləʊ ˈfɑːnzwɜːθ/
Pizza World /ˈpiːtsə wɜːld/
the Pridelands
/ðə ˈpraɪdlændz/
the Queen /ðə ˈkwiːn/
the Queen Victoria
/ðə ˌkwiːn vɪkˈtɔːriə/
Rat and Parrot
/ˌræt‿ən ˈpærət/
Red Nose Day /red ˈnəʊz deɪ/
Rihanna /riˈænə/
Robbie Williams
/ˌrɒbi ˈwɪljəmz/
Robinson Crusoe
/ˌrɒbɪnsən ˈkruːsəʊ/
Rover /ˈrəʊvə/
Ruth Wakefield
/ˌruːθ ˈweɪkfiːəld/
Sally Brown /ˌsæli ˈbraʊn/
Scar /skɑː/
Simba /ˈsɪmbə/
Sir Ector /sɜː ˈektə/
St. Paul's Cathedral
/sənt ˌpɔːlz kəˈθiːdrəl/
Thomas Edison
/ˌtɒməs‿ˈedɪsən/
Time Out Magazine
/taɪm‿aʊt ˈmægəˌziːn/
Tom Hanks /tɒm ˈhæŋks/
Tower Bridge /ˌtaʊə ˈbrɪdʒ/
Usain Bolt /juˌseɪn ˈbəʊlt/
Victoria Station
/vɪkˌtɔːriə ˈsteɪʃn/
Wellington Hospital
/ˌwelɪŋtən ˈhɒspɪtl/
Westminster Abbey
/ˌwestmɪnstər‿ˈæbi/
Whitcomb Judson
/ˌwɪtkəʊm ˈdʒʌdsn/
William Ellis School for Boys
/ˌwɪljəm‿ˌelɪs skuːl fə ˈbɔɪz/
Windsor Castle /ˌwɪnzə ˈkɑːsl/
the Wright Brothers
/ðə ˈraɪt ˌbrʌðəz/

Geographical names

Abercrave /ˌæbəˈkreɪv/
Aberdeen /ˌæbəˈdiːn/
Africa /ˈæfrɪkə/
Arlington Road /ˈɑːlɪŋtən rəʊd/
the Atlantic (Ocean)
/ðiˌətˌlæntɪk(‿ˈəʊʃn)/
Australia /ɒˈstreɪliə/
Austria /ˈɒstriə/
Belfast /ˌbelˈfɑːst/
Berlin /ˌbɜːˈlɪn/
Birmingham /ˈbɜːmɪŋəm/
Blackheath /ˌblækˈhiːθ/
Bombay /ˌbɒmˈbeɪ/
Bone Cave /ˌbəʊn ˈkeɪv/
Brighton /ˈbraɪtən/
Bristol /ˈbrɪstl/
Britain /ˈbrɪtn/
Cambridge /ˈkeɪmbrɪdʒ/
Camden /ˈkæmdən/
Camden High Street
/ˌkæmdən ˈhaɪ striːt/
Canada /ˈkænədə/
Canterbury /ˈkæntəbəri/
Cardiff /ˈkɑːdɪf/
the Caribbean /ðə ˌkærɪˈbiːən/
Carol Street /ˈkærəl striːt/
Cathedral Cave
/kəˌθiːdrəl ˈkeɪv/
China /ˈtʃaɪnə/
Cornwall /ˈkɔrnwəl/
Cotswolds /ˈkɒtswəʊldz/
Dan-yr-Ogof Cave
/ˌdænərˌɒgɒv ˈkeɪv/
Dover /ˈdəʊvə/
Dublin /ˈdʌblɪn/
Eastbourne /ˈiːstbɔːn/
Edinburgh /ˈedɪnbərə/
England /ˈɪŋglənd/
Europe /ˈjʊərəp/
France /frɑːnts/
the Giant's Causeway
/ðə ˌdʒaɪənts ˈkɔːzˌweɪ/
Glencoe /glenˈkəʊ/
Great Britain /ˌgreɪt ˈbrɪtn/
Greater London
/ˌgreɪtə ˈlʌndən/
Greenwich Park
/ˌgrenɪtʃ ˈpɑːk/
Haverstock Hill /ˈhævəstɒk hɪl/
the Himalayas
/ðə ˌhɪməˈleɪəz/
Holloway /ˈhɒləweɪ/
India /ˈɪndiə/
Indonesia /ˌɪndəʊˈniːʒə/

Iran /ɪ'rɑːn/
Ireland /'aɪələnd/
the Irish Sea /ði‿ˌaɪrɪʃ 'siː/
Italy /'ɪtəli/
Jamaica /dʒə'meɪkə/
Loch Ness /ˌlɒk 'nes/
London /'lʌndən/
Malaysia /mə'leɪziə/
Manchester /'mæntʃɪstə/
Mexico /'meksɪˌkəʊ/
Mount Snowdon /ˌmaʊnt 'snəʊdən/
New York /njuː 'jɔːk/
New Zealand /nju 'ziːlənd/
Newcastle /'njuːˌkɑːsəl/
North Wales /ˌnɔːθ 'weɪlz/
Northern Ireland /ˌnɔːðn‿'aɪələnd/
Notting Hill /ˌnɒtɪŋ 'hɪl/
the Pacific (Ocean) /ðə pəˌsɪfɪk(‿əʊʃn)/
Plymouth /'plɪməθ/
Poland /'pəʊlənd/
River Dee /ˌrɪvə 'diː/
Russia /'rʌʃə/
Scotland /'skɒtlənd/
Seattle /si'ætəl/
Sheffield /'ʃefiːəld/
South Africa /saʊθ‿'æfrɪkə/
Spain /speɪn/
St John's Park /sənt ˌdʒɒnz 'pɑːk/
Stonehenge /ˌstəʊn'hendʒ/
Swansea /'swɒnzi/
Turkey /'tɜːki/
UK (= United Kingdom) /ˌjuː'keɪ, juːˌnaɪtɪd 'kɪŋdəm/
USA (= United States of America) /ˌjuːes'eɪ, juːˌnaɪtɪdˌsteɪts‿əv‿ə'merɪkə/
Wales /weɪlz/
Wembley /'wembli/
Westbourne Grove /'westbɔːn grəʊv/
Westbourne Street /'westbɔːn striːt/
Wiltshire /'wɪltʃə/
York /jɔːk/

Numbers

Cardinal numbers

0	zero /'zɪərəʊ/	12	twelve /twelv/	30	thirty /'θɜːti/
1	one /wʌn/	13	thirteen /ˌθɜː'tiːn/	40	forty /'fɔːti/
2	two /tuː/	14	fourteen /ˌfɔː'tiːn/	50	fifty /'fɪfti/
3	three /θriː/	15	fifteen /ˌfɪf'tiːn/	…	
4	four /fɔː/	16	sixteen /ˌsɪks'tiːn/	90	ninety /'naɪnti/
5	five /faɪv/	17	seventeen /ˌsevn'tiːn/	100	one hundred /'wʌn ˌhʌndrəd/
6	six /sɪks/	18	eighteen /ˌeɪ'tiːn/	…	
7	seven /'sevn/	19	nineteen /ˌnaɪn'tiːn/	900	nine hundred /'naɪn ˌhʌndrəd/
8	eight /eɪt/	20	twenty /'twenti/	1,000	one thousand /'wʌn ˌθauznd/
9	nine /naɪn/	21	twenty-one /ˌtwenti'wʌn/		
10	ten /ten/	…			
11	eleven /ɪ'levn/				

Ordinal numbers

1st	first /fɜːst/	14th	fourteenth /ˌfɔː'tiːnθ/	30th	thirtieth /'θɜːtiəθ/
2nd	second /'sekənd/	15th	fifteenth /ˌfɪf'tiːnθ/	31st	thirty-first /ˌθɜːti'fɜːst/
3rd	third /θɜːd/	…		…	
4th	fourth /fɔːθ/	20th	twentieth /'twentiəθ/	40th	fortieth /'fɔːtiəθ/
5th	fifth /fɪfθ/	21st	twenty-first /ˌtwenti'fɜːst/	50th	fiftieth /'fɪftiəθ/
6th	sixth /sɪksθ/	22nd	twenty-second /ˌtwenti'sekənd/	60th	sixtieth /'sɪkstiəθ/
7th	seventh /'sevnθ/	23rd	twenty-third /ˌtwenti'θɜːd/	70th	seventieth /'sevntiəθ/
8th	eighth /eɪtθ/	24th	twenty-fourth /ˌtwenti'fɔːθ/	80th	eightieth /'eɪtiəθ/
9th	ninth /naɪnθ/	…		90th	ninetieth /'naɪntiəθ/
10th	tenth /tenθ/			100th	one hundredth /'hʌndrədθ/
11th	eleventh /ɪ'levnθ/				
12th	twelfth /twelfθ/				
13th	thirteenth /ˌθɜː'tiːnθ/				

infinitive	simple past	past participle	German
be /biː/	was/were /wɒz/wɜː/	been /biːn/	sein
become /bɪˈkʌm/	became /bɪˈkeɪm/	become /bɪˈkʌm/	werden
begin /bɪˈgɪn/	began /bɪˈgæn/	begun /bɪˈgʌn/	anfangen, beginnen
bend /bend/	bent /bent/	bent /bent/	biegen
bite /baɪt/	bit /bɪt/	bitten /ˈbɪtn/	beißen
break /breɪk/	broke /brəʊk/	broken /ˈbrəʊkən/	(zer)brechen
bring /brɪŋ/	brought /brɔːt/	brought /brɔːt/	(mit)bringen
build /bɪld/	built /bɪlt/	built /bɪlt/	bauen
burn /bɜːn/	burnt/burned /bɜːnt/bɜːnd/	burnt/burned /bɜːnt/bɜːnd/	(ver)brennen
buy /baɪ/	bought /bɔːt/	bought /bɔːt/	kaufen
catch /kætʃ/	caught /kɔːt/	caught /kɔːt/	fangen; festnehmen; erwischen, kriegen
choose /tʃuːz/	chose /tʃəʊz/	chosen /ˈtʃəʊzn/	auswählen
come /kʌm/	came /keɪm/	come /kʌm/	kommen
cost /kɒst/	cost /kɒst/	cost /kɒst/	kosten
cut /kʌt/	cut /kʌt/	cut /kʌt/	schneiden
do /duː/	did /dɪd/	done /dʌn/	machen, tun
draw /drɔː/	drew /druː/	drawn /drɔːn/	zeichnen
drink /drɪŋk/	drank /dræŋk/	drunk /drʌŋk/	trinken
drive /draɪv/	drove /drəʊv/	driven /ˈdrɪvn/	fahren
eat /iːt/	ate /eɪt/	eaten /ˈiːtn/	essen
fall /fɔːl/	fell /fel/	fallen /ˈfɔːlən/	fallen
feed /fiːd/	fed /fed/	fed /fed/	füttern, zu Essen geben
feel /fiːl/	felt /felt/	felt /felt/	(sich) fühlen
fight/faɪt/	fought /fɔːt/	fought /fɔːt/	(be)kämpfen
find /faɪnd/	found /faʊnd/	found /faʊnd/	finden
fit /fɪt/	fit/fitted /fɪt/ˈfɪtɪd/	fit/fitted /fɪt/ˈfɪtɪd/	passen (zu)
fly /flaɪ/	flew /fluː/	flown /fləʊn/	fliegen
forget /fəˈget/	forgot /fəˈgɒt/	forgotten /fəˈgɒtn/	vergessen
get /get/	got /gɒt/	got/gotten/gɒt/ˈgɒtn/	erhalten, bekommen; (an)kommen; verstehen; holen; werden
give /gɪv/	gave /geɪv/	given /ˈgɪvn/	geben
go /gəʊ/	went /went/	gone /gɒn/	gehen; fahren
grow /grəʊ/	grew /gruː/	grown /grəʊn/	wachsen
hang /hæŋ/	hung /hʌŋ/	hung /hʌŋ/	(auf)hängen
have /hæv/	had /hæd/	had /hæd/	haben; essen
hear /hɪə/	heard /hɜːd/	heard /hɜːd/	hören
hide /haɪd/	hid /hɪd/	hidden /ˈhɪdn/	(sich) verstecken
hit /hɪt/	hit /hɪt/	hit /hɪt/	schlagen; treffen; stoßen (gegen)
hold /həʊld/	held /held/	held /held/	halten
keep /kiːp/	kept /kept/	kept /kept/	(be)halten; aufbewahren
know /nəʊ/	knew /njuː/	known /nəʊn/	wissen; kennen
lead /liːd/	led /led/	led /led/	(an)führen, leiten
learn /lɜːn/	learnt/learned /lɜːnt/lɜːnd/	learnt/learned /lɜːnt/lɜːnd/	lernen

leave /liːv/	left /left/	left /left/	verlassen; abfahren; lassen
let /let/	let /let/	let /let/	lassen
lie /laɪ/	lay /leɪ/	lain /leɪn/	liegen
lose /luːz/	lost /lɒst/	lost /lɒst/	verlieren
make /meɪk/	made /meɪd/	made /meɪd/	machen
mean /miːn/	meant /ment/	meant /ment/	bedeuten; meinen
meet /miːt/	met /met/	met /met/	(sich) treffen; kennenlernen
mow /məʊ/	mowed /məʊd/	mowed/mown /məʊd/məʊn/	mähen
pay /peɪ/	paid /peɪd/	paid /peɪd/	(be)zahlen
put /pʊt/	put /pʊt/	put /pʊt/	setzen, legen, stellen
read /riːd/	read /red/	read /red/	lesen
ride /raɪd/	rode /rəʊd/	ridden /ˈrɪdn/	fahren; reiten
ring /rɪŋ/	rang /ræŋ/	rung /rʌŋ/	klingeln, läuten
run /rʌn/	ran /ræn/	run /rʌn/	laufen, rennen
say /seɪ/	said /sed/	said /sed/	sagen
see /siː/	saw /sɔː/	seen /siːn/	sehen
sell /sel/	sold /səʊld/	sold /səʊld/	verkaufen
send /send/	sent /sent/	sent /sent/	(zu)schicken
shine /ʃaɪn/	shone /ʃɒn/	shone /ʃɒn/	scheinen (Sonne)
show /ʃəʊ/	showed /ʃəʊd/	shown /ʃəʊn/	zeigen
sing /sɪŋ/	sang /sæŋ/	sung /sʌŋ/	singen
sit /sɪt/	sat /sæt/	sat /sæt/	sitzen
sleep /sliːp/	slept /slept/	slept /slept/	schlafen
speak /spiːk/	spoke /spəʊk/	spoken /ˈspəʊkən/	sprechen, reden
spell /spel/	spelt/spelled /spelt/speld/	spelt/spelled /spelt/speld/	buchstabieren
spend /spend/	spent /spent/	spent /spent/	ausgeben *(Geld)*; verbringen *(Zeit)*
spit /spɪt/	spit/spat /spɪt/spæt/	spit/spat /spɪt/spæt/	spucken
stand /stænd/	stood /stʊd/	stood /stʊd/	stehen; ertragen, aushalten
steal /stiːl/	stole /stəʊl/	stolen /ˈstəʊlən/	stehlen, klauen
stick /stɪk/	stuck /stʌk/	stuck /stʌk/	kleben
swim /swɪm/	swam /swæm/	swum /swʌm/	schwimmen
swing /swɪŋ/	swung /swʌŋ/	swung /swʌŋ/	schwingen, schaukeln
take /teɪk/	took /tʊk/	taken /ˈteɪkən/	(mit)nehmen; bringen; brauchen
teach /tiːtʃ/	taught /tɔːt/	taught /tɔːt/	unterrichten; beibringen
tear /teə/	tore /tɔː/	torn /tɔːn/	(zer)reißen
tell /tel/	told /təʊld/	told /təʊld/	erzählen; sagen
think /θɪŋk/	thought /θɔːt/	thought /θɔːt/	denken, glauben, meinen
throw /θrəʊ/	threw /θruː/	thrown /θrəʊn/	werfen
understand /ˌʌndəˈstænd/	understood /ˌʌndəˈstʊd/	understood /ˌʌndəˈstʊd/	verstehen
wear /weə/	wore /wɔː/	worn /wɔːn/	tragen *(Kleidung)*
win /wɪn/	won /wʌn/	won /wʌn/	gewinnen
write /raɪt/	wrote /rəʊt/	written /ˈrɪtn/	schreiben

QUELLENVERZEICHNIS

Bildquellen

Umschlagfoto Dirk Schmidt/dsphotos.de; Vorsatz vorn Technisch-Grafische Abteilung Westermann; Vorsatz hinten Zwick, Joachim, Gießen; 15, 34 StockFood GmbH, München (Davorin Marjanovic) (bread); alamy images, Abingdon/Oxfordshire (©Valentyn Volkov) (fish); TopicMedia Service, Putzbrunn (pm) (fruits); fotolia.com, New York (©Gina Sanders) (vegetables); 16 alamy images, Abingdon/Oxfordshire (© Frances Roberts); 17 u. alamy images, Abingdon/ Oxfordshire (Dennis MacDonald); 20 m.l. alamy images, Abingdon/Oxfordshire (© foodfolio); 20 m.r. alamy images, Abingdon/Oxfordshire (Anthony Thorogood); 20 o. alamy images, Abingdon/Oxfordshire (Kevin Foy); 20 u.l. alamy images, Abingdon/Oxfordshire (SHOUT); 20 u.r. alamy images, Abingdon/Oxfordshire (©Andrew Fox); 21 fotolia.com, New York (Carmen Steiner) (fish and chips); StockFood GmbH, München (Peter Howard Smith) (English breakfast); fotolia.com, New York (©Joe Gough) (Sunday roast); Coverpicture, Berlin (Michaela Begsteiger) (The Cambridge); alamy images, Abingdon/ Oxfordshire (Chris Howes/Wild Places Photography) (fish and chips restaurant); Bildagentur Schapowalow, Berlin (Stefano Amantini) (pub); 21 u.l. fotolia.com, New York (moonrun); 23 Meinhardt, Annika, Braunschweig; 24 mauritius images GmbH, Mittenwald (Foodpix) (1); fotolia.com, New York (Julián Rovagnati) (2); Corbis, Düsseldorf (Creativ Studio Heinemann/ Westend61) (4); fotolia.com, New York (rdnzl) (5); fotolia.com, New York (TrudiDesign) (6); 25 Schmitt, André, Braunschweig (A–F); 26 o. Verlagsarchiv, Braunschweig; 26 u. alamy images, Abingdon/Oxfordshire (©Gerry Walden); 27 mauritius images GmbH, Mittenwald (Rene Truffy) (B); alamy images, Abingdon/Oxfordshire (©Nordicphotos) (C); Fotoagentur Lade/BIM (D); Katja Nandorf, Frankfurt (E); 31 Corbis, Düsseldorf (©Royalty-Free) (1); ullstein bild, Berlin (Imagebroker.net) (2); Corbis, Düsseldorf (©Royalty-Free) (3); 31 u. alamy images, Abingdon/Oxfordshire (© funkyfood London – Paul Williams); 32 iStockphoto.com, Calgary (©travellinglight) (chicken tikka); fotolia. com, New York (©Joe Gough) (curry vindaloo); fotolia.com, New York (©Ildi) (daal); adpic Bildagentur, Bonn (H. Leitner) (naan); 33 CartoonStock Ltd, GB-Bath (Bucella, Marty) (1); CartoonStock Ltd, GB-Bath (Bucella, Marty) (2); CartoonStock Ltd, GB-Bath (Kes) (3); 36 o., 179 iStockphoto.com, Calgary (©Sarsmis); 36 u. Bulls Pressedienst GmbH, Frankfurt am Main; 37 o., 41 o. Picture-Alliance GmbH, Frankfurt/M. (AP Photo); 39 o. F1online digitale Bildagentur GmbH, Frankfurt/M. (Juice Images); 39 u. Getty Images, München (Joe Mcbride); 40 Fotoagentur SVEN SIMON Gmbh & Co. Pressefoto KG, Mülheim an der Ruhr (Frank Hoermann) (Bolt); Picture-Alliance GmbH, Frankfurt/M. (empics/Stephen Pond) (Messi); vario images, Bonn (J. Wolter) (Novitzki); Picture-Alliance GmbH, Frankfurt/M. (Rauchensteiner/Augenklick) (Theiss); Picture-Alliance GmbH, Frankfurt/M. (dpa/Büttner) (Vettel); Getty Images, München (Bongarts/Mark Sandten) (Williams); 41 u. Picture-Alliance GmbH, Frankfurt/M. (epa Geoff Caddick); 43 l. alamy images, Abingdon/ Oxfordshire (©Alamy Celebrity); 43 r. alamy images, Abingdon/Oxfordshire (Carolyn Jenkins); 47 u. Verlagsarchiv, Braunschweig; 49 alamy images, Abingdon/Oxfordshire (©David Crausby); 52 o. Corbis, Düsseldorf (Leo Mason); 52 u. alamy images, Abingdon/Oxfordshire (©Adrian Muttitt); 53 Picture-Alliance GmbH, Frankfurt/M. (Actionplus); 55, 170 Panther Media GmbH (panthermedia.net), München (Christophe Schmid); 56 m.l. CartoonStock Ltd, GB-Bath (©Wiley); 56 o.r. dreamstime.com, Brentwood (©Steve Allen); 58 Picture-Alliance GmbH, Frankfurt/M. (ZB/M. Gröning) (1); Bettermann, Antje, Wendhausen (2); Tönnies, Frauke, Laatzen (3); 62 Picture-Alliance GmbH, Frankfurt/M. (The Advertising Archives); 63 fotolia.com, New York (©richirik) (rose garden); mauritius images GmbH, Mittenwald (alamy) (restaurant); alamy images, Abingdon/Oxfordshire (Clynt Garnham Education) (juggling); Caro Fotoagentur GmbH, Berlin (Teich) (jugger); 64, 57 u.r. alamy images, Abingdon/Oxfordshire (©epa european pressphoto agency b.v.); 65 Getty Images, München (©Franck BONHAM); 66 m. vario images, Bonn; 66 o.l. vario images, Bonn; 66 o. r. Shutterstock.com, New York (Tadeusz Ibrom); 66 u.l. iStockphoto.com, Calgary (Jacek27); 66 u.r. vario images, Bonn; 67 m.l., o.r. Shutterstock.com, New York (Bikeworld travel); 67 m.r. iStockphoto. com, Calgary (vladimirzahariev); 67 o.l. iStockphoto.com, Calgary (Manuel Velasco); 67 u.l., 57 u.l. vario images, Bonn; 67 u.r. iStockphoto.com, Calgary (jon11); 70 Museum of Modern Art (MoMA), New York/Scala, Florence (Gemälde von Henri Rousseau. Die schlafende Zigeunerin); 74 dreamstime. com, Brentwood (Gorgios) (A); alamy images, Abingdon/Oxfordshire (Rex Features/Tom Watkins) (B); ullstein bild, Berlin (Vidler) (C); 82 iStockphoto.com, Calgary (nimblewit) (axe); alamy images, Abingdon/Oxfordshire (©ST-images) (first aid kit); fotolia.com, New York (RRF) (matches); Shutterstock.com, New York (Seregam) (rope); alamy images, Abingdon/Oxfordshire (studiomode) (seeds); fotolia.com, New York (djama) (soap); fotolia.com, New York (Birgit Reitz-Hofmann) (spade); iStockphoto. com, Calgary (EasyBuy4u) (sweets); Superbild – Your Photo Today, Taufkirchen (trumpet); Uhrenfabrik Junghans GmbH & Co.KG (watch); fotolia.com, New York (svort) (toothbrush); fotolia.com, New York (Sven Hoppe) (scissors); iStockphoto.com, Calgary (Rouzes) (sunglasses); Druwe & Polastri, Cremlingen/Weddel (book); iStockphoto. com, Calgary (Michael Flippo) (knife); 85 fotolia.com, New York (©Light Impression); 86 Meinhardt, Annika, Braunschweig; 91 Panther Media GmbH (panthermedia.net), München; 95 o. Cinetext Bildarchiv, Frankfurt am Main; 95 u. ullstein bild, Berlin (Reuters); 98 Getty Images, München (GK Hart/Vikki Hart); 99 o., u.l., u.m. Grimm, Dr. Anne, Braunschweig; 99 u.r. alamy images, Abingdon/Oxfordshire (Alex Segre); 101 fotolia.com, New York (maconga); 104 o.l., u.l., u.r. Science & Society Picture Library, London; 104 o.r. alamy images, Abingdon/Oxfordshire (Alistair Laming); 106 iStockphoto.com, Calgary (mustafa deliormanli) (TV); iStockphoto.com, Calgary (Shaun Lowe) (telephone); iStockphoto.com, Calgary (Eivaisla) (light bulb); fotolia.com, New York (©sergio37_120) (cookie); F1online digitale Bildagentur GmbH (Drives Images) (car); fotolia.com, New York (300dpi) (computer); fotolia.com, New York (Tribalstar) (matches); iStockphoto. com, Calgary (JazzIRT) (dishwasher); 106, 113 fotolia.com, New York (Emin Ozkan) (microwave); Eastham, Katharine, Oxford (bike); alamy images, Abingdon/ Oxfordshire (stamp); fotolia.com, New York (Gstudio Group) (zipper); 107 Picture-Alliance GmbH, Frankfurt/M. (91020) (Bell); akg-images GmbH, Berlin (Benz); INTERFOTO, München (Mary Evans/Photo Researchers) (Cochrane); akg-images GmbH, Berlin (Edison); Getty Images, München (Underwood Archives) (Farnsworth); Getty Images, München (Hulton Archive) (Mauchly, Eckert); INTERFOTO, München (Neon 2) (Wakefield); INTERFOTO, München (Science & Society) (Walker); 108 o.l. fotolia.com, New York (trekandphoto); 108 o.m. fotolia.com, New York (okinawakasawa); 108 o.r. Caro Fotoagentur GmbH; 108 u.m. Eastham, Katharine, Oxford; 108 u.r. Hammersen, Bettina, Braunschweig; 113 u. wikipedia. org; 118 fotolia.com, New York (©pico); 119 m. wikimedia.commons; 119 o. Studio Schmidt-Lohmann, Gießen; 119 u. ullstein bild, Berlin; 120 o. iStockphoto. com, Calgary (PeteKlinger); 120 u. ullstein bild, Berlin (Imagebroker.net/ Rosseforp); 121 m.l. F1online digitale Bildagentur GmbH, Frankfurt/M. (sodapix); 121 m.r. iStockphoto.com, Calgary (dd72); 121 o.l. alamy images, Abingdon/Oxfordshire (©Mary Evans Picture Library); 121 o.r. Shutterstock. com, New York (Hein Nouwens); 121 u.l. fotolia.com, New York (Martin Konz); 121 u.r. fotolia.com, New York (©viennapro); 123 laif, Köln (Modrow) (biking); action press, Hamburg (castle); alamy images, Abingdon/Oxfordshire (©Helene Rogers) (station); alamy images, Abingdon/ Oxfordshire (©Chris Howes) (walking); 123 u. alamy images, Abingdon/ Oxfordshire (©Richard Nicholls); 125 mediacolors Bildagentur & -Produktion, Zürich (Stillo) (A); dreamstime.com, Brentwood (B); F1online digitale Bildagentur GmbH, Frankfurt/M. (Johner) (C); Picture-Alliance GmbH, Frankfurt/M. (ZB/A. Lander) (D); 130 iStockphoto. com, Calgary (barsik) (Brian); Shutterstock.com, New York (Monkey Business Images) (Ciaran, Fiona); iStockphoto.com, Calgary (bsauter) (Penny); 130 u.l. iStockphoto.com, Calgary (Matt Gibson); 130 u.r. Picture-Alliance GmbH, Frankfurt/M.; 131 o.l. fotolia.com, New York (daskleineatelier); 131 o.r. Corbis, Düsseldorf (©Sebastian Wasek); 131 fotolia.com, New York (Gail Johnson) (castle); 131 alamy images, Abingdon/ Oxfordshire (©foodfolio) (bakestone); alamy images, Abingdon/Oxfordshire (Nick Gregory) (biking); alamy images, Abingdon/Oxfordshire (©Jeff Morgan 07) (cheese); alamy images, Abingdon/ Oxfordshire (©Paul Francis) (daffodil); fotolia.com, New York (Ayzek) (flag); alamy images, Abingdon/Oxfordshire (©neil setchfield – food) (fruit cake); alamy images, Abingdon/Oxfordshire (©Andrzej Tokarski) (leek); Technisch-Grafische Abteilung Westermann (map); actionplus sports images, London (Neil Tingle) (rugby); 132 m.l. Shutterstock. com, New York (stephen); 132 m.r. Clipdealer GmbH, München (speedfighter); 132 o.l. Picture-Alliance GmbH, Frankfurt/M.; 132 o.r. alamy images, Abingdon/Oxfordshire; 132 u.l. iStockphoto.com, Calgary (matthewleesdixon); 132 u.r. alamy images, Abingdon/Oxfordshire (James Osmond); 133 m.l. iStockphoto.com, Calgary; 133 m.r. iStockphoto.com, Calgary (mirrormere); 133 o.l. LOOK-foto, München (The Travel Library); 133 o.r. alamy images, Abingdon/Oxfordshire (©Adam Burton); 133 u.l. ullstein bild, Berlin (AISA); 135 alamy images, Abingdon/Oxfordshire (©Emin Ozkan); 136 alamy images, Abingdon/Oxfordshire; 137 l. alamy images, Abingdon/ Oxfordshire (Jeff Morgan 16); 137 r. alamy images, Abingdon/Oxfordshire (Michael Olivers); 138 l. action press, Hamburg (Oedia Sarl); 138 r. alamy images, Abingdon/Oxfordshire (©Jupiterimages); 139 Meinhardt, Annika, Braunschweig; 141 F1online digitale Bildagentur GmbH (1), Frankfurt/M. (Image Source/tabato); alamy images, Abingdon/Oxfordshire (©Paul Kingsley) (2); iStockphoto.com, Calgary (IS_ImageSource) (3); iStockphoto.com, Calgary (©slobo) (4); iStockphoto.com, Calgary (©Juanmonino) (5); alamy images, Abingdon/Oxfordshire (David R. Frazier Photolibrary, Inc.) (6); 143 m. StockFood GmbH, München; 143 o.l. alamy images, Abingdon/Oxfordshire (©Food Feature); 143 o.r. www.joyzine. org (Jo Williams); 143 u.l. alamy images, Abingdon/Oxfordshire (Cephas picture library); 143 u.r. alamy images, Abingdon/Oxfordshire (©Food Features); 144 ddp images GmbH, Hamburg (pwe Kinoarchiv); 146, 147 Picture-Alliance GmbH, Frankfurt/M. (KPA); 148 Penguin Books (UK) Ltd, Essex (Jill McDonald/ Puffin Books Cover illustrated by Martin Simpson); 149 fotolia.com, New York (©GigiPeis); 150, 151 Tonn, Dieter, Bovenden-Lenglern.

Textquellen

116/117 from „How Nearly Everything Was Invented" by the Brainwaves, illustrated by Lisa Swerling and Ralph Lazar (Dorling Kindersley 2008); reproduced by permission of Penguin Books Ltd.; 146/147 from "About a Boy" ©Nick Hornby, 2005; reproduced by permission of Penguin Books Ltd.; ; 148 from "Monstroso" by Charlie Higson (Puffin 2010), ©1945 Charlie Higson; reproduced by permission of Penguin Books Ltd.

Seite 16 1 A food and drink ABC

a) **A** apple
B banana, bread, bad, broccoli, breakfast
C cake, cheese, chicken, chips, crisps
D delicious, dinner
E eat, egg
F feed, fresh, flour
G gum, glass of milk
H honey, hot chocolate, ham
I ice cream
J jam
K knife
L lemonade, lunch
M meat, milk, muesli
N noodles
O orange
P potato, pizza
Q quiche
R recipe, rice
S sweets, sandwich, salad
T tomato, toast
U unsalted
V vegetables
W water
X –
Y yoghurt, yummy
Z zucchini

c) **fruit:** apple, banana, orange, tomato
vegetable: potato, vegetable, zucchini
for breakfast: jam, honey
drink: lemonade, water
snacks: cake, gum, ice cream, sweets
dinner: meat, noodles, quiche
eating words: eat, feed, knife, recipe, delicious

Seite 16 2 Places to eat

a) My favourite place to eat is the pizza place in our street. It's called Mamma Mia. You can put as many things as you like on your pizza, and the music is always great.

b) I'd like to go to Burger Queen because it's not too expensive. Also, my favourite food is onion rings, and you can order those with your burger. I'd also like to go to Burger Queen because I'd like to try the Sweet Queen Donut – it sounds delicious!

c) **S1:** How many desserts are there at the Windsor Castle?
S2: There are four desserts.
S1: How much is the Pizza Verde?
S2: Regular or large?
S1: I'm very hungry – large, please!
S2: £12.25. Can you have chips at the Windsor Castle?
S1: No, you can't. There are no chips on the menu.

d) I'd like to go to the Windsor Castle. For fifteen pounds I can have the vegetarian lasagne and the apple and blackberry crumble. I'd like to try the chocolate and strawberry cake, too, but I don't have enough money!

Seite 18 3 Friday evening

a) I think Mrs Collins, Gillian and Charlie are talking about what they are going to eat on Friday evening.

c) They are talking about Burger Queen, Pizza World, the Windsor Castle and Bengal Tiger.
Burger Queen has got delicious burgers and isn't very expensive.
Pizza World has got pizza, of course!
The Windsor Castle has got salads and other great food.
Bengal Tiger has got Indian food./hot and spicy food.

d) Mrs Collins wants to go to the Windsor Castle. She wants to eat a salad. She doesn't want to go to Burger Queen.
Gillian wants to go to Burger Queen. She wants to eat burgers. She doesn't want to go to Pizza World. She also wants to eat Indian food.
Charlie wants to go to Pizza World. He doesn't want to go to Burger Queen.

Seite 19 5 Any ideas?

a)

	Who says it?	in German
Have you got any other ideas?	Mrs Collins	Habt ihr noch andere Ideen?
I really don't want any pizza today.	Gillian	Ich habe heute echt keine Lust auf Pizza.
They've got some delicious burgers on the menu.	Gillian	Sie haben leckere Burger auf der Speisekarte.

b)

+	–	?
They've got some delicious burgers on the menu.	I really don't want any pizza today.	Have you got any other ideas?
I'm going to have some at Dad's house tomorrow.	I haven't done any shopping this week.	Do you know any other good places to eat?
I really fancy some Indian food tonight.	We don't have to buy any drinks.	Can we please order some takeaway food from Bengal Tiger, Mum?
We can have some ice cream for dessert.		

c) In bejahten Aussagesätzen verwendet man **some,** in verneinten Aussagesätzen und in Fragen **any.** Für **something** und **anything** gelten dieselben Regeln.

Seite 22 6 In a restaurant

a)

waiter/waitress	guest
That's £..., please. What would you like to eat? Anything else? Here you are. Anything to drink? What would you like to drink? Are you ready to order? Thank you.	I'd like ..., please. How much is that, please? Thank you. Could you bring the bill, please? I'll have ..., please. Can I have the menu, please?

b) **S1:** I think the guest says "How much is that, please?"
S2: I agree with you. The guest always pays. I think the waiter says "Thank you".
S1: I don't agree with you. The guest says "Thank you" for the food.
S2: But the waiter says "Thank you" for the money at the end. "Thank you" can be in both lists.

c) That's £9.50, **please.**
I'd like a soup, **please.**
What would you like to drink?
Could you bring the bill, please?
I'll have a glass of mineral water, please.
Anything to drink?
Are you ready to order?

d) **S1:** Good evening. Are you ready to order?
S2: Yes, I think so.
S1: Great. What would you like to eat?
S2: I'll have the fish pie, please.

S1: And what would you like to drink?
S2: I'd like a glass of lemonade, please.
S1: Of course. Anything else?
S2: Some water would be great.
S1: No problem.
S2: Could you bring the bill, please?
S1: Of course, here you are. That's £9.20. (nine pounds twenty)
S2: Thank you. Here's £10 (ten pounds). Keep the change.
S1: Thank you very much. Enjoy the rest of your day.

Seite 22 7 Choose an activity

My perfect menu
Main courses: – tuna pizza with salad
– vegetable curry with rice
– chicken fajitas with tomato salsa and cheese
– prawns with a French sauce
Dessert: – chocolate ice cream, with brownies and chocolate sauce
– apple pie
– fruit salad

Menu for a/your pet
Here is a menu for my dog Sammy.
I have drawn chicken and bones because they are his favourite food.
There is a picture of Sammy up here to show you that it is his menu.

Seite 23 8 Clever, isn't he?

a) Rajiv and Charlie are eating lunch/having lunch in the school cafeteria.
Rajiv is eating healthy food, I think. I can see some pasta on his plate and a side order of salad.
There is a glass of water on his tray.
Charlie is eating chips, fried eggs and a lot of tomato ketchup. There is a glass of lemonade on the table.
Charlie looks very happy with his food. Rajiv looks surprised.
b) …, stimmt's?
…, gell?
…, wa?

Seite 23 9 Hands up!

b) Twelve people in our class always have breakfast before school.
Seven eople in our class sometimes bring a snack to school.
Fifteen people in our class never eat fruit at break time.

Seite 24 10 Good for you?

a) **S1:** I think spinach is healthy.
S2: I agree. I also think that yoghurt is healthy.
S1: I don't agree. There is a lot of sugar in yoghurt. I think cereal is healthy.
S2: I don't agree. There is no sugar in natural yoghurt. But there is a lot of sugar in cereal.
b) It is new to me that you should eat five portions of fruit and vegetables each day.
I didn't know that some smoothies contain a lot of sugar.

Seite 24 11 Lunch at school

a)

name	likes	doesn't like
Karla	pasta, dessert	potatoes

b)

name	likes	doesn't like
Jack	meat, rice, potatoes, desserts, chips	vegetables, salads
Shima	vegetables, salads, fruit, rice, potatoes, vegetable lasagne	pasta with tomato sauce

d) I like the food at our school. The waffles with cream are my favourite snack at our school cafeteria because they're warm and sweet. But I don't like the bananas because they're always really old and brown.
I don't like the food at our school. I'm OK with the snacks but I don't like the warm meals. They don't taste fresh.

Seite 25 12 A school lunch recipe

a) B – D – F – E – A – C

b)

things you use	what you do	food you need
knife tablespoon pan stove plate	cook wash cut into small pieces cut open take out dry cut off the ends cut into thin strips mix add heat stir break take off pour put on	pasta tomatoes green or red chillies parsley leeks olive oil paprika powder salt pepper black cumin seeds feta cheese water

Seite 26 13 Very British?

a) I love Turkish food. On Fridays I always go to my friend Eva's house and her mum makes Turkish pizza for us – it's delicious!

b) **S1:** Have you ever tried sushi?
S2: Yes, I have. It was disgusting. Why don't they cook the fish first? Have you ever tried it?
S1: Yes, I have. It was great, I loved it! Have you ever drunk green tea?
S2: No, I haven't but I have drunk black tea with milk. Have you ever eaten fish and chips?
S1: Yes, I have. It was OK. I ate it in London last summer. Have you ever had currywurst?
S2: Yes, I have! I often have one after school. I like it, but not every day.

Seite 26 14 Eating habits around the world

b) My parents are Greek, and a typical meal from Greece is moussaka. People in Greece normally eat moussaka hot. In Turkey you eat it cold.

Seite 27 15 Choose an activity

(food diary)

Monday: (breakfast) cornflakes with milk, orange juice
(lunch) salami sandwich with crisps and a salad, coke
(dinner) chicken fajitas, water; (snacks) banana, chocolate bar

Tuesday: (breakfast) scrambled egg and bacon, tea
(lunch) chicken and salad sandwich, crisps, lemonade
(dinner) prawn curry with rice, apple juice
(snacks) Nutella on toast

Wednesday: (breakfast) special flakes with milk, water
(lunch) tuna pizza, carrot sticks, orange juice
(dinner) cheese and tomato salad with bread, water
(snacks) grapes, carrot sticks with a yoghurt dip

Thursday: (breakfast) cheese and tomato sandwich, tea
(lunch) macaroni cheese with peas, coke
(dinner) chicken salad with bread, orange juice
(snacks) chocolate bar, pretzel

Friday: (breakfast) bacon sandwich with tomato ketchup, water
(lunch) hamburger with chips, water
(dinner) spaghetti bolognese, apple juice
(snacks) bread and butter, apple

Saturday: (breakfast) fried eggs, bacon, tomatoes and mushrooms, toast, orange juice
(lunch) cheese and tomato sandwich, water
(dinner) chicken curry, apple juice

Sunday: (breakfast) Nutella on toast, orange juice
(lunch) roast pork with vegetables and potatoes, lemonade
(dinner) cheese on toast, tea

(presenting different food items: healthy or unhealthy?)

Eggs are very healthy because they make you feel full and will stop you from wanting chocolate for dessert. However, many things that you have with eggs, like bacon and cheese, have a lot of salt – so be careful!

I think that cheese is healthy because it has lots of milk in it. But my friend says that cheese is bad for you because there is a lot of fat and a lot of salt in it.

(favourite recipe) My favourite recipe is chicken curry with rice.

Ingredients (for 4 people)

- 4 chicken breasts
- 1 tbs olive oil
- 1 large onion
- 1 bag of spinach
- half a tin of chickpeas
- 2 green chillies
- 4 cups of rice

- 8 cups of boiling water
- 1 jar of curry sauce (500ml)
- salt and pepper

1. Cut the chicken breasts into small pieces. On a different plate chop the onions and chillies with a sharp knife.
2. Add the oil to a pan and heat for two minutes. Then add the chicken to the pan and cook on a medium heat for 8–10 minutes, until the chicken is a light brown colour.
3. Mix the onions and chillies with the chicken and heat for five minutes.
4. Add the curry sauce and let it boil. After that turn down the heat and cook on a low heat for 30 minutes. Make sure that you stir the curry with a spoon every five minutes!
5. While the curry is cooking, add the rice to a pan of boiling water. Cook for 20 minutes on a medium heat.
6. After 30 minutes add the spinach, chickpeas and some salt and pepper to the curry.
7. Turn up the heat to a medium temperature and stir the ingredients well. Serve on a plate and enjoy!

My favourite recipe comes from India. My grandparents lived in India before they moved to Hamburg. My grandma often makes me this curry when I have a cold because it makes me feel better.

Seite 28 P1 Food words

a)

English	German
carrot	Karotte
salad	Salat
pizza	Pizza
apple	Apfel
banana	Banane
melon	Melone
chocolate	Schokolade
soup	Suppe

Seite 28 P3 Sound check

b)

/ʃ/	/dʒ/	/tʃ/
shopping	fridge	chips
delicious	age	Charlie
sure	juice	question
dish	German	chocolate
English	enjoy	cheeseburger
she		ketchup

Seite 29 P5 A special burger

a) tomatoes, lettuce, onions, cheese, mayonnaise

b) **S1:** I like some tomatoes, some lettuce, some onions and some mayonnaise on my burger. I don't like any eggs or mushrooms on it. What about your burger?
S2: I like some meat, some cucumber, some cheese and some mayonnaise on my burger. I don't like any ketchup on it.

Seite 29 P6 So many questions

b) **S1:** How many eggs have you eaten this week?
S2: I haven't eaten any eggs this week. – How much water do you drink each day?
S1: I usually drink three glasses of water each day. I should drink more. – How many meals do you have each day?
S2: I normally have two meals a day. I never eat breakfast. – Guess: How much time do you spend eating each day?
S1: I think I normally spend thirty-five minutes eating each day – ten minutes for breakfast, ten minutes for lunch and fifteen minutes for dinner. – What do you think: How many students in this class can cook spaghetti?
S2: I think everyone can cook spaghetti, but only five students can make spaghetti bolognese. – How much money do you spend on sweets every week?
S1: I spend all my pocket money on sweets: so that's ten euros.

Seite 30 P8 Give me five!

5 things you can use to eat food: **knife, fingers, fork, chopsticks, bowls**
5 kinds of vegetables: **cucumber, onions, mushrooms, carrots, broccoli**
5 kinds of fruit: **oranges, apple, banana, blackberry, strawberry**
5 adjectives to talk about food: **delicious, hot, spicy, healthy, sugary**
5 drinks: **wine, coffee, tea, soft drinks, smoothies**

Seite 31 P11 Have you tried it?

I have tried tomato soup but I didn't like it. It was disgusting.
I have had spaghetti and I liked it. It was great.
I have tried a baked potato and I liked it. It was good because you could choose different toppings.
I have had chicken curry but I didn't like it. It was too spicy for me.

Seite 31 P12 A recipe from India

Für dieses Rezept braucht man
300g Hähnchenbrust,
150g Joghurt,
1 Esslöffel Currypaste,
Salz,
Pfeffer,
2 Zwiebeln,
1 rote Chili,
Öl.
Zuerst schneidet man die Hähnchenbrust in Stücke und mischt den Joghurt mit der Currypaste.
Anschließend würzt man die Hähnchenstücke mit Salz und Pfeffer, legt sie in eine flache Auflaufform und bedeckt sie mit der Joghurtmischung.
Dann schneidet man die Zwiebeln und die rote Chili in dünne Scheiben und brät sie in Öl an.
Dann gibt man die Hähnchenstücke mit in die Pfanne und lässt das Ganze 40 Minuten köcheln.
Am Ende serviert man das Gericht mit Reis.

Seite 32 M1 Indian food in Britain

a) I tried Indian food when I was in Berlin last year. It was delicious! The meat tasted really good and I liked the rice and the poppadums. But I know that Indian food can be quite spicy.

b) curry with vegetables or meat in a special sauce, curry vindaloo, daal, naan bread, chicken tikka masala

c) a word or phrase that people shout or sing many times: **chant**
red or green hot fruits: **chillies**
another word for kind or sort: **type**
not hot: **mild**
a restaurant selling meals that you can take home: **takeaway**

d) 1. Many Indians live in Britain.
2. Indian curry is a meal with vegetables or meat in a special sauce. You eat it with rice.
3. Lots of different spices are used, such as chillies, which are really hot.
4. Vindaloo is a very hot curry dish.
5. daal, naan bread and chicken tikka masala
6. CTM is probably the first Indian dish that started to make Indian food popular in Britain.

I've read an article about Indian food in Britain. I found out that Indian food is popular in Britain because there are so many Indians in Britain. – The Indian curry is a meal with vegetables or meat in a special sauce, and you usually eat it with rice. – You will find lots of different spices in Indian food, such as chillies. Chillies are very hot! – One of the hottest curries is called curry vindaloo, and it became popular in Britain during the 1998 World Cup. – Other types of Indian food popular with British people include daal, naan bread and chicken tikka masala, also called CTM. Chicken tikka masala is special because it is probably the first Indian dish that started to make Indian food popular in Britain.

Seite 33 M2 Friday evening

a) **S1:** Let's go out for dinner. What do you think?
S2: That's a great idea. Who wants to go to a Chinese restaurant?
S3: I can't stand Chinese food. Have you got any other ideas?
S1: What about the pizza place in our road?
S2: I had pizza yesterday, so I don't want it again. What about a burger place? We all like chips.
S3: That's no good, I'm trying to be healthy this week. Why don't we try the new sushi restaurant in town? I've never had sushi before.
S1: Good idea! I'd like to try it. What do you think?
S2: Sounds good. So let's go there!

Seite 33 M3 In a restaurant

a) It's an Italian restaurant.

b)

Can I have the menu, please?	**And please can I see the menu?**
Are you ready to order?	**Can I take your order?**
I'll have ..., please.	**And please can I have ...?**
Anything to drink?	**Would you like a drink with that?**
Here you are.	**Here you go.**
Could you bring the bill, please?	**Excuse me, could I have the bill, please?**
That's £..., please.	**That comes to £..., please.**

Seite 33 M4 Anything else?

1. Cat on the left: "I'll have the caviar and the lobster, please."
   Waiter (thinking): "You've got more money than sense."
2. Witch: "Why won't this machine give me my favourite chocolate bar? I'll have to use magic to get it."
3. Waiter: "C-c-c-an I t-t-t-ake your oooorder?"
   Skeleton (thinking): "Why is everyone scared of me? All I want is pizza ..."

Seite 34 M5 A healthy food plate

a) cucumbers, tomatoes, carrots, yellow peppers, mushrooms, herbs, bananas, grapes, lemons, kiwis, coconuts, milk, cheese, eggs, fish, meat, chicken, bread, rice, pasta and water

b) 1. wrong 2. wrong
   3. right 4. right

c) I'd like to talk to you about my ideas for a healthy meal plan.
   Your day should start off with a banana, some bread and some eggs for breakfast.
   At lunchtime you can have fish with a tomato and cucumber salad.
   For dinner I would serve you some chicken with carrots and cucumber.
   Followed by a fruit salad with kiwis, grapes and coconut for dessert.
   It isn't difficult to follow a healthy meal plan. Try it: it's fun!
   Thank you for listening.

Seite 34 M6 Rajiv's curry party

a) The children are in a kitchen. They are preparing/cooking something to eat.
   Caroline is adding something red to the food on the stove.
   Karla has just tried the food: it's too hot and spicy!
   Charlie is giving Karla some bread against the hot spices.
   Rajiv is looking at Gillian. He's helping his friends with the curry.
   Gillian is crying because she is cutting onions. I think she has cut her finger.

b) In the end the curry tastes very hot and burns Gillian's mouth. The curry is too spicy.

c) **who:** Rajiv, Gillian, Charlie, Caroline, Karla
   where: Rajiv's house, in the kitchen
   when: Saturday
   what: The friends are making a curry. The recipe is from Rajiv's grandmother. When Gillian is cutting the onions, she starts to cry and then cuts her finger. Then Rajiv and Caroline put too much extra-hot chilli paste in the curry.

d) I think Caroline will suggest that they add some yoghurt or some water to the curry so that it's milder and not so strong.
   I think Caroline will suggest that they add some more tomatoes to the curry and cook some extra rice.

e) I don't think it's a good idea to add yoghurt to the curry because that will change the taste too much.
   I think they should add water to the curry and cook it for longer.
   I agree with Karla that they should get something from the snack bar next door or from Bengal Tiger because the curry is just too hot to eat. I think they should go to Bengal Tiger because that would be easy.
   I don't agree with Karla because it would be a waste of money to buy more food. They should eat the hot curry.

Seite 35 M7 It's different, isn't it?

a) Yes, I do. / Yes, I agree.

b) 1. You don't cut spaghetti with a knife, do you?
2. The Chinese use chopsticks, don't they?
3. Chopsticks aren't very expensive, are they?
4. You can't read a Chinese menu, can you?
5. A chapati is a kind of flatbread, isn't it?
6. Peas are the most popular vegetable in Britain, aren't they?
7. Germans love sauerkraut, don't they?

c) Your cat is called Archibald. → Your cat is called Archibald, isn't it?
We don't break any school rules. → We don't break any school rules, do we?
Bayern Munich have the best footballers in Germany. → Bayern Munich have the best footballers in Germany, don't they?

Seite 36 Did you get it all?

Why don't Gillian, her mum and Charlie cook dinner at home? **Gillian's mum hasn't done any shopping this week, so there isn't anything in the fridge to cook.** (→ TB 3, TB Seite 18)

What is Gillian's favourite restaurant? **Burger Queen** (→ TB 3, TB Seite 18)

What kind of restaurant is the Windsor Castle? **a pub** (→ TB 3, TB Seite 18)

What does Rajiv eat in the school cafeteria? **pasta and a salad (and he drinks mineral water)** (→ TB 8, TB Seite 23)

Who likes to eat desserts in the school cafeteria? **Karla** (→ TB 11, TB Seite 24)

What is Shima's favourite dish at school? **vegetable lasagne** (→ TB 11, TB Seite 24)

How do many British people eat their peas? **They put them onto the back of a fork with a knife.** (→ TB 14, TB Seite 26)

Where do people use chopsticks for eating? **in China** (→ TB 14, TB Seite 27)

Seite 38 1 Test your fitness

c) Jumping up and down for 30 seconds was easy.
Walking backwards was no problem.
Running up and down 20 stairs quickly was really hard.
Balancing for 15 seconds was difficult.
Pressing my back against the wall for one minute was too hard. I couldn't do it!

Seite 39 2 All kinds of sports

alone: swimming / skateboarding / horse riding
with a partner: tennis / boxing / badminton
in a team: football / hockey / running
inside: karate / gymnastics / handball
outside: cycling / rugby / running

Seite 39 3 Favourite sports

a)

name	age	what sport?	why do they like it?	other information
Telisha	15	hockey	– exciting and fast – you don't need special equipment like helmets or special clothes	– trains twice a week – likes playing outside – nicer than being in a sports hall
Amar	13	skateboarding	– you can do it whenever you want	– started five years ago – skate park near house – meets his friends at skate park after school
Caitlin	11	mini-triathlon	– you can do different kinds of sports in short amount of time	– first mini-triathlon last week – triathlon has three parts: swimming, running, cycling – bike broke down in middle of race – was the fastest swimmer – can't wait for next triathlon

c) I play tennis. I like it because you have to run a lot and every game is different. I train three times a week. I started two years ago.

Seite 40 4 Karate with Jessica

b) 1. wrong (She started karate training **eight** years ago.)
3. wrong (It **always** starts with a warm-up.)

d) Jessica's belt is blue. That means that she is pretty good. But she still has a number of things to learn on her way to the black belt.

Seite 40 5 Different sports

Someone who plays football must be fast.
Someone who goes swimming must be fit.
Someone who does karate doesn't have to be tall.
Someone who goes cycling doesn't have to be slim.
Someone who plays tennis doesn't have to be young.

Seite 40 6 A sportsperson

a) **Name:** Andy Murray
Age: 28
Country: Great Britain / Scotland
Sport: Tennis
Titles: Olympic Gold Medal in the Men's Singles in 2012, US Open champion in 2012, Wimbledon Champion in 2013
Other information: At the moment Andy Murray is the world number 6. He was the first British man to win Wimbledon in almost 77 years. His brother Jamie is a professional tennis player, too. / The two brothers from Scotland enjoyed playing and training together when they were kids but Andy was always the more competitive of the two. He didn't like losing to his brother, so he was determined to train harder and become better than him. / Andy Murray got married in 2015.

b) **S1:** I think Pepe Reina is the most successful goalkeeper.
S2: I don't think so. I think Manuel Neuer is faster and fitter than Reina.
S3: I think Michael Phelps is the most famous swimmer.
S4: I think so, too. And I think Usain Bolt is the fastest athlete. Nobody is faster than him!

Seite 41 7 Sports chants

b) I know a British sports chant for Tranmere Rovers FC. It goes 'And it's Tranmere Rovers, Tranmere Rovers FC. They're by far the greatest team the world has ever seen!'

Seite 42 8 A friendly match

a) I can see a football match. All the players are wearing red noses.
I think they are playing football for fun or for charity.
Charlie is one of the players. He is wearing white shorts and a grey T-shirt.

Seite 43 9 An interview

b) – football training 2x a week / correction: Charlie only trains once a week.
– in skateboarding club / correction: Charlie likes skateboarding, but he isn't in a club.
– special food / correction: He doesn't eat any special food. (He loves hamburgers and chips.)

Seite 43 10 Choose an activity

My favourite sportsperson is Andy Murray. He is 27 years old. He plays tennis and is Britain's number one. He won Wimbledon in 2013 and the 2012 Olympics. (He was the first British man to win Wimbledon in almost 77 years!) In 2012 he also won the US Open.
I like Andy Murray because he works very hard. He is very close to his mum, who coached him when he was a boy. His brother Jamie is a professional tennis player, too.
Sports chant: Don't give up (name), don't give in. Fight to the end – we want to see you win!

Seite 44 12 At the doctor's

a) wehtun – **to hurt**
geprellt – **bruised**
geschwollen – **swollen**
Verband – **bandage**
gebrochen – **broken**
Röntgenbild – **X-ray**
Rezept – **prescription**
Salbe – **cream**

Seite 45 13 After the friendly match

2. He has to wear a bandage.
3. He mustn't run during the breaks.
4. He can watch sports on TV.
5. He has to put on cream twice a day.
6. He can go to the cinema with his friends.
   He mustn't forget to put on cream twice a day.
   He mustn't do any sports.
   He has to sit and watch his team's match against Hendon School next Saturday.

Seite 46 14 What's the problem?

a) I can see a receptionist and people who want to see the doctor. They are all thinking about how they got ill or hurt.
   The woman in purple and pink stepped on some broken glass on the grass.
   The old man has a bandage on his leg. A dog bit him.
   The man with the red scarf has a cold. He was out in the rain and wearing only a T-shirt.
   The old lady has stomach ache. She ate too much.
   The boy in the red T-shirt has broken his arm. He fell off his bike.
   The girl with the red shoes has hurt her back. She fell off her chair.
b) The old lady has stomach ache.
   The man with the red scarf has a bad cold.
   The woman in the pink T-shirt has a cut foot.
   The old man has a sore leg.
   The man with the red hair has a broken arm.
   The girl with the red shoes has backache.
c) I think the old lady has eaten too much.
   I believe the man with the red scarf has been out in the rain.
   I think the woman in the pink T-shirt/with the black hair has stepped on some broken glass.
   I think a dog has bitten the old man.
   I believe the man with red hair has fallen off his bike.
   I think the girl with the red shoes has fallen off a chair.
d) advice for **the old lady:** You should take some medicine.
   advice for **the man with the red scarf:** You should stay in bed.
   advice for **the girl in the pink T-shirt:** Don't do any sports for a few days.
   advice for **the old man:** You should put on this cream.
   advice for **the man with red hair:** You shouldn't ride your bike until your arm is better.
   advice for **the girl with blonde hair:** Don't stand on a chair again. But you can go to school.

Seite 47 15 Too bad

a) The old lady is not able to eat very much.
   The man with the red scarf is not able to play basketball.
   The girl in the pink T-shirt is not able to go dancing.
   The old man is not able to clean the windows.
   The man with red hair is not able to ride a bike.
   The girl with blonde hair is not able to go to work.
b) When I had a bad cold, I wasn't able to go to school. I had to stay in bed all day.
   When I had a broken arm, I wasn't able to play tennis or ride my bike.
   When I had stomach ache, I wasn't able to eat anything.

When I had a cut foot, I wasn't able to wear my favourite shoes.
When I had a sore leg, I wasn't able to walk normally.
When I had a broken arm, I wasn't able to take a shower for four days.

Seite 47 16 Choose an activity

perfect prescription for a bad cold: You should watch films. You absolutely have to lie on the sofa all day. Drink lots of hot chocolate and listen to music. Remember to chat with your friends. You can watch a football match if you like. You should eat your favourite food and have a hot, long bath.

Seite 48 P1 A sports word web

favourite sport: swimming
things you need: swimming costume, bathing cap, goggles, water
where you do it: swimming pool, lake near my house, ocean
why you like it: wakes me up, clears my head, I feel free when I'm in the water

Seite 48 P2 Sports poems

Hockey
Our team
Ready to score
Let's win!
Hockey

Seite 48 P4 Swimming is ...

a) Swimming is boring.
Playing hockey can be dangerous.
Cycling is not difficult.
Doing karate is fun.
Running isn't very interesting.
b) **S1:** I think swimming is fun.
S2: I think so, too. I think skateboarding can be dangerous.
S1: I don't agree. I think skateboarding is OK. You just have to practise! I don't think cycling is very interesting.
S2: I agree. I think it's boring.

Seite 49 P5 Fit, fitter, the fittest

a) happy, happier, (the) happiest
clean, cleaner, (the) cleanest
fast, faster, (the) fastest
strong, stronger, (the) strongest
small, smaller, (the) smallest
successful, more successful, (the) most successful
bad, worse, (the) worst
exciting, more exciting, (the) most exciting
good, better, (the) best
famous, more famous, (the) most famous
b) Football players are more famous than swimmers.
Tennis is more exciting than karate.
Gareth Bale is as fast as Lionel Messi.

Tennis players are as strong as basketball players.
Bayern Munich fans are happier than Eintracht Braunschweig fans.
I'm the worst swimmer in our family.

Seite 49 P7 A special day

Die Schüler durften am Red Nose Day, 15. März, gegen die Schulregeln verstoßen.
Sie mussten zum Beispiel keine Schuluniform tragen und keine Hausaufgaben machen.
Allerdings mussten sie für jeden Regelverstoß 2 Pfund bezahlen.
Insgesamt kamen so über 900 Pfund zusammen.
Dieses Geld wurde dann für einen guten Zweck gespendet.

Seite 50 P10 Rules for Gillian

b) When I am ill, I don't have to go school.
I can eat lots of chocolate and watch films.
But I mustn't see my friends. That makes me sad and sometimes angry.
I have to take medicine until I get better.

Seite 51 P11 Oh, Mum!

a) Have you drunk your tea?
Have you eaten your fruit?
Have you slept enough?
Have you taken your medicine?
Have you watched TV?

b) Yes, I've drunk three cups.
No, I haven't. I want chocolate, not sweets!
Yes, I have. I slept for three hours this afternoon.
No, I haven't. I forgot, sorry!
Yes, I've watched two films.

Seite 51 P12 A broken leg

George is able to read comics.
George is not able to play football.
He is able to play computer games.
He is able to watch films.
He is not able to walk to school.
George is not able to go swimming.
He is able to do his homework, but he isn't able to walk to school.

Seite 51 P13 Can you help?

How often should I use the cream? – You should use the cream in the morning and in the evening. You should also put a bandage around your hand.
When can I see the doctor? – You can see Dr Large on Mondays, Tuesdays and Thursdays.

Seite 52 M1 The London Marathon

a) A marathon is a race over about 42 kilometres. The New York Marathon and the London Marathon are two very famous marathons.
I'd like to take part in a marathon one day, but I'd have to train very hard. I think I'd do a run over 10 kilometres first.
b) There are four races: the Elite Race, the Mass Race, the Wheelchair London Marathon and the Mini Marathon.
The runners collect money for charities. This year the charities are The Children's Trust and the British Heart Foundation.

c) – **Who is in the race?** About 30,000 people run the London Marathon each year. Elite runners, normal people, wheelchair athletes and children all take part.
– **When does the race start?** The first race starts at 9am; that's the women's Elite Race. The other races start at 9.30 am, 9.45 am, 9.25 am and 11 am.
– **Where is the start?** There are three starting points. There is the Blue Start in Blackheath, the Red Start in Greenwich and the Green Start in St John's Park.

Seite 52 M2 Henry's big day

a) – **What was Henry's result in the Mini Marathon?** eighteen minutes and two seconds
– **What does he think about his result?** He wanted to be faster than eighteen minutes, but it didn't work out. But it's OK – it was great just to take part.
– **How did he prepare for the marathon?** trained for one month; ate lots of fruit, vegetables and pasta. He also drank lots of water and sometimes special sports drinks after training.

Seite 53 M3 A sportsperson

a) + b)
How old are you? – She was born in 1995.
When did you start running? – She started when she was ten years old.
Why do you like sprinting? – She has a real talent for it.
What's been your fastest time? – There's no info in the text. But at the 2012 Paralympics in London she finished the 100 m final in sixth place.
What happened to your left hand/arm? – She was born like that. Her left arm didn't develop from below the elbow.
How often do you train? – Before London 2012, Sally Brown trained six days a week; she ran three times a week and did strength and conditioning work.

c) **Name:** Sally Brown
Age: 20 (Stand 2015)
Country: UK (Northern Ireland)
Sport: sprinting
Titles: bronze medal in the 200 m at the 2011 Paralympic World Championships
6th place in the 100 m at the 2012 London Paralympics
Other information: – her left arm didn't develop from below the elbow
– biggest sacrifice is her social life
– has to eat healthy food
– hopes to go to university one day and become Paralympic champion

d) **S1:** Where did the 2011 Paralympic World Championships take place?
S2: They took place in New Zealand.
S1: What is the biggest sacrifice you have to make for your sport?
S2: The biggest sacrifice is that I can't go out on a Saturday night with my friends.
S1: When were you born?
S2: In 1995.
S1: Why do you want to become a Paralympic Champion?
S2: I want to prove that although I'm disabled, I can run as fast as people who aren't.
S1: How has your life changed since the World Championships in New Zealand?
S2: Training has got a lot tougher and journalists now want to know all about me.

Seite 54 M4 After the friendly match

Hi Uncle Joe,
How are you? I'm OK. But my knee isn't, haha.
Last week the Arsenal club at my school played a friendly match against William Ellis School for Boys. (We raised about £250 for Red Nose Day!) It all started well. After ten minutes I scored the first goal for our team. But in the second half Thomas West, a player from the WES team, ran into me and knocked me down. I was able to get up with the help of another WES player and was able to play the rest of the match (I even scored another goal for our team!) but my knee really hurt. The next day I went to see Dr Thompson because my knee still hurt. She took an X-ray to see what the problem is. A few minutes later she told me that my knee isn't broken, just bruised. She gave me a prescription for some cream and put a bandage on my knee.
Now I mustn't play football for two weeks! Can you imagine, two weeks!!! Our next match is against Hendon School on Saturday. (Oh, before I forget: Our match against WES ended 3-3.)
Hope to see you this week. Talk soon, Charlie

Seite 54 M5 In the surgery

a)

doctor
Now, what's the problem?
Does this hurt?
I'll be with you in a few minutes.
Let me see.
We'll have to take an X-ray of your (knee/ arm/...) so we can see what the problem is.
The X-ray room is the second door on the right.
Your X isn't broken, just bruised.
You should put on this cream.
I'll give you a prescription for (some cream).
I'll put a bandage on your X.
You should/shouldn't ...
And listen: You mustn't ... for two weeks.

patient
I've got a bad cold.
My (head/leg/arm/...) hurts.
I can't move my (leg/arm/...) at all.
I've got stomach ache.
I've cut my foot.
I've got a headache.
I've got backache.
I've got a sore (leg/arm/...).
I think I've broken my (leg/arm/...).
Ouch!
My (knee/elbow/...) is swollen/bruised.
I've got a cut (finger/foot/...)
I've got toothache.

b) **S1:** Hello, Rebecca. Now, what's the problem?
S2: Hello. I've cut my foot. I stepped on some broken glass in the park yesterday.
S1: Let me see. Does this hurt?
S2: A little bit, yes.
S1: OK. It's nothing to worry about. I'll put a bandage on your foot. You should keep the bandage on for about a week. It shouldn't get wet. After that, you should put on a cream twice a day. I'll give you a prescription for the cream.
S2: Thank you. When will I be able to wear my favourite shoes again?
S1: You shouldn't wear them for about a week. After that you'll be fine.
S2: Thank you very much, doctor. Bye.
S1: Goodbye.

Seite 54 M6 Helping out at the doctor's

a) – leg is swollen and hurts when she walks
- difficult to go downstairs
- she was running in the park when she hit a stone and fell
- jogged home and felt fine, but today her leg feels terrible and is black and blue

b) Katies Bein ist geschwollen und schmerzt beim Gehen, sie kam heute Morgen kaum die Treppe hinunter. Sie ist gestern beim Joggen im Park über einen Stein gestolpert und hingefallen. Gestern war noch alles gut, sie ist sogar nach Hause gejoggt. Aber heute hat sie starke Schmerzen und das Bein ist blau. Sie hat Sorge, dass das Bein gebrochen ist.

Seite 55 M7 I won't give up!

a) In 2009 the Formula 1 driver Felipe Massa had a bad accident in the Hungarian Grand Prix. He had to have an operation on his head, and he wasn't able to drive for the rest of the year. Fortunately, he is now able to take part in races again.
Michael Schuhmacher had a skiing accident at the end of 2013.
An Australian cricket player was hit by a cricket ball in November 2014. The ball hit his head, and he died two days later.
Rafael Nadal could not play tennis for a while because he hurt his back.
Andy Murray had an operation on his back in September 2013. After that he wasn't able to play tennis for a few months.

b) Leroy was very worried when he wasn't allowed to swim because swimming is his life.
When he found out that he couldn't take part in the Nationals, he felt that all his dreams were ruined. But he also knew that he is a fighter!
At the Nationals, he tried to feel happy for his friend Michael but it was difficult.
He was very frustrated because he wasn't allowed to take part in the Nationals.
Leroy felt down, but his coach cheered him up with the story of Usain Bolt's return from injury.

c) Leroy wasn't allowed to take part in the Nationals.
He had to do different exercises three times a day.
Leroy's biggest problem was that he was worried he wouldn't be able to swim anymore. /
The biggest problem for him was feeling down and thinking that he wasn't going to get better.

Seite 56 Did you get it all?

What sports do you have to do in a triathlon? **swimming, running, cycling** (→ TB 3, TB Seite 39)
Who scored the first goal in the friendly match between Haverstock and William Ellis School? **Charlie** (→ TB 8, TB Seite 42)
What was the score at the end of the match? **3-3** (→ TB 8, TB Seite 42)
When is Red Nose Day? **once every two years in March** (→ Land & Leute, TB Seite 43)
What day does Charlie go to the doctor? **Monday** (→ TB 8 und 11, TB Seite 42 und 44)
What does the doctor do to help Charlie? **gives him a prescription for some cream and puts a bandage on his knee** (→ TB 12, TB Seite 44)
How long must Charlie wait to play football again? **two weeks** (→ TB 12, TB Seite 44)
Who was bitten by a dog? **the old man in the doctor's waiting room** (→ TB 14, TB Seite 46)

Seite 58 1 Where YOU live

a) In my area there is a station./a sports centre./an indoor swimming pool./a cinema.
There are parks./supermarkets./cafés and shops./bus stops.

b) I would like to have a youth club in my area.

Seite 58 2 Different places

a) **In picture A** I can see a busy street.
There are lots of people. They are all doing different things.
The man and the woman on the right are sitting outside a pub.
The man next to them is serving them./is bringing them something to drink.
In the middle of the picture a boy is crossing the road. He is carrying a pizza.
The two girls/women on the left are looking at some clothes in a shop window.
At the bottom two people, a man and a woman, are talking on their mobile phones.
A young mum is waving hello to a woman on a motorbike.
A woman in a green suit is carrying her dog across the road.
A tourist in shorts is taking a photo of the London bus.
A man is reading the takeaway menu of a snack bar.
In picture B I can see a village with a village shop.
The boy and the girl on the right are feeding ducks in a little river.
The boy is taking a photo of the ducks with his phone.
In the middle of the picture some children are riding their skateboards.
On the left some boys are playing football.
A man and a woman are chatting. The woman is holding shopping bags.
A boy on his bike is waving to someone in a garden.
The cows at the top are eating grass.
A man is driving his red car into the village.
The young child on the left is playing with a big dog.

b) I like picture B better because it looks quieter and greener. The people don't look as busy as in picture A. I enjoy feeding ducks. I would like to be in the picture and feed the ducks.

Seite 59 3 The city-village rap

b) I live in a village, but I would like to live in a city because there isn't much to do in a village.
I would like to live near a cinema, and I would like to go shopping every weekend.

c) Living in Frankfurt,
For me it is just great,
A cool view at night,
Delicious food to go,
Lots to do and see at the weekend.
City life yeah –
I like living this way.

Seite 60 4 A chat

b) Karla's parents want to go to the Science Museum.
Gillian says there is a concert at the youth club on Saturday.
Caroline's mum has a surprise for Caroline.
Karla says that she and Gillian could go to a car boot sale near her grandma's house.

c) In my area you can go to the park – that doesn't cost any money! You can also go skateboarding. If you don't like sports, you can go and read books in the library.

Seite 60 5 A car boot sale

a) books, jewellery, boots, trainers, keyboards, computers, inline skates, mobile phones, a guitar, a football, a basketball, a clock, knives, forks, plates, spoons, cups, vases, magazines, a skateboard, jeans, gloves, toys, scarves, watches, baseball caps, a camera, a T-shirt, posters, a bag

Seite 61 7 Buying and selling

a)

customer	seller
I need something for my friend's birthday. Have you got any ...? Does it work? What size are they? How much is it? What would you like for this? Oh, that's too expensive. Have you got anything cheaper? I think I'll take it.	It's a special offer. What do you think about this? It's £5. OK. Let's say £4. Sorry, I don't have any ... but I have some ... Here's your change.

c) **S1:** Hey there, can I interest you in this vase?
S2: It looks quite old to me. I'm sorry, but I prefer modern things.
S1: Well, what about this mobile phone? It's only three months old – my brother doesn't want it anymore so I'm selling it here today.
S2: Does it work?
S1: Oh yes! It works just fine.
S2: How much do you want for it?
S1: £40.
S2: Oh, that's too expensive. Never mind. I'll be going now, have a nice day.
S1: Wait! I'll make you a special offer. How about £25? For a new mobile phone, that's not bad!
S2: £25? OK, I'll take it! Here's £30.
S1: Great, thanks. Here's your £5 change. Enjoy the rest of your day.
S2: Thanks. Bye.

Seite 62 8 A musical

a) I would like to see the musical because it sounds very exciting. I really like live music and I think the costumes would be beautiful.

b) **Mufasa** is a powerful lion and the king of the Pridelands in Africa.
Simba is Mufasa's son.
Scar is Simba's uncle and Mufasa's brother.
Nala is Simba's friend.

c) **Mufasa:** good king / all the animals look up to him / saves his son's life twice
Simba: will be the next king / runs away because he thinks he has killed his father / kills Scar in a fight
Scar: is jealous of Simba / tries to kill Simba
Nala: tells Simba that Scar is King / asks Simba to come back / becomes Simba's wife

Seite 62 9 A closer look

a) **words I know:** lion, Africa, kill, father
words I can guess: trample down, hyena, panic, makes believe

words I don't know: jealous, rescue, valley, almost

b) **almost** – fast, beinahe; **jealous** – eifersüchtig; **rescue** – retten; **valley** – Tal

Seite 64 11 The Notting Hill Carnival

What can you see at the carnival?

- National Steel Band competition
- Children's Day Parade: children and teenagers parade through the streets in colourful costumes
- on the last day, the Monday, there is the Main Parade: groups and clubs in costumes dance to the rhythms of mobile sound systems or steel bands

Seite 64 12 At the carnival

b) crowds of people: walk, dance and sing in the streets of Notting Hill
many tourists: take photos
dancers: dance to the rhythm of the steel drums
singers and bands: play Caribbean music
pickpockets: try to steal wallets and watches
police: put up posters which tell everybody to be careful
Sharon: takes part in the Children's Day Parade; runs over and gives Charlie a big hug

c) I would feel very excited because I love wearing cool costumes and dancing. But I think I would also be a bit nervous because so many people go to watch and the music is so loud.

Seite 65 13 Lots to see

a) There are steel bands which play great music.
There are police officers who help people.
There is a programme which tells you what's on.
There are tourists who take photos of the parade.
There is a Children's Day Parade which you can watch on Sunday.
There are pickpockets who steal wallets and watches.

Seite 66 14 Welcome to the carnival!

a) food stands, tourists, dancers, people in costumes, a float, a band, percussion, a group of drummers, children, many people

b) I would like to go to the Notting Hill Carnival because it sounds really exciting! I love steel drums and costumes. But I wouldn't want to go in the rain. It's important that the weather is sunny!

Seite 68 15 A narrow escape

a) In the first picture people are watching the carnival parade. A pickpocket/young man is stealing/taking something from a man's trouser pocket.
In picture number 2 the thief/pickpocket is running away and a boy is falling in front of the wheels of a float. Maybe the pickpocket hit the little boy.
In the third picture the mother is helping her son/saving her son's life.

c) ist gerade noch einmal davongekommen – had a narrow escape
konnte ihren Sohn gerade noch wegziehen – managed to pull her son away
stieß den Jungen unter einen Festwagen – knocked the boy under a float
bevor das Vorderrad des Festwagens ihn überrollte – before the float ran him over
befragen zurzeit einen jungen Mann – are now questioning a young man
wer weitere Informationen hat – anybody with further information

Seite 69 16 A police interview

a) The police officer is talking to a young man. (He thinks that the boy is the pickpocket.)
b) He was playing football.
He was watching TV.
He wasn't watching the parade.
He wasn't stealing wallets.
He wasn't wearing the same jacket.
c) The police officer thinks that the young man is the pickpocket.
I think the police officer is right. The young man can't tell the police officer what he was watching on TV, so I think he is lying. He wasn't watching TV, he was at the parade.
It's difficult to tell if the police officer is right. Maybe the young man is just nervous.

Seite 69 17 A project – YOUR festival

Speyerer Brezelfest
We have a fantastic festival in summer every year. It's at the second weekend in July. It starts late afternoon on Thursday and ends late on Tuesday night.
There's a big fair near the cathedral where you can do all sorts of things: eat food and go on rides. There is always a Ferris wheel (= Riesenrad) there.
On Sunday afternoon there is a parade through Speyer. Not only groups from Speyer take part in the parade but also groups, clubs and bands from further away, like Kaiserslautern or Rülzheim.
The Brezelfest ends with some very colourful fireworks on Tuesday night, at 10:30 pm.
I sometimes walk in the Sunday parade with my hockey club but I don't go to the fair. I don't enjoy fairs that much.

Seite 70 P1 City or country?

a) **city:** airport, department store, factory, park, rubbish, sightseeing, theatre, youth club
country: farm, nature, fresh air, forest, chicken
b) **city:** many people, traffic, noise, dirt, busy, dangerous, motorbikes, tall buildings, library
country: quiet, boring, cows, slow

Seite 70 P3 A painting

b) ... is called "The Sleeping Gypsy". It shows a woman who is sleeping and a **lion** which is standing behind her. The sky is **blue** and there aren't any clouds. The moon is **on the right.**
The woman has long hair and she is wearing **a colourful dress.** She is holding a stick in her **right** hand. At the bottom you can see a musical instrument. Next to the musical instrument there **is a vase.**
c) I like the painting because it's interesting. Is the lion going to attack the sleeping woman? We don't know. But I don't think so. The lion looks happy, and the woman looks happy.
I don't like the painting. I think it's boring and I prefer watching films.

Seite 71 P4 Pocket money

a) + b)
How often do you get pocket money? – I get pocket money each Friday.
Do you get money for good marks at school? – I sometimes get ten euros for good marks in maths, but I don't get any money for good marks in any other subject.
Do you get extra money? – No, I don't.
What jobs do you do to earn money? – I hoover the living room and do the ironing.

c) I spend my money on downloads and sweets.
I don't want to spend all my money but I'm not very good at saving money.
I sometimes save my money for tickets for concerts and plays.
I always need to know what I'm saving money for. I'm not good at saving for a rainy day.

Seite 71 P5 Last weekend

a) On Saturday morning Karla went to the youth club.
After that she spent some time with her brother.
In the afternoon she read in bed.
Then she played with her rabbit.
In the evening she wrote lots of emails.
After that she watched basketball on TV.

b) Last weekend I went shopping with my friends. I bought a new skirt.
On Saturday evening I went to an Italian restaurant with my family. I had pizza for my main course and tiramisu for dessert.
On Sunday I played football with my brother and his best friend.
In the evening I did some homework and then I watched TV until bedtime.

Seite 71 P6 A poster

Die Haverstock Schule veranstaltet einen Car Boot Sale – das ist eine Art Flohmarkt.
Er findet statt am Sonntag, den 27. Mai, von 9 bis 16 Uhr neben der Turnhalle der Schule.
Es kostet 20p für Erwachsene. Kinder müssen keinen Eintritt zahlen.
Wer etwas verkaufen möchte, kann seinen Stand ab 8 Uhr aufbauen.
Die Standgebühr beträgt 7 Pfund, wenn man im Voraus bucht, und 10 Pfund am Tag selbst.

Seite 72 P10 Check your spelling

Verdopplung des letzten Buchstabens	Wegfall des -e	nur -ing wird angehängt
run → running	have → having	watch → watching
put → putting	drive → driving	happen → happening
sit → sitting	take → taking	talk → talking
swim → swimming	make → making	listen → listening
	write → writing	visit → visiting
	dance → dancing	do → doing

Seite 73 P11 What were YOU doing?

S1: What were you doing at seven o'clock this morning?
S2: I was cleaning my teeth. And you?
S1: I was drying my hair.
S2: What were you doing at four o'clock yesterday afternoon?
S1: I was doing my homework. And you?
S2: I wasn't doing my homework. I was playing on the computer.
S1: And what were you doing at eight o'clock last Saturday night?
S2: I was watching a film with you! What were you doing?
S1: I was doing the same thing, silly!

Seite 73 P12 What a class!

Aisha and Debbie were talking on their mobile phones.
John was shouting at Joey, who was throwing things out of the window.
Tommy was writing in his book.
Kim was doing her make-up.
Patty was listening to music.
Lemmy was reading a comic.
Sid and Eric were playing cards.
Jack was sitting on the desk.
Ginger was drawing on the board.

Seite 73 P13 Tips for the carnival

Man soll nicht mit dem Auto hinfahren, sondern mit Bus oder U-Bahn. Man sollte bequeme Schuhe tragen. Man soll keine wertvollen Gegenstände bei sich haben und Handy und Geldbörse nicht in die hintere Hosentasche stecken. Bei Hitze sollte man viel trinken. Und man sollte immer bei seiner Gruppe bleiben.

Seite 74 M1 Teenagers talking about London

b)

:)	:(
so much to do	very expensive
music: the best bands come and play in London	air isn't very clean
many different people and cultures	traffic and noise
Camden Market	too much rubbish on the streets
different food: kebabs, fish & chips, donuts, muffins	
sights and museums	
lots of shops	
the parks: big, lots of trees and ponds, can meet friends, sit in the sun, read a book, go horse-riding	

Seite 74 M2 Money problems

a) have a car boot sale
bake cakes and sell them at school
do jobs around the house and be paid by our parents
play music in town and ask people walking past for money
do a paper round
help our teachers set up their smartphones
clean our teachers' shoes/bikes/cars
go shopping for a busy neighbour
babysit
repair people's bikes

c) We've talked about how to raise money for a class trip. These are our three best ideas.
Number one: We could sell the class computer. We don't need it anymore because we all have smartphones.
Number two: Florian can make brownies and we can sell them at school.
Finally, we could all do some tasks at home and ask for money from our parents.

Seite 75 M3 An advert

Babysitting: My name is Nadine. I'm 13. I go to Karl-Marx-Gesamtschule. I offer to look after babies and young children in the afternoon and at weekends. I've got a little sister and I have looked after children before. I'm happy to work at weekends.
Phone Nadine on: 0172 873 638

Seite 75 M4 King of the musicals?

a) **what people liked**
- full of colour and surprises
- wonderful singing and music
- the acting, the costumes and the make-up

what people didn't like:
- tickets far too expensive
- quality of singing bad; background singing not loud enough
- actors were cold and the show had no feeling
- lots of mobile phones were ringing during the performance

b) bnorth25: ★★★★
Max4u: ★★★★★
Anonymous: ★★★
kiki1234: ★
Sus@n: ★★★★

c) The film 'Wreck it Ralph' is one of the best films I've ever seen. The animation and the story were really exciting. I hope they'll make a 'Wreck it Ralph 2'! The only negative thing is that I think the music could be better.

Seite 76 M5 At the carnival

a) It is the Children's Day Parade. The friends are excited because they are waiting to see Charlie's sister Sharon in the parade.

b) people: walk, dance and sing
tourists: take photos
pickpockets: try to steal wallets and watches and mobile phones
police: put up posters which tell everybody to be careful
Nick: plays Caribbean music in children's steel band
Sharon: takes part in the Children's Day Parade; dances to the rhythm of the steel drum; runs over and gives Charlie a big hug

c) I would like to play the steel drums, because I love music.
I would feel very excited, but also quite nervous. There are a lot of people watching.

Seite 76 M6 Better safe than sorry

b)

dos	don'ts
take the tube or the bus	no high heels
wear trainers or other shoes that are good for walking	no car
take a map of the carnival route	no mobile phones
find out where the toilets are	don't bring a lot of money with you
check where you can find police and doctors	
stay together with your friends	

Seite 77 M7 The pickpocket

a) The pickpocket is young, maybe nineteen or twenty.
He has blonde hair.
He was wearing a green baseball cap and green trousers, a black T-shirt and a beige jacket at the parade. He was also wearing white trainers with a bit of blue.

b) This pickpocket has lots of tattoos on his arms. He's wearing yellow trainers, green trousers, a white T-shirt and a blue baseball cap. He has some piercings. (That's pickpocket number 1.)
This pickpocket has blonde hair and a little beard. He's wearing a pink shirt, a grey T-shirt, black trousers and black shoes. He looks older than the other five.(That's pickpocket number 2.)
This pickpocket is wearing green trousers, a black T-shirt under a beige jacket and a green baseball cap. (That's pickpocket number 3.)
This pickpocket has red hair and a red goatee. He's wearing a gold necklace and has tattoos on his arms. He also has some piercings. He's wearing blue trousers, black shoes and a yellow T-shirt. (That's pickpocket number 4.)
This pickpocket is tall, the tallest of them all. He's wearing a green hoodie, a black T-shirt, black shoes and long yellow trousers. He has tattoos on his arms. (That's pickpocket number 5.)
This pickpocket is wearing a yellow hat, a grey T-shirt, brownish-yellow trousers and white trainers. (That's pickpocket number 6.)

Seite 77 M8 What Mr Harley saw

Well, this morning I went to the Children's Day Parade.
I was watching the floats when suddenly I felt a hand in my (back) pocket.
I turned round and there was a pickpocket with my wallet.
He started to run away. I shouted after him. He knocked a young boy under a float. Terrible!
He was wearing a jacket and a green baseball cap, I think. I'm afraid that's all I can remember.

Seite 77 M9 Guess what it is

a) 1. a float
2. a wallet or a purse
3. a tourist
4. a (steel) drum/an instrument
5. a police officer
6. a costume or a headdress
7. a pickpocket
8. a bird of paradise

b) You use 'who' for people, and 'which' for things and 'that' for people and for things.

c) It is a thing that you wear around your hand or arm. (bracelet)

Seite 78 Did you get it all?

How much pocket money does Gillian have left? **five pounds** (→ TB 4, TB Seite 60)
Where does Karla's grandma live? **in a small village north of London** (→ TB 4, TB Seite 60)
Who becomes the new lion king? **Simba** (→ TB 8, TB Seite 62)
Who is Simba's new wife? **Nala** (→ TB 8, TB Seite 62)
When is the Children's Day Parade? **Sunday, August 25, 9 am to 7 pm** (→ TB 11, TB Seite 64)
What does Sharon wear at the Children's Day Parade? **a colourful skirt and a fantastic headdress of flowers and feathers** (→ TB 12, TB Seite 64)
How old is John Scott? **six years** (→ TB 15, TB Seite 68)
What did the pickpocket steal? **a wallet** (→ TB 15, TB Seite 68)

Seite 80 1 Robinson Crusoe

a) I have heard of Robinson Crusoe. He was alone on an island. He lived there for many years.
He became friends with a man called Friday.

c) In picture 1 I think Robinson felt excited.
In picture 2 I think Robinson felt happy.
In picture 4 I think Robinson felt scared.
picture 1: excited, nervous
pictures 2 and 3: seasick, bored
picture 4: scared, helpless
picture 5: exhausted, hungry, homesick
picture 6: shocked, scared
picture 7: lonely, sad, homesick
picture 8: shocked, worried
picture 9: brave, angry
picture 10: interested, curious, proud
picture 11: helpful, surprised, hungry
picture 12: hurt, scared, helpless
picture 13: happy, excited
picture 14: glad, safe, proud

d) – he was born in York, England
– was a slave for two years
– then became a rich man in Brazil
– wanted to buy slaves in Africa
– slept in a tree

Seite 82 2 The story of Robinson

a) Well, I left my parents in York on 1st September 1651.
I boarded a ship to the Caribbean on 1st September 1659.
One day, there was a storm and the ship hit some rocks.
I swam to an island.
I built a raft and collected a few things from the wreck.
After some time I was able to begin a new life on the island.
I lived alone for many years.
One day some cannibals came to the island.
I rescued one of their prisoners.
I called him Man Friday because I found him on a Friday.
I taught him to speak English, and soon we were able to talk to each other.
He taught me how to fish and how to use plants as medicine.
One day, in 1686, an English ship sailed by and rescued us.
I decided to take Man Friday back home to England with me.
We were really happy when we arrived back in England in June 1687.

b) Robinson left his parents in York on 1st September 1651.
He boarded a ship to the Caribbean on 1st September 1659.
One day, there was a storm and the ship hit some rocks.
Robinson swam to an island. He built a raft and collected a few things from the wreck.
After some time he was able to begin a new life on the island.
He lived alone for many years.
One day some cannibals came to the island.

Robinson rescued one of their prisoners.
He called him Man Friday because he found him on a Friday.
Robinson taught Friday to speak English, and soon they were able to talk to each other.
Friday taught Robinson how to fish and how to use plants as medicine.
One day, in 1686, an English ship sailed by and rescued them.
Robinson decided to take Man Friday back home to England with him.
They were really happy when they arrived back in England in June 1687.

Seite 82 3 YOUR survival kit

a) a rope, a knife, a spade, a first aid kit
b) chocolate, a tent, toothpaste
c) **S1:** I think a rope is very important. What about you?
S2: I agree. We absolutely need a rope. I think we should also take a knife.
S3: I agree. If we have a knife, we won't need a pair of scissors.
S4: Hm, I'm not so sure. A pair of scissors is always useful.
S3: I agree that a pair of scissors is useful but it's not necessary.
S4: Well, OK, I think you're right.

Seite 83 5 What is home?

a) Home is where the heart is. – You are at home when you are with the people you love.
There is no place like home. – Home is the best place in the world.
My home is my castle. – Home is the place where I am safe and in control.
Home, sweet home. – I love being at home.
East, west – home is best. – Home is always the best place.
b) **play:** computer games, board games, table tennis
read: books, magazines
my family: brother, sister, mum, dad, grandmother
my street: cars, bus stop, trees
c) I love my room. I can read my books there in the evening.
I like playing computer games in the living room.
I hate my street. There are too many cars and it's really noisy.

Seite 83 6 Choose an activity

(message in a bottle)
Please help! My name is Simon and I'm alone on this island. Please send a ship to rescue me as soon as possible! I miss my family and I don't want to eat any more coconuts! Thanks for reading. Simon
(20 English words)
good – so that Man Friday can say that he likes something
no – so that Man Friday can say when he doesn't like something
hello – so that Man Friday can be friendly when he sees Robinson in the morning
ship – so that Man Friday can tell Robinson when a ship sails by
(fact file) Daniel Defoe
Born: 1659 or 1660, London
Nationality: British
Jobs: writer and journalist
Wife: Mary Tuffley
Number of children: eight

Seite 84 8 Different people – different problems

b) I think the answer to letter number 1 is quite good.
I think the answer to letter number 2 is not very helpful.
I think the answer to letter number 3 is not very helpful.
I think the answer to letter number 4 is very good.

Seite 86 9 Caroline's family

a) Mr Lambraki doesn't have a job. He is looking for a new job but it is very difficult.
Caroline's mother is often tired. She has to work very hard because the family needs the money.
George doesn't like to help with the housework. He doesn't work very hard for school.
Caroline is worried about her family. She worries about her father's job and her family's future.

b) **Mr Lambraki:** engineer, out of work, does the housework and the cooking, checks newspaper and Internet for a new job, will get frustrated soon
Mrs Lambraki: nurse at Wellington Hospital, works hard, loves job, looks after patients, often tired, needs money
George: Caroline's twin brother, 13, never cleans or helps around the house, plays football or computer games, doesn't do homework, will maybe get a bad report
Caroline: 13, loves pets and friends, best friend Gillian, listens to music and talks about boys, worries about father's job, house, mother's work, sometimes very worried

c) Hi everyone. I would like to present Caroline Lambraki to you.
She's 13. She loves pets. Gillian is her best friend. Caroline is worried about her family. What will happen if her father doesn't find a new job soon? She is worried that they will have to move to a smaller house and that her mother will have to work even more.
So that's Caroline. Thanks for listening.

Seite 87 10 What will happen?

b) 1. Wenn Mr Lambraki nicht bald neue Arbeit findet, wird er sehr frustriert sein.
2. Wenn ihr Mann nicht bald eine neue Stelle hat, muss Mrs Lambraki noch mehr arbeiten.
3. Wenn George nicht mehr für die Schule tut, bekommt er kein gutes Zeugnis.
4. Wenn ihr Vater nicht bald neue Arbeit findet, wird Caroline sich noch mehr Sorgen machen.
5. Wenn Mrs Lambraki noch mehr arbeitet, wird sie keine Zeit mehr für ihre Familie haben.

c) If Mr Lambraki finds a new job, Mrs Lambraki will work less./will have more time for her family.
If Mr Lambraki finds a new job, Caroline will be happy again./won't be worried anymore.
If Mr Lambraki finds a new job, George will get more pocket money.
If Mr Lambraki finds a new job, he will be happy again.
If Mr Lambraki finds a new job, the Lambraki family will be happy again.
If Mr Lambraki finds a new job, the Lambraki family will go on holiday to Greece next year.
If Mr Lambraki finds a new job, life for the Lambraki family will be a lot easier.

Seite 87 11 Welcome to my life

b) I think the song is about someone who feels sad and angry.
I don't like the melody but the lyrics are good.
The music often sounds sad but also angry.
The singer sounds angry and strong at the same time.

Seite 88 12 How to deal with problems

a) I talk to my friends.
I listen to music.

I write emails to my older sister.
I write emails to my aunt.
I do yoga.
I bake a cake.
I do sports.
I go shopping with my best friend.
I run as fast as I can until I'm tired.
I read a book.
I cry for a bit.

Seite 88 13 Girls talk

a) I think they are talking about problems and about Gillian's parents, about how sad Gillian was when her dad moved out. I think they are talking about how to deal with problems.

Seite 89 14 YOUR favourite music

a) I listen to the Talking Heads a lot. I think they're great.
My favourite band member is Tina Weymouth, who plays the bass guitar.
I like the band because their songs always have special meanings.

Seite 89 15 Choose an activity

(sentences for a dialogue)

Mr Lambraki: You can't go to football practice today.
George: Why? We have a very important match soon and I need to practice.
Mr Lambraki: Your teacher has just given me your class test and you got a bad mark. You should stay at home and do your homework!
George: OK, Dad. I'll go to practice after I've finished my homework.
Mr Lambraki: That's a good boy.

Seite 90 P1 Missing letters

b) r _ _ _ _ e (rescue) w _ _ _ _ _ d (worried)
b _ _ _ n (begin) h _ _ _ _ _ _ k (homesick)

Seite 90 P2 Working with words

a) difficult–**easy** happy–**sad** fast–**slow** early–**late**
boring–**interesting/exciting** unfriendly–**friendly** expensive–**cheap** good–**bad**
fair–**unfair** right–**wrong** small–**big** terrible–**amazing/great**

b) difficult tests, a sad film, slow music, in the early morning, an interesting idea, a friendly waiter, expensive clothes, a good report, the wrong answer, a terrible headache

Seite 90 P4 Verb search

a) swim – swam
build – built
leave – left
collected – collected
hit – hit
begin – began
live – lived
be – was
come – came
find – found
have – had
show – showed
give – gave
rescue – rescued
teach – taught
sail – sailed

Seite 91 P5 The story in short

a) 1. Robinson began a new life on an island.
2. He lived alone for many years.
3. One day cannibals came to the island.
4. Robinson rescued their prisoner.
5. Robinson taught Man Friday to speak English.
6. Man Friday taught Robinson how to fish.
7. A ship sailed by and rescued them.

Seite 91 P6 A message in a bottle

Von wem ist die Flaschenpost? – Sie ist von Rajiv Patel.
Warum hat der Junge sie geschrieben? – Es ist Teil eines Wissenschaftsprojekts in der Schule.
Es dreht sich um Ozeane und Menschen in fernen Ländern.
Was sollen wir als Finder jetzt tun? – Rajiv Datum und Ort mitteilen, wo wir die Flasche gefunden haben.
Wozu braucht der Junge unsere Adresse? – Damit er uns ein Bild von sich schicken und uns sagen kann, wo und wann er die Flaschenpost aufgegeben hat.

Seite 91 P7 What did they say?

Gillian, Charlie und Rajiv möchten auf eine tropische Insel, so wie Robinson Crusoe.
Gillian würde aber nicht alleine hinfahren wollen, sondern würde gerne einen Freund oder eine Freundin mitnehmen. Sie verrät aber nicht, wen.
Charlie wäre gerne alleine dort und hofft, vielleicht Man Friday zu treffen.
Rajiv hätte nichts dagegen, dort ein Girl Friday kennenzulernen.

Seite 92 P9 Finding words

a)

-oo-	-ea-	-ie-	-ou-
choose	heard	worried	proud
look	seasick	friendship	about
toothbrush	learn	believe	found
book	each	patient	would, should
room	speak	Charlie	group
school	heart		mountain

Seite 92 P11 I guess ...

I think Patty will speak to her friend again.
I guess Jason will visit a dogs' home.
I'm sure Tommy will talk to his parents about the things that worry him.
I'm sure Jason won't get a cat.
Maybe Susan will receive more horrible messages.
Maybe Susan will tell her parents, teachers and friends.

Seite 93 P13 On Sunday

2. If Mr Lambraki doesn't check the newspaper, he will watch TV.
3. If it is sunny, George will play football.
4. If it is rainy, Caroline will listen to music.

5. If no one plays with Patch, he will sleep.
6. If Caroline opens the cage, Daisy will come out and play with a ball.

Seite 93 P14 A letter

Jan writes that his sister never helps at home.
Jan takes out the rubbish on Mondays and Tuesdays and he unloads the dishwasher.
It's his sister's turn on Wednesdays and Thursdays, but she doesn't do it.
She meets her friends or plays with her mobile phone.
He wants to know what to do and asks for help.

Seite 94 M1 Interviewing Robinson Crusoe

b) What did you miss most? – A lot of things – the houses, the people, the food!
What did you like about the island? – I liked the weather and hearing the sea when I woke up.
Would you go there again? – Yes, I would! But only for a holiday, not forever.
How did you teach Man Friday to speak English? – Well, I pointed to things and told him the word.
How did you brush your teeth? – With a small stick.
What did Man Friday teach you? – He taught me how to fish and use plants as medicine.

c) Did you feel lonely? – Oh yes. The first few months and years were very difficult.
When did you go to sleep each night? – I didn't have a clock or a watch, so I can't really tell you. But I usually went to bed when the sun went down. And I got up when the sun came up the next morning.
What did you normally eat? – I ate a lot of fish. Man Friday taught me how to fish.
How did you find water to drink? – There was a little waterfall on the island.
Did you miss your family? – Of course I did. My parents are now dead. I still miss them.
What did you miss most about home? – The food. I can't wait to have roast beef and Yorkshire pudding again. I've told Man Friday so much about it.
Did you ever give up hope? – Oh yes, many times.

Seite 94 M2 The story of Robinson

Hi. My topic today is the story of Robinson Crusoe.
I will start off by telling you the story.
I will then move on to tell you what I like and don't like about the story.
But before I start telling you the story, here's some information about the author.
The English writer Daniel Defoe wrote the adventure story "Robinson Crusoe" in 1719. That's almost three hundred years ago.
"Robinson Crusoe" is about a man called Robinson Crusoe, who is shipwrecked on an island.
But let me start at the beginning:
Robinson Crusoe leaves England in September 1659, on a ship to the Caribbean.
One day, there is a storm and the ship hits some rocks.
Robinson is able to swim to an island.
With the help of a raft he collects a few things from the wreck and begins a new life on the island.
At first he feels scared, but he learns how to survive.
After a few years, he rescues a prisoner from some cannibals and calls him Man Friday, because they met on a Friday.
Man Friday teaches Robinson how to fish and use plants as medicine, and Robinson teaches Man Friday to speak English.
The years go by and the two men become good friends.

Then one day an English ship sails by and rescues them.
They arrive back in York in June 1687. Robinson was away from home for twenty-eight years.
I like the story because it's exciting. And it makes you think how you would feel, alone on an island.
But I don't like how the story ends. I think Robinson and Man Friday should stay on the island.
I don't think Man Friday will be happy in England. It's too cold and there is too much rain.
Thank you very much for listening. Any questions?

Seite 95 M3 Cast Away

a) I wouldn't like to watch Cast Away. It sounds boring. There is only one person and a volleyball. I prefer films with lots of interesting characters.

b)

similar	different
Chuck Noland and Robinson Crusoe are both on an island.	Robinson Crusoe meets people on the island.
They are both rescued.	Robinson Crusoe is shipwrecked and Chuck Noland is in a plane crash.
They both build a raft.	Cast Away is a modern story and Robinson Crusoe is three hundred years old.

Seite 95 M4 Oh, yeah!

a) They are talking about a perfect island.
b) **Rajiv** wants to live on an island with lots of trees so he could build his own house.
Gillian wants to live on an island with a high mountain because then she could climb up and look out for ships to rescue her. She would also like a big waterfall on her island, so she could have a shower every morning and wash her hair.
Charlie wants to live on an island with a beautiful lake and a dry cave, because he wants to be nice and cool in the day and cosy and warm at night.

Seite 95 M5 A diary entry

I don't know what day it is today. Monday or maybe Tuesday? I'm on this island and I think I'm here all alone. I'm sitting in a cave. Lots of big spiders! Miss my warm bed at home.
Life is quite relaxed. I get up and go fishing. Then I cook the fish. In the afternoons I just explore the island or lie around in the sun. I'm quite happy but would like to go home soon. I hope a ship will sail by and rescue me. I look out for ships all the time. Maybe tomorrow I'll see one.

Seite 96 M6 A problem letter

a) Dear Sarah,
I need your help because I am really worried. I have a problem with my clothes. They're all really old and horrible. I want to buy new ones but I don't have enough pocket money.
I'm afraid that my friends will laugh at me. Please help me.
Mandy, 13, Potsdam

b) Dear Mandy,
Don't worry about your clothes! If your friends are nice, they won't care and they will like you anyway. But if you really want some new clothes, you could go to a second-hand shop – sometimes you can find really cool things there, and it's really cheap. I hope this advice helps.
Sarah

Seite 96 M7 A message from Gillian

b) I think Gillian wants to talk about her dad. Maybe he wants to move to another city.

Seite 96 M8 A phone call

a) Rajiv is calling Gillian to tell her that he is coming to the Canal Café at 5.
b) What does Rajiv want to know? **if Gillian wants to tell them something serious**
Who does Gillian want to talk about later? **about her dad**
Who else is coming to the Canal Café? **Caroline and Charlie**

Seite 97 M9 At the café

a) Gillian's dad is going to marry his girlfriend Ronda, and Gillian doesn't like her.
Ronda is pregnant.
b) **Gillian:** Dad, can I talk to you about something?
Gillian's dad: Of course, Gillian. What's the matter?
Gillian: I'm worried. When Ronda and you have a baby, I won't fit into your life anymore.
Gillian's dad: Gillian, don't be silly! You'll always be my first daughter and that's so important to me. You'll always be welcome to come and see me and Ronda.
Gillian: But I want time with just you and me – not with Ronda.
Gillian's dad: Really? I didn't know you felt like that. Well, we can do that, too. Why don't we go to the park this weekend for a game of football?
Gillian: That sounds good.
Gillian's dad: Great. Everything will be OK, Gillian, I promise. So, would you like dessert?
Gillian: Yes please! Shall we have some ice cream?
Gillian's dad: Good idea. How about the strawberry flavour ...

Seite 97 M10 What if ...?

1. If Gillian talks to her father, he will understand her better.
2. If Gillian goes to the wedding, Ronda and her dad will be very happy.
3. If Gillian gets a baby brother, she will play with him a lot.
4. If her dad, Ronda and the baby go on holiday, Gillian will go with them.
5. If her dad and Ronda go out in the evening, Gillian will look after the baby.
6. If Gillian has a problem, her dad will listen and try to help her.

Seite 98 Did you get it all?

Who wrote "Robinson Crusoe"? **Daniel Defoe** (→ TB 1, TB Seite 80)
What did Man Friday teach Robinson? **how to fish and how to use plants as medicine** (→ TB 1, TB Seite 81)
When did Robinson return to England? **11th June 1687** (→ TB 1, TB Seite 81)
What is Patty's problem? **her best friend is going out with the boy Patty likes** (→ TB Seite 85)
What is Sarah's advice for Jason? **visit a dogs' home in your town** (→ TB Seite 85)
Why is Mr Lambraki looking for a new job? **He lost his job two months ago.** (→ TB 9, TB Seite 86)
Where does Mrs Lambraki work? **at Wellington Hospital** (→ TB 9, TB Seite 86)
How does Caroline deal with her problems? **She likes listening to music.** (→ TB 11, TB Seite 87)

Seite 100 1 Computer words

a) email, internet, printer, mouse, website, laptop, download, chat, software, hardware, screen, click, online, DVD, CD, USB stick, tablet

Seite 100 2 Computers & Co.

b)

	computer	mobile phone	TV	tablet	smartphone
order tickets	✓	✗	✗	✓	✓
download music	✓	✗	✗	✓	✓
watch films	✓	✗	✓	✓	✓
chat with friends	✓	✓	✗	✓	✓
play games	✓	✓	✗	✓	✓

c) **S1:** Have you got a computer?
S2: Yes, I've got a computer.
S1: How often do you use the computer?
S2: I don't use it very often.
S1: What do you use it for?
S2: I sometimes use it for my homework and I play computer games on it. I also use it when I want to download music. What about you?
S1: Yes, I've got a computer, too. It's a tablet. I use it every day.
S2: What do you use it for?
S1: I use it when I want to listen to music. I also use it to chat with my friends in the evening.

Seite 101 4 Text messages

a) – Hi Nick, how are you?
The weather is great today.
Do you want to come to the park with me and play football?
– Hi Charlie, I have to stay at home and tidy up my room. Boring!
So no football today, but maybe tomorrow.

b) Hi Em. Do u want 2 go 2 the cinema l8r?
We cud c da nu Till Schweiger film.
Let me no.
Sarah xx

Seite 102 5 Home alone

a) Yes, I play video games. I like the stories and playing against my friends. It's fun!

d) Hi Nick,
Tidy up your room, please. As discussed!
Your grandmother is coming at 12. She is taking you out for lunch.
Make sure you're ready in time. NO COMPUTER GAMES!
Love, Mum xx

Seite 103 6 Lunch with grandma

c)

what they can do	things they have
go to restaurants	TV in their rooms
go out in the evenings	computer
meet friends on Sundays	Internet
go shopping after school	
do sports	
play computer games	
chat to friends online	
go to the library	

Seite 104 8 At the Science Museum

a) 1. seven
2. on the second floor
3. café/restaurant in the basement and on the ground and third floors
4. yes (there are lifts and accessible toilets)
5. twelve
6. in the museum shop on the ground floor

b) If you want to learn about the future, you should go to the third floor.
If you are hungry, you can have a meal in the café or restaurant.
If you are interested in computers, you should go to the second floor.
If you can't walk, you can take the lift.
If you love farms, you should go to the first floor.

c) I think Foucault's Pendulum would be interesting.
I'd go to the first floor first because I'm interested in space, and they have a 'Cosmos & Culture' part there.

Seite 104 9 Around the museum

a) Jessica and Pranav are at the Science Museum. First they are looking at the cars, especially the Volkswagen "Beetle" from 1965.
Then they come to the Apollo 10 Command Module. It travelled around the moon in 1969. (The Apollo 11 that came after it was the one that landed on the moon.)
Then they see the Apple 1 home computer, from 1976.
After that the clip shows the hands-on galleries, where you can learn about the brain, for example. You can also take a look into the future there.
And finally, the clip shows the cafeteria, where you can go if you need a break.

c) A: **Agriculture:** Tractor → 1st floor
B: **Exploring space:** Apollo 10 → ground floor
C: **Energy:** Computer terminals → 2nd floor
D: **Flight:** Propeller plane → 3rd floor

Seite 106 10 Inventions

a) I use my computer every day.
I never use matches. I sometimes use a stamp.
My family and I use the car a lot.
I use zips every day. There are zips on my jacket and on my jeans.
I often eat chocolate chip cookies. I could eat them all day.

b) The computer is very important for me.
Matches are good to have.
The bike is more important than the stamp.
Chocolate chip cookies are not important for me.

c) 1. mobile phone
2. light bulb
3. bike
4. computer
5. microwave

Seite 107 11 Successful inventors

a) The light bulb was invented by Thomas Edison. It was invented in 1879.
The dishwasher was invented by Josephine Cochrane. It was invented in 1886.
Matches were invented by John Walker. They were invented in 1826.
Chocolate chip cookies were invented by Ruth Wakefield. They were invented in 1930.
The car was invented by Karl Benz. It was invented in 1876.
The television was invented by Philo Farnsworth. It was invented in 1928.
The telephone was invented by Alexander Graham Bell. It was invented in 1876.
The computer was invented by John Mauchly and John Eckert. It was invented in 1945.

b) My computer was made in China.
Our car was made in Germany.
My schoolbag was made in China.
My phone was made in China.
My shoes were made in Turkey.
My T-shirt was made in Malaysia.
My skirt was made in Turkey.

Seite 108 12 Life without electricity

a) toaster, kettle, oven, TV, telephone, lamp, computer, fridge, smartphone, washing machine, dishwasher, microwave, smoothie machine, electric toothbrush, hair dryer

b) I need electricity for the lamp on my desk.
I need electricity for drying my hair.
We need electricity for keeping our food cool.
We need electricity for our smoothie machine.

c) Without electricity you can't listen to CDs.
Without electricity we have to eat cold food.
Without electricity I can't watch TV.

Seite 109 13 Paper plane

First you have to fold a piece of A4 paper in half.
Then you have to open the paper again and fold the corners into the centre.
Now you fold again to the centre line.
After that you turn the plane over. Fold it along the centre line so that the sides are together.
The next thing you have to do is make a mark 3 cm from the bottom line.
Draw a line to the tip and stick the bottom parts together.
After that do the same with the other wing.
Now, listen carefully: Make small cuts in both wings.

Seite 109 14 Choose an activity

(a tour through the Science Museum) First we will look at the Making of the Modern World exhibit on the ground floor. I really want to see the Apollo 10, it looks awesome! Then we will definitely go up to the third floor and try the Fly Zone Simulator so we can feel like we are flying in a jet. After that we should go to the IMAX cinema and watch a 3D film about life underwater. It is even narrated by Johnny Depp!

(Tell your class about a museum)

At the Natural History Museum in Braunschweig (Brunswick), you can experience many different kinds of animal, as well as the skeletons of dinosaurs! On the top floor you can see the skeleton of a large dinosaur, many fossils and other animals that do not live anymore. On the floor below, there is an exhibit about insects, such as snails and bees. In the basement there is an aquarium, where you can see fish that live in the Amazon River. There are even snakes in the aquarium so it is a really interesting place to go.

(quiz cards)

Some people use this every day. It has four wheels and takes you from one place to another. (car)
This object creates wind. Sometimes it can turn around by itself. (fan)
I use this every day by standing in it. It makes me clean. (shower)

(an invention that doesn't exist but should exist)

I think that the Homework Finisher 3000 should be invented because I hate doing homework! It would be really helpful to have a machine that does all my homework and then feeds all the information into my brain. This would mean that I could spend more time playing football with my friends and watching TV.

Seite 110 P1 Odd one out

b) 3. "Radio" is the odd one out because you don't see it, you listen to it.
   4. "Cook" is the odd one out because you can't do it on the computer.
   5. "Bandage" is the odd one out because it has nothing to do with computers.
   6. "Music" is the odd one out because you can't write it.

c) car – bus – motorbike – plane ("Plane" is the odd one out because it can fly.)

Seite 110 P2 All kinds of words

a) alone, bad, bored, forget, fridge, game, glad, grandmother, hide, hungry, kitchen, lunch, remember, save, think

Seite 111 P6 Texting rules

Man soll beim Schreiben von SMS darauf achten, höflich zu sein.
Man sollte sie nicht schreiben, wenn man verärgert ist.
Wenn du gemeine SMS bekommst, zeige sie deinen Eltern oder Lehrern.
Man sollte denen helfen, die Mobbing-Botschaften bekommen.
Man soll beim Essen oder im Unterricht keine SMS schicken und auch nicht, wenn man gerade im Gespräch mit jemandem ist.
Man soll keine SMS schicken, während man mit dem Rad fährt oder die Straße entlanggeht.
Man soll nachts das Handy ausschalten.

Seite 111 P7 What did she say?

Sie sagt, dass man früher in die Bücherei gehen musste, wenn man Informationen gesucht hat. Es gab damals ja noch kein Internet. Sie ist immer gerne in die Bücherei gegangen, weil sie dort ihre Freundin Lilly getroffen und mit ihr über die Lieblingsbücher der beiden gesprochen hat.

Seite 112 P10 How verbs become nouns

a)

verbs	nouns
invent	invention
teach	teacher
decorate	decoration
play	player
celebrate	celebration
dream	dreamer
invite	invitation
train	trainer
report	reporter
work	worker
imagine	imagination
sing	singer
drive	driver
present	presentation
ride	rider

b) **things:** invention, decoration, celebration, invitation, imagination, presentation
people: teacher, player, dreamer, trainer, reporter, worker, singer, driver, rider
The people words end in -er, the "thing" words end in -tion.

Seite 113 P11 Invented by?

The stamp was invented by James Chalmer. It was invented in Scotland in 1838.
The microwave was invented by Percy Spencer. It was invented in the USA in 1946.
The bike was invented by Karl Drais. It was invented in Germany in 1817.
The zip was invented by Whitcomb Judson. It was invented in the USA in 1893.

Seite 113 P13 Josephine Cochrane

Josephine Cochrane erfand die Spülmaschine, weil sie gerne Gäste zum Abendessen einlud und das anschließende Geschirrspülen ihre Angestellten viel Zeit kostete und dabei manchmal auch Geschirr zu Bruch ging.
Nachdem niemand sonst auf die Idee kam, eine Lösung für dieses Problem zu suchen, erfand sie die Geschirrspülmaschine eben einfach selbst.

Seite 114 M1 The history of ...

c) Stone Age: People made sounds and signs with their hands to 'talk' to each other.
5,000 years ago: The Egyptians invented the first paper and the first letters.
600 years ago: People started to write letters and send it with the first kind of post.
1876: The telephone was invented by Alexander Graham Bell.
20th century: The computer was invented. There were many other inventions in the world of communication, too.

Seite 115 M2 The talking computer

a) the kids go inside the computer – parents are worried – the kids have an adventure (pirates! aliens!) – they find money – when they return to their room, the money is gone

b) It is Friday evening. Gina and Tim Davis are alone at home. Their parents have gone out. They switch on the computer, and it starts talking to them! It tells them that they can come inside their adventure game. Tim is a bit frightened, but Gina says 'Come on, Tim! It'll be fun!' So they jump into the computer.
A little while later, their parents come back home, and they can't find Gina or Tim. They are very worried.
But Gina and Tim are having an amazing adventure inside the computer. They meet pirates and aliens and at the end they find lots of money. 'Let's take this home!' says Tim. 'Great!' says Gina. But when they leave the computer, the money is not there anymore, and they meet their angry parents. What a nightmare! But they will try again tomorrow ...

c) I liked your story because it was exciting. You also used good English words. I would change the ending – Gina and Tim should take the money out of the computer and go shopping with it.

Seite 115 M3 Computer games: good or bad?

a)

good	bad
– learn a lot – teach you things you don't learn at school – fun: some of the games are really great	– lots of killing and shooting – dangerous for young people – sitting in front of a computer alone is not good for you

b)

good	bad
– You can play even when it's raining.	– unhealthy if you play for too long
– more interesting than homework – help you think – good exercise: quick reactions	– a waste of time – bad for your eyes – expensive

Seite 116 M4 Visiting the Science Museum

Wie viel kostet der Eintritt? – Der Eintritt ist umsonst, aber manche Aktivitäten kosten Geld.
Wann ist das Museum geöffnet? – Täglich von 10 bis 18 Uhr.
Wo können wir unsere Jacken und Rucksäcke lassen? – In einem Schließfach am Eingang.
Kann man im Museum etwas zu essen kaufen? – Ja, im Eat Drink Shop im Keller. Schulgruppen dürfen die Cafés aber nicht besuchen.
Können wir im Museum auch Filme ansehen? – Ich denke schon. Es wird jedenfalls auch ein Kino erwähnt.

Seite 116 M5 Inventions

S1: What do you need a zip for?
S2: You need a zip to close up your jacket or a tent. Right, what is a bike for?
S1: A bike helps you to travel around quickly. And what do you need matches for?
S2: To start fires! What do you need chocolate chip cookies?
S1: You need them to make you happy on a sad day. What do you use a dishwasher for?
S2: You need it to clean your plates, glasses, knives and forks. What do you use a stamp for?
S1: You use it to send letters and postcards to your friends.

Seite 116 M6 Fantastic inventions?

b) My favourite invention is the Amphicar. Then I could drive to America on the water.

c) What does Karen Waterman think about the Amphicar? **she thinks the Amphicar is beautiful: she is very enthusiastic**
What does the reporter think about it? **he thinks it's cool, but doesn't think 65 kilometres per hour is very fast; when he's on the water, he feels sick**
What new information can you get about the Amphicar? **You steer the Amphicar with a steering wheel, and underwater the wheels work like a rudder. / There is a water pump to pump out the water when the car is back on land.**

Seite 117 M7 Are YOU a successful inventor?

My invention is a pair of walk-on-walls boots.
They are used to walk up walls.
They have special glue so that you don't fall down.
They are used for painting and cleaning very big windows.
You can use walk-on-walls boots every day if you like – they are always fun!

Seite 118 Did you get it all?

Who sends a text message to Nick? **Charlie** (→ TB 4, TB Seite 101)
What is Nick's favourite computer game? **Boom Trader** (→ TB 5, TB Seite 102)
Where did Nick's mother put her note? **on the kitchen table** (→ TB 5, TB Seite 102)
Where does Nick's grandmother want to take Nick? **for lunch** (→ TB 5, TB Seite 102)
Can you learn about maths at the Science Museum? **yes, on the 2nd floor** (→ TB Seite 105)
On which floor of the Science Museum can you see planes? **the 3rd floor** (→ TB Seite 105)
What did Ruth Wakefield invent? **chocolate chip cookies** (→ TB 11, TB Seite 107)
Who invented the television? **Philo Farnsworth** (→ TB 11, TB Seite 107)

Seite 119 The invention of the bike

1. In the year 1815 there was a large volcanic eruption in Indonesia.
   The weather all over the world changed because of that.
   This is why food in Europe did not grow well in 1816, and, as a result, people couldn't feed their horses anymore.
   As a result, people had to find a new way of travelling around.
   So somebody invented the bike!
2. The Running Machine is different from a modern-day bike because it doesn't have any pedals and it doesn't have a chain. Riders had to push themselves forward with their feet.
   The Running Machine was made of wood. Today's bikes are made of metal.

Seite 120 The development of the bike

1. The problem with Drais's invention was that it was heavy and difficult to ride.
   Many of the Running Machines didn't have any brakes.
   The Boneshaker was invented by a Frenchman, Pierre Lallement. The problem with Lallement's invention was that his bikes weren't very comfortable.
   The problem with the Penny Farthing was that there were no brakes so you couldn't stop. You had to jump off, which was sometimes very difficult and dangerous.
2. The back wheel on the Rover was bigger than the Penny Farthing's back wheel.
   The Rover also had a chain which linked the pedals to the back wheel.
   It was faster than the Penny Farthing because it was easier to ride.
3. The bike still changed a lot after 1880.
   In 1888 rubber tyres were replaced by pneumatic tyres.
   From 1890 the safety bike was mass produced.
   In 1900 the first gear change system was invented.
   In the late 1950s the bike was replaced by the car as the most popular vehicle.
   The first BMX bikes were produced in the early 1970s and by the late 1970s the first mountain bikes were produced.
   In the early 1990s the first modern electric bikes were produced.
   I also noticed that the first Tour de France took place in 1903: So the bike was probably already quite popular around that time.

Seite 122 How the bike changed the world

1. The bike changed the world in so many ways. It has been a very useful invention.
   Bikes meant a big difference for people's clothes, because women could not wear a dress and ride a bike at the same time. They started wearing trousers.
   Bikes made women more independent. Then, once they were more independent, they asked for more freedom and respect.
   The technology used in bikes also played a big role in the manufacturing of other machines, such as the car.
   However, bikes are still a very popular means of transport, as you can see from the diagram.
   In China, for example, there are 450 million bikes. In Germany there are more than 50 million.
2. In a city with only bikes there are fewer accidents because there are no cars.
   There is a lot less pollution because bikes don't need any petrol.
   People have more money, too. They don't have to pay for fitness studios because they their bikes to go everywhere. And people are healthier. They don't get angry as often.
   Cycling is good for your body and good for your feelings and for your mind.
   We think that this would be a great city! We would like to live there.

Seite 124 1 Holiday

b) no work, fun and laughter, no worries, sun, sea, doing things you want to do

Seite 124 2 YOUR summer holidays

S1: In the summer holidays I'm going to go to the zoo. And you?
S2: I'd like to go to Berlin.
S3: In the summer holidays I'm going to stay with my grandparents. And you?
S4: I'd like to spend some time with my friends. And you?
S5: I'd like to sleep until lunchtime every day.

Seite 124 3 Holidays without parents

a) There are some families in the picture. The parents are saying goodbye to their children. The children are getting on a bus/coach and they're going on holiday/on a school trip.
b) The parents are thinking that their children will do some interesting activities, like walking in the woods.
I think the parents are sad to say goodbye to their children but they're happy because they know that their children will have a lot of fun while they're away.
The children are thinking that they will have a party while they're on holiday. I think they are happy to get away from their parents for a few days.
Parents and children have different ideas of what the holiday will look like for the children.
The parents are thinking of walks through the forest. The children are thinking of party time.

Seite 125 4 Choosing a camp

a) B – D – A – C
First they talk about the football and rugby camp.
Then they talk about the musical star camp.
After that they talk about the water sports camp.
And finally, they talk about the climbing camp.
b) I would like to go to the water sports camp because I like being outside. I think it would be fun to go rafting and windsurfing. I enjoy extreme sports so I think I would also enjoy water sports.

Seite 125 5 Charlie's application form

a) climbing camp
b) Geburtsdatum – **date of birth**
Postleitzahl – **postcode**
Anmeldeformular – **application form**
weiblich – **female**
Einverständnis – **agreement**
Nachname – **surname**
männlich – **male**
Unterschrift – **signature**
Alter – **age**
Erziehungsberechtigte/r – **parent/guardian**
c) If Charlie breaks the rules, a camp instructor can send him home.

Seite 126 6 At the station

a) Where are the ticket counters? – They're opposite the telephone boxes.
Where is the escalator? – It's in front of the toilets.
Where are the platforms? – They're opposite the ticket counter.
Where is the cash machine? – It's next to the ticket counter.
Where is the information point? – It's near the snack bar.
Where is the coach station? – It's on the right, near the information point.
Where are the toilets? – They're behind the escalator.

Where are the accessible toilets? – They're where the other toilets are, behind the escalator.
Where is the exit? – It's next to the ticket counters.
Where are the telephone boxes? – They're opposite the escalator.

b) When does the next train to Bristol leave? – It leaves at 15:47.
Which platform does the train from Plymouth arrive at? – It arrives at platform 10.
Which platform does the train to Bristol leave from? – It leaves from platform 12.
When does the next train from Plymouth arrive? – It arrives at 16:48.
Which platform does the train to Cardiff leave from? – It leaves from platform 8.
Which platform does the train from Brighton arrive at? – It arrives at platform 4.
When does the next train to Swansea leave? – It leaves at 13:18.

Seite 128 9 Friends in foreign countries

Who is it? – It's my aunt, my mum's sister.
Where does she live? – She lives in New York.
Have you ever visited her? – Yes, we visited her when I was eight years old.
Has she ever visited you? – Yes, she comes and visits us every year.
What else do you know about her? – She loves New York. She doesn't want to live in Germany.

Seite 128 11 Friends from the USA

a) At the beginning the people are at the airport.
After that they are at home/at Gillian's and her mum's home.

Seite 130 13 Four places – four things to see

I find Loch Ness the most interesting because it looks beautiful in the picture. I love walking in the mountains and maybe you can swim in the lake when you're there. I would also like to look for the Loch Ness monster. Another reason is that I like listening to people with a Scottish accent.

Seite 134 P1 Word groups

b) **school:** teacher, lessons, exercise book, pen
animals: dog, horse, sheep, tiger
holidays: sun, sea, airplane, hotel
food and drink: water, apples, chocolate, orange juice

Seite 135 P4 Plans

a) This afternoon I'm going to meet my friends after school and play football.
Then we're going to get an ice cream and after that I'm going to go home.
This evening I'm going to do my homework.
Later my family and I are going to eat dinner, and then I'm going to watch TV.

b) Are you going to do your homework? – Yes, I am.
Are you going to send text messages to your friends? – Yes, I am.
Are you going to play computer games? – No, I'm not.
Are you going to visit your grandparents? – No, I'm not.

Seite 135 P6 A ticket machine

- Was muss man denn hier zuerst machen? – Man muss auswählen, was für eine Fahrkarte man kaufen möchte.
- Da steht **One day bus pass.** Ist der nur heute gültig? – Nein, er ist ab sofort gültig und gilt bis morgen 16 Uhr 30.

- Was ist denn ein **Single journey bus ticket?** – Das ist eine Fahrkarte für eine Einzelfahrt. (Die Fahrt muss innerhalb von einer Stunde angetreten werden und die Karte gilt für nur eine Fahrt ab dieser Haltestelle.)
- Gibt der Automat Wechselgeld? – Nein.

Seite 136 P7 Give me five!

5 countries in Europe: **England, Scotland, France, Austria, Italy**
5 countries which are not in Europe: **USA, Canada, Mexico, India, Jamaica**
5 countries where English is spoken: **England, USA, Scotland, Wales, Ireland**
5 things to do or see in London: **St. Paul's Cathedral, Westminster Abbey, the London Eye, Tower Bridge, museums**
5 cities in the UK: **London, Edinburgh, Aberdeen, Newcastle, Brighton**

Seite 136 P10 Sound check

b)

/æ/	/e/
land	ten
unhappy	spend
family	many
candy	then
plan	welcome
activity	any

Seite 137 P12 So many questions

1. How was your flight to London?
2. Are you tired after the flight?
3. What would you like to see in London?
4. Where would you like to go first?
5. Do you want to visit a museum?
6. Why don't we all go to Edinburgh?

Seite 137 P13 Caves and dinosaurs

- **Was gibt es dort zu sehen?** drei Höhlen, die mehr als 315 Millionen Jahre alt sind; außerdem einen Dinosaurier-Park mit 200 Modellen in Lebensgröße
- **Gibt es in den Höhlen auch Dinosaurier?** nicht in den Höhlen, aber im Park
- **Wie sind denn die Öffnungszeiten?** täglich 10 bis 15 Uhr, aber nur von März bis November
- **Was kostet der Eintritt?** 13 Pfund 75 für Erwachsene; 8 Pfund 50 für Kinder von 3 bis 16
- **Warum steht dort „sweatshirt"?** Man soll ein Sweatshirt oder etwas anderes Langärmeliges tragen, weil es in den Höhlen kühl ist. Die Temperatur beträgt dort durchgängig 12°C.

Seite 138 M1 Away from home

Yes: Last year I went to Spain with my best friend and her family. We stayed in a hotel at the beach for a week. We had a wonderful time. The weather was really warm and sunny so we were able to go swimming in the sea every day. My friend and I were allowed to go to the ice cream café at the end of the street alone, which was really fun. I didn't miss my mum and dad much but it was nice to see them again when I got back home.

No: I have never been away from home without my parents. I would like to go on holiday with my friends but we always go on holiday with my family. I like going on holiday with my parents and my sister but I think it would also be fun to go away with my best friend. Maybe it will happen next year. Our volleyball club are organising a training camp for a long weekend in June. I would like to take part. And I hope my best friend will take part, too. It's only three days.

Seite 138 M2 Summer camps

1. between 10 and 16 years
2. There are 23 camps.
3. You can click on the activities to find out more.
4. People can stay at the camps for one week.
5. I think the most interesting activities are 'Creative Writing' and 'Lights, Camera, Action'. I'm really interested in films and books so I think these activities would be a lot of fun. I think I would learn a lot about writing and making films, which is what I want to do when I'm older.

Seite 139 M3 Camp rules

b) I'd like to talk to you about my ideas for camp rules at the climbing camp.
I think it's important to have the right clothes at climbing camp, especially shoes. I don't think you're allowed to wear trainers or sandals. The children should wear comfortable clothes.
The food should be healthy at the camp so that the children have a lot of energy to go climbing. They aren't allowed too many fizzy drinks or too many sweets and crisps.
The children must clean their rooms and they should switch the lights off at 11pm.
I also think the children should leave their mobile phones in their rooms during the day.
It'll be interesting to hear about your ideas. Thank you for listening.

Seite 139 M4 At the ticket counter

1. Hello. I'd like two tickets to Cardiff, please.
2. Would you like single or return tickets?
3. Return, please.
4. That's £108 altogether, please. (one hundred and eight pounds)
5. OK, here you are. Which platform does the train leave from?
6. Platform 8.
7. Thank you very much. When does the next train to Cardiff leave?
8. You'll have to hurry: it leaves in five minutes.

Seite 139 M5 Welcome to the camp

a) He talks about camp activities, camp rules and meal times.
b) **Meal times:**
   - breakfast between 7:30 and 8:30
   - lunch at 12
   - dinner at 7
   - no food if you're late
   - don't have to pay for main meals but have to pay for dessert

   Free time: sometimes between 8 and 10 pm but not allowed to leave the camp
   Bedtime: 11 pm; no talking after that
   Weather: looks good for most of the week

Seite 140 M6 Making a reservation

a)

customer	receptionist
– Have you got three rooms free for Friday and Saturday night? – How much does that cost altogether? – What time is breakfast? – Could you make a reservation for me? – Thank you very much for your help.	– How can I help you? – Let me check. Yes, three rooms are free. – Would you like to make a reservation? – OK, I've made a reservation for Friday and Saturday. – No problem. Glad I could help.

b) Have you got three rooms for Friday and Saturday night?
Let me check. Yes, three rooms are free.
Would you like to make a reservation?
I've made a reservation for Friday and Saturday.

c) **S1:** Good morning, Central Hotel. This is Rebecca Coles speaking. How can I help you?
S2: Good morning. This is Amelie Vogel. My friends and I would like to stay at your hotel this week. Have you got two rooms free for Thursday and Friday night?
S1: Let me check. Yes, two rooms are free. Would you like me to make a reservation?
S2: Yes, please. How much does that cost altogether? There are four of us. The name is Vogel.
S1: That's £150. (one hundred and fifty pounds)
S2: OK. Thank you very much for your help.
S1: No problem at all. Glad I could help.
S2: Goodbye.
S1: Goodbye. See you on Thursday.

Seite 140 M7 YOUR phrase book for travelling

a) – making a (hotel) reservation
– at the doctor's
– in a café
– on the phone
– meeting someone new for the first time/making friends

b) **Going shopping**
– Excuse me, I'd like to buy some ... Where can I find them, please?
– I'm looking for ... Can you tell me where to find them, please?
– How much is that altogether?
– Can I pay cash?
– Do you have them in a size (X)?

In a restaurant
– Can I have the menu, please?
– I'd like ..., please.
– I'll have ..., please.
– Could I have the bill, please?/Could you bring the bill, please?
– How much is that, please?

At the doctor's
– I can't move my (leg/arm/foot/...) at all.
– I think I've broken my (leg/arm/foot/...).
– My (leg/arm/foot/...) (really) hurts.

Seite 141 M8 Different Englishes

a) Brian Fallon: **Australia** Sheila Murphy: **Ireland** Oliver Kumalo: **South Africa**
Sue Monkhouse: **USA** Sunit Nandi: **India** Barbara Harmer: **England**

b) **Brian Fallon:** Melbourne, Australia; on a business trip; waiting for a flight to Manchester
Sheila Murphy: Kerry in Ireland; on her way home from a trekking holiday in the Himalayas
Oliver Kumalo: Cape Town, South Africa; has never been to London; excited about seeing the famous sights in London
Sue Monkhouse: Houston, Texas; has come for some sightseeing and to visit family
Sunit Nandi: India; going to visit his friend in Poland; hasn't seen his friend for a long time so is really excited
Barbara Harmer: lives near London and is a pilot; has just arrived from New York; is going home for the weekend

Seite 141 M9 More interesting places

a) I would like to visit the northwest of Scotland because it would be great to try and look for the Loch Ness Monster.
Manchester also sounds like a lot of fun because a lot of people play football there and there are two famous football teams, Manchester United and Manchester City. I would be really excited if I could go to a Manchester United match.
After that we could get the train to the southwest of England and do some surfing. I didn't know you could surf in England.

b) When you think of **Loch Ness,** the first thing that you will think of is the Loch Ness Monster. However, there is a lot more to do and see in the area. Although it is only seven miles from the nearest city, the countryside around the loch is very beautiful. You can do many sports, such as cycling, swimming and canoeing in and around the loch. There are also many things to see, for example Urquhart Castle, the local wildlife (animals) and waterfalls. At the end of the day, you can enjoy a dance evening (Ceilidh) and try some traditional food, such as Scottish haggis.
I would like to introduce **Brighton** to you. It sounds like the place we would all like. It's a town on the south coast of Great Britain. It's not too far from London, so you get many people who live in Brighton but work in London. They take the train to London every day. The fastest trains between Brighton and London take just under an hour. Brighton is famous for its lovely beaches. In the summer Brighton is packed with holidaymakers.

Seite 142 Did you get it all?

What do Charlie and Rajiv want to do in the summer holidays? **go to a summer camp** (→ TB 4, TB Seite 125)
What is the English word for Geburtsdatum? **date of birth** (→ TB 5, TB Seite 125)
Where do trains leave and arrive at a train station? **a platform** (→ TB 6, TB Seite 126)
Where do Charlie and Rajiv buy their train tickets? **at Victoria Station** (→ TB 6, TB Seite 126)
Who visits Gillian and her mother in the summer holidays? **Gloria Hill and her family** (→ TB 10 und 11, TB Seite 128f.)
What is Mrs Collins' great idea? **that they could all go to Edinburgh** (→ TB 11, TB Seite 129)
What is the American English word for "holiday"? **vacation** (→ TB 11, TB Seite 129)
Who laughed at the Irish giant Finn McCool? **the Scottish giant Benandonner** (→ TB 13, TB Seite 130)

READING IS FUN

Seite 143 A Traditional British specialities

Shepherd's pie: a meat pie with a crust of mashed potato; bottom layer: minced beef; top layer: mashed potato; often made from leftovers
trifle: a dessert; bottom layer: biscuit fingers soaked in fruit; top layer: custard

Seite 145 C Country Mouse and City Mouse

What do you think the story is about?
I think the story is about two mice. One mouse lives in the city and the other mouse lives far away from the city. I think they are good friends but they have got problems with their friendship. Sometimes it is difficult to be friends when you live far away from each other.

Seite 146 D About a Boy

Would you like to read the whole book?
- No, I wouldn't. It sounds like a sad story, and I don't like sad stories. Marcus sounds lonely and depressed. His mother doesn't sound very nice.
- Yes, I would. It sounds a lot like my life. It helps me when I know others have the same kind of life.

Describe the two lives Marcus's mum talks about. Life before Marcus's parents split up and life after his parents split up. Life before was quiet, stable, maybe a bit boring. Life after is chaotic, strange, a bit lonely, quite sad but also interesting because Marcus is never sure what is going to happen next.

Seite 149 F The Giant's Causeway

Which moral fits the story best?
- I find that the moral "A big giant isn't always the most intelligent giant" fits the story best. It was pretty stupid of Benandonner to believe Finn's wife so easily.
- If you ask me, I think the moral "Always think before you build something" fits the story best. Finn didn't really think much. He just got angry and didn't think. I think I would even change the moral to "Always think before you do".
- In my opinion, the moral "Women have always got the best ideas" fits the story best. Finn's wife Oonagh saved Finn with a very simple trick. I don't think Finn is as clever as his wife.

(possible different parts)
Benandonner (lines 1–10)
Finn builds a path (lines 11–26)
Oonagh's plan (lines 27–31)
A shock for Benandonner (lines 32–end)

Seite 150 G The Sword in the Stone

How the raven got its black feathers (a Native American legend)
At the beginning of time all the birds were the same colour. The raven wanted to make the birds all different from one another, so he went to the four Great Spirits in the sky with his idea. He said, "The birds are all the same colour. They look so uninteresting. I will paint all of the birds different colours if you give me the paints and the brushes."
The Spirits agreed and then the raven said, "If I do all this work for you, I will want you to paint me so that I am the most beautiful bird in the world." The Spirits agreed again and the raven

started painting the birds. When he had finished, each bird was different and their feathers were all the colours of the rainbow: red, orange, yellow, green, blue and violet.
The raven went to the four Great Spirits and said, "I have kept my promise, now you must keep yours." So the first Great Spirit painted the raven with wonderful colours and made him the most beautiful bird in the world. But the raven said, "I don't think you have painted me very well. I'm no different from the other birds."
The raven hoped the Spirits would make him even more beautiful. So each of the other three Great Spirits added even more beautiful colours to the first Great Spirit's work but the raven still said, "I'm no different from the other birds."
After the fourth Great Spirit had finished painting, the raven said, "You have played a trick on me. I kept my promise and painted all the birds. You haven't kept your promise to make me the most beautiful bird in the world."
When the Great Spirits heard this, they were very angry. They poured all of their paint over the raven so that all the colours mixed together. The result was a dark, dark black. Then they sent the raven back home. This is how the raven got its black feathers.

Stn.
Station (Railway)
Station (Underground)
Park / open space
0 mile
1/4
1/2
0 km
0,5
1
Hendon
Camd
Camden
Primrose Hill
Prince Albert Road
Grand Union Canal
London Zoo
Regent's Park
Albany Street
London
Wellington Road
Maida Vale
Grove End Road
Park Road
Maida Vale
Marylebone Stn.
Mme. Tussaud's
Marylebone
Road
Edgware
Road
Westway A 40 (M)
Baker Street
Marylebon
Paddington Stn.
Bayswater
Notting Hill
Chepstow Rd
Pembridge Rd.
Wigmore Street
Oxford Str
New Bond Street
Bayswater
Road
Bayswater
Road
Park
Park
Lane
Lane
Mayfair
Notting Hill Gate
Kensington Church Street
Kensington Gardens
Hyde Park
Kensington
Round Pond
The Serpentine
Piccadilly
Green Park
Holland Park
Kensington Road
Knightsbridge
Buckingham Palace
Grosvenor Place
Royal Albert Hall
Road
Sloane Street
West
Museums
Brompton
Natural History Museum
Cromwell Road
Victoria Stn.